Criminalizing Disobedience

Recent Titles in

Studies in Penal Theory and Philosophy
R.A. Duff, General Editor

Just Sentencing
Principles and Procedures for a Workable System
Richard S. Frase

Popular Punishment
On the Normative Significance of Public Opinion
Jesper Ryberg and Julian V. Roberts

Taming the Presumption of Innocence
Richard Lippke

Sentencing Multiple Crimes
Edited by Jesper Ryberg, Julian V. Roberts and Jan W. de Keijser

Playing Fair
Political Obligation and the Problems of Punishment
Richard Dagger

Hate, Politics, Law
Critical Perspectives on Combating Hate
Edited by Thomas Brudholm and Birgitte Schepelern Johansen

Criminal Law in the Age of the Administrative State
Vincent Chiao

Punishment and Citizenship
A Theory of Criminal Disenfranchisement
Milena Tripkovic

Beyond Punishment?
A Normative Account of Collateral Restrictions on Offenders
Zachary Hoskins

Neurointerventions, Crime, and Punishment Ethical Considerations
Jesper Ryberg

The Metamorphosis of Criminal Justice
A Comparative Account Jacqueline S. Hodgson

Guilty Acts, Guilty Minds
Stephen P. Garvey

Sentencing and Artificial Intelligence
Jesper Ryberg and Julian V. Roberts

Punishment for the Greater Good
Adam J. Kolber

Criminalizing Disobedience

YOUNGJAE LEE
I. Maurice Wormser Professor of Law, Fordham University School of Law, USA

OXFORD
UNIVERSITY PRESS

OXFORD
UNIVERSITY PRESS

Oxford University Press is a department of the University of Oxford.
It furthers the University's objective of excellence in research, scholarship,
and education by publishing worldwide. Oxford is a registered trade mark of
Oxford University Press in the UK and in certain other countries.

Published in the United States of America by Oxford University Press
198 Madison Avenue, New York, NY 10016, United States of America.

Library of Congress Cataloging-in-Publication Data
Names: Lee, Youngjae author
Title: Criminalizing disobedience / Youngjae Lee.
Description: New York : Oxford University Press, 2026. |
Series: Studies in penal theory and philosophy |
Includes bibliographical references and index.
Identifiers: LCCN 2025048966 (print) | LCCN 2025048967 (ebook) |
ISBN 9780197617144 hardback | ISBN 9780197617151 updf |
ISBN 9780197617175 online | ISBN 9780197617168 epub
Subjects: LCSH: Civil disobedience—Law and legislation | Obedience (Law) |
Criminal law—Philosophy | Punishment—Philosophy | Political obligation | Rule of law
Classification: LCC K258 .L44 2026 (print) | LCC K258 (ebook)
LC record available at https://lccn.loc.gov/2025048966
LC ebook record available at https://lccn.loc.gov/2025048967

DOI: 10.1093/9780197617175.001.0001

Printed by Integrated Books International, United States of America

The manufacturer's authorized representative in the EU for product safety is
Oxford University Press España S.A. of Parque Empresarial San Fernando de Henares,
Avenida de Castilla, 2 – 28830 Madrid (www.oup.es/en or product.safety@oup.com).
OUP España S.A. also acts as importer into Spain of products made by the manufacturer.

To my parents

Contents

Preface

In June 2025, while finishing this book, I picked up Albert Camus's *The Fall*, for reasons that had nothing to do with writing this book. At one point in *The Fall*, the protagonist says something that is very much relevant to this book, and it is this passage:

> Somebody has to have the last word. Otherwise, every reason can be answered with another one and there would never be an end to it. Power, on the other hand, settles everything.[1]

This book is an attempt to capture the tension present in the Camus passage—that on any given issue, there can be arguments and counterarguments but that what it means to have power is to *cut* through all that, *decide once and for all*, and have the *last word*, despite the likely presence of objections and despite the state violence that could result from the exercise of power—and examine this tension as it plays out in many different contexts of criminal law.

I have been thinking and writing about this topic ever since the summer and fall of 1998, when, as a law student, I read—and wrote a student piece about—*United States v. Bajakajian*, which had just been decided by the US Supreme Court.[2] *Bajakajian* was about a man who was convicted of the crime of failing to report $357,144 in cash, which he attempted to carry out of the United States in a suitcase with a false bottom. I continued to think about disobedience in criminal law after the Supreme Court decided *Ewing v. California*, a 2003 case about punishing those who reoffend after having been convicted of and punished for a crime in the past.[3] Writing about the questions that the *Ewing* case raised in my mind led to a series of articles in the early 2000s as I began my career as a legal academic, and several articles followed on related themes.

However, I did not think seriously about writing a book on criminalizing disobedience until one morning in the summer of 2020. That summer, the first summer of the COVID-19 pandemic, I had unexpectedly found myself to be the director of "Camp Daddy," when no other options for summer schools or camps

[1] Albert Camus, *The Fall*, trans. Justin O'Brien (Alfred A. Knopf, Inc., 1956; repr., Vintage International, 1991), 45.

[2] United States v. Bajakajian, 524 U.S. 321 (1998).

[3] Ewing v. California, 538 U.S. 11 (2003).

for children were readily available. Academics who are parents of small children know that those quiet morning hours before the children wake up are golden—and fleeting—for scholarly work. The book took shape in my mind little by little on those mornings in that anxious summer. Shortly afterward, I encountered the stunning painting that is on the cover of this book when I visited the Clark Art Institute (and the serene Tadao Ando–designed Clark Center) with my sons in Williamstown, Massachusetts, one rainy, leafy day in the fall of 2020. I made steady progress on the book in the subsequent five years as the world emerged from the pandemic and I finished out my term as the Dean for Research at Fordham.

The book is, therefore, a product the origin of which can be traced back to a point over twenty years ago, and it has developed over time since the beginning of my legal academic career until it came together in the last five years. I have accumulated many debts from many individuals and institutions as I developed and refined ideas contained in this book over all those years. I acknowledge them here in rough reverse chronological order.

I would like to first thank Kezia Johnson at Oxford University Press for shepherding the project from start to finish with much patience and supportiveness and the two anonymous reviewers of the book proposal and one anonymous reviewer of the full manuscript for their extremely helpful comments.

NOMOS: The American Society for Political and Legal Philosophy (and Deborah Hellman and Micah Schwartzman of NOMOS) hosted a workshop on the book manuscript in May 2025 after the penultimate manuscript was completed. Questions, challenges, and suggestions from Debbie and Micah, as well as from Daniel Fryer and Alex Sarch, both of whom served as probing and supportive commentators, and from Michelle Dempsey, Doug Husak, Alec Walen, and Ben Zipursky led me to revisit and rework some of the thorniest issues present in the manuscript. I believe the manuscript improved as a result, and I am very thankful to the organizers and participants.

Edmond & Lily Safra Center for Ethics at Harvard University (and its Director, Eric Beerbohm) hosted me in the academic year 2024–25 as a visitor as I finished the book manuscript. The Center, as well as providing a friendly, welcoming, and intellectually rich environment for the year, put on a workshop for a part of the manuscript, and pushes and insights from Eric, as well as from Tommie Shelby and Eliza Wells, who served as commentators, and others participating in the workshop, especially Selim Berker, helped me see the need to rewrite and clarify important parts of Chapter 2. I would also like to thank Steve Koh and Richard Re for their helpful comments at the workshop and Emily Bromley and Yuuka McPherson for helping my visit go smoothly and successfully throughout the year.

Antony Duff has supported this project from its inception. He advised me on the book proposal as it came together and read the entire manuscript, and his feedback improved the manuscript immeasurably. I would also like to take this opportunity to highlight the contributions of Antony and Doug Husak (mentioned above) to the world of criminal law and philosophy. Their influence on my work should be evident throughout the book, but, in addition, the current field of criminal law and philosophy and its global community of scholars would not exist without their pathbreaking work, intellectual leadership, and support for junior colleagues. Their written works have inspired and continue to inspire my work, and their feedback and support for my work and career over the years have been invaluable. The academic vibrancy and personal warmth of the community of criminal law and philosophy scholars are in major part due not only to their masterful academic work but also to their ability to cultivate and maintain a welcoming and supportive community of scholars. As someone just starting out in the field, I met them both at the conference, "Justifications and Excuses: Legal and Philosophical Perspectives," at the Rutgers Institute for Law and Philosophy in 2004, and ever since then they have been a constant source of support for which I am eternally grateful.

The said community of criminal law and philosophy scholars has provided me with an extended academic family that has sustained my work for many years. At the Rutgers Conference mentioned above, I also met Kimberly Ferzan, to whom I have turned many times since then for inspiration, straight talk, and counsel. In addition, I have learned much from many conversations with those in the community, especially, in addition to those already mentioned, Mitch Berman, Vincent Chiao, Stuart Green, Adil Haque, Tatjana Hörnle, Adam Kolber, Sandra Marshall, Gabe Mendlow, Alice Ristroph, Victor Tadros, François Tanguay-Renaud, Malcolm Thorburn, Ekow Yankah, and Leo Zaibert. I thank them all for their ideas, energy, sparring, and friendship, and I am happy to see that the community continues to grow each year with new entrants.

Reading David Pozen's recent work on drug laws helped me tremendously with related chapters in the book, and I thank him for his insightful comments on parts of the manuscript. Conversations with the Colombian Constitutional Court's former Chief Justice Manuel Cepeda, who spent a semester at Fordham in the spring of 2024, helped me think through the drug law discussions in the book. I also thank the European University Institute in Florence for hosting me as a visitor in 2008–09. There, I wrote the article that turned out to be the first version of what would eventually evolve into Chapters 8 and 9 of this book. That article also benefited from my stint at University of Chicago Law School immediately after Florence, especially from conversations with Bernard Harcourt, Adam Hosein, Brian Leiter, Martha Nussbaum, and Ariel Porat, and also from comments from Elizabeth Cohen, Simon Keller, and John Kleinig. Cécile Fabre's recent engagement with that work in her own work on treason and espionage and subsequent back-and-forth with her helped me refine my arguments in the same chapters.

Fordham Law School has been my professional home since 2005, and I have a long list of people to thank. It probably surprises no one that Ben Zipursky has been the most important interlocutor among my colleagues at Fordham. Ben is not only a giant in his field (along with his co-author John Goldberg) but also an incredibly helpful and generous colleague. What is remarkable about Ben's brilliance, incisiveness, and willingness to give his time is that there are many people on my faculty writing in many different areas who would also consider him to be *their* most important interlocutor on the faculty. Abner Greene has been an enthusiastic and thoughtful commentator on this project, and I always appreciate and learn from his input. I am also grateful to Tom Lee and Ethan Leib for their feedback on my work over the years, for their reliably insightful and stimulating conversations, and for being all-around fun colleagues. I value their sharp and fertile intellect, deep expertise, and warm friendship. It's been a joy to talk legal philosophy with Courtney Cox since she joined our faculty several years ago, and the manuscript benefited from her comments. My Fordham criminal law and legal theory colleagues past and present, all with very strong and distinctive academic personalities, have kept Fordham an intellectually rich and provocative setting in which to think and write about criminal law as a theorist. Along these lines, I thank, in addition to those already mentioned, Aditi Bagchi, Bennett Capers, Dan Capra, Deborah Denno, Bruce Green, Russ Pearce, John Pfaff, Dan Richman, and Ian Weinstein. I have also learned much from Kimani Paul-Emile's work on drug laws, and I am grateful for her comments on parts of the manuscript. I thank the Deans Bill Treanor, Michael M. Martin, Matthew Diller, and Joe Landau for their unwavering support. I thank the Fordham Law Library staff for their help and patience with me, especially Juan Fernandez and Herbert Mayner, as well as my faculty assistants, Daphne Lightburn and Diane Pinero. I also thank my research assistants (from Fordham and elsewhere) who helped with different aspects of the book as well as related work over the years, and they are: Sam Adler, Abigail Carbajal, Joon-Sung Choe, Jillian Foley, Chehak Gogia, Clarissa Gowandi, Katherine Huffman, Sun Kim, Sophia Lattanzio, Juliet Liu, Lauren ReVeal, Diane Shin, Abbott Van Doren, Amy Walker, Ryan Whyte, Chrystel Yoo, and Susu Zhao.

Before coming to Fordham, I developed my scholarly voice and identity as an Alexander Fellow at NYU Law School in 2003–05. NYU had an incredibly supportive community for criminal law scholars at the time, which was cultivated and maintained by the late Jim Jacobs and the late Jerry Skolnick. Jim and Jerry, along with others including Rachel Barkow and David Garland, provided the most nurturing environment for young criminal law scholars that one could imagine. They, along with Noah Feldman, Larry Kramer, and Liam Murphy, guided me as I took my first crucial steps as a legal scholar. It is my good fortune that Nicola Lacey happened to be visiting NYU for a semester around then from London, and she has been an important source of support and mentorship since then. I thank them all for their guidance, past and continuing.

I could not have completed this book without the research leave I received in 2024–25 from Fordham University, and I am grateful for the support. I also thank the staff at the New York Society Library and the bar staff at Sant Ambroeus on Madison Avenue for keeping me productive with steady supplies of quiet and caffeine during that year.

This being my first book, I would like to use this space to acknowledge those who have shaped me in the early days. I did not think about writing as a craft until I had Ann Kashiwa for US History and did not appreciate literature and its potential for philosophical explorations until I had Bill Costello for English Literature, both at Mariner High School (before it split up to create Kamiak High School near my then home) in the suburbs of Seattle. The lights they lit all those years ago are still alive in me. I first imagined pursuing a life in academia when I fell in love with my studies at Swarthmore College. I thank my teachers and mentors for their guidance and encouragement, especially Rick Eldridge, Hugh Lacey, Hans Oberdiek, and Rich Schuldenfrei from the Philosophy Department, Barry Schwartz from the Psychology Department, and Mark Kuperberg and Steve O'Connell from the Economics Department. The discussions they led back then continue to inform my thinking to this day. The late Jerry Frug and the late David Charny helped me continue to grow intellectually by shaking my world loose and turning it upside down at Harvard Law School. I am grateful for their provocations, love of ideas old and new, and mentorship.

Early versions of different parts of this book have been presented, in addition to the venues already mentioned, at: Theorizing Criminal Law Conference at the Max Planck Institute for the Study of Crime, Security and Law in Freiburg, Institute of Criminology at Cambridge University, Maastricht Law and Philosophy Seminar, Roundtable on Global and Criminal Justice at Boston College School of Law, Conference on Desert at Centre for Moral Political Philosophy of the Hebrew University, Mini-Conference on Law and Epistemology hosted by *Noûs*, Criminal Defending Conference at the University of Illinois College of Law, Conference on Douglas Husak's Contribution to Criminal Law and Philosophy at Rutgers University, Conference on Proportionality in the Criminal Law at Georgetown Law Center, Symposium on R. A. Duff's *The Realm of Criminal Law* at King's College London, the Oxford Jurisprudence Discussion Group, Criminal Justice Roundtable at Yale Law School, and Conference on Proportionality in Theory and Practice at Goethe-University Frankfurt. I thank the organizers and participants at these meetings, especially Dick Arneson, Kevin Davis, Sharon Dolovich, Margareth Etienne, Jeff Fagan, Jim Forman, Alex Guerrero, Miri Gur-Arye, John Hasnas, Tatjana Hörnle, Heidi Hurd, Chimène Keitner, Martin Kelly, Steve Koh, Issa Kohler-Housmann, Jennifer Lackey, Ryan Liss, Ellie Mason, Tracey Meares, Lucas Miotto, Julie O'Sullivan, Joshua Pike, Massimo Renzo, Dan Richman, Julian Roberts, Re'em Segev, Andrew Simester, David Sklansky, and John Tasioulas.

Fragments of the book draw from previously published articles, and they are: "Reconceptualizing Incomplete Attempt," *Criminal Law Forum* 36, no. 3 (2025); "Proportionalities," *Notre Dame Law Review Reflection* 99, no. 3 (2024); "*Mala Prohibita*, the Wrongfulness Constraint, and the Problem of Overcriminalization," *Law and Philosophy* 41, no. 2 (2022); "*Mala Prohibita* and Proportionality," 15 *Criminal Law and Philosophy*, no. 3 (2021); "The State's Right to Evidence and Duties of Citizenship," *Philosophical Issues (A Supplement to* Noûs*)* 31, no. 1 (2021); "Punishing Disloyalty?: Treason, Espionage, and the Transgression of Political Boundaries," *Law and Philosophy* 31, no. 3 (2012), and "Recidivism as Omission: A Relational Account," *Texas Law Review* 87, no. 3 (2009). I am grateful to the publishers of these journals for permission to use these materials.

Finally, I'd like to express gratitude for my family. I am fortunate to have as my life partner Julie Chi-hye Suk, an extraordinary and astonishingly multitalented thinker and doer. And nothing brings more joy to me than seeing my two sons, Emile and Niccolo, grow and find their footing. They are everyday miracles of my life.

This book is dedicated to my parents who, contrary to the powerful norms that surrounded them, never demanded obedience from me and my sister as they raised us.

Introduction

This book is about laws that criminalize disobedience. Consider the following offenses:

- resisting arrest
- contempt
- perjury
- obstruction of justice
- receipt of stolen items
- money laundering
- failure to report child or sexual abuse
- failure to register as a sex offender
- violation of environmental regulations
- violation of food, drug, and medical devices regulations
- possession of guns
- possession of drugs
- espionage
- export control violation
- sanctions violation

Laws defining these offenses criminalize disobedience in the sense that the main reason to refrain from such conduct is that the government has prohibited it. That is, they do not involve conduct like murder or rape—conduct in which no one should ever engage, even in the absence of laws prohibiting such conduct.

This book takes a systematic look at the ways in which the state, through criminal law, demands obedience, threatens to punish people for disobedience, and carries out its threats. This book is concerned with the following questions. How should we think theoretically about disobedience? Is disobedience of the state blameworthy? In what ways does the state criminalize and punish disobedience? And what should be the limits to the state's power to demand obedience and punish disobedience?

The laws that create these offenses are not obscure laws that reside in little corners of the legal system, or legal oddities that are rarely enforced and the stuff

Criminalizing Disobedience. Youngjae Lee, Oxford University Press. © Oxford University Press 2026.
DOI: 10.1093/9780197617175.003.0001

of joke books about stupid laws. These are familiar laws, most of which are routinely enforced and reported in the news daily. These laws also tend to be controversial, and many of them have attracted criticism at one time or another from different parts of the ideological spectrum.

However, it is rare to find a person who is enthusiastic about or averse to *all* of them. It is much more likely to find a person who likes some of these laws but not others. For instance, a person may be in favor of tough enforcement of environmental regulations but critical of sex offender registration laws. A person may be in favor of tough gun laws but against tough drug laws. A person may be against laws criminalizing resisting arrest but may act outraged when someone defies judicial orders or obstructs legal proceedings, though that might also depend on which judicial orders and which legal proceedings are at issue. And so on and so forth.

Should the state be able to enact such prohibitions and back them up with criminal sanctions? Again, the answer to that question often seems to depend on which laws we are talking about, and one might be tempted to pick and choose which laws to support and which laws to oppose or ignore. However, it is not a straightforward matter to support only some of these laws and not others in a principled manner.

To see this, consider the following two statements:

1. The state should not be permitted to criminalize and punish morally innocent conduct.
2. Unless a law requires one to conform one's behavior to certain demands of morality (such as, for example, not engaging in murder or rape), mere disobedience of a law is morally innocent; therefore, when the state criminalizes and punishes such disobedience, it criminalizes and punishes morally innocent conduct.

If Statements 1 and 2 are correct, then there is potentially a problem with all of the laws designating conduct listed above as crimes *if* they are crimes of disobedience. Therefore, endorsing Statements 1 and 2 might threaten the validity of all these laws, and arguments relied upon to criticize laws that criminalize disobedience in some contexts may do the same in other contexts.

Here is a statement that takes a different position from Statement 2:

3. Even if a law does not require one to conform one's behavior to certain demands of morality (such as, for example, not engaging in murder or rape), mere disobedience of a law can be morally blameworthy; therefore, when the state criminalizes and punishes such disobedience, it may do so without criminalizing and punishing morally innocent conduct.

If Statement 3, as opposed to Statement 2, is true, then there is at least an argument to be made that *all* the laws designating conduct listed above as crimes are defensible. However, again, defending some instances of criminalization of disobedience with Statement 3 might entail defending other such instances.

There are two lessons to draw from this discussion. First, it is not easy to support only some of these laws and not others in a principled fashion by simply invoking either the duty to obey the law or lack thereof. Second, whether the crimes listed at the beginning are correctly characterized as crimes of disobedience matters because if they are, then the question whether mere disobedience can be criminalized and punished becomes a pressing issue when considering the merits of the laws.

Now, one may reject Statement 1 and adopt the view that it is okay for the state to criminalize and punish the morally innocent. Once that step is taken, then all the laws defining crimes above can be kept intact without having to embrace the view that mere disobedience is morally blameworthy. But let us set that possibility aside for now. For those of us who think that the state should not criminalize and punish the morally innocent, then keeping at least some of these laws intact would require embracing the view that disobedience can be morally blameworthy.

However, that is not the end of the story because Statement 2 encapsulates an understandable worry. There *is* something quite troubling about the idea of the state criminalizing and punishing mere disobedience. That is, once one seeks to defend at least some of these laws by embracing the notion that disobedience can be morally blameworthy, it immediately raises the question as to what sorts of limitations should exist on the state's ability to criminalize and punish disobedience.

That is, again, unlike laws that criminally prohibit, say, murder or rape, laws that criminalize mere disobedience seem to need special limitations. For instance, there is no individual right to commit murder, but there might be a right to possess a gun or recreational drugs, to resist arrest at times, or to leak state secrets to blow the whistle on government misbehavior. Criminalizing murder does not seem to be a disproportionate response on the part of the government to the possibility of people killing one another for no good reason, but criminalizing regulatory violations may be disproportionate at times. Characterizing an offense as a disobedience offense also raises the question whether the state that makes a demand to be obeyed has standing to do so, how it can earn and maintain such a standing, and how it may lose its standing to set rules, demand obedience, and punish disobedience. If the offenses listed at the beginning of this discussion are indeed disobedience offenses, then these questions become important.

This book is about such questions and defends the following propositions. First, the state should not be permitted to criminalize and punish morally innocent conduct. Second, broad swaths of criminal laws criminalize and punish disobeying the state, not necessarily for harming or risking harm to other people (like killing), but for merely disobeying. Third, disobedience of the state can be morally blameworthy; therefore, when the state criminalizes and punishes disobedience, it can do so without criminalizing and punishing morally innocent conduct. Fourth, because of the nature of disobedience offenses as disobedience offenses, the question of limitations on the state's ability to criminalize and punish disobedience is critical, and such limitations may take the form of individual rights, proportionality, and the requirement of what I will call "cooperation-worthiness" for the state to demand obedience.

The following is how the discussion unfolds, chapter by chapter.

Chapter 1 is devoted to the argument that the state should not criminalize and punish morally innocent conduct. The school of thought that is commonly associated with this position is "legal moralism," or the view that criminal wrongs and moral wrongs are closely related. Chapter 1 explains what is meant by legal moralism in this book and defends it. I should add that while the rest of the book's analysis assumes a certain shape due to concerns driven by legal moralism, the value of its discussions is not entirely dependent on the truth of legal moralism. The questions addressed in Chapters 2 to 12, whether a person who is being punished for violating a criminal law has behaved morally wrongfully and why, how the state can legitimately demand obedience and punish disobedience, and what limitations should be placed on such powers to criminalize and punish should interest and concern even those who are not persuaded by the particular account of legal moralism that is defended here or by legal moralism generally.

Chapter 2 describes the main topic of this book—criminalizing disobedience—by discussing what disobedience is and what it means to criminalize and punish disobedience. In short, to criminalize and punish disobedience is to criminally prohibit and punish acting, or failing to act, in ways that are counter to the law, when the relevant conduct is not morally wrongful, except for the fact that the law prohibits it. Under this definition, criminalizing and punishing murder would not count as an instance of criminalizing and punishing disobedience because murder is wrong whether the law prohibits it or not. On the other hand, criminalizing and punishing running a stop sign when there is no one around would count as criminalizing and punishing disobedience because running a stop sign when there is no one around is not really a wrong, except for the fact that the state has prohibited it. This formulation will be refined in Chapter 2, as the moral significance of one's conduct may change due to the law. For instance, if the law requires cars to drive on the right side of the road, then driving on the left side of the road when there are other cars around is dangerous and is morally wrong for that reason and is not a mere disobedience offense, even though there is a sense in which driving on the left side is not a wrong except for the fact that the state has prohibited it. A traditional way of discussing these sorts of ideas is the *malum prohibitum–malum in se* distinction, and Chapter 2 explains how this book's analysis relates to this distinction.

Chapter 2 also identifies the wrongfulness of disobedience that can provide a basis for its criminalization. Namely, Chapter 2 argues that the state serves a number of crucial functions, including ensuring physical security, coordinating behaviors of individuals and entities, resolving disputes, and providing numerous social services, and it often engages in these pursuits by formulating rules of behavior and enforcing them in various ways and addressing problems that arise. For the state to engage in these projects, it needs not only to formulate, announce, and enforce rules of behavior but also to authorize public entities and officials to devise programs and implement them with state instruments that they have at their disposal. Disobeying the law, then, can be blameworthy because there is a duty to support the state as it carries out its tasks, as the state cannot function and provide conditions for peaceful coexistence of strangers over a territory without cooperation of the governed. While each individual's effort makes little difference for the state to function successfully, each person has an obligation to do their fair share as the state seeks to do its work. Mistakes by the state, and disagreements among those impacted, about the wisdom and justice of the state's laws and actions are to be expected, but that reality, by itself, does not negate the duty to obey the law. However, this position need not commit one to the proposition that there is a general duty to obey the law.

Chapters 3 through 9, the bulk of this book, are devoted to showing the ways in which the state criminalizes and punishes disobedience. The discussions throughout the chapters are interpretive in the sense that they are a blend of description and normative evaluation of laws that criminalize disobedience, where more normatively defensible readings that are consistent with the legal materials are favored.

As mentioned above, laws that criminalize and punish disobedience cover a wide range. Chapters 3 and 4 discuss administration of justice crimes, which are crimes of interfering with or failing to support administration of justice. Chapter 3 focuses on interference offenses, such as contempt of judicial and administrative proceedings, disobedience of law enforcement officers, obstruction of justice, perjury, and false statements to government agents. Chapter 4 focuses on offenses relating to a failure to support law enforcement, such as hindering prosecution, receiving stolen property, money laundering, failure to report crimes, and failure to register as a person with relevant criminal history. Chapters 3 and 4 argue that administration of justice offenses are disobedience offenses because the commands do not invite individuals to make their own judgments even though whatever the law or legal actors demand may not be the best course to pursue all things considered, and challenges against such commands are met with a response that refers to the state's authority to determine which courses to pursue. Yet the laws demand obedience and require noninterference with and assistance of law enforcement and may punish failures to satisfy such requirements.

Chapter 5 shifts the focus from administration of justice crimes to regulatory offenses. The world of regulatory offenses is vast, as regulatory offenses can be generated from anything that the state regulates, which is just about everything. Regulatory offenses typically exist because regulatory schemes exist, implementing regulatory schemes often involves rules, and such rules are criminally enforced at times. Chapter 5 discusses as examples two broad areas of regulation: environmental protection and preservation on one hand and drugs and devices for medical use on the other. Chapter 5 shows that rule violations in such contexts do not necessarily result in direct endangerment of the public but might still interfere with regulatory schemes established by the government, which both sets the relevant standards and commands compliance with them. That is the sense in which regulatory offenses frequently turn out to be disobedience offenses.

Chapters 6 and 7 address the topic of preventive offenses, or offenses that criminalize conduct that may be harmless on its own but has a certain relationship to harm, which is the basis for its criminalization. Chapter 6 focuses on the crime of incomplete attempt. Chapter 6 is more revisionist than interpretive, as it contributes to a large existing body of theoretical work on attempt and argues against the prevailing view that the wrongfulness of incomplete attempt lies in the wrongfulness of trying to commit a wrongful act. Chapter 6 argues that we should instead conceptualize the offense of incomplete attempt as something akin to a regulatory offense, as the purpose of laws criminalizing incomplete attempt is to reduce the amount of risk of harm that exists in society. Incomplete attempt is a disobedience offense, then, because the wrongfulness of committing an incomplete attempt does not consist of *trying* to engage in a wrongful act (such as harming others) but interfering with the government's program of managing risks.

Chapter 7, the second chapter on preventive offenses, focuses on possession offenses, especially laws criminalizing possession of guns, certain addictive drugs, and child pornography. Chapter 7 argues that criminalizing possession serves many different purposes. First, it is a way of identifying those about to harm other people, especially when intent to harm is present or thought to be present. Second, it is a regulatory mechanism that disallows some people from possessing something in order to reduce the amount of risk from potentially harmful objects, like guns. Third, it is a tool the government enlists to fight the existence of markets that harm society, such as those for child pornography or illicit drugs. Despite the variety, what these possession offenses have in common is that they are all best understood as disobedience offenses. That is, the laws do not criminalize the wrong of harming or risking harm to others but rather criminalize the wrong of interfering with the government's attempt to reduce the overall amount of harm in society. That is the sense in which possession offenses are disobedience offenses.

Chapters 8 and 9 discuss national security offenses. Chapter 8 focuses on the crime of treason and Chapter 9 on espionage offenses. Chapter 8 argues that while treason criminalizes the wrong of betrayal for government officials who are given access to power and information in exchange for their commitment to work on behalf of a political community, the wrongfulness of treason is less straightforward for ordinary citizens. For such people, the chapter argues, the best account of the wrongfulness of treason is that they are going against the state's command not to engage in certain acts of disloyalty in the realm of national security even when the morality of taking the side of one's own nation may be questionable. In this way, treason is a crime of disobedience.

Chapter 9, on espionage, export control, and international sanctions, starts by discussing several famous cases of espionage, such as those of Klaus Fuchs, Ethel and Julius Rosenberg, Robert Hanssen, Aldrich Ames, Daniel Ellsberg, Chelsea Manning, and Edward Snowden, and argues that we should interpret the wrong of espionage offenses as involving not betrayal or risking harm, but usurpation. The relevant wrong is rooted in the idea of separation of powers between individuals and the state, and we should conceive of these national security crimes as crimes of usurpation or "foreign relations vigilantism," which is in its essence a failure to respect the lines drawn and areas designated as off limits by the state to those not otherwise authorized by the state to enter. Chapter 9 explains the wrongness of export controls and international sanctions violations in the same way.

As alluded to above, that an act of disobedience can be blameworthy does not necessarily mean that criminalization and punishment of it is warranted. The last three chapters, 10 through 12, explore several principles that provide sources of limitation on the state's power to criminalize and punish disobedience. Chapter 10 argues that while the state may set down all kinds of rules to make the project of living together possible in a way that is consistent with the principle of punishing only the morally blameworthy, the state's power to criminalize and punish disobedience should be further limited in order to preserve a sphere of autonomy in which people can move about and pursue their ordinary life projects free of the state's interference. Some such limitations may take the form of constitutional rights, such as freedom of thought, freedom of speech and expression, freedom of association, right to privacy, privilege against self-incrimination, and so on, but they need not be, as the liberty interest of individuals does not disappear just because we are not dealing with fundamental rights recognized by constitutions.

Chapter 11 focuses on limitations on the state's power to criminalize and punish based on different principles of proportionality, primarily the principle of proportionality in punishment and the principles of proportionality and necessity in self-defense and war. This chapter discusses some special difficulties of applying the principle of proportionality in punishment in the context of disobedience offenses and sketches what it would mean to apply other principles of proportionality to the question of criminalization in the context of disobedience offenses, especially as they may manifest in the idea of criminal law as a last resort, or *ultima ratio*.

Chapter 12 then argues that the state at times may find itself in a situation where its laws seek to criminalize and punish disobedience, yet it lacks standing to demand obedience because it is not cooperation-worthy. In such situations where the state lacks standing to demand obedience, it may need to refrain from punishing individuals for mere disobedience. Chapter 12 then argues that the state, in order to avoid such uncomfortable and corrosive situations where a law is broken but it does not have the standing to enforce the law against the person who has broken the law, must work continually to earn its cooperation-worthiness and maintain its standing to set rules and demand obedience and punish disobedience.

Finally, a note about the source of laws discussed in this book. While this book is written as a book of criminal law and philosophy that has applicability in different legal systems, the book's primary focus is on state and federal criminal laws of the United States. That the book focuses mostly on laws based in the United States should not be taken to suggest that this book is only for those concerned with the status of disobedience crimes in the United States. The general arguments are meant to apply to any jurisdiction that may criminalize and punish disobedience.

1

Criminal Wrongs and Moral Wrongs

I. Introduction

A book about criminal law and disobedience can be written in many different ways, and this book takes an approach that I will call "legal moralism." That is, the main question that I will be asking about the criminal laws under scrutiny in this book is whether the laws in question criminalize and punish moral wrongs. That the legal moralist perspective is legitimate and fruitful as a scholarly methodology is something that should be defended, not just assumed. The purpose of this chapter is to justify this book's approach to these laws.

The phrase "legal moralism" has been unfortunately associated with Lord Patrick Devlin's 1959 lecture, later republished as a book called *The Enforcement of Morals*,[1] and H. L. A. Hart's criticism of it in *Law, Liberty, and Morality*,[2] and with the notion that it is the proper function of the law to enforce morality, which sounds illiberal and oppressive.[3] Legal moralism as an idea has moved far beyond that debate in contemporary criminal law theory, and it is not my aim here to devise a proper definition of the phrase and defend a particular version over all others.[4] In this book, I use the phrase to refer to the idea that there is a close relationship between criminal wrongs and moral wrongs and that criminal laws should be evaluated by asking whether whatever they criminalize are genuine moral wrongs.[5]

[1] Patrick Devlin, *The Enforcement of Morals* (Oxford University Press, 1965).

[2] H. L. A. Hart, *Law, Liberty, and Morality* (Stanford University Press, 1963).

[3] Recent revelations about Devlin's decade-long sexual abuse of his daughter also render him a poor spokesperson for legal moralism and make his association with this school of thought even more unfortunate than it was pre-revelations. See, e.g., Beatrix Campbell, "'Our Silence Permits Perpetrators to Continue': One Woman's Fight to Expose a Father's Abuse," *Guardian*, July 25, 2021.

[4] For a detailed discussion, see R. A. Duff, *The Realm of Criminal Law* (Oxford University Press, 2018), 52–101.

[5] Some have used the metaphor of "mirror" to illustrate the close relationship between criminal law and morality. Douglas Husak, for instance, has argued that "the rules and principles of the criminal law should mirror morality in the absence of good reason to the contrary." Douglas Husak, *Ignorance of Law: A Philosophical Inquiry* (Oxford University Press, 2016), 41. James Edwards and Tarek Yusari have called this "the mirror principle," which they describe as the view that "the norms of the criminal law should be such that they have counterparts with the same content in morality" and that, in part, "legal wrongs that are offences should be moral wrongs." James Edwards and Tarek Yusari, "The Internal Morality of Criminal Law," *Oxford Journal of Legal Studies* 43, no. 3 (2023): 478. The image of a "mirror" is useful to convey the close relationship between criminal law and morality, and I will be using it occasionally as a shorthand. However, the "mirror" metaphor is also misleading,

Criminalizing Disobedience. Youngjae Lee, Oxford University Press. © Oxford University Press 2026.
DOI: 10.1093/9780197617175.003.0002

More specifically, there is a distinction here to be made between negative and positive legal moralism, where negative legal moralism emphasizes that the law should criminalize *only* moral wrongs and that a criminal law that criminalizes something that is not morally wrong is defective for that reason, whereas positive legal moralism considers moral wrongfulness of something to be a reason to criminalize it.[6] The phrase "legal moralism" is used in both negative and positive senses in this book, and the basis for that outlook is elaborated in the rest of this chapter. I should add, though, that much of the book is motivated by negative moralism and is thus focused on the question whether a given law criminalizes a moral wrong and satisfies what has been called "the wrongfulness constraint."[7]

Legal moralism, understood in the more general sense of positing a close relationship between legal and moral concepts, characterizes the methodology of much of the scholarship in many areas of the law, not just criminal law. This is to be expected given that, as Oliver Wendell Holmes pointed out long ago, the law is "full of phraseology drawn from morals," such as "rights, and duties, and malice, and intent, and negligence, and so forth."[8] Criminal law, in particular, is awash with morality. Murder, rape, and assault are obviously criminal wrongs that are also moral wrongs. Seen that way, legal moralism in criminal law seems to require no special justification.

As Holmes also warned, though, moral terms in law, "by the mere force of language continually invite[] us to pass from one domain to another without perceiving it," and "nothing is easier . . . than to take these words in their moral sense . . . and . . . to drop into fallacy."[9] Holmes is correct to emphasize that law is one thing and morality is quite another, and criminal law is no exception. So the question remains. Why should criminal law have anything to do with morality? Holmes's admonition is about the need to be careful not to confuse moral and legal meanings of terms that sound alike, but the lesson can be extended to the task of understanding the proper content of criminal law. More specifically, does the fact that moral wrongs and criminal wrongs generally share at least some

as the term suggests a one-way relationship, where morality is fixed and it is the law's task to reflect it accurately. An important phenomenon this book highlights is the *moral* significance of the *legal* act of prohibiting or requiring something in criminal law. The moment that happens, the relevant legal act can turn a hitherto morally innocent conduct into a morally wrongful conduct, and the image of a "mirror" has trouble efficiently expressing such a dynamic, two-way-street nature of the relationship between criminal law and morality. However, to the extent the "mirror principle" stands for the idea that "legal wrongs that are offences should be moral wrongs," the principle correctly represents the meaning of legal moralism as used in this book.

[6] See Duff, *The Realm of Criminal Law*, 55–58.

[7] Douglas Husak, *Overcriminalization: The Limits of the Criminal Law* (Oxford University Press, 2008), 66 (defining the "wrongful constraint" as the principle that "[c]riminal liability may not be imposed unless the defendant's conduct is (in some sense) wrongful").

[8] Oliver Wendell Holmes Jr., "The Path of the Law," *Harvard Law Review* 10, no. 8 (1897): 459–60.

[9] Holmes, "The Path of the Law," 459–60.

superficial resemblance imply that that is the way things ought to be? And should criminal laws be written in a morally inflected way, and should the law criminalize only what is morally wrongful?

II. Criminal Law as a Distinctive Mode of Harm Prevention

We first have to define our subject. What is criminal law? Here is a working definition: criminal law is the body of laws that prohibit (or require) certain acts and impose punishment on those who fail to comply with such prohibitions or requirements. And what is criminal law for? A popular understanding of criminal law is that it is a means to prevent people from harming other people. But if minimizing the incidence of people harming other people is a goal to be pursued, it can be done in any number of ways with and without using criminal law and punishment issued and administered by the state.

First, a society may prevent certain harmful behaviors not by using criminal law but by devoting resources to numerous other basic goods and services, such as education, health care for physical and mental health, job training, employment, child care, welfare benefits, universal basic income, and community organizations. Such early interventions are different from criminal law and punishment. In addition, this method of preventing harm leaves the government's role in it undefined, as these kinds of services may be provided by the public or private sector.

Second, people also engage in prevention of harm by taking steps to avoid becoming targets of certain behaviors. People put locks on doors and fences around properties, place valuable items in cars out of plain view, refrain from walking alone at night in certain neighborhoods, hold onto their bags and wallets tightly in crowded places, and so on. Toy and electronics stores have anti-theft packaging, and drug and liquor stores place certain items in locked cabinets. These devices prevent certain undesired behaviors, too, but do so without using criminal law and punishment, and, again, need not involve the government.

Third, as the existence of quarantine facilities and mental institutions shows, we can prevent people from harming other people by placing those who carry risks of harming others in places where they are not able to inflict harm. This method of preventing harm may be present in criminal law, but incapacitation of those who are too dangerous to be out and about does not require criminal laws, as it merely requires identifying and incapacitating those who are likely to end up harming others. In other words, while we may use criminal law and punishment in order to incapacitate, we may also incapacitate without criminal law and punishment. But because this method of preventing harm can take the form of physical—often coercive and violent—interventions, government involvement is often needed to execute the method lawfully.

Finally, we can prevent harmful behaviors by attaching unpleasant consequences to certain risky or harmful conduct. Property owners have guard dogs or automatic guns that are set up to attack intruders. Unless such owners are sadists who want to harm others or see themselves as doling out private punishment to trespassers, the purpose of such additions to property is to prevent, not harm, intruders, and the prevention is achieved by warning the would-be intruders of negative consequences of intruding. Similarly, people who park illegally, run red lights, or go over the speed limit can get caught by cameras and receive traffic tickets that demand payment, and failures to pay can result in their licenses to drive being suspended. Such disincentives change people's behaviors. More generally, a society may have rules that tell people to do or refrain from doing some things and enforce such rules by imposing fines or prison sentences on transgressors. And sometimes the law may discourage harmful behavior by providing remedies in the shape of civil lawsuits, like in torts. Some of these strategies are recognizable as state punishment that enforces criminal laws, though not all, but they all have in common the basic feature of preventing harm by attaching disincentives to harmful conduct and inducing people to adjust their behaviors in response.

Among these four strategies of harm prevention, only the last two resemble what is conventionally classified as criminal law, and they are forms of incapacitation and deterrence, two commonly mentioned functions of criminal law and state punishment. And, between the two, only the latter, deterrence, naturally renders itself to the form of commands issued by the government and followed by sanctions and thus bears the most resemblance to the commonsense understanding of criminal law. Incapacitation, by contrast, need not involve any commands to conform one's behavior, as the point is not to induce people to adjust their behaviors but to keep those who pose danger away from others. A person's failure to comply with state commands may be taken as evidence of the need for the state to incapacitate that person, but such commands are generally incidental to the project of incapacitation.[10]

[10] There are some exceptions, such as the "Disqualification Clause" of the Fourteen Amendment, Section 3 of the US Constitution, which provides in part:

> No person shall be a Senator or Representative in Congress, or elector of President and Vice-President, or hold any office, civil or military, under the United States, or under any State, who, having previously taken an oath, as a member of Congress, or as an officer of the United States, or as a member of any State legislature, or as an executive or judicial officer of any State, to support the Constitution of the United States, shall have engaged in insurrection or rebellion against the same, or given aid or comfort to the enemies thereof.

U.S. Const. amend. XIV, § 3. This type of incapacitation appears to be a hybrid, as it may deter, incapacitate, and punish all at once.

So, to go back to the original question about the relationship between moral wrongs and criminal wrongs, that question is not about all the different ways of preventing people from harming other people but only about criminal law, a state institution. The basic picture it assumes is a system where the government issues a set of rules and demands that the people to whom the rules apply comply with such rules. A subset of such rules is criminal law, and it is the content of that law that I seek to examine in this book.

To be clear, not all laws that we think of as belonging to criminal law take the form of commands backed up with sanctions. Some "criminal laws" define how the overall criminal justice system is to be organized, designed, and administered, including how law enforcement officers are to behave and what rights defendants have during the criminal process, and a collection of such laws is typically labeled "criminal procedure," to be contrasted against "criminal law" or "substantive criminal law." When I ask whether there is a close relationship between criminal wrongs and moral wrongs, I am talking only about substantive criminal law and not criminal procedure.

Some may wonder at this point, after having looked at the different modes of harm prevention, why one would want to single out "criminal law" defined as such as an object of study and focus on the question of the relationship of criminal wrongs and moral wrongs. Criminal law is just one of many modes of harm prevention, and it does not seem that it is necessary for there to be a close relationship between criminal wrongs and moral wrongs. Anything in theory can be criminalized and paired with negative consequences, and behaviors that we do not like—whether they are morally wrongful or not—can be threatened with sanctions, and such threats can be carried out in order to reform, deter, and incapacitate people. The content of what we call "criminal law" and the content of morality would of course overlap, but that is only because serious moral wrongs to others often have the feature of doing harm to others. Criminal law, in other words, may be seen simply as one of many levers the government can press to pursue its policy objectives, especially the objective of preventing people from harming others. What that means is that sometimes criminal law targets moral wrongs but sometimes it does not, and the question whether there is a close relationship between criminal wrongs and moral wrongs is not a very interesting question.

We could just leave things at that, but, in my view, doing so would be a mistake, as it would result in a woefully deficient understanding of criminal law, precisely in that it misses the important relationship between criminal wrongs and moral wrongs. But how are they related? We in fact have no shortage of accounts that posit a close relationship between criminal and moral wrongs.

III. Desert

According to one common view, the purpose of criminal law is to give people what they deserve. People who do bad things should get what they deserve, and criminal law is well positioned to give people what they deserve. If criminal law fails to deliver in this regard, we might experience that as deeply disappointing and consider the law to have failed.[11]

The most well-known theoretical articulation of a perspective like this is perhaps the one by Michael Moore, who has argued that "criminal law is a functional kind whose function is to attain retributive justice" where "[r]etributive justice demands that those who deserve punishment get it."[12] According to this view, criminal law's purpose is to give people what they deserve, namely, punishment, and what that in turn means is that criminal wrongs have to be moral wrongs. Criminal law must be written to capture moral wrongs because, in Moore's words, "[t]o deserve punishment, . . . one must have done a wrongful action, and one must have done so culpably."[13] Call this the "Desert Thesis" for the view that there is a close relationship between criminal wrongs and moral wrongs.

> *Desert Thesis*: Criminal wrongs and moral wrongs should be closely related because (1) criminal law's essential function is to give people what they deserve, and (2) in order for criminal law to give what people deserve, the law should criminalize what is morally wrong.

Let us bracket the questions that may arise from the fear that the Desert Thesis may be another way of stating Devlin's thesis that criminal law should enforce morality. That is, we will ignore the question whether the law should criminalize *all* moral wrongs or only *some* moral wrongs and focus on a different problem.[14]

A serious problem with the Desert Thesis is that it is not clear whether we can go from the idea that some people deserve to be punished to the conclusion that criminal law therefore ought to give people what they deserve. One plausible understanding of the idea that people should get what they deserve is the "whole life view" of desert, which means that what a person deserves should be determined by looking at that person's life as a whole, not just what that person has done on a given day.[15]

[11] See, e.g., Amber Rose Carlson, "Is There a Rational Punishment for My Rapist?," *New York Times*, October 23, 2017.

[12] Michael S. Moore, *Placing Blame: A Theory of Criminal Law* (Clarendon Press, 1997), 33.

[13] Moore, *Placing Blame*, 33.

[14] For a discussion of the distinction between private and public moral wrongs, see Duff, *The Realm of Criminal Law*, 168–76, 187–89.

[15] See Victor Tadros, *The Ends of Harm: The Moral Foundations of Criminal Law* (Oxford University Press, 2011), 68–73. For an argument against the "whole life" understanding of desert, see

However, it is odd, once desert is understood in this way, to think that criminal law ought to be designed to give people what they deserve. As a general matter, the state is not in the business of ensuring just deserts. Bad things may happen to good people, just as some people may achieve far more success than they deserve. But it is not the state's job to intervene and take from those who have more than they deserve and give to those who have less than they deserve. Such skepticism is warranted, especially considering that saying that a person deserves something rarely imposes an obligation for anyone to make sure that person gets what they deserve.[16]

In other words, the problem with desert-based accounts of state punishment is that it is obscure as to why the state is tasked with the project of giving people what they deserve and why only what they *negatively* deserve. In addition, because the connection between desert and the state's role is not robustly made under the account, the theory opens itself up to the idea that it does not matter much *who* does the punishing. The operating principle is that people who are bad or have done bad things should receive the punishment they deserve, which appears indifferent as to *who* gives them what they deserve.

We will need something more than just the idea of desert to give an account of state punishment, and if the desert-based account of state punishment is thus a nonstarter, then the view that criminal wrongs ought to mirror moral wrongs cannot be based on that account.

IV. State Displacement of Private Vengeance

Having rejected the Desert Thesis, we might start with another commonly given purpose of criminal law, which is to *displace* personal vengeance by punishing wrongdoing.[17] As John Gardner evocatively has put it, "The blood feud, the vendetta, the duel, the revenge, the lynching: for the elimination of these modes of retaliation, more than anything else, the criminal law as we know it today came into existence."[18] In other words, a core purpose of criminal law and punishment

Göran Duus-Otterström, "Do Offenders Deserve Proportionate Punishments?" *Criminal Law and Philosophy* 15, no. 3 (2021): 463–80.

[16] Douglas N. Husak, "Why Punish the Deserving?" *Noûs* 26, no. 4 (1992): 447–64; see also Joel Feinberg, "Justice and Personal Desert," in *Doing and Deserving* (Princeton University Press, 1970), 60 ("[A] person's desert of *X* is always a reason for giving *X* to him, but not always a conclusive reason.").

[17] See, e.g., John Gardner, "Crime: In Proportion and in Perspective," in *Offences and Defences: Selected Essays in the Philosophy of Criminal Law* (Oxford University Press, 2007), 213.

[18] Gardner, "Crime: In Proportion and in Perspective," 213; see also Scott Hershovitz, "Vindicating Criminal Law," in *From Morality to Law and Back Again: A Liber Amicorum for John Gardner*, ed. Michelle Madden Dempsey and François Tanguay-Renaud (Oxford University Press,

is to manage the punitive and retaliatory emotions of those who have been victims of wrongdoers (as well as others in the community who feel indirectly victimized) and to sublimate, displace, and provide an outlet for feelings of resentment toward the wrongdoers.

The displacement function of criminal law is relevant for our purposes because it provides a way of explaining the relationship between criminal wrongs and moral wrongs. Given the displacement function, the state, when it convicts and punishes, must act in a way that adequately replaces and improves upon a system of private vengeance. It follows that a properly functioning system must speak in a voice that is recognizable from the perspective of ordinary moral intuitions about wrongdoing, and the success or failure of a society's criminal law system thus depends on how well it responds to the punitive emotions of its people.[19] The criminal wrongs-moral wrongs connection, then, is not a feature that flows from the general principle that people ought to receive what they deserve. Rather, it is a requirement that stems from the very reason for the state's takeover of the task of adjudicating wrongs away from individuals' hands. Let us call this the Displacement Thesis.

> *Displacement Thesis*: Criminal wrongs and moral wrongs should be closely related because: (1) criminal law's essential function is to displace private responses to wrongdoing by creating and maintaining state institutions that respond to such acts of wrongdoing, and (2) for such state responses to constitute an adequate substitute for private responses, they must convey the wrongness of the acts to which the state is responding.

The Displacement Thesis has its problems, however. An obvious one is its seeming endorsement of people's desire for vengeance and its assumption that a measure of the state's success is to be anchored in satisfaction of such desires. Given the enormous amount of harm that the state can bring about in people's lives through its uses of power to criminalize and punish, that the state is doing so in order to satisfy the people's thirst for revenge is not the most flattering story to tell about the institution of criminal law and punishment.

That is, state punishment may be thought of as a way of replacing private vengeance, but if whatever state punishment is replacing is morally unjustified, then to the extent that the state produces outcomes that resemble those that it

2023), 139 ("[A]ccording to Gardner, . . . criminal law is worth having, in no small part, because it dampens retaliatory impulses.").

[19] See Gardner, "Crime: In Proportion and in Perspective," 216 ("[T]he criminal law's medicine must be strong enough to control the toxins of bitterness and resentment which course through the veins of those who are wronged, or else the urge to retaliate in kind will persist unchecked.").

replaces, state punishment seems morally suspect as well. What is needed is an additional step of justifying the response demanded by the people. Without such a justificatory step, the government's use of power becomes merely a version of keeping the people satisfied, no matter how morally suspect their demands may be.

What would such a justificatory step look like? There are two possibilities. The first possibility is to resist the description of private responses to wrongdoing as vengeance or retaliation but as legitimate enforcement of rights by individuals. Gardner's invocation of words like "blood feud," "revenge," and "lynching" suggests that "these modes of retaliation" are evils to be eliminated. That may well be the case, but putting it that way may obscure the natural right of punishment each person has in the state of nature. It is this natural right to punish that gets transferred to the state when the state forms, so there is nothing embarrassing about the state simply drawing from each person's right to punish.[20] It would be a mistake, under this view, to see the state punishment as retaliation to satisfy the people's bloodthirst.[21]

The second possibility, which does not rely on the natural right to punish in the state of nature, is for the state to be careful to respond punitively only to wrongdoing, instead of simply following what the people want.[22] This limitation is in some tension with the need for criminal law to achieve stability through responding to wrongdoing on victims' behalf, as the state's own moral judgments may end up frustrating the victims, but that is the way it has to be for the Displacement Thesis if the "displacement" is to be an improvement over private vengeance.

Even if the Displacement Thesis survives in one of these two ways, there is another problem, which has to do with the breadth of criminal law. We will revisit these offenses more in detail in later chapters, but consider crimes like the crime of giving investment advice without a license[23] and the crime of failing to declare that one is carrying more than $10,000 in cash when leaving the country.[24] When one thinks of crimes, paradigmatic offenses are those that tend

[20] Cf. A. John Simmons, "Locke and the Right to Punish," *Philosophy and Public Affairs* 20, no. 4 (1991): 311.

[21] I thank Richard Arneson for this point.

[22] Cf. Duff, *The Realm of Criminal Law*, 53–54.

[23] 15 U.S.C. § 80b-3 ("[I]t shall be unlawful for any investment adviser, unless registered under this section, . . . to make use of the mails or any means or instrumentality of interstate commerce in connection with his or its business as an investment adviser."); 15 U.S.C. § 80b-2 ("'Investment adviser' means any person who, for compensation, engages in the business of advising others . . . as to the advisability of investing in, purchasing, or selling securities."); 15 U.S.C. § 80b-17 ("Any person who willfully violates any provision of this subchapter, or any rule, regulation, or order promulgated by [the Securities and Exchange] Commission under authority thereof, shall, upon conviction, be fined not more than $10,000, imprisoned for not more than five years, or both.").

[24] 31 U.S.C. § 5316(a)(1)(A).

to mirror offenses that are, one might say, "found in nature." Killing another person is morally wrongful "in nature," and the crime of murder in our criminal codes seems to merely formalize and legally recognize what is already found "in nature." The Displacement Thesis goes well with these sorts of offenses. The kinds of examples just given, however, do not appear to be found "in nature." For there to be offenses like failure to declare export of currency or practicing investment advising without a license, nonnatural entities like the government, laws, agencies, and regulations must be in place. It is only when such nonnatural, manmade, artificial institutions come into existence the possibility of such offenses comes into being.

The problem is that it is not clear whether something like the Displacement Thesis, which may be compelling in its own way in explaining criminal laws having to do with conduct like murder and rape, has much explanatory power in a world where the government has its hands, often using criminal law, in many more aspects of our lives than simply those having roughly to do with living next to one another without harming one another. Therefore, the Displacement Thesis does not look so plausible when placed next to the sheer breadth of criminal law.[25]

We may at this point attempt to save the Displacement Thesis by limiting its scope. Perhaps it explains some criminal laws but not all and will remain at best an incomplete theory. But we would then need an account of how important the Displacement Thesis is, as it may end up explaining the criminal wrongs–moral wrongs connection in only a highly limited way, as its scope seems quite narrow. That is, it is not that the Displacement Thesis does not look plausible but that its significance seems limited and out of touch with today's criminal law. So we will have to give another account of the relationship between criminal wrongs and moral wrongs.

V. Censure and Condemnation

A. Censure Thesis

Joel Feinberg has sketched one way of thinking about criminal law that may avoid the difficulty of imagining the state as being in the business of giving people what they deserve or displacing private vengeance. He describes the criminal law process as being "in its very nature a kind of complex 'moral machine,'" where "[a]pprehended suspects are fed into one of the process and either emerge, status

[25] Cf. Vincent Chiao, "Two Conceptions of the Criminal Law," in *The New Philosophy of Criminal Law*, ed. Chad Flanders and Zachary Hoskins (Rowman & Littlefield International, 2016), 23.

unchanged, through various escape hatches along the way, or are processed right through to the other end of the machine, where the moral stigma is stamped on both by a judge's solemn pronouncements and the reprobatory symbolism of their confinement."[26] Buying into this picture does not commit one to the view that the purpose of criminal law is to give people what they deserve or to replace private vengeance. Instead, Feinberg imagines taking the criminal justice system built in that particular way and asking: "Here is the complex moral machine . . . ; now, for what purposes only should we use it?"[27]

That the criminal justice system has the feature of attaching "moral stigma" to those who are subject to it is a commonly held view, though not everyone puts it in terms of "moral stigma." Feinberg's articulation elsewhere that punishment is "a conventional device for the expression of attitudes of resentment and indignation" is canonical.[28] Another well-known statement comes from Henry Hart, who has argued that "[w]hat distinguishes a criminal from a civil sanction and all that distinguishes it . . . is the judgment of community condemnation which accompanies and justifies its imposition."[29]

These ideas remain prevalent to this day. Douglas Husak, writing decades after Feinberg and Hart, has noted that "quarantine, deportation, civil commitment, and any number of unwanted practices that deprive persons of one or more rights should not be construed as modes of punishment" as "they neither intend to, nor succeed in stigmatizing persons who are subject to them."[30] R. A. Duff has similarly written that criminal convictions carry a certain meaning—namely, "censure or condemnation" and that "censurable wrongfulness is integral to criminal law in a way that it is not integral to a system of non-criminal regulation."[31] The US Supreme Court has endorsed this interpretation of the criminal process as well. When it held in *In re Winship* that the US Constitution requires "proof beyond a reasonable doubt of every fact necessary to constitute the crime" for a conviction, it justified its decision partly on "the certainty that [the accused] would be stigmatized by the conviction."[32]

These formulations are all slightly different, but it does appear to be the case that if this picture of the criminal justice system is correct, then there is a reason

[26] Joel Feinberg, "Some Unswept Debris from the Hart-Devlin Debate," *Synthese* 72, no. 2 (1987): 255.

[27] Feinberg, "Some Unswept Debris from the Hart-Devlin Debate," 256; see also A. P. Simester and Andreas von Hirsch, *Crimes, Harms and Wrongs: On the Principles of Criminalisation* (Hart Publishing, 2014), 10 (describing criminal law as a "morally loaded sledgehammer").

[28] Joel Feinberg, "The Expressive Function of Punishment," *The Monist* 49, no. 3 (1965): 400.

[29] Henry M. Hart, "The Aims of the Criminal Law," *Law and Contemporary Problems* 23, no. 3 (1958): 404.

[30] Douglas N. Husak, "Already Punished Enough," *Philosophical Topics* 18, no. 1 (1990): 84.

[31] Duff, *The Realm of Criminal Law*, 18, 19.

[32] In re *Winship*, 397 U.S. 358, 363 (1970).

to believe that criminal law should target moral wrongdoing.[33] Let us call this the "Censure Thesis."

> *Censure Thesis*: Criminal wrongs and moral wrongs should be closely related because (1) conviction and punishment of a person through the criminal process express censure, and (2) the law should criminalize (only) what is censurable so that the legal conclusion that supports such a governmental action is based on a judgment about what is properly censurable in a person's conduct.

Perhaps this account is more plausible than, say, the idea that it is the state's job to give people what they deserve or to displace private vengeance. However, there are at least two questions to raise about it. First, is it really the case that the criminal process is a "complex moral machine"? It seems that we would have to do some interpretive work to reach that conclusion.[34] Second, even if the criminal process is plausibly described as a complex moral machine, that does not settle the question as to whether that is the way it should be. There may be good reasons not to have the state operate a complex moral machine.

B. Is Censure What Makes Criminal Conviction Distinctive?

Let's take the first question. The question whether the censure aspect correctly describes the criminal justice system—the first part of the Censure Thesis—is not a simple matter.

One source of confusion is that the idea that criminal conviction and punishment express censure is often combined with the observation that censure is what makes criminal conviction and punishment *distinctive*. This combination can give one the impression that examples of governmental actions that stigmatize individuals in noncriminal settings can serve as counterexamples. A simple fix to that is to point out that just because criminal conviction and punishment express censure does not mean that is the only way for the government to express censure, but that answer can raise more questions about how widespread the phenomenon of government expressions of censure outside the criminal law setting is and what that means. If the supposedly distinctive feature of criminal conviction and punishment turns out not to be so distinctive, then it cannot be used as a reliable way to generate conclusions about what criminal law ought to be without committing one to broader implications that may well get out of

[33] Duff, *The Realm of Criminal Law*, 19.

[34] Some have said that punishment conveys censure by definition. See Simester and von Hirsch, *Crimes Harms and Wrongs*, 11 ("We take it to be conceptually true that punishment connotes blame.").

hand. So, instead of quickly disposing of the issue of criminal law's distinctiveness by deeming it irrelevant, it is worth examining some of the complications of the idea that criminal conviction and punishment censure.

Counterexamples to the idea that censure or moral stigma is what makes criminal convictions distinctive abound. For instance, in *Kansas v. Hendricks*, the US Supreme Court considered the Kansas Sexually Violent Predator Act, which provides for civil commitment of someone who has been "convicted or charged with a sexually violent offense and who suffers from a mental abnormality or personality disorder which makes the person likely to engage in the predatory acts of sexual violence."[35] The Court held in the case that the civil commitment scheme is "nonpunitive" and is civil in nature.[36] It seems, though, that to be deprived of liberty because of the state's judgment that one's "personality disorder" makes it likely one will engage in "predatory acts of sexual violence" can be stigmatizing, even if the deprivation of liberty is styled "civil," not "criminal."

Also consider sex offender registration requirements. In *Smith v. Doe*, the US Supreme Court looked at the Alaska Sex Offender Registration Act, which requires those who have been convicted of sex offenses to register as sex offenders. When the law was challenged at least partly for "resembl[ing] shaming punishments," the Court acknowledged that the law "may cause adverse consequences for the convicted defendant, running from mild personal embarrassment to social ostracism" but still held that the registration requirement was "civil" and "nonpunitive."[37] A few lower courts since then have held otherwise and declared the sex offender registration requirements that are more intrusive than the one at issue in *Doe* to amount to punishment,[38] but the point remains. Sex offender registration was acknowledged to be potentially stigmatizing by the Supreme Court but was still classified as civil in nature.

What these two examples show is that it is an overstatement to say that criminal conviction is distinctive because it stigmatizes. Feinberg's complex moral machine seems to be at work in these civil contexts as well. One possible response is to say that the distinctiveness of criminal law lies in that the stigma is *intended* in that context because expressing censure is one of the purposes of criminal law. Preventive detention and sex offender registries may be stigmatizing, but only as a byproduct of governmental efforts to prevent harm, as there is no state intent to express censure about those who are subject to such treatments. However, this

[35] Kansas v. Hendricks, 521 U.S. 346, 352 (1997).

[36] Hendricks, 521 U.S. at 369.

[37] Smith v. Doe, 538 U.S. 84, 99 (2003).

[38] See, e.g., Does 1-5 v. Snyder, 834 F.3d 696 (6th Cir. 2016); see also Jane Ramage, "Reframing the Punishment Test through Modern Sex Offender Legislation," *Fordham Law Review* 88, no. 3 (2019): 1099.

way of defending the idea that criminal law is distinctive because of its censuring aspect has a number of difficulties.

First, there is the question whether we can coherently maintain that the state has "intentions" in a way that is at least analogous to the way persons have intentions.[39] Without an ability to articulate what it means for the state to have an "intention," it appears difficult, at least at first glance, to make any important distinctions on the basis of what the state supposedly "intends." Second, even if we can coherently ascribe intentions to the state, its intent to express censure may be unreliable as a way of marking out what is distinctive about criminal law, given that the state uses criminal law for all kinds of reasons. The state may be interested in not only punishing but in managing and surveilling certain populations. Issa Kohler-Hausmann, for instance, has argued that a study of misdemeanor prosecutions in New York City shows that "the animating goal" behind the city's misdemeanor prosecution is "using various tools to sort and regulate the population of people who flow through the courts," as opposed to "determining guilt or innocence and imposing sanctions accordingly."[40] And this is only one example among many; entire legal and sociological literatures are devoted to the topic of what the state seeks to achieve through criminal law and punishment.[41] This means that if the intent to express censure is taken up as a way to demarcate the line between criminal law and other laws, much of what we understand to be criminal law would fall outside the line.

Third, putting too much emphasis on what the state intends has a way of encouraging the notion that we need not worry about consequences the state does not intend. Clearly, if there *is* an intent to express censure, it would be highly relevant to determining whether censure and condemnation are being expressed by a governmental act in a given instance, but even if there is (purportedly, one might add, at least sometimes) no such intent, a given treatment by the government may still carry such a meaning. And when a governmental action expresses censure and stigmatizes a person, whether the state intends it or not, it ought to be held responsible for such consequences instead of hiding behind the distinction between intended and unintended consequences.[42] Hence, two of the factors that the Supreme Court appropriately considers when determining whether something constitutes punishment are whether "it has historically been regarded as punishment" and "whether the behavior to which it applies is

[39] See, e.g., Jeremy Waldron, *Law and Disagreement* (Clarendon Press, 1999), 119–46.
[40] Issa Kohler-Hausmann, "Managerial Justice and Mass Misdemeanors," *Stanford Law Review* 66, no. 3 (2014): 611.
[41] For a quick summary, see Alexandra Natapoff, *Punishment without Crime: How Our Massive Misdemeanor System Traps the Innocent and Makes America More Unequal* (Basic Books, 2018), 195–201.
[42] Cf. David Enoch, "Intending, Foreseeing, and the State," *Legal Theory* 13, no. 2 (2007): 69.

already a crime," both of which appear to be designed to get at the way in which a government act is perceived and understood by observers to be punitive.[43]

So, the simple answer that turns on whether the state intends stigma is no good. A better response is to note that the reason the sex offender registration and civil commitment provisions carry such stigma is precisely because of the ways in which these "civil" devices are often closely related to criminal convictions. Civil commitment in *Hendricks* and sex offender registration laws in *Doe* are both devices that immediately follow convictions, and the stigma from the civil actions is parasitic on the stigma from the related criminal actions. Therefore, the fact that these "civil" devices seem to carry the kind of stigma more closely associated with criminal devices does not disprove the thesis that there is a close relationship between criminal wrongs and moral wrongs; it in fact reinforces it by highlighting the ways in which the censure expressed in the criminal realm can overflow and spill over to the civil realm.

We should of course acknowledge that the government ends up stigmatizing individuals through different types of government actions, some punitive, some not punitive. Furthermore, we should erect procedural protections the strength of which is commensurate with the impact of governmental actions, so that even "civil cases" are sometimes accompanied by protections that are typically associated with criminal cases.[44] For our purposes, the important conclusion is that the validity of the Censure Thesis does not turn on a claim about the *distinctiveness* of criminal conviction and punishment, and *Hendricks* and *Doe* thus cannot serve as counterexamples that challenge the Censure Thesis.

C. Should the State Be in the Business of Censure?: Some Criticisms

The second, more serious, challenge comes from the view that the state should not be in the censuring business in the first place. That is, as noted above, we could ask not only whether the criminal process is a "complex moral machine" but also whether it is a good thing that it is a complex moral machine that stamps

[43] Kennedy v. Mendoza-Martinez, 372 U.S. 144, 168 (1963). The full list of factors is: "[w]hether the sanction involves an affirmative disability or restraint, whether it has historically been regarded as a punishment, whether it comes into play only on a finding of *scienter*, whether its operation will promote the traditional aims of punishment—retribution and deterrence, whether the behavior to which it applies is already a crime, whether an alternative purpose to which it may rationally be connected is assignable for it, and whether it appears excessive in relation to the alternative purpose assigned." *Id.*

[44] See, e.g., Vincent Chiao, *Criminal Law in the Age of the Administrative State* (Oxford University Press, 2018), 208 ("[T]he allocation of procedural rights should not be limited to officially imposed restrictions or disabilities, but should take into account expected social stigma, even of an informal nature.").

people with moral stigma. Critics of moralism in criminal law, like Erin Kelly and Vincent Chiao, forcefully argue that the answer to that question is no.[45]

Kelly gives many reasons to reach her conclusion, and one chief argument that she makes is that criminal law employs "specification of the conditions under which one is subject to legal punishment [that] departs from the morality's specification of when a person can be blamed."[46] She argues that the practice of blaming requires "a complete and nuanced account of the circumstances of each wrongdoer's wrong," and criminal law systematically fails to achieve that.[47] To give an example, in our everyday moral blaming practice, the motive behind one's actions often makes a big difference, but criminal law, as a general matter, does not take motives into account.[48] Blaming also involves taking a certain view on a person's attitudes, but criminal law is generally concerned more with what actions people take toward one another and not what attitudes people hold.[49] Also, many of the most relevant factors in individual blaming situations are difficult to access because they depend on particular situations, emotions, and attitudes, and if they are often difficult in intimate interpersonal relationships, the difficulties are even more pronounced in situations among strangers and of government actors relating to individuals.[50] In short, for Kelly, the state in the censuring business would be taking on a project it could not possibly handle and often handles poorly by design.

Kelly has also argued that "[t]he state may forbid us from acting against interests of society, but it risks overstepping its proper bounds when it scrutinizes people's motives and condemns them for their personal moral flaws."[51] Chiao has similarly expressed astonishment at "a conception of coercive state power as simply large-scale manifestation of private moral relationships," as this view of punishment seems to endorse a vision where "public institutions . . . would be in the business of making remarkably intrusive, potentially demeaning, and in any case highly contentious judgments about a person's actions, character, and personality, and backing those judgments with overpowering force."[52] So for both Kelly and Chiao, using the Feinbergian complex moral machine would be a literally violent intrusion into people's internal worlds and would amount to a highly improper use of state power in a liberal state.

[45] Another contemporary theorist who is highly and frequently critical of legal moralism is Malcolm Thorburn, whose work is discussed below.

[46] Erin I. Kelly, *The Limits of Blame: Rethinking Punishment and Responsibility* (Harvard University Press, 2018), 38.

[47] Kelly, *The Limits of Blame*, 38.

[48] Kelly, *The Limits of Blame*, 102–05.

[49] Kelly, *The Limits of Blame*, 109–14, 119–20.

[50] Kelly, *The Limits of Blame*, 114–20.

[51] Kelly, *The Limits of Blame*, 102.

[52] Chiao, *Criminal Law in the Administrative State*, 29.

What is clear from these criticisms is that the criminal wrongs–moral wrongs relationship cannot be assumed simply by making the sociological observation that the criminal process is a complex moral machine. A normative case as to why that is the way it ought to be needs to be made. The next part makes that case and shows, in addition, that even vehement critics like Kelly and Chiao have trouble doing without state censure in criminal law.

D. Should the State Be in the Business of Censure?: Communitarian-Theses

Thus far, we have discussed the various ways in which the Desert Thesis and the Displacement Thesis are deficient and have arrived at the view that the censure aspect of conviction and punishment in the criminal setting cannot simply be taken as a given but needs to be defended as a normative matter. Here is one way in which one might go about it, which I will call the "Communitarian Thesis."

> *Communitarian Thesis*: Criminal wrongs and moral wrongs should be closely related because: (1) criminal law's essential function is to articulate and enforce norms of conduct that enable members of a society to live together, and (2) the state's responses to violations of those norms can serve as adequate responses only if they effectively communicate the moral wrongness of the acts to which they respond.

Perhaps the most developed communitarian account is the one advanced by R. A. Duff. According to Duff's theory, criminal law makes "a formal declaration of the norms" that are to guide the citizens' "civic conduct."[53] In other words, "criminal law can be seen . . . as a code of civic ethics, dealing with what is to count as civically right or wrong conduct within the distinctive practice of civil life—the enterprise of living together as a political community."[54] Once a polity formally declares such norms, it stands ready to publicly respond to violations of such norms as that is what it means to "take values seriously."[55] Nicola Lacey, similarly, imagines a community where criminal law is "employed primarily to preserve the framework of values perceived as necessary to the maintenance, stability and peaceful development of the community."[56] In that community, criminal laws would be "instituted as a response to behavior which directly violates

[53] Duff, *The Realm of Criminal Law*, 207.
[54] Duff, *The Realm of Criminal Law*, 87, 145.
[55] Duff, *The Realm of Criminal Law*, 208–09.
[56] Nicola Lacey, *State Punishment: Political Principles and Community Values* (Routledge, 1988), 176.

socially acknowledged fundamental interests,"[57] and punishment would be "a means of making the standards of the criminal law *real*,"[58] an "affirmation of social values" through "denunciation of the behavior involved in the offence."[59] If this is a purpose of criminal law, then its close relationship to morality, having to do with how we ought to treat one another, seems to follow.

Accounts like these do not rely on the idea that the state's job is to give people what they deserve. Neither do they see punishment as an institutionalized form of private vengeance. Plus, while the question I alluded to above about which wrongs are properly within the scope of criminal law remains, it appears that under this understanding of criminal law, there is potentially room to include offenses other than just those that would exist in the state of nature. Certain criminal prohibitions—like the law against murder—would of course be necessary in a view like this simply by virtue of the fact that the enterprise of living together activates those aspects of morality that have to do with the question of how people ought to treat one another. As to offenses that may be more regulatory in nature, wrongness of such offenses could be articulated in terms of what is needed for the enterprise of living together.[60]

The censure aspect of conviction and punishment fits well with the Communitarian Thesis, and in fact, we may combine the two to create the "Communitarian-Censure Thesis."

> *Communitarian-Censure Thesis*: Criminal wrongs and moral wrongs should be closely related because: (1) criminal law's essential function is to articulate and enforce norms of conduct that enable members of a society to live together; (2) the state's responses to violations of those norms can serve as adequate responses only if they effectively articulate the moral wrongness of the acts to which they respond; (3) conviction and punishment of a person through the criminal process should thus express censure; (4) whenever governmental action expresses censure, the legal conclusion supporting it should rest on a judgment about what is properly censurable in a person's conduct, which in turns means that the law should criminalize (only) conduct that is, in this sense, morally wrong.

One may object to the picture presented here with the argument that the Communitarian Thesis does not entail the Censure Thesis. Would it be possible

[57] Lacey, *State Punishment*, 176.
[58] Lacey, *State Punishment*, 182.
[59] Lacey, *State Punishment*, 183.
[60] This is briefly and tentatively put, as we will be revisiting this very question throughout the book. The point here is mainly that there is more room for different types of crimes in this account than in the displacement of private vengeance account.

to endorse one and not the other, given that doing so would make it possible to avoid Kelly's and Chiao's criticism that the state should not be in the censuring business?

To answer this question, we should start by recalling that not all harm prevention strategies involve criminal law's mode of announcing standards of conduct and expecting conformity to such standards. As discussed above, we may prevent harms by investing in social services like education, health care, job training, and universal basic income, by engaging in preventive behaviors like locks and fences, and by identifying those who are likely to harm others and incapacitating them. And then there is the harm-prevention strategy that raises the cost of harming others by attaching disincentives to certain conduct. As Andrew Ashworth and Andrew von Hirsch once put it in (admittedly provocative) terms, this way of thinking about punishment is consistent with the idea of treating people "as beings that have to be restrained, intimidated, or conditioned into compliance" as if they are "beasts . . . in a circus."[61] The problem of the state being in the business of censure would disappear if the state employed only these four strategies of harm prevention, as there would be no occasion to express censure.

Censure comes into play, though, if we assume that we have a system where the government issues norms of conduct that are important enough to be enforced with criminal law and expects people to be able to recognize why criminal wrongs are wrongs and to guide their lives accordingly. Thinking of criminal law as being about wrongs, as opposed to just harms, gives us a way of thinking of people as agents capable of responsibility rather than just as entities that may produce harm and need to be controlled as a form of risk management. As Duff puts it, criminal law may "address us as responsible citizens" and by "address[ing] us in terms of those very reasons that should . . . guide our conduct."[62] Ashworth and von Hirsch, too, have emphasized the importance of treating individuals in the criminal justice system as "agent[s] capable of moral deliberation," who may be "confronted with disapproval in virtue of the wrongfulness of [their] conduct."[63] If that is the picture we assume about what people are capable of, it is only natural to respond to violations of these norms with disapproval and censure.

This general picture is easy to abandon for those who seek to engage in harm prevention primarily through early intervention, incapacitation, and deterrence with unpleasant consequences. However, it is not so easy to scrub from existence once we think of people as capable of deliberation and of being guided by reasons and see criminal laws as addressing them as such.

[61] Andrew Ashworth and Andrew von Hirsch, *Proportionate Sentencing: Exploring the Principles* (Oxford University Press, 2005), 18.
[62] Duff, *The Realm of Criminal Law*, 208.
[63] Ashworth and von Hirsch, *Proportionate Sentencing*, 17.

Consider Kelly, a censure skeptic, again. According to her favored theory of punishment, "punishment would be used only to prevent and to redress the harms caused by criminal wrongdoing, especially the criminal violation of individual rights,"[64] and the theory "permits us to apply criminal sanctions to a person who has committed a serious wrong in order to protect, to reduce, and to remediate harm to the basic rights of other people."[65] So far, this deterrence notion need assume merely that people respond to disincentives. However, she then goes further. She says her proposed framework is "sensitive to a person's capacity to make choices that satisfy the requirements of law," given that "[a]s moral agents, we are, generally speaking, capable of guiding our choices with practical reasoning, including reasoning that takes the requirements and sanctions of law into account."[66] The law should "express[] reasons most people can and usually do take into account, reasons that guide rational and reasonable people to act appropriately," and this means that "a legal system that is at least minimally just is designed for human beings who can recognize and guide themselves by relevant reasons, moral or prudential."[67] That is, "the law's default position should be one of rational address," and "[b]eings capable of purposeful action might be persuaded by reasons to refrain from acting in ways that violate one another's rights."[68] Under this framework, "[p]eople who fail to respect the rights of other people or the fundamental interests of society may be held accountable to action-guiding norms . . . ."[69]

These quotes are admittedly selected to emphasize one strain in Kelly's proposal and to de-emphasize aspects of her thinking that stress deterrence as the main rationale, but it is still striking how similar she sounds to censure-friendly theorists like Duff and Ashworth and von Hirsch. Similarities of Kelly's preferred outlook with censure-friendly theories do not end there. She also says her proposal "seems naturally to incorporate a morally expressive function" given that "[w]e punish to discourage certain kinds of wrongdoing, and in so doing we express our disapproval of acts of that kind."[70] Punishment can "communicate a moral judgment," where "[t]he object of the moral judgment . . . would be the wrongdoer's act," and "[i]n judging an act to be wrong and worthy of criminal sanctions, we display publicly our moral rejection of acts of that type and call attention to the reasons we take them to be objectionable."[71]

[64] Kelly, *The Limits of Blame*, 122.
[65] Kelly, *The Limits of Blame*, 129.
[66] Kelly, *The Limits of Blame*, 128.
[67] Kelly, *The Limits of Blame*, 128–29.
[68] Kelly, *The Limits of Blame*, 129–30.
[69] Kelly, *The Limits of Blame*, 130.
[70] Kelly, *The Limits of Blame*, 145.
[71] Kelly, *The Limits of Blame*, 145.

I noted previously that another vehement critic of moral censure by the state in criminal law is Chiao. Chiao's preferred theory of criminal law focuses on "ex ante social programming" through things like education as opposed to "punishment ex post."[72] The phrase "social programming" suggests that people are to be shaped and programmed to become harmless, and Chiao notes that his views thus may be thought of as promoting "the indefinite detention of the dangerous, the medicalization of the idiosyncratic, and aggressive policing and mass surveillance for everybody else."[73] However, Chiao urges that we "sharply distinguish" his arguments from "the idea that people are not responsible agents."[74] He further suggests that "non-punitive, preventive means can potentially be superior to punitive ones at fostering responsible agency" given that "[g]iving people a decent education may better develop responsible agency than blaming, resenting, and punishing them for the bad choices they make."[75]

However, once people are seen as responsible agents, it is not clear whether Chiao can escape the grasp of the view that the state should express censure when it enforces criminal laws. In fact, Chiao ends up conceding that "because the criminal law is able to sustain cooperation over the long haul by publicly establishing rules of conduct that are widely regarded to be legitimate, the criminal law's expressive function is likely to be of crucial importance"[76] and that "[t]here is indeed value in responding to deliberate rule-violations, perhaps by communicating censure and imposing punishment."[77] He adds that "the urge to condemn and punish those who do wrong is itself grounded in its ability to sustain social cooperation."[78]

Both Kelly and Chiao then, because of their commitment to the idea that individuals are agents capable of responsibility, seem to end up in a place that is very close to the Communitarian-Censure Thesis,[79] though it may be the case that the following, which de-emphasizes the idea of censuring the person while retaining the idea of condemning the act, is more likely to be acceptable to them.

[72] Chiao, *Criminal Law in the Administrative State*, 230.
[73] Chiao, *Criminal Law in the Administrative State*, 225.
[74] Chiao, *Criminal Law in the Administrative State*, 226.
[75] Chiao, *Criminal Law in the Administrative State*, 229–30.
[76] Chiao, *Criminal Law in the Administrative State*, 242.
[77] Chiao, *Criminal Law in the Administrative State*, 243.
[78] Chiao, *Criminal Law in the Administrative State*, 243.
[79] For an insightful and interesting attempt to sever the connection between responsibility and censure while acknowledging "the force of the intuition that punishment is only justified if the offender has the capacity for responsible agency and hence is blameworthy for wrongdoing or harm perpetrated," see Nicola Lacey and Hanna Pickard, "From the Consulting Room to the Court Room? Taking the Clinical Model of Responsibility without Blame into the Legal Realm," *Oxford Journal of Legal Studies* 33, no. 1 (2013): 5.

> *Communitarian-Condemnation Thesis*: Criminal wrongs and moral wrongs should be closely related because: (1) criminal law's essential function is to articulate and enforce norms of conduct that enable members of a society to live together; (2) the state's responses to violations of those norms can serve as adequate responses only if they effectively articulate the moral wrongness of the acts to which they respond; (3) conviction and punishment through the criminal process should thus express disapproval or condemnation of the person's conduct; and (4) whenever governmental action expresses such disapproval, the legal conclusion supporting it should rest on a judgment about what is properly subject to disapproval, which in turn means that the law should criminalize (only) conduct that is, in this sense, morally wrong.

The main difference between the Communitarian-Censure Thesis and the Communitarian-Condemnation Thesis is that the former may be read to take more interest in judging a person who has engaged in wrongdoing as a person, whereas the latter condemns the wrongdoing while carefully avoiding making comments about the person. The difficult question is whether it is possible to announce standards of conduct, treat people to be individuals capable of moral deliberation and acting for reasons, and respond with disapproval when they violate such standards, without also implying that the wrongful conduct they engaged in reflect badly on them given the way in which treating people as responsible agents entails positing a tight relationship between them and their chosen acts.

Consider the debate surrounding the character theory of culpability. The idea that the law may condemn the act but not the person is more commonly expressed as the idea that criminal law may punish what people do but not who they are. That may well be the case, but not all acts are the same. For instance, the duress defense requires, under one influential formulation, that the kind of threat that has brought about the crime be something "a person of reasonable firmness in his situation would have been unable to resist."[80] According to this standard, even if a person genuinely feels that he has no choice other than to commit a crime to prevent a serious harm to himself by someone else, the duress defense would not be available to him if he did not live up to the standard of behavior set by the hypothetical "person of reasonable firmness." Persons of reasonable firmness are those who recognize the wrongness of the crime they are being pressured to commit and are courageous enough to resist the pressure to a reasonable extent. If someone who commits a crime meets the requirement of the duress defense, the message the legal system communicates is that the crime does not reflect badly on the offender because the source of the criminality is

[80] Model Penal Code § 2.09(1) (American Law Institute, 1985).

something external to the offender's self, and giving in to the threat of harm is not to be condemned because the offender has behaved in the way a reasonable person would have.[81]

Conversely, if the duress defense is not applicable in a particular offender's situation, the legal system judges the offender for being the sort of person who either does not live up to the society's expected standard of fortitude and resistance to criminal temptations or threats, or does not care sufficiently about the seriousness of the values that the law protects, or both. Of course, this is not to say that the law is punishing the offender *for* being a coward; rather, the punishment is for the crime itself. Implicit in the punishment, however, is the proposition that whatever pressure the offender might have felt to commit the crime is something that should have been resisted, and the failure to resist it shows a defect in the actor's character.

This idea—that holding a person criminally responsible for an act entails a judgment that the act reflects badly on that person—implies that a criminal justice system may punish people only for "actions that are in a real sense *their own*."[82] Only when actions are "their own" can we justify blaming persons for what they do. Theories of culpability that bridge the gap between an actor and an act through the notion of "character" derive some of their persuasive force from this idea of one's ownership of one's acts. According to this account, character plays both inculpatory and exculpatory roles in criminal culpability. It is appropriate to punish persons for their acts if the bad acts can be traced to their character defects.[83] It is inappropriate to punish persons for their acts if the circumstances surrounding their actions are such that the acts cannot be explained as resulting from their character defects.[84]

There are many questions here, and an extensive literature on the relevance of character to criminal culpability has grown around the debate among "choice," "character," and "capacity" theories of culpability.[85] To give a full account of the current state of that debate here would be out of place. Further, my purpose here

[81] R. A. Duff, "Choice, Character, and Criminal Liability," *Law and Philosophy* 12, no. 4 (1993): 358–59; R. A. Duff, "Rule-Violations and Wrongdoing," in *Criminal Law Theory: Doctrines of the General Part*, ed. Stephen Shute and A. P. Simester (Oxford University Press, 2002), 63–68.

[82] See, e.g., Lacey, *State Punishment*, 71; Duff, *The Realm of Criminal Law*, 369–78.

[83] Cf. David Hume, *A Treatise of Human Nature* (Oxford University Press, 1978; originally published 1739), 264 ("Actions are by their very nature temporary and perishing; and where they proceed not from some cause in the characters and disposition of the person, who perform'd them, they infix not themselves upon him, and can neither redound to his honour, if good, nor infamy, if evil.").

[84] Victor Tadros, *Criminal Responsibility* (Oxford University Press, 2005), 48.

[85] See, e.g., H. L. A. Hart, *Punishment and Responsibility: Essays in the Philosophy of Criminal Law* (Clarendon Press, 1968); Jeremy Horder, "Criminal Culpability: The Possibility of a General Theory," *Law and Philosophy* 12, no. 2 (1993): 193; Duff, "Choice, Character, and Criminal Liability," 345–46; Michael Bayles, "Character, Purpose, and Criminal Responsibility," *Law and Philosophy* 1, no. 1982 (1982): 5.

is not to declare that the character theory of culpability is superior to competing accounts, nor is it to solve all the problems that the character theory of culpability raises. It does, however, seem to me that character theorists are correct when they argue that *criminal law punishes persons for their actions only when those actions reflect badly on the actors in the sense that the actions display their character defects.* Without an account along these lines, it is difficult to explain what makes up the relationship between actors and their acts, and why it is that we have no trouble connecting our condemnation of a bad act to the agent who performed it. In short, this is the sense in which it is correct to say that criminal law punishes people for what they do *and* for who they are.

But we must be careful. As Duff has pointed out, there is a difference between treating character as a "condition of liability" and as an "object of liability."[86] The formulation that we punish people for actions only when they reflect their character defects can mean one of two things. First, it may be argued that it is unfair to hold persons responsible for actions not flowing from their character defects. Alternatively, it may be argued that the legal system is ultimately interested more in character defects as objects of condemnation, and that actions that express bad character are significant only to the extent they provide a window into persons' characters. The account of the role of character in criminal culpability I have given thus far does not appear to go beyond the former formulation, in which case it would be misleading to state that we punish people for being who they are as opposed to what they do. It would be more accurate to say instead that we punish people for what they do, but only to the extent that what they do reflects who they are. Does this threaten my conclusion that we *do* punish people for who they are and not just for what they do?

Not exactly. And that is because it is doubtful that we can neatly separate out the two roles—condition of liability versus object of liability—played by character in culpability determination. Once character defects are thought to be behind the bad actions condemned by the criminal justice system, and it is this link that satisfies the condition of liability, then it is difficult to imagine how the character defects can escape the reach of condemnation. The reasons we take character defects seriously as conditions of liability do not suddenly cease to operate when it comes to objects of liability as if there is some on-off switch. When a malicious act is condemned as it reflects a malicious character, a cruel act is condemned as it reflects a cruel character, or a reckless and indifferent omission is condemned as it reflects a callous character indifferent to suffering, there is no way for the criminal justice system to avoid commenting on the actor's bad character trait as well as the bad act.

[86] R. A. Duff, "Virtue, Vice, and Criminal Liability: Do We Want an Aristotelian Criminal Law?" *Buffalo Criminal Law Review* 6, no. 1 (2002): 175.

For these reasons, I am doubtful that there is a real difference between the Communitarian-Censure Thesis and the Communitarian-Condemnation Thesis. But for our purposes, the choice between the two theses is not important, as they both deliver articulations of the integral, not just incidental, connection between criminal wrongs and moral wrongs.

VI. Conclusion

This chapter has defended the theoretical orientation of this book, which is legal moralism, and has in the process (1) pointed out the ways in which criminal law is a distinctive mode of harm prevention involving a system where the government issues a set of rules and demands that the people to whom the rules apply comply with such rules; (2) rejected the desert theory of criminal law; (3) highlighted the limits of the displacement of private vengeance theory of criminal law; and (4) defended the view that conviction and punishment of a person through the criminal process express censure or condemnation of what that person has done.[87]

[87] Malcolm Thorburn's criticisms of legal moralism—see Malcolm Thorburn, "Punishment and Public Authority," in *Criminal Law and the Authority of the State*, ed. Antje du Bois-Pedian, Magnus Ulväng, and Petter Asp (Hart Publishing, 2017), 7 (declaring legal moralism to be a failure)—do not threaten the picture presented in this chapter, as what he calls "legal moralism" is highly stylized and different from the way the phrase is used here.

According to Thorburn, legal moralism has three features. First, legal moralists argue that in "a criminal trial, . . . we are *simply* doing in a *somewhat more* formal way what we do privately all the time," that "the practices of the criminal justice system are *nothing more than* formalized versions of the private practice of calling others to account," that "the criminal process is *simply a formalized version* of private practices," and that "there is *nothing importantly different* about the criminal justice system and the extra-legal moral practices." Malcolm Thorburn, "Criminal Law as Public Law," in *Philosophical Foundations of Criminal Law*, ed. R. A. Duff and Stuart Green (Oxford University Press, 2011), 22, 23, 29, 37 (emphases added). Second, legal moralism is "an attempt to justify the state's coercive criminal justice powers as *mere* tools for doing to moral wrongdoers what morality requires." Thorburn, "Punishment and Public Authority," 7 (emphasis added). Third, by naming his own alternative theory a "public law account," he implies that legal moralism is something other than a "public law account." Thorburn, "Criminal Law as Public Law," 24.

Legal moralism, which I defined above as the idea that there is a close relationship between criminal wrongs and moral wrongs and that criminal laws should be evaluated by asking whether whatever they criminalize are genuine moral wrongs, has none of these features.

First, legal moralism need not endorse the idea that criminal law is "nothing more" than, "nothing importantly different" from, and "simply" a formal version of what we do privately, though a part of the problem here is that the significance of terms like "nothing more" and "simply" is somewhat obscure, more rhetorical than substantive.

Second, justifying hard treatment need not be a priority for legal moralism. Thorburn complains that legal moralism does not have the resources to "justify the practice of criminal punishment" because it "cannot explain why the state should be entitled to communicate its message of moral censure *through the means of hard treatment*." Thorburn, "Punishment and Public Authority," 10, 12 (emphasis in original). He similarly argues that "it has proven extremely difficult [for legal moralists] to show why the state should be morally entitled to impose coercive punishment as a response to . . . moral wrongs." Malcolm Thorburn, "Criminal Punishment and the Right to Rule," *University of Toronto Law Journal* 70, Supplement 1 (2020): 52.

But these complaints assume that justifying hard treatment is important for legal moralism. In fact, it seems to me to be a feature, not a bug, of legal moralism that "many legal moralists turn out to be something very close to punishment abolitionists," Thorburn, "Criminal Punishment and the Right to Rule," 52, and that "[o]n the . . . legal moralist account, criminal punishment not only cedes centre stage . . . it actually fades away from the picture almost entirely" and "[t]he . . . legal moralist project seems to come very close to eliminating the place of legitimate coercion in the criminal justice process altogether." Thorburn, "Criminal Law as Public Law," 28–29. Justifying coercion and incarceration appears to be a priority for Thorburn, but it is not for legal moralism, at least not the version of legal moralism used in this book.

Third, the implication of Thorburn's terminological decision to call his approach the "public law account" is that legal moralists do not think of criminal law as public law and that his approach is unique in this respect compared to others writing in the field, but that is inaccurate. See, e.g., Duff, *The Realm of Criminal Law*, 187 ("[W]e must begin with political theory, and must theorize criminal law as a public institution (as 'public law')."); see also Duff, *The Realm of Criminal Law*, 186 ("We are not short of accounts of . . . criminal law grounded in political theory of various kinds."). (Vincent Chiao commits the same wrong with his terminological choice. See Chiao, "Two Conceptions of the Criminal Law," 19 (contrasting between a "public law" and "private law" conception of criminal law). I agree with Leora Dahan Katz's criticism of this aspect of Chiao's theory. See Leora Dahan Katz, "Criminal Law: Political or Moral? Defending a Complementary Conception of Criminal Law in the Age of the Administrative State," *Jerusalem Review of Legal Studies* 17, no. 1 (2018): 112 (arguing that Chiao's "constructed opposition . . . is both unnecessary and undesirable").

Finally, I note that despite his purported stance against legal moralism, Thorburn himself acknowledges that "states have many good reasons to prohibit" conduct like "murder, rape, assault, and the like," "not least of [such reasons] is that they constitute serious wrongs to other persons" and that his preferred account "does not deny the moral significance of the underlying interpersonal wrong that the offender might have committed." Thorburn, "Criminal Punishment and the Right to Rule," 63.

2
Criminalizing Disobedience: General Considerations

I. Introduction

To examine the topic of criminalizing disobedience, we first need to know what disobedience is and what it means to criminalize it. This chapter first discusses what it means to criminalize something, generally speaking. This chapter then discusses what disobedience is and what it means to criminalize it and relates the discussion to the traditional distinction between *mala in se* and *mala prohibita* offenses. Next, this chapter gives examples of criminalizing disobedience in different contexts. This chapter then identifies the wrongfulness of disobedience that can serve as a basis for its criminalization. Finally, this chapter previews a later discussion on potential limitations on the power to criminalize and punish disobedience.

II. Criminalizing *X*

For the state to criminalize something, the way the term is typically understood, is for the state to, through law, prohibit something by treating that thing as the object of criminal prohibition. That is, to criminalize something (usually some conduct) is to pick it out and criminally prohibit it by listing the elements that identify that thing. In addition, to criminalize something is to label an official determination that an offense in violation of the prohibition has taken place as a *conviction*, to make available criminal sanctions, such as imprisonment and fines (and even death in some jurisdictions), as responses to violations, and to label certain official responses imposed on those who are criminally responsible for the violations as *punishments*.

However, the term "criminalizing" can be used in another sense. When a state criminally prohibits something and a person engages in the prohibited act, the *wrongdoing* that is committed may not be explicitly captured by the elements of the crime definition at issue. That is, a person may commit a crime by engaging in some conduct that satisfies the definition of a crime but the wrong committed

Criminalizing Disobedience. Youngjae Lee, Oxford University Press. © Oxford University Press 2026.
DOI: 10.1093/9780197617175.003.0003

through the conduct may be something different from (though of course related to) what is given as the definition of the crime. In such a situation, the state is criminalizing not just the conduct as defined in the crime definition (which is criminalization in one sense) but also the wrongdoing that is implicated when the person engages in the prohibited conduct (which is criminalization in another sense).

Sometimes the object of criminal prohibition and the wrongdoing targeted are one and the same. Homicide laws criminalize killing human beings and the wrongdoing that is implicated in killing a human being is killing a human being.[1] By contrast, take the crime of driving while intoxicated, which is defined in New York as "operat[ing] a motor vehicle while such person has .08 of one percentum or more by weight of alcohol in the person's blood."[2] In this example, the object of criminal prohibition is driving when one's blood alcohol concentration is above a certain level—that is what is prohibited—but the wrongdoing that is implicated is driving dangerously or imposing risks of harm to other people.[3] It would not make sense in this example to say that a person who is convicted of the crime of driving while intoxicated is *convicted* of driving dangerously or being a danger to others, since the person can be convicted only of the crime as defined by the elements listed above. However, the question of what response is appropriate may depend on understanding the exact *wrong* that is implicated in violating the prohibition. So, while it would be inaccurate to say that a person in a typical case of driving while intoxicated was convicted of the crime of driving dangerously since that is not how the crime is defined, it would not be inaccurate to say about a person convicted that either the person was punished *for* driving while intoxicated or the person was punished *for* driving in a dangerous manner (assuming the person was in fact driving dangerously). This means that, through criminalizing driving when one's blood alcohol concentration is above 0.08 percent, the state has also criminalized driving while intoxicated and driving in a dangerous manner.[4]

[1] There is a question here as to how to identify the relevant wrongdoing and which level of generalization is the correct one. One stark answer is the one proposed by Larry Alexander and Kimberly Ferzan, who say the following: "To us, there is really only one injunction that is relevant to criminal culpability: choose only those acts for which the risks to others' interests—as you estimate those risks—are sufficiently low to be outweighed by the interests, to yourself and others, that you are attempting to advance (discounted by the probability of advancing those interests)." Larry Alexander and Kimberley Kessler Ferzan, *Crime and Culpability: A Theory of Criminal* Law (Cambridge University Press, 2012), 263. Contrast this view against John Gardner's, who has argued that "maiming, blinding, disfiguring, and so on" are all "different actions, with different intrinsic features, which do not owe their wrongness . . . to any unifying principle." John Gardner, "On the General Part of the Criminal Law," in *Philosophy and the Criminal Law*, ed. Antony Duff (Cambridge University Press, 1998), 246–47.

[2] N.Y. Vehicle and Traffic Law § 1192.

[3] Cf. Gabriel S. Mendlow, "The Elusive Object of Punishment," *Legal Theory* 25, no. 2 (2019): 105.

[4] The example of drunk driving will be revisited in Chapter 11.

So, criminalizing *x* can mean either to treat something as the object of criminal prohibition (by outlining elements of the crime) or to single out something as a relevant wrongdoing that is implicated when a person does what is prohibited, in which case the punishment imposed is for that wrongdoing. In this book, I will use the term "criminalizing" in both senses, with each context determining which of the two senses is being employed. That the term "criminalize" can be used in these two different senses is important for the purposes of this book because, among other things, the book will advance the argument that some laws criminalize disobedience even though that is not what it may look like at first from the elements. For example, the drug possession laws criminalize possession of certain drugs, but they also, we will see, simultaneously criminalize disobedience, and the term "criminalize" is being used in two different ways in that statement.

III. Disobedience

A. Disobedience Defined

To define disobedience, it is useful to start with the idea of lawbreaking. Lawbreaking and disobeying are two different phenomena. If individuals go around in life never killing or raping, do they "obey" the laws that prohibit such conduct? In a sense, yes, they do because they do not break these laws. On the other hand, they do not "obey" or "follow" the law; they merely behave in a way that does not involve committing an act that is prohibited. They may be lazy and never do anything that takes the kind of energy involved in most cases of rapes and murders. Also, especially for these kinds of offenses, many people would behave the same way with or without laws that prohibit them, simply because they are people for whom the thought of doing wrongful acts is not even a live possibility, or they are people who may refrain from certain acts simply because they are wrong. These individuals seem to "obey" the law in these instances in only a very weak sense.[5]

[5] See also Michael Sevel, "Obeying the Law," *Legal Theory* 24, no. 3 (2018): 200 ("If all that is required to obey the law is . . . merely doing the actions required, . . . , there may be little connection between the issuance of a legal rule or order on the one hand, and an action that amounts to obeying it on the other. . . . For that reason, the view has bizarre implications. It would open up the possibility that a person could obey the law while being completely oblivious to the fact that she is doing so, indeed, while completely unaware of the fact that there is a system of legal rules that applies to her conduct."). Sevel's argument is a contribution to an ongoing debate within jurisprudence about what it means to obey the law, and the debate typically takes place in terms of the distinction between compliance and conformity with a reason, as articulated in Joseph Raz's

Obedience of the law, in other words, implies that a person does or refrains from doing something for reasons that have to do with the existence of a law that applies to them. The purest instance of obedience would be the act of doing something or refraining from doing something just because that is what the law requires. This is not the only kind of obedience, however. People may also be prudent and obey the law because they want to avoid bad consequences that follow from disobeying. These people are not following the law because that is what the law requires. These people are following the law because the consequences of not following it would be unpleasant. Both instances of following the law should be considered instances of obedience because the actors behave in ways that the law requires, either because that is what the law requires or to avoid the sanctions attached to violations of what the law requires. The difference between the two is primarily attitudinal. The former respects the law or treats it as binding, whereas the latter need not have any particular attitude toward the law. But both obey the law.

The flip side of this discussion is that disobedience can also show up in different ways. People who break the law without realizing it are disobeying the law in the sense that they do what they are told not to do, but the term "disobeying" implies *knowingly going against an applicable legal directive that one is aware of.* A person who receives a toy drone as a present and takes it out for a spin without realizing that flying drones in his town is banned may have broken the law, but he has not disobeyed the law. In other words, it is possible for one to break the law without disobeying the law. It may also be possible to disobey the law without breaking the law. If a person with a toy drone who knows about the ban decides to defy the law by flying it without realizing that the law exempts the particular type of drones he owns, he may have disobeyed the law but has not broken the law. Perhaps a situation like this is better characterized as an instance of attempted disobedience, but the point still stands. Disobedience and lawbreaking are two different phenomena.

work. See Joseph Raz, *Practical Reason and Norms*, 2nd ed. (Oxford University Press, 1999), 178–79; see also Scott Hershovitz, "The Authority of Law," in *The Routledge Companion to Philosophy of Law*, ed. Andrei Marmor (Routledge, 2012), 67; Laura Valentini, "The Content-Independence of Political Obligation: What It Is and How to Test It," *Legal Theory* 24, no. 2 (2018): 138; Stephen R. Perry, "Political Authority and Political Obligation," in *Oxford Studies in Philosophy of Law: Volume 2*, ed. Leslie Green and Brian Leiter (Oxford University Press, 2013), 13–14. This debate is certainly related to the issues addressed throughout this book and this chapter in particular. However, as will become quickly clear below, this chapter and this book work with my own, distinctive way of conceptualizing disobedience in the criminal law context, and it is not part of my project to reconcile my views with views held by those participating in that particular debate in philosophy of law.

B. Disobedience, Mistake of Law, and Strict Liability

This discussion already takes some controversial positions, as it crashes into two longstanding issues in criminal law: strict liability and mistake of law.[6] Namely, this conception of disobedience, which is described in terms of knowingly going against an applicable legal directive, seems to require recognizing a mistake of law defense when criminalizing disobedience. If a person is not going against a legal requirement that they are aware of, then disobedience seems to be an inaccurate description of what is going on. And to the extent that some strict liability offenses involve situations where a person does something not realizing that what he is doing is criminally prohibited, those offenses do not seem to have much to do with disobedience, either.

Limiting punishment of disobedience to situations where a person knowingly goes against an applicable legal directive also has a normative justification. As we will see throughout this book, the laws that criminalize disobedience often criminalize conduct that is not always obviously wrongful. The normative significance of prohibited conduct can be obscure, and the supposed wrongfulness of it can be unintuitive until one becomes aware of the law prohibiting it. (The same is not the case for more traditional crimes like murder, which is not a crime of disobedience, as we will see in Part IV.) Therefore, punishing those who do not realize that what they are doing is legally prohibited would raise serious fair notice concerns.[7]

While this limitation of the scope of the discussion may raise some eyebrows, it does not skew the discussion by leaving out too many important instances of criminalizing disobedience. Certain offenses like regulatory offenses or "public welfare offenses"[8] are often associated with strict liability crimes, but it is important not to exaggerate the connection. In the United States at least, it is a common legislative practice in the context of regulatory offenses to insert terms like "knowingly" or "willfully" in offense definitions to avoid convicting the unaware,[9] and when the legislation fails to do so, courts often, though not

[6] Cf. Douglas Husak, *Ignorance of Law: A Philosophical Inquiry* (Oxford University Press, 2016).

[7] There is a line-drawing question here as to whether the concept of disobedience should apply to a situation where a person breaks a law without necessarily meaning to because of a failure to be aware of the existence of applicable directives one should have been aware of through reasonable investigation. That person may not have investigated either because of insufficient concern about the law or because of a simple lack of awareness of the potential illegality. Such a person may be a reckless or negligent disobedient, which is a theoretical possibility. Relatedly, a person may be aware that he may be engaging in *some* kind of lawbreaking without knowing exactly what, and that might also count as a form of criminal disobedience. I will not attempt to resolve here the doctrinal line-drawing questions of whether such instances are "disobedient" enough to qualify as disobedience and whether a criminal prohibition that covers such instances provides sufficient notice.

[8] Morissette v. United States, 342 U.S. 246, 255 (1952).

[9] See, e.g., 22 U.S.C. § 2778(c); 50 U.S.C. § 1704(c); Bryan v. United States, 524 U.S. 184, 191–92 (1998) ("[I]n order to establish a 'willful' violation of a statute, the Government must prove that the defendant acted with knowledge that his conduct was unlawful") (citation and quotation marks

always, step in to imply mens rea terms.[10] So, even though defining disobedience as involving knowingly going against an applicable legal directive takes strict liability offenses off the table at the outset, there is much in the world of criminalizing disobedience, including the so-called public welfare offenses, that remains as an object of our scrutiny. This limitation does mean that there are some strict liability laws that cannot be characterized or justified (or criticized for that matter) *as laws that punish disobedience*, though they may be justified on some other ground.

C. Disobedience as Conduct or Attitude

The term "disobedience" suggests a defiant attitude, but one may engage in an act of disobedience with different attitudes, such as defiance, disrespect, indifference, or regret. Therefore, we need to distinguish between conduct and attitude when discussing disobedience. Disobedience may be the conduct of acting contrary to an applicable legal directive or the attitude of a lack of respect.

Even though conduct is often distinguished from thoughts, that need not be the case, as one may engage in either physical or mental acts. A research psychologist performing experiments on subjects may give a number of instructions that are meant to direct people's mental acts, such as "try not to think about the racial characteristics of a person you are about to meet," or "reevaluate your initial instincts after giving the matter some time," and such instructions can be obeyed or disobeyed through a series of mental acts.[11]

We need to make another distinction here, between punishing disobedience as a crime on its own or punishing disobedience as a culpability-enhancer. The attitude–conduct distinction and the crime–culpability distinction are orthogonal. One may punish insubordination—or an act of disobedience—as a distinct crime or as a culpability enhancer, and one may punish a lack of respect—or a disobedient view or attitude—as a distinct crime or as a culpability enhancer. There are, therefore, four possibilities: punishing disobedience as conduct as an independent wrong; punishing disobedience as conduct as a culpability

omitted); see also Richard J. Lazarus, "Meeting the Demands of Integration in the Evolution of Environmental Law: Reforming Environmental Criminal Law," *Georgetown Law Journal* 83, no. 7 (1995): 2448–50, 2454, 2468–71.

[10] Susan R. Klein and Ingrid B. Grobey, "Debunking Claims of Over-Federalization of Criminal Law," *Emory Law Journal* 62, no. 1 (2012): 9–10, 70–71.

[11] See Douglas Husak, "Does Criminal Liability Require an Act?," in *Philosophy and the Criminal Law: Principle and Critique*, ed. Antony Duff (Cambridge University Press, 1998), 87 (discussing mental acts).

enhancer; punishing disobedience as attitude as an independent wrong; and punishing disobedience as attitude as a culpability enhancer.

By putting things this way, I am not necessarily endorsing all four possibilities. The category of punishing defiant, disrespectful, or disobedient attitudes is especially problematic. The idea of the state punishing "attitudes" is disturbing and invokes the image of government officials trying to control people's thoughts by imprisoning those without "correct" attitudes. Often in cases where such attitudes are present, it would not be clear whether there is any wrong to punish, and even if there were, there is a good case for a constitutional scrutiny and at times prohibition of practice of criminalizing and punishing attitudes. At the same time, as we already saw in the previous chapter, it is often difficult to separate out one's conduct from one's character (or, if "character" is too contested as a concept, one's attitudes and emotions), and a blanket prohibition of punishing attitudes is neither desirable nor realistic.

As an illustration, consider the ways in which criminal law treats the act of killing a person differently depending on the mental state of the person who kills. A person may kill on purpose after a period of reflection or in the "heat of passion" after encountering a particularly upsetting situation. A person may kill by "perpetrating an act eminently dangerous to others and evincing a depraved mind, without regard for human life,"[12] or simply recklessly. A person may simply beat up another person or engage in the same act while spewing racial epithets. In these instances, the same conduct is accompanied by different attitudes, and the law may treat them differently for that reason. One could object to such laws by arguing that the law is punishing attitudes and thoughts, but such an objection would have to simply ignore the ways in which the criminal law, in many instances, takes people's emotional states, motives, and attitudes into account, even if such accounting is not done in a consistent and theoretically coherent way.[13] In short, we should think about "punishing attitudes" not in terms of punishing bare attitudes, but as punishing attitudes as they are reflected in conduct, or as punishing in recognition of the ways in which different attitudes can change the badness of what may appear to be the same conduct externally.

While for reasons just given, I would not rule out the idea of punishing attitudes, the focus of this book will be on disobedience as conduct—that is, the act that constitutes going against an applicable legal directive—for the most part.

[12] Minn. Stat. § 609.195(a).

[13] This feature of criminal laws has been well documented in debates over hate crimes laws. See, e.g., Paul Robinson, "Hate Crimes: Crimes of Motive, Character, or Group Terror?," *Annual Survey of American Law* 1992, no. 4 (1992): 605; see also Carol Steiker, "Punishing Hateful Motives: Old Wine in a New Bottle Revives Calls for Prohibition," *Michigan Law Review* 97, no. 6 (1999): 1857.

IV. Isolating Sites of Criminalization of Disobedience

Because our topic is criminalizing disobedience, we need to understand when criminalization of disobedience occurs in criminal laws. There is a sense in which disobedience is present whenever a person breaks a law, which suggests disobedience is criminalized in all crime definitions. For instance, a sane person who kills another person on purpose most likely knows that there is a law against killing another human being but does it anyway. That person appears to be engaged in an act of disobedience.

However, if that is all there is to the idea of criminalizing and punishing disobedience, the idea as an analytic category is not going to be very useful or illuminating. We can make some headway away from that from the legal moralist perspective, which looks for moral wrongfulness in criminal wrongs. What is odd about describing murder as a crime of disobedience is that murder is already a wrong whether the state criminally prohibits it or not.[14] This means we can look for instances of criminalizing disobedience where such moral wrongfulness, without the state's prohibition, seems to be absent. That is, we can start with the view that the state criminalizes disobedience when it lays down a set of prohibitions that do not necessarily implicate moral wrongfulness and convicts and punishes people for going against such prohibitions.

The *malum in se–malum prohibitum* distinction is often used to express this idea. Some offenses, like murder, are wrongs "in themselves" (*in se*), whereas other offenses, like investment advising without registering as an advisor, are wrongs because they have been prohibited (*prohibitum*). Advising a person on how to invest his or her funds and accepting a fee for the advice without registering with the government does not seem harmful or wrongful, so long as no fraud is involved, the relevant parties understand the risks, and so on. But practicing investment advising without registering is a crime for which one may be convicted and punished. So, if a person breaks this law by giving investment advice for compensation without a license, depending on the facts of the case, the wrong implicated seems to arise solely because the government has prohibited the practice.

However, that explanation, which draws the *malum in se–malum prohibitum* line by simply asking if the state is absent (*in se*) or present (*prohibitum*) in explanations of relevant criminal wrongs, is too simplistic. First, even some conduct that is morally innocent absent state involvement may turn out to be

[14] Cf. Joseph Raz, "The Obligation to Obey: Revision and Tradition," in *Ethics in the Public Domain: Essays in the Morality of Law and Politics* (Oxford University Press, 1994), 343 ("I would feel insulted if it were suggested that I refrain from murder and rape because I recognize a moral obligation to obey the law. We expect people to avoid such actions whether or not they are legally forbidden, and for reasons which have nothing to do with the law.").

morally wrongful once the state speaks on the matter. For instance, there is nothing inherently morally wrong about driving on the left side of the road, but once the state coordinates individuals' behaviors by setting down rules of the road that require people to drive on the right side, then driving on the left side of the road when there are other cars around risks injury to others. So, it is a mistake to try to imagine *mala in se* offenses as only those offenses that would exist *in nature* without the state or civil society. Another example has to do with property offenses. In order for there to be a crime of theft, we first need to have laws that define ownership and assign ownership interests to different individuals and entities. So what constitutes theft in most cases necessarily makes references to the state's prior detailed determinations of what belongs to whom, yet theft is typically thought to be a moral wrong and a *malum in se* offense.[15] Therefore, just because the wrongfulness of a crime cannot be explained without reference to the state's prior actions and decisions, such as enactment of the rules of the road or the marketplace, does not necessarily make that crime a *malum prohibitum* offense.

Second, even a crime like murder, a paradigmatic *malum in se* offense that seems to be morally wrong whether the state bans it or not, assumes a distinct shape once the state gets involved and starts drawing lines. Consider, for example, the case of Judy Norman. Norman was a battered woman who killed her husband after suffering from years of abuse and was convicted for the act because her killing failed to satisfy the self-defense law's requirement of happening while facing an "immediate threat," even though the killing appears to have been necessary to avoid her own death by her husband at *some* point in the near future.[16] Or imagine a case of assisted suicide or mercy killing, where a person assists a suicide by injecting a person with poison or goes beyond assisting a suicide and kills a terminally ill person to quicken the person's death and end their suffering. These acts may not be morally wrongful but may nevertheless be criminally prohibited. In both cases, those who kill knowing that what they are doing is criminal even though they see themselves as—correctly, let us assume—morally

[15] For a discussion, see, e.g., A. P. Simester and G. R. Sullivan, "On the Nature and Rationale of Property Offences," in *Defining Crimes: Essays on the Special Part of the Criminal Law*, ed. R. A. Duff and Stuart Green (Oxford University Press, 2005), 171 ("[I]n most modern societies, property rights are not pre-legal. This is not to deny that the legal structure of property rights may, analytically and historically, be a development of pre-legal norms and rights . . . ."); John Gardner and Stephen Shute, "The Wrongness of Rape," in *Oxford Essays in Jurisprudence*, ed. Jeremy Horder (Oxford University Press, 2000), 201 ("My having[] property right over my old clothes . . . does not come of any value . . . *to me* but of the contribution which my having such a property right makes to the perpetuation of a *system* of optimal . . . value."); A. P. Simester and Andreas von Hirsch, *Crimes, Harms and Wrongs: On the Principles of Criminalisation* (Hart Publishing, 2011), 40–43.

[16] For a discussion, see Kimberly Kessler Ferzan, "Defending Imminence: From Battered Women to Iraq," *Arizona Law Review* 46, no. 2 (2004): 213; Benjamin C. Zipursky, "Self-defense, Domination, and the Social Contract," *University of Pittsburgh Law Review* 57 (1996): 579.

justified in killing would be disobeying the state's directives not to kill on purpose even in such situations. That is the sense in which even murder can be a *malum prohibitum* offense.

To explore a more promising way of thinking about criminalizing disobedience through the *malum in se–malum prohibitum* distinction, we might start by looking at traffic laws again. This time, take the crime of going over the speed limit. Is it a *malum in se* or a *malum prohibitum* offense? The crime appears to be both *malum in se* and *malum prohibitum*. The *malum in se* component has to do with endangering others by driving in an unsafe manner, not only because everyone else is roughly driving at about the same speed and it is dangerous to be an outlier but also because driving too fast can lead one to lose control over one's vehicle. But, as everyone knows, a sober, competent driver may drive above the speed limit on purpose with due care without imposing any unwarranted risk on others, if the speed limit is set too low or if the surrounding conditions are such that there is no additional risk of harming others by speeding. That would still be an offense because the speed limit means what it says and there is a prohibition on driving over a certain speed. In that situation, speeding is a *malum prohibitum*. Speeding may not be a wrong in and of itself because an instance of speeding may not increase the risk of harm to others unwarrantedly, though it may still be a wrong because it is prohibited.

Even crimes that are commonly and squarely classified as *mala prohibita* offenses often have *mala in se* components. An example might be an environmental regulatory offense where dumping a certain amount of chemicals may increase the risk of people nearby getting sick, which would make the offense *malum in se*, though the same act may not risk harming anyone unwarrantedly yet still go against a legal directive, which makes it *malum prohibitum*. Or, consider a weapons possession case. One might say that having a gun in one's possession is not a moral wrong but only a legal wrong because merely having it does not harm others. However, the matter may be more complicated than that. First, by having a gun, one would be increasing the amount of risk that exists in one's community. Second, by having a gun, one may be encouraging others to obtain one, which can also increase the risk of gun-related violence.[17]

We may then think about culpability of various offenses by applying the following formula:

$$C_t = C_d + C_a$$

C_t is the "Total Culpability," C_a is culpability attributable to the badness of the prohibited act itself (for example, driving dangerously), and C_d is culpability

[17] Larry Alexander and Kimberly Kessler Ferzan, *Reflections on Crime and Culpability: Problems and Puzzles* (Cambridge University Press, 2018), 17–60.

attributable to the act of disobeying a prohibition (the portion of culpability having to do with doing something that is counter to the law, like going over the speed limit). As we will see in Chapter 11, some complications arise when we try to make individual culpability determinations with this formula. But for now, the important point is that, rather than classifying offenses as *mala prohibita* or as *mala in se* offenses, it is better to think of offenses as having *mala prohibita* and *mala in se* components.[18] Once crimes are broken down into those components, we can isolate the *mala prohibita* components as involving disobedience.[19]

The fact that crimes have *mala in se* and *mala prohibita* components to varying degrees might invite the objection that *mala prohibita* or disobedience offenses do not constitute a distinctive category. One might argue, for instance, that even murder may be considered a *malum prohibitum* offense because explaining why murder is a crime necessarily refers to prior determinations by the state about when a human life begins or ends and what a human person is, and those determinations are not to be discovered "in nature" but are to be made by the state. This might be a reason to question the *in se–prohibitum* distinction and the coherence of the category of criminalization of disobedience altogether.

However, one can preserve the *malum in se–malum prohibitum* distinction while conceding the point that crime definitions contain both components. The state's role in defining, say, murder as a criminal wrong is only on the margins, where the law can play the role of reflecting morality for the core of the relevant legal prohibition while drawing lines as necessary or assigning a legal official to do so for reasons of the rule of law.[20] By contrast, in the *malum prohibitum* context, instead of declaring pre-legal wrongs as offenses, the state determines how to employ the state's institutional apparatus to achieve various ends and to define whatever interferes with such efforts as offenses, so the nature of the wrongdoing at its core has to do with how a person interacts with the state's exercises of its powers. The wrongfulness of the act does not derive from the moral wrongfulness of, say, harming another person, as is the case in the homicide context, but from going against the manner in which the state uses its powers.[21] Therefore,

18 I am not the first to make this suggestion. See, e.g., Douglas Husak, "*Malum Prohibitum* and Retributivism," in *Defining Crimes*; R. A. Duff, *The Realm of Criminal Law* (Oxford University Press, 2018), 313–22 ("pure and impure"); Stuart P. Green, *Lying, Cheating, and Stealing: A Moral Theory of White-Collar Crime* (Oxford University Press, 2006), 120 ("*mala in se* and *mala prohibita* qualities").

19 While the term "component" might give the impression that different elements of crime definitions can be neatly assigned to different components, C_d and C_a, that is not the intended reading of the formulation. The idea is that an act may be wrong for different reasons, having to do with the underlying badness of the act and disobedience manifested in the act. Such reasons do not necessarily correspond to different, discrete parts of the relevant crime definition.

20 Cf. James Edwards, "Criminalization without Punishment," *Legal Theory* 23, no. 2 (2017): 77; John Gardner, "Reply to Critics," in *Offences and Defences: Selected Essays in the Philosophy of Criminal Law* (Oxford University Press, 2007), 239.

21 For a similar discussion that grapples with the difficulties of defining the *malum in se–malum prohibitum* distinction, see Ambrose Y. K. Lee and Alexander F. Sarch, *The Moral Prerequisites of*

the phenomenon of the state drawing such lines as necessary for reasons of the rule of law does not turn a *malum in se* offense into a *malum prohibitum* offense, though it may introduce a *malum prohibitum* element into what is predominantly a *malum in se* offense. Crimes can still be classified as a *malum in se* or a *malum prohibitum* offense depending on which component predominates the relevant offense definition.

V. Varieties of Criminalization of Disobedience

Now that we have a way of identifying instances of criminalization of disobedience, let us look at some examples of them.

A. Disobedience of Government Officials

We can start with one of the more familiar examples of criminalization of disobedience, the crime of contempt. For instance, a US federal court can punish a person for "[d]isobedience or resistance to its lawful writ, process, order, rule, decree, or command."[22] Disobedience of law enforcement officers can be a crime as well. In New York, it is a crime to "congregate[] with other persons in a public place and refuse[] to comply with a lawful order of the police to disperse" with "intent to cause public inconvenience, annoyance or alarm, or recklessly creating a risk thereof."[23] Provisions like these criminalize disobedience and convict people for their failures to obey commands by legal authorities in certain situations; the fact that one does not do what one is told to do—even if the commands may not prescribe what is optimal in a given situation—is precisely at the heart of this type of criminality.

B. Obstruction of Justice and Similar Offenses

The contempt and disobedience laws discussed above are closely related to obstruction of justice offenses. We can start with a general obstruction of justice provision, which makes it a crime for a person to "corruptly . . . influence[], obstruct[], or impede[], or endeavor[] to influence, obstruct, or impede, the due

the Criminal Law: Legal Moralism and the Problem of Mala Prohibita (Cambridge University Press, 2023), 4.

[22] 18 U.S.C. § 401.
[23] N.Y. Penal Law § 240.20.

administration of justice."[24] Then there are more specific obstruction of justice laws such as perjury, which is defined in the US federal law as a situation where a person "willfully and contrary to . . . oath states . . . any material matter which he does not believe to be true."[25] These laws and laws like them criminalize disobedience of the state because they prohibit conduct that would frustrate the government's efforts to enforce the law despite the government's specific commands not to do so, no matter the merits of given enforcement efforts.

C. Evasion of Justice and Failures to Cooperate

Closely related to obstruction of justice laws are laws that criminally prohibit certain activities because criminalizing them helps the state combat other activities. For example, it is a federal crime in the United States to engage in "a monetary transaction in criminally derived property of a value greater than $10,000 [where the property] is derived from specified unlawful activity."[26] The term "specified unlawful activity" covers a variety of offenses such as drug offenses, bribery, and human trafficking.[27] The state also imposes certain affirmative duties in order to aid law enforcement. For instance, information-gathering offenses like the requirement that one declare the amount of currency one is carrying abroad over a certain minimum is a way of criminalizing something in order to unveil illicit conduct, like running an unlawful business.[28] These types of offense frequently also require reports of signs of suspicious activities by other people, as we see in various anti–money laundering laws that bind financial institutions. These laws are similar to obstruction of justice laws but tend to go further in that they prohibit conduct that makes the state's job of enforcing the laws more difficult or require people to engage in conduct that makes the state's job of enforcing the laws easier, and the obligation to support the state does not turn on the merits of the relevant laws or the enforcement efforts.

D. Regulatory Offenses

The phrase "regulatory offenses," sometimes also known as "public welfare offenses," refers to a type of criminal offense that the government enacts as a way of enforcing its regulation of various aspects of our lives—air quality, food

24 18 U.S.C. § 1503.
25 18 U.S.C. § 1621.
26 18 U.S.C. § 1957.
27 18 U.S.C. § 1956(c)(7).
28 31 U.S.C. § 5316(a).

safety, environmental preservation, and so on. In the United States at the federal level, typically, a statute would authorize an agency (or authorize the president to authorize an agency) to promulgate regulations to implement the statute and specify that certain violations of the statute or the regulations are crimes.[29] Regulatory offenses often have to do with regulations of potentially harmful substances and products, but not always. Consider for instance the requirement noted above that those who give investment advice for compensation do so only after registering as an investment advisor,[30] or similar licensing requirements for drivers and inspection requirements for cars. Perhaps these do not look like disobedience offenses at first glance. However, the relationship between doing something prohibited and imposing a harm or risk of harm to others may not always be clear, whereas it is clear that people are expected to follow the state's determinations regarding required behaviors in relevant regulated spaces.

E. Risk Creation and Other Inchoate Offenses

Harm prevention is one of the state's core tasks, and the state criminalizes not just directly causing harm but also risking harm in order to prevent people from harming others. One way in which criminal law is used to manage risks is through regulations, as just mentioned. More generally, though, the state often criminalizes conduct that might lead or contribute to harm by, say, enabling further acts by the actor or others. Various possession offenses—drugs and weapons—may be categorized in this group of offenses. Those who have these items in their possession may not be harming or wronging anyone, but may still be going against clear commands not to have them. Such laws may seem to be about risk management and public safety, but wrongness of violation of these laws can often be more about disobedience than about risk creation.

F. National Security Offenses

There are many crimes with national security implications. Here are some examples from the United States. The most well-known, while rarely prosecuted, is the crime of treason, which prohibits those who "ow[e] allegiance to the United States" from "levy[ing] war against" the United States or "adher[ing]"

[29] See, e.g., 31 U.S.C. § 5322; 15 U.S.C. § 80b-17; see also Lazarus, "Environmental Criminal Law," 2441 ("[A]t the federal level, Congress has virtually criminalized civil law by making criminal sanctions available for violations of otherwise civil federal regulatory program.").
[30] 15 U.S.C. §§ 80b-3, 80b-2, 80b-17.

to the enemies, "giving them aid and comfort."[31] More common are espionage crimes[32] that prohibit a variety of information gathering and disclosure acts with, for instance, "intent or reason to believe" that the information is "to be used to the injury of the United States or to the advantage of a foreign nation."[33] Some national security offenses take place in the more mundane setting of export controls, where certain items are prohibited from being exported without authorization for reasons of national security.[34] These crimes can be thought of as disobedience crimes in the sense that they command persons subject to the laws to take one side in international relations and act in ways that benefit the United States or not in any ways that hurt the United States, no matter the merits of individual actions the state chooses to take in matters of foreign relations and national security.

VI. Disobedience and the Question of Wrongfulness

A. General Duty to Obey the Law and Civil Disobedience

Given the legal moralist perspective this book assumes, criminalization of disobedience is going to be problematic if the case that disobedience is morally wrong cannot be made. Some might argue that there is a simple answer to this question—namely, that it cannot be done.[35] One might, for example, argue that there is no general duty to obey the law and that we cannot criminalize disobedience on the basis of its wrongfulness. Others might argue that one should never be punished for disobedience given the tradition of civil disobedience in liberal democracies. Neither argument settles the issue.

Let's start with the argument that there is no general duty to obey the law. There is a voluminous philosophical literature on this question, and much of this literature is critical of the idea that there is a general duty to obey the law.[36] And

[31] 18 U.S.C. § 2381.

[32] See, e.g., 18 U.S.C. §§ 793–798.

[33] 18 U.S.C. § 794.

[34] 50 U.S.C. §§ 4811, 4813, 4819.

[35] Some make it too easy. As will be discussed in more detail below, Stephen Garvey, for example, says: "A well-functioning democratic state possesses legitimate authority over its citizens. . . . When it declares that doing this or that is a crime it thereby makes it wrong to do this or that (assuming it was not wrong before the state spoke)." Stephen P. Garvey, "Was Ellen Wronged?," *Criminal Law and Philosophy* 7, no. 2 (2013): 211. This is not my view as I do not think a mere act of criminalization of something can render it morally wrongful, without saying more about the content of the legislation.

[36] See, e.g., Leslie Green, *The Authority of the State* (Oxford University Press, 1988), 232–34; Joseph Raz, "The Obligation to Obey the Law," in *The Authority of Law: Essays on Law and Morality* (Oxford University Press, 1979), 233–49; Raz, "The Obligation to Obey: Revision and Tradition," 341–42; A. John Simmons, *Moral Principles and Political Obligations* (Princeton University Press, 1979), 191–201.

I will take it as a given that there is no such general duty. But if it were indeed the case that there is no such duty, would this mean that it is unjust to criminalize and punish disobedience?

The answer is no. The obligation to obey that is discussed in the literature is "a general obligation applying to all the law's subjects and to all the laws on all the occasions to which they apply."[37] This leaves open the following possibilities: there is an obligation to obey that applies to all the law's subjects with regard to *some* laws on all the occasions to which they apply; there is an obligation to obey that applies to *some* of the law's subjects with regard to all laws on all the occasions to which they apply; there is an obligation to obey that applies to all the law's subjects with regard to all laws on *some* occasions to which they apply; or some other combination. And in some of these instances, not only may the duty to obey exist but the violation of the duty (as distinct from the violation of the law) may be the basis to punish. In short, a proof against the existence of a general duty to obey the law cannot help us answer when a duty to obey exists and when a violation of such a duty is punishable.

As for civil disobedience, in liberal democratic societies, in which disobedience is sometimes thought to be an acceptable and valuable form of political participation,[38] the vision of the government's punishing its own citizens for disobeying seems distasteful and dangerous. The romantic images of courageous lawbreakers participating in lunch-counter sit-ins or refusing to move to the back of the bus resonate powerfully. There is a debate over how the law should respond to such situations of justifiable lawbreaking,[39] but there is a distinction between punishing civil disobedients *for engaging* in acts that the law prohibits—such as trespassing—and punishing them *for being* disobedient or defiant. The former may be deemed reasonable for rule-of-law reasons; the latter smacks of authoritarianism. Thinking along such lines, one may arrive at the view that it is unjust for the state to punish disobedience.

However, the problem with the argument based on civil disobedience is that civil disobedience is typically understood to be a special kind of lawbreaking that should be distinguished from ordinary offenses. And those who have defended

[37] Raz, "Obligation to Obey the Law," 234; see also William A. Edmundson, "State of the Art: The Duty to Obey the Law," *Legal Theory* 10, no. 4 (2004): 215–16 (observing that the duty to obey the law as debated in the philosophical literature is a duty that is "comprehensively applicable" and "universally borne"); Abner S. Greene, *Against Obligation: The Multiple Sources of Authority in a Liberal Democracy* (Harvard University Press, 2012), 15–17.

[38] See, e.g., Ronald Dworkin, *A Matter of Principle* (Harvard University Press, 1985), 104–05; John Rawls, *A Theory of Justice*, rev. ed. (Harvard University Press, 1999), 336.

[39] See generally Ronald Dworkin, *Taking Rights Seriously* (Harvard University Press, 1977), 206–22; Dworkin, *A Matter of Principle*, 113–14; Kent Greenawalt, *Conflicts of Law and Morality* (Oxford University Press, 1989), 271–85; Kimberly Brownlee, *Conscience and Conviction: The Case for Disobedience* (Oxford University Press, 2012); Candice Delmas, *A Duty to Resist: When Disobedience Should Be Uncivil* (Oxford University Press, 2018).

the use of civil disobedience are eager to place strict conditions on permissible forms of lawbreaking under the banner of justifiable civil disobedience. As Joseph Raz has summarized, it has been argued by various theorists that civil disobedience, in order for it to be justified,

> must be used as a measure of last resort . . . ; it must be non-violent; it must be openly undertaken; and its perpetrators must submit to prosecution and punishment; such acts must be confined to those designed to publicize certain wrongs and to convince the public and the authorities of the justice of one's claims; it should not be used to intimidate or coerce.[40]

We can have a debate over whether all of these conditions must be met for an act of lawbreaking to be a genuine act of civil disobedience, but eliminating all or most of these conditions would erase the distinction between civil disobedience and ordinary lawbreaking. Given the importance of this distinction, whatever doubts one may have about punishing disobedience *as a general matter* cannot be drawn from inspiring examples of civil disobedience from history.

In short, neither skepticism about the existence of the duty to obey the law nor recognition of civil disobedience as an important form of political advocacy has the reach to show that the government is not permitted to punish disobedience. What the debates do show is that there are times when lawbreaking is desirable or even mandatory, but it is too quick to go from that conclusion to the conclusion that punishment of disobedience is unjust as a general matter.[41]

[40] Joseph Raz, "A Right to Dissent? I. Civil Disobedience," in *Authority of Law*, 269; see also Greenawalt, *Conflicts of Law and Morality*, 226–43 (discussing various factors that justify disobedience); Rawls, *A Theory of Justice*, 320 (defining civil disobedience as "a public, nonviolent, conscientious yet political act contrary to law usually done with the aim of bringing about a change in the law or policies of the government"); H. A. Bedau, "Civil Disobedience and Personal Responsibility for Injustice," in *Civil Disobedience in Focus*, ed. H. A. Bedau (Routledge, 1991), 51 (describing "paradigm cases" of civil disobedience as acts that are illegal; are committed openly, nonviolently, conscientiously, and within the framework of the rule of law; and are committed "with the intention of frustrating or protesting some law, policy, or decision . . . of the government"). It has further been observed:

> There is all the difference in the world between the criminal's avoiding the public eye and the civil disobedient's taking the law into his own hands in open defiance. This distinction between an open violation of the law, performed in public, and a clandestine one is so glaringly obvious that it can be neglected only by prejudice or ill will. It is now recognized by all serious writers on the subject and clearly is the primary condition for all attempts that argue for the compatibility of civil disobedience with law and the American institutions of government.

Hannah Arendt, "Civil Disobedience," in *Crises of the Republic* (Harcourt Brace Jovanovich, 1972), 75; see also Dworkin, *A Matter of Principle*, 5–13 (asserting that for civil disobedience to be acceptable, it must embrace a working theory that rests not on the mere wickedness of a law, but instead on the persuasiveness that disobedience is the appropriate response of those who view a certain law or political decision as immoral or wrong).

[41] One might argue that another lesson from the civil disobedience example is not just that there are special kinds of lawbreaking that we ought to recognize as an acceptable form of activism but

B. Wrongfulness of Disobedience

To say something generally about wrongfulness of disobedience, consider again the example of speeding. Traffic laws that regulate velocities of vehicles exist to ensure a reasonably safe driving environment for everyone on the road primarily by signaling the speed at which the driving is likely to be too risky. Setting the speed limit communicates the speed at which maneuvering the vehicle starts to become too difficult and also coordinates drivers' behaviors so that vehicles' movements are predictable, which both help avoid accidents. So the law appears to be about safety.

Let's revisit this formula:

$$C_t = C_d + C_a$$

To illustrate how this framework would apply to the speeding context, take four drivers in two different sets, each set with two drivers. The first set has drivers who are driving over the speed limit, and the other set has drivers driving within the speed limit. We can express the universe of possibilities as shown in Table 2.1. Let's first take the drivers in Quadrant II and Quadrant IV. They are both driving within the speed limit, so neither is disobeying, but the driver in Quadrant II is driving dangerously, whereas the driver in Quadrant IV is not driving dangerously. The driver in Quadrant II is not in violation of the law against speeding, though it is possible that there is some other safety-related law of which the driver is in violation. The driver in Quadrant IV is driving safely and is law-abiding. As to the drivers in Quadrants I and III, the driver in Quadrant I is disobeying and driving dangerously, whereas the driver in Quadrant III is driving safely, though he is driving over the speed limit. The driver in Quadrant III then has the C_a of zero, but his disobedience makes him blameworthy.

Or does it? Perhaps the safe driver should not be punished at all, given that he is, after all, a safe driver. Is the safe driver who disobeys the speed limit

Table 2.1 Conduct-Disobedience Culpability Matrix

	$C_d > 0$	$C_d = 0$
$C_a > 0$	I	II
$C_a = 0$	III	IV

that it is good when individuals refuse to surrender their judgment or to obey blindly. Cf. Robert Paul Wolff, *In Defense of Anarchism* (Harper & Row, 1970); Michelle Madden Dempsey, "Authority, Obedience, and Justification," *University of Cincinnati Law Review* 90, no. 2 (2021): 411–12. I will return to this point below.

blameworthy? The answer to that question could be that a person who drives over the speed limit but is nevertheless not imposing any unwarranted risk on others is still blameworthy if they go against a known legal directive, meaning that a law designed to promote safety may end up punishing a safe driver. In that case, speeding may not be a wrong in and of itself because an instance of speeding may not increase the risk of harm to others unwarrantedly, though it may still be a wrong because it is prohibited.

This speeding example illustrates a perennial and familiar problem in the law that has to do with overinclusiveness of rules.[42] An overinclusive law presents the problem of punishing a morally innocent person—a person who does not do anything wrong. Throughout the book, we will see many examples of situations where a person may reasonably believe they are justified in doing what they are doing, even though they are going against a legal directive. There could also be reasonable disagreements about what the state ought to do and what the rules ought to say, and an individual facing a speed limit may reasonably believe that the state came to the wrong conclusion, while others may reasonably disagree with that individual.[43]

So where is the wrong in such situations? Theorists who have addressed this issue have said many different things over the years, and ideas like "civic arrogance"[44] and "failure to show sufficient respect to rule-of-law values"[45] have been considered.[46] Such arguments come uncomfortably close to

[42] For discussions, see, for example, Frederick Schauer, *Playing by the Rules: A Philosophical Examination of Rule-Based Decision-Making in Law and in Life* (Clarendon Press, 1991), 128–34; Larry Alexander, "Can Law Survive the Asymmetry of Authority?," *Quinnipiac Law Review* 19, no. 3 (2000); Larry Alexander, "The Gap," *Harvard Journal of Law and Public Policy* 14, no. 3 (1991); Heidi M. Hurd, "Justifiably Punishing the Justified," *Michigan Law Review* 90, no. 8 (1992): 2203. An underinclusive criminal law, a law that fails to capture those that the law is trying to capture, could also be a problem. That is, it may present the problem of ineffectiveness, and that, counter-intuitively, may also present the problem of overpunishment in the sense that the people who are being punished may be being punished in vain—to advance a governmental program that is bound to fail to produce the effects it seeks. At the same time, underinclusiveness may be by design. It may be thought that the law would be more effective if it was underinclusive for reasons having to do with particulars of the situation. Alternatively, undereffectiveness may simply be a way of limiting the reach of criminal laws, given other relevant concerns like civil liberties.

[43] Along these lines, consider Joseph Raz's argument that while "laws concerning safety at work, regulations regarding standards of manufactured goods such as cars, pharmaceuticals, and the like, rules concerning safe maintenance of cars, or concerning standards of safe driving, qualifications required for engaging in certain occupations, and many more" may "make[] a difference to one's moral obligations," if one is, say, "the greatest living expert on pharmaceuticals, then the law has no authority over [that person] regarding the safety of pharmaceuticals." Consequently, there is no duty for that person to obey laws regarding the safety of pharmaceuticals. Raz, "Obligation to Obey: Revision and Tradition," 348.

[44] R. A. Duff, "Crime, Prohibition, and Punishment," *Journal of Applied Philosophy* 19, no. 2 (2002): 97, 104.

[45] Alexander and Ferzan, *Crime and Culpability*, 311.

[46] For a recent discussion of various attempts, see Lee and Sarch, *The Moral Prerequisites of the Criminal Law*, 47–69.

arguments in favor of punishing attitudes and should thus be disfavored. More recently, R. A. Duff has proposed that we take the following steps when thinking about wrongness of *mala prohibita* offenses that criminalize conduct like speeding: "[W]e must first justify the regulation in question, by showing that it efficiently serves some aspect of the common good, or averts some mischief that properly concerns the polity, and does so without laying unreasonable burdens on those who are required to obey it; we must then argue on that basis that those who breach the regulation thereby commit a censure-worthy public wrong."[47] Andrew Simester and Andreas von Hirsh have similarly argued: "The wrongfulness of a rule-violation depends on the moral force of the rule. In the case of a *malum prohibitum* rule, the moral force comes from its instrumental value; which depends, in turn, on the purposes the rule serves and how well it serves them. It depends, that is, on whether the creation of the rule itself is justified."[48]

We may elaborate on these types of arguments as follows. A typical definition of a state is that it is a set of political institutions that, organized to govern a particular territory, successfully lays claim to the monopoly of legitimate violence within the territory.[49] The state serves a number of crucial functions, including ensuring physical security, coordinating behaviors of individuals and entities, resolving disputes, and providing various social services (like, just to name a few, building and maintaining infrastructure, public transportation, protecting against—and facilitating recovery after—natural disasters, and so on). For the state to engage in these projects, it needs to formulate, announce, enforce rules of behavior (deterring undesirable behaviors with monitoring and threats of unpleasant consequences, investigating them after they happen, following through with the said consequences), and address problems that arise.[50] In doing so, it needs to authorize public entities and officials to devise programs and implement them with state instruments that they have at their disposal. The duty to obey certain laws, then, may be premised on the idea that the state cannot function well in carrying out such tasks without cooperation of the governed.

In addition, the people who do the work of governing, even if they are working in good faith, are fallible and may also be working in situations of

[47] Duff, *Realm of Criminal Law*, 333.

[48] Simester and von Hirsch, *Crimes, Harms and Wrongs*, 27.

[49] Leslie Green, *The Authority of the State* (Oxford University Press, 1988), 63–88; George Klosko, *Political Obligations* (Oxford University Press, 2005), 17–59.

[50] For a similar argument, see Christopher Heath Wellman, "Rights Forfeiture and *Mala Prohibita*," in *The Constitution of the Criminal Law*, ed. R. A. Duff et al. (Oxford University Press, 2013), 84–85; see also Raz, "Obligation to Obey: Revision and Tradition," 348 (observing that laws often set "[s]tandards for the preservation of the environment, for the protection of scarce resources, for the raising of revenue through taxation to finance public projects, welfare services, or other valuable projects").

disagreements about what ought to be done, and the programs and the laws they enact and implement may be flawed (or flawed from the perspective of some but not others) in any number of ways.[51] But fallibility of the state and disagreements among those impacted are to be expected even when the state is just and well-functioning, and the state cannot govern and sustain itself and provide conditions that produce necessary stability for the people's lives for the long haul if individuals subject to its powers resist the state every time the state is mistaken or is facing disagreement about soundness of its governance. From all of these considerations, we might attempt to draw out the duty to obey the law and the corresponding wrong of disobedience even when one reasonably and even correctly disagrees with the state's policies, rules, and implementations.

The normative core of such arguments may find its articulation in the following well-known passages from John Rawls:

> From the standpoint of justice as fairness, a fundamental natural duty is the duty of justice. This duty requires us to support and to comply with just institutions that exist and apply to us. It also constrains us to further just arrangements not yet established, at least when this can be done without too much cost to ourselves. Thus if the basic structure of society is just, or as just as it is reasonable to expect in the circumstances, everyone has a natural duty to do his part in the existing scheme.[52]

And here is another:

> The main idea is that when a number of persons engage in a mutually advantageous cooperative venture according to rules, and thus restrict their liberty in ways necessary to yield advantages for all, those who have submitted to these restrictions have a right to a similar acquiescence on the part of those who have benefited from their submission. We are not to gain from the cooperative labors of others without doing our fair share.[53]

Now, a problem with this account is that the fact that the state is justified in carrying out such valuable projects by enacting various laws by itself does not

[51] Cf. Joseph Raz, *The Morality of Freedom* (Clarendon Press, 1986), 78–79 ("The existence of the occasional bad laws enacted by a just government does not by itself establish much. However just a government may be, it is liable to pass undesirable and morally objectionable laws from time to time. This need not be due to any moral shortcomings in the government. Even assuming complete good will and unimpeachable moral convictions, inefficiency, ignorance and other ordinary facts of life will lead to objectionable laws being passed.").

[52] Rawls, *A Theory of Justice*, 99.

[53] Rawls, *A Theory of Justice*, 96.

establish an obligation on the part of individuals not to disobey these laws. If we assume that it is the case that every time a person breaks a law, the person undermines or at least negatively impacts the law's functioning, we might conclude that the person engages in a wrong, but that assumption is false. As Raz has pointed out multiple times, "it is a melodramatic exaggeration to suppose that every breach of law endangers, by however small a degree, the survival of the government, or of law and order."[54] If an act of obedience does not impact the law, then it is unclear where the wrong is. In other words, just because it makes good sense to have a rule in place does not show that it is wrong for an individual to disobey it.

The answer to this challenge can be found in the last sentence of each of the quoted passages from Rawls, which contains the idea of doing one's "part" or "fair share."[55] The importance of those phrases is that they do not imply a causal notion of supporting or disobeying the state. In a group activity, a person whose contribution or lack thereof makes absolutely no difference can still be described as either doing their fair share or not. The fact that each individual makes little to no difference is irrelevant to the issue of doing one's fair share, and the duty not to disobey when it comes to *mala prohibita* offenses can be based on this idea of doing one's part or fair share.[56]

I emphasize that this is not to say that there is a general duty to obey the law that applies to all laws and to all people to which the laws apply. First, even

[54] Raz, *Morality of Freedom*, 102; Raz, "Obligation to Obey: Revision and Tradition," 349 ("Law breaking is liable to undermine the effectiveness of the government in many cases. In others, violations of law have no such effect."); Raz, "Obligation to Obey the Law," 238–39 ("There are . . . countless offences the commission of which is never known. . . . [O]ne's violation of the law does not always affect anybody, however minimally and however indirectly."); see also Wellman, "Rights Forfeiture and *Mala Prohibita*," 85; Lee and Sarch, *The Moral Prerequisites of the Criminal Law*, 56.

[55] The phrase "one's part" or "fair share" need not mean that only citizens are subject to such obligations.

[56] Cf. Duff, *Realm of Criminal Law*, 320 (sketching an argument to require obedience on the basis of "an idea of solidarity with fellow citizens," which would be the view that "I accept this modest burden that most citizens must accept, because it serves the common good, even though my obedience is not strictly necessary to that end; I do not seek to make an exception for myself"); A. P. Simester, *Fundamentals of Criminal Law: Responsibility, Culpability, and Wrongdoing* (Oxford University Press, 2021), 241–42 (arguing that when given a choice between getting a license for a dangerous activity and seeking an exemption from it on grounds of one's personal expertise, the person "has moral reasons" to get the license and "the state has good reason to require him to do so" in order to maintain and protect the scheme of licensing the way it is set up given "[t]he constraints imposed by limited state resources and practicalities of enforcement," which "may then entail that individual nuances cannot be evaluated"); Wellman, "Rights Forfeiture and *Mala Prohibita*," 87 ("If a citizen exceeds the designated speed limit, then he or she is not doing his or her fair share to contribute to the benefits that these laws provide . . . ."); see also Christopher Heath Wellman, "Toward a Liberal Theory of Political Obligation," *Ethics*, 111, no. 4 (2001): 737. For a discussion of Duff, Simester, and Wellman along these lines, see Lee and Sarch, *The Moral Prerequisites of the Criminal Law*, 57–60, 61–69. Duff, Simester, and Wellman's arguments are compatible with the argument presented here, though it would take us too far afield for me to spell out which parts of their broader theoretical commitments I endorse and which I deny.

within the Rawlsian framework, the duty to support is framed in terms of "just institutions" and "mutually advantageous cooperative venture[s]" that "yield advantages for all." We need not adopt these exact formulations, but the basic idea here is that the assumption of "just institutions" and "advantages for all" places a limit on even the relatively expansive notion of the duty not to disobey defended here. For one thing, as Rawls has said, "we are not required to acquiesce in the denial of our own and others' basic liberties," and there is no duty to comply with laws that "exceed certain bounds of injustice."[57] Second, we would still need to give an account as to why a law prescribes what it does the way it does, what good or bad the particular law in question does, and what policies the particular law is supposed to advance on a case-by-case basis before determining that there is a duty to obey *that* law, as there are situations where the duty not to disobey may be weak or nonexistent according to those considerations.

This also means that it should be kept clear that none of the arguments made so far counsels in favor of blind obedience, meek acceptance of the law, or "a surrender of judgment."[58] One can, and indeed should, always be alert to how the state exercises its powers, whether such exercises can be defended, if deferring to the state on any matter is appropriate all things considered, whether the law extends beyond "certain bounds of injustice," whether civil disobedience is appropriate, and even whether there is a duty to disobey. The arguments made here do not challenge such attitudes and practices of vigilance. Being alert to injustices can coexist with the duty not to disobey even erroneous laws. As noted above, one can disobey with different attitudes, and it is also the case that one can obey with a variety of attitudes, including attitudes critical of the very laws being obeyed.

In the next several chapters, I will discuss different areas of the law where the state criminalizes disobedience. What I have sought to show so far is that in instances where the law criminalizes disobedience, there are ways to make the case that such laws criminalize genuine moral wrongs, and the considerations given here show how such cases may be made. That, however, does not mean that the case for wrongfulness of disobedience in a particular context can be successfully made for every law I discuss. Nor does it show that it makes sense to criminalize every time there is wrongful disobedience. Therefore, the presentations given in the following chapters should not be understood necessarily as defenses of these laws. I will say more about this in the next part.

[57] Rawls, *A Theory of Justice*, 312; see also Tommie Shelby, *Dark Ghettos: Injustice, Dissent, and Reform* (Harvard University Press, 2016), 219.
[58] Raz, *Morality of Freedom*, 38–39.

C. Why Disobedience?

One thought that may arise at this point is that what is going on here is not criminalization of disobedience but of something else. Take for instance the crime of contempt, or "[d]isobedience or resistance to [a federal court's] lawful writ, process, order, rule, decree, or command."[59] The law is written in terms of disobedience to be sure, but one may be tempted to think that that is not what it really is about. The basic idea may instead be that, in order to function, the legal system depends on the cooperation of those who are subject to it. That is, a failure to obey government officials in certain situations interferes with the government's ability to carry out the functions of the state. The core wrong of "disobedience" in these situations, some might accordingly argue, is interference with the workings of a legal system, not disobedience per se. In other words, these laws do not in fact criminalize the wrong of disobedience but criminalize *undermining*.[60] The two wrongs are different. Even offenses that appear to be pure disobedience offenses like contempt may be wrong because of their potential to undermine the legal system. What all this means is that, one might argue, disobedience is not the best way of describing the nature of the wrong involved, as every instance of disobedience can be redescribed as an instance of undermining.

Does it really matter whether we talk in terms of disobeying or undermining? Perhaps not, as the distinction between disobedience and undermining will make little difference for much of the analysis that this book will undertake. One may frequently undermine cooperative ventures by disobeying, and one may obey in order to avoid undermining. The ideas overlap in application considerably.

Yet it is a mistake to de-emphasize the disobedience aspect by characterizing relevant transgressions as undermining as opposed to disobeying. For one thing, the term "undermining" is a causal notion that implies actual impact, but, as discussed above, disobedience need not result in any actual undermining at all to be wrongful. More importantly, consider the following. Establishing and operating social schemes typically requires governmental institutions. When such institutions get to work, they advance their goals often by issuing binding directives. Therefore, it is by obeying such directives one does one's fair share of supporting the institutions, and that aspect should not be obscured in our analyses. In other words, lawmakers and law enforcers determine what policies

[59] 18 U.S.C. § 401.

[60] Cf. Simester, *Fundamentals of Criminal Law*, 242 (arguing that in certain situations "nonconformity is a moral wrong not because of any risk of harm that the regime is designed to prevent" but because "[i]t is a wrong of indirectly undermining the regime, a regime that is itself valuable, which protects against harm, and which deserves to be upheld").

to pursue with what programs and tools, and when a person goes against such policies and interferes with state programs and uses of tools, they go against what those public officials have determined to be the way the people ought to behave, and that is disobedience.

But is it still not the case that the wrong of disobedience derives from the wrong of undermining of state institutions and programs? Put that way, it seems that the wrong of undermining is more fundamental than the wrong of disobedience. This is a fair point, but we should remember that the state, as mentioned above, can get things wrong. That is, law is fallible. The laws and the way they are enforced by the state may be unjust, stupid, do more harm than good, and so on. When a person goes against a legal prohibition, they may be either not undermining anything the state or the relevant political community cares about or may be undermining something that ought to be undermined because of some defect or injustice in the law, program, or policy. Yet the law still demands obedience, and still may punish the disobedient conduct, even in the absence of any undesirable undermining. The talk of undermining fails to capture this important dimension of *mala prohibita* offenses.

That the law is fallible yet demands obedience and even criminalizes disobedience is the tension that will run throughout the book and the key question in many difficult situations. The problem with characterizing *mala prohibita* components of offenses as being about the wrong of undermining as opposed to the wrong of disobeying is that it takes the spotlight off the distinctive problem that is presented when the state criminalizes disobedience. Given the fact that the phenomenon that is to be morally analyzed is the state making commands and expecting to be obeyed, we should not frame the debate in such a way that the most morally problematic aspects that are undoubtedly present drop out. In other words, given the subject matter, disobedience should remain the focus of our analysis of these laws.

VII. Criminalizing Disobedience: Limiting Principles?

That the law criminalizes disobedience on a regular basis and that disobedience can be wrongful does not mean that every instance of criminalization of disobedience is justifiable. As mentioned above, the duty not to disobey may be weak or nonexistent in certain areas of criminal law. For the state to criminalize and punish a person for disobeying when there is no duty to obey would be in violation of the wrongfulness constraint of legal moralism. Also, as a general matter, just because we identify a wrong that is properly within the domain of criminal law does not mean it is appropriate to criminalize it. There may be times when criminalizing disobedience unjustifiably infringes upon a person's rights, and for the state to criminalize and punish a person in such instances would be in violation of individual rights. Furthermore, criminalization and punishment of disobedience may at times be disproportionate in multiple ways.

We will return to these more particular reasons to place limits on the state's ability to criminalize and punish disobedience in Chapters 10 through 12, and some of the general considerations going into the choice between criminal law and other tools will also be discussed in Chapter 11. Before we get to those discussions, however, it is important to see all the ways in which the state does criminalize disobedience, so that will be the main task of Chapters 3 through 9. Once we see the role that criminalization of disobedience plays in our legal system, we can fully understand not only the usefulness of criminalization of disobedience for achieving important social objectives but also the potential excess and injustice of it. By categorizing certain instances of criminalization as instances of criminalization of disobedience, we will be in a better position to diagnose what exactly might be the problem with the state's use of criminal law in certain situations. For example, to the extent that the problem of criminalization and punishment of disobedience in an instance has to do with the state's loss of standing to demand obedience, the state that demands obedience and wields brute force to ensure compliance in such a situation would be acting unjustly. But we are getting ahead of ourselves. A more detailed discussion is reserved for the last chapters of the book.

VIII. Conclusion

This chapter has scrutinized the idea of criminalizing disobedience. In short, to criminalize and punish disobedience is to criminally prohibit and punish acting, or failing to act, in ways that are counter to the law, when the relevant conduct is not morally wrongful, except for the fact that the law prohibits it. This chapter has argued that crimes have *mala in se* and *mala prohibita* components and that the *malum prohibitum* component criminalizes disobedience. Next, after giving examples of criminalizing disobedience in different contexts, this chapter has identified the wrongfulness of disobedience that can serve as a basis for its criminalization. Namely, disobeying the law can be blameworthy because there is a duty to support the state as it carries out its tasks, as the state cannot function and provide conditions for peaceful coexistence of strangers over a territory without cooperation of the governed. While each individual's effort makes little difference for the state to govern successfully, each person has an obligation to do their fair share as the state seeks to do its work. There are limits to be imposed on the state's power to criminalize and punish disobedience, and they will be discussed later in the book.[61]

[61] The discussion in this chapter should make clear that the view defended here should be distinguished from the views of some contemporary theorists who emphasize the state's right to rule and to punish lawbreakers who defy the state. Stephen Garvey and Malcolm Thorburn exemplify such an approach.

Garvey distinguishes between the "moral model" and the "political model" and says that under the moral model, it would be wrong for the state to punish a person for committing a *malum prohibitum* offense like money laundering because "money laundering is . . . no wrong in the mind of morality," whereas the political model says that the state does the person "no wrong" when it punishes the person for violating the law against money laundering since the state "possesses the power or capacity to create and impose moral obligations where morality itself does not." Garvey, "Was Ellen Wronged?," 211. Garvey's solution to the concern that punishing people for *mala prohibita* offenses may involve punishing the morally innocent is to simply embrace the political model and dismiss the moral model. The fact that the state is a "well-functioning democratic state" and has prohibited money laundering is sufficient to permit the punishment, subject to certain limitations to be placed on democracy, such as those derived from "liberal rights." Garvey, "Was Ellen Wronged?," 210. For Garvey, no additional step of identifying the moral wrongfulness of money laundering is needed, other than perhaps the wrong of "defy[ing]" "the will of all" and sending the "false and arrogant" "message to [the] compatriots" that "I am better than you." Garvey, "Was Ellen Wronged?," 210. Garvey even says that "[t]he state always has at least one good reason to punish within the political model: to uphold or vindicate its authority." Garvey, "Was Ellen Wronged?," 211 n.116.

Thorburn is similar. We already saw in the previous chapter that Thorburn rejects legal moralism. Like Garvey, Thorburn dismisses the moral model and says "we suffer criminal condemnation and punishment for contravening the demands of the positive law with mens rea, *whether or not the law in question identifies a form of conduct that is morally wrongful*." Malcolm Thorburn, "Punishment and Public Authority," in *Criminal Law and the Authority of the State*, ed. Antje du Bois-Pedain et al. (Hart Publishing, 2017), 13 (emphasis added). Second, Thorburn argues that "criminal punishment" is essential because it is "a legal remedy that can vindicate the state's claim to be the exclusive holder of the right to rule in the jurisdiction." Malcolm Thorburn, "Criminal Punishment and the Right to Rule," *University of Toronto Law Journal* 70, Supplement 1 (2020): 48. He explains: "Where someone takes it upon himself to act contrary to the demands of the state's laws because he is acting instead upon his own view . . . , he is directly challenging the state's claim to have the exclusive right to make the law around here," and "[b]y choosing to act as he pleases notwithstanding the law's rules, the offender has threatened the state's claim to have an exclusive right to rule." Thorburn, "Criminal Punishment and the Right to Rule," 55, 59.

So, while Thorburn's talk of punishing disobedience bears a superficial resemblance to the view advanced in this book, the contrast between his perspective and this book is stark. Punishing disobedience is, this book will argue throughout, a pervasive feature of our criminal laws, and it is *both* justifiable *and* highly problematic from the legal moralist perspective, while Thorburn, while otherwise rejecting legal moralism, says that the core wrong in "criminal wrongdoing" is "against the state's right to set down the positive law," or "a wrong against the state in its exclusive right to make the law around here." Disobedience, for Thorburn, is thus at *the core* of *all instances of* criminal wrongdoing, as opposed to an element that is either minimally present or absent in many instances of criminal wrongdoing, and punishing *disobedience* is not only unproblematic but is in fact *the* central feature of state punishment. Thorburn, "Criminal Punishment and the Right to Rule," 62; see also Thorburn, "Punishment and Public Authority," 17–25 (making similar arguments with analogies to parental authority and king's authority). I should also add that I am with Shachar Eldar and Vincent Chiao when they say that the picture of the citizen-state relationship that Thorburn paints (and Garvey, too, for that matter) is authoritarian and unappealing for that reason. Shachar Eldar, "Criminal Law, Parental Authority, and the State," *Criminal law and Philosophy* 12, no. 4 (2017): 699–700; Vincent Chiao, *Criminal Law in the Age of the Administrative State* (Oxford University Press, 2019), 241 n.41.

3

Administration of Justice Crimes I: Offenses of Interference

I. Introduction

Law criminalizes disobedience in numerous ways, and some of the most obvious instances are when people come in direct contact with the legal system. Courts give commands of various kinds and back them up with the power to punish. Police officers give commands, the disobedience of which can be a crime. Government agencies and legislatures can, too, order individuals to cooperate with their investigations, defiance of which can give rise to criminal charges. These instances of criminalizing disobedience spell out how people ought to relate to legal actors and institutions and enable certain actors in the legal system to impose duties on people to cooperate.

II. Types of Interference Offenses

A. Disobedience of Courts, Legislative Bodies, and Government Agencies

In the United States, federal courts have the power to "punish by fine or imprisonment, or both, . . . such contempt of [their] authority . . . as . . . [d]isobedience or resistance to [their] lawful writ, process, order, rule, decree, or command."[1] Closely related is the crime commonly known as "bail-jumping," and the federal version criminalizes "knowingly fail[ing] to appear before a court as required by the conditions of release."[2]

Similar provisions are ubiquitous throughout the states. In California, "[w]illful disobedience of the terms, as written, of a process or court order or out-of-state court order, lawfully issued by a court" is a misdemeanor, as are

[1] 18 U.S.C. § 401; Fed. R. Crim. P. 17; see also 28 U.S.C. § 636(e); 18 U.S.C. § 3613A (compliance with order to pay fines); 18 U.S.C. § 922 (requiring attendance of a parent or a legal guardian in proceedings involving juvenile possession of firearms).

[2] 18 U.S.C. § 3146.

Criminalizing Disobedience. Youngjae Lee, Oxford University Press. © Oxford University Press 2026.
DOI: 10.1093/9780197617175.003.0004

"[r]esistance willfully offered . . . to the lawful order or process of a court" and "contumacious and unlawful refusal of a person to be sworn as a witness or, when so sworn, the like refusal to answer a material question."[3] It is a crime in Delaware to "knowingly violate[] or fail[] to obey any provision of a protective order issued by: the Family Court; or a court of any state, territory, or Indian nation in the United States."[4]

From the early days of the United States, such power was thought to be inherent in the judicial power. In the 1812 case of *United States v. Hudson*, the Supreme Court noted that "[c]ertain implied powers must necessarily result to our Courts of justice from the nature of their institution" and named the power to "fine for contempt—imprison for contumacy—inforce the observance of order" as examples of "powers which cannot be dispensed with . . . because they are necessary to the exercise of all others" and concluded that courts "no doubt possess [such] powers."[5] In Ex Parte *Robinson* from 1874, the Court similarly declared that "[t]he power to punish for contempts is inherent in all courts; its existence is essential to the preservation of order in judicial proceedings, and to the enforcement of the judgements, orders, and writs of the courts, and consequently to the due administration of justice."[6] More recently, one hundred years later in *Young v. United States ex rel. Vuitton et Fils, S. A.*, decided in 1987, the Court held that contempt prosecutions are "designed to serve the limited purpose of vindicating the authority of the court," as "[i]n punishing contempt, the Judiciary is sanctioning conduct that violates specific duties imposed by the court itself, arising directly from the parties' participation in judicial proceedings."[7] When "misconduct occurs in open court, the affront to the court's dignity is more widely observed," and in such instances, the Court held in *Pounders v. Watson* in 1997, the court may "find summary contempt and impose punishment."[8]

In fact, attached to every government action is the possibility of punishment of contempt for disobeying. Under the US Code, one can be punished for contempt for refusing to testify to either House of Congress after having been summoned to testify or produce documents.[9] The Tax Court similarly

[3] Cal. Penal Code § 166.

[4] 11 Del. C. § 1271A.

[5] United States v. Hudson, 11 U.S. (7 Cranch) 32, 34 (1812).

[6] Ex Parte Robinson, 86 U.S. (19 Wall.) 505, 510 (1874); see also Bessette v. W.B. Conkey Co., 194 U.S. 324, 327 (1904) (stating that the "power to punish for contempt is inherent in all courts" and noting that the purpose of criminal—as opposed to civil—contempt law is to "preserve the power and vindicate the dignity of the courts and to punish for disobedience of their orders"); Michaelson v. United States ex rel. Chi., St. Paul, Minneapolis & Omaha Ry. Co., 266 U.S. 42, 65 (1924) ("That the power to punish for contempts is inherent in all courts, has been many times decided and may be regarded as settled law. It is essential to the administration of justice.").

[7] Young v. U.S. ex rel. Vuitton et Fils S.A., 481 U.S. 787, 800 (1987).

[8] Pounders v. Watson, 521 U.S. 982, 987–88 (1997).

[9] 2 U.S.C. § 192 ("Every person who having been summoned as a witness by the authority of either House of Congress to give testimony or to produce papers . . . willfully makes default, or who . . . refuses to answer any question pertinent to the question under inquiry, shall be deemed guilty of a

has the power to punish "disobedience or resistance" to its commands,[10] as do the Court of Appeals for Veterans Claims[11] and the Court of Federal Claims.[12] Military courts have the power to "punish for contempt any person who . . . willfully disobeys" them under the Uniform Code of Military Justice.[13] The Federal Arbitration Act gives arbitrators the power to summon witnesses, and the power is backed up with the power to punish for contempt.[14]

Government agencies are also empowered to engage in fact-finding and compel cooperation. Here is a typical provision governing powers of the Federal Retirement Thrift Investment Board, which administers the Thrift Savings Plan, a tax-deferred retirement savings plan for federal employees. The Executive Director of the Board "may issue subpoenas commanding each person to whom the subpoena is directed to produce designated books, documents, records, electronically stored information, or tangible materials in the possession or control of that individual."[15] The law further provides that "[w]hen a person fails to obey a subpoena" issued under the section, "the district court of the United States for the district in which the investigation is conducted or in which the person failing to obey is found, shall on proper application issue an order directing that person to comply with the subpoena," and the "court may punish as contempt any disobedience of its order."[16] The law also authorizes the Federal Labor Relations Authority to "issue subpenas requiring the attendance and testimony of witnesses and the production of documentary or other evidence"[17] and provides that "[i]n the case of contumacy or failure to obey a subpena issued" under this section, a federal court "may issue an order requiring such person to appear at any designated place to testify or to produce documentary or other evidence" and "[a]ny failure to obey the order of the court may be punished by the court as a contempt thereof."[18]

Similar provisions are found in laws governing numerous agencies. Just to name a few, the Federal Trade Commission,[19] Internal Revenue

misdemeanor . . . ."); see also Josh Chafetz, *Congress's Constitution* (Yale University Press, 2017), 180 ("[F]or a legislative house to be able effectively to perform any of its functions, it must have access to information. . . . Indeed, if it is essential that courts have the power to compel testimony and evidence in order to render justice in particular cases, then it must be at least as essential for the houses of Congress to have this power, whether they are pondering impeachment, judging the elections, returns, and qualifications of members, conducting oversight, appropriating, considering legislation, or carrying out any of their other functions.").

[10] 26 U.S.C. § 7456.
[11] 38 U.S.C. § 7265.
[12] 28 U.S.C. § 2521.
[13] 10 U.S.C. § 848.
[14] 9 U.S.C. § 7.
[15] 5 U.S.C. § 8480.
[16] 5 U.S.C. § 8480.
[17] 5 U.S.C. § 7132.
[18] 5 U.S.C. § 7132.
[19] 15 U.S.C. § 49; 42 U.S.C. § 6299.

Service,[20] Federal Communications Commission,[21] Securities and Exchanges Commission,[22] Federal Election Commission,[23] Environmental Protection Agency,[24] National Labor Relations Board,[25] Small Business Administration,[26] Patent and Trademark Office,[27] Bureau of Consumer Financial Protection,[28] and many others can enlist the aid of a federal court to compel testimony and punish refusals to do so. The president[29] and other agency officials, such as the secretary of treasury,[30] secretary of commerce,[31] secretary of labor,[32] secretary of housing and urban development,[33] secretary of interior,[34] secretary of transportation,[35] secretary of agriculture,[36] federal energy administrator,[37] comptroller general,[38] secretary of energy,[39] attorney general,[40] director of national intelligence,[41] secretary of the army,[42] administrator of the Transportation Security Administration,[43] administrator of the Federal Aviation Administration,[44] and administrative law judges,[45] too, can invoke the aid of a court to enforce their orders with regard to various matters.

B. Disobedience of Law Enforcement Officers

Disobedience of law enforcement officers can be punished as well. In New York, it is a crime to "congregate[] with other persons in a public place and refuse[] to

[20] 26 U.S.C. § 7604.
[21] 47 U.S.C. § 409.
[22] 15 U.S.C. §§ 77v, 78u, 80a-41, § 80b-9.
[23] 52 U.S.C. § 30107; 52 U.S.C. § 30109.
[24] 15 U.S.C. § 2610.
[25] 29 U.S.C. § 161.
[26] 15 U.S.C. §§ 687b, 634.
[27] 35 U.S.C. § 24.
[28] 15 U.S.C. § 1714.
[29] 22 U.S.C. § 286f; 15 U.S.C. § 3364; 42 U.S.C. §§ 9609, 9622; 50 U.S.C. § 4555.
[30] 21 U.S.C. § 969; 26 U.S.C. § 7604; 31 U.S.C. § 5318.
[31] 19 U.S.C. § 1677f; 15 U.S.C. §§ 330c, 5408, 8709, 16 U.S.C. §§ 973f, 1540, 1858, 2437, 5507; 50 U.S.C. § 4820.
[32] 29 U.S.C. § 657; 30 U.S.C. § 813; 38 U.S.C. § 4323, 4326, 5711; 41 U.S.C. § 6507; 5 U.S.C. § 3330a.
[33] 42 U.S.C. § 5413.
[34] 30 U.S.C. § 1717; 16 U.S.C. § 1540.
[35] 46 U.S.C. § 50306; 33 U.S.C. § 206; 49 U.S.C. §§ 502, 13301, 30166, 32307, 32505, 432706, 32907, 32910; 46104, 60120.
[36] See, e.g., 7 U.S.C. § 2909; 7 U.S.C. § 6412; 16 U.S.C. § 1174.
[37] 15 U.S.C. § 796.
[38] 31 U.S.C. § 716; 15 U.S.C. § 771; 42 U.S.C. § 1320a-4, 6384.
[39] 42 U.S.C. § 6299.
[40] 21 U.S.C. § 876; 31 U.S.C. §§ 3733, 5318; 52 U.S.C. § 10101; 15 U.S.C. § 78dd-2; 18 U.S.C. § 3486; 42 U.S.C. § 2281; 50 U.S.C. § 1881a.
[41] 50 U.S.C. § 1881a.
[42] 33 U.S.C. § 1319.
[43] 49 U.S.C. § 46104.
[44] 49 U.S.C. § 46104.
[45] 16 U.S.C. § 3373.

comply with a lawful order of the police to disperse" with "intent to cause public inconvenience, annoyance or alarm, or recklessly creating a risk thereof."[46] In Alaska, a person commits the crime of "disorderly conduct" if "in a public place, when a crime has occurred, the person refuses to comply with a lawful order of a peace officer to disperse" or if "in a private place, the person refuses to comply with an order of a peace officer to leave premises in which the person has neither a right of possession nor the express invitation to remain of a person having a right of possession."[47] In Massachusetts, it is a crime to "refuse[] or neglect[] to obey [a] command" to "assist in arresting . . . rioters or persons . . . unlawfully assembled, or in suppressing such riot or unlawful assembly."[48] In Ohio, it is a crime to "[f]ail to obey the lawful order of any law enforcement officer engaged in the law enforcement officer's duties at the scene of or in connection with a fire, accident, disaster, riot, or emergency of any kind."[49]

"Resisting arrest" is also a crime. In California, for example, it is a crime to "willfully resist[], delay[], or obstruct[] any public officer."[50] In Texas, it is a crime for a person to "intentionally refuse[] to give his name, residence address, or date of birth to a peace officer who has lawfully arrested the person and requested the information."[51] In Utah, it is a crime to "flee[] from or otherwise attempt[] to elude a law enforcement officer . . . after the officer has issued a verbal or visual command to stop . . . for the purpose of avoiding arrest."[52]

C. Obstruction of Justice

Closely related offenses are obstruction of justice offenses. Under the federal law in the United States, it is a crime to "corruptly . . . influence[], obstruct[], or impede[] . . . the due administration of justice,"[53] where "the due administration of justice" has been interpreted by courts as "pending judicial or grand jury proceeding."[54] It is also a crime to "corruptly . . . influence[], obstruct[], or impede[] . . . the due and proper administration of the law under which any pending proceeding is being had before any department or agency of the United States, or the due and proper exercise of the power of inquiry under which any inquiry or investigation is being had by either House, or any committee of either House

[46] N.Y. Penal Law § 240.20.
[47] Alaska Stat. § 11.61.110.
[48] Mass. Gen. Laws ch. 269 § 2.
[49] Ohio Rev. Code § 2917.13(3).
[50] Cal. Penal Code § 148(a)(1).
[51] Tex. Penal Code § 38.02.
[52] Utah Code 1953 § 76-8-305.5.
[53] 18 U.S.C. § 1503.
[54] United States v. Quattrone, 441 F.3d 153, 170 (2d Cir. 2006).

or any joint committee of the Congress."[55] These provisions thus cover the three branches of the government and prohibit obstructing "the due administration of justice" within any of the three branches.

There are equivalent provisions throughout the United States. In Oregon, the relevant law provides that "[a] person commits the crime of obstructing governmental or judicial administration if the person intentionally obstructs, impairs or hinders the administration of law or other governmental or judicial function . . . ."[56] In the District of Columbia, "[a] person commits the offense of obstruction of justice if that person . . . [c]orruptly, or by threats of force, any way obstructs or impedes . . . the due administration of justice in any official proceeding."[57] In Vermont, it is a crime to "corruptly or by threats of force or by any threatening letter or communication, obstruct[] or impede[] . . . the due administration of justice . . . ."[58] In New Jersey, "[a] person commits an offense if he purposely obstructs, impairs or perverts the administration of law or other governmental function."[59]

There are more specific prohibitions as well. It is a federal crime in the United States to "knowingly . . . corruptly persuade[] another person, . . . with intent to influence, delay, or prevent the testimony of any person in an official proceeding[,] . . . cause or induce any person to . . . withhold testimony . . . from an official proceeding . . . ,"[60] where an "official proceeding" is defined as, among other things, a proceeding before a judge, Congress, or a federal agency.[61] It is also a crime to "knowingly alter[], destroy[], mutilate[], conceal[], cover[] up, falsif[y], or make[] a false entry in any record, document, or tangible object with the intent to impede, obstruct, or influence the investigation or proper administration of any matter within the jurisdiction of any department or agency of the United States . . . , or in relation to or contemplation of any such matter or case."[62]

Again, there are similar provisions in states. In Nebraska, "[a] person commits the offense of tampering with a witness . . . if, believing that an official proceeding or investigation of a criminal or civil matter is pending . . . , he or she attempts to induce or otherwise cause a witness . . . to [t]estify or inform falsely; [w]ithhold any testimony . . . ; [e]lude legal process . . . ; or [a]bsent himself or herself from any proceeding or investigation to which he or she has been legally summoned."[63] In North Dakota, "[a] person is guilty of a . . . felony if he uses force, threat, deception, or bribery: [w]ith intent to influence another's testimony in an official

[55] 18 U.S.C. § 1505.
[56] Or. Rev. Stat. § 162.235.
[57] D.C. Code § 22-722(a)(6).
[58] Vt. Stat. 13, § 3015.
[59] N.J. Stat. § 2C:29-1.
[60] 18 U.S.C. § 1512(b).
[61] 18 U.S.C. § 1515(a).
[62] 18 U.S.C. § 1519.
[63] Neb. Rev. Stat. § 28-919.

proceeding; or [w]ith intent to induce or otherwise cause another [t]o withhold any testimony, information, document, or thing from an official proceeding. . . ."[64] And in New York, "[a] person is guilty of tampering with physical evidence when . . . [b]elieving that certain physical evidence is about to be produced or used in an official proceeding . . . , and intending to prevent such production or use, he suppresses it by any act of concealment, alteration or destruction, or by employing force, intimidation or deception against any person."[65]

Because these laws are so broadly worded, it is worth pausing here to consider some examples. Judge Bruce Selya once memorably described "loansharking" as at times involving "employment . . . of unorthodox collection measures," such as "the breaking of bones."[66] In the same way, obstruction of justice can involve the breaking of bones of, say, potential witnesses, and the law describes such tactics as obstruction of justice "by threats or force"[67] or by "intimidation."[68] When such violent means are employed to prevent a person from testifying, we are outside the realm of criminalization of mere disobedience, as unjustified acts of violence against persons are morally wrongful whether the government says so or not. However, there are other ways of obstructing justice, such as destroying documents or persuading a person not to testify, that can be characterized as disobedience offenses in the sense that the core of the offense lies in their interference with official proceedings within the government.

For instance, in *United States v. Baker*, an owner of a brothel under investigation for his business told his employees not to talk to the FBI or the grand jury and offered his lawyer's services to the employees.[69] At one point, the owner and his lawyer even gave one of the employees a card spelling out her Fifth Amendment constitutional privilege against self-incrimination. The court ruled that the owner's conduct amounted to an obstruction of justice because he "corruptly" "endeavor[ed] to influence, obstruct, impede[] the due administration of justice" despite the fact that the employee had a right not to testify under the Constitution. One might argue that if a person has a right not to testify, telling that person to exercise that right should not amount to a crime. The court disagreed and held that the defendant's "motive and intent in advising them to interpose their right not to incriminate themselves . . . was to further his interest and conceal his crime and not to protect them against self-incrimination," and that motive rendered his "endeavor to impede . . . corrupt."[70] That is, even if a

[64] N.D. Cent. Code § 12.1-09-01.
[65] N.Y. Penal Law § 215.40.
[66] United States v. Cintolo, 818 F.2d 980, 984 (1st Cir. 1987).
[67] 18 U.S.C. §§ 1503, 1505; see also 18 U.S.C. § 1512 ("whoever kills or attempts to kill" and "whoever uses physical force or the threat of physical force" and "intimidation").
[68] 18 U.S.C. § 1512.
[69] United States v. Baker, 611 F.2d 964 (4th Cir. 1979).
[70] Baker, 611 F.2d at 968. The defendant had also drugged one of the employees.

person is merely asking another person to do something that the person has a right to do, if it is a way of interfering with a legal proceeding that is driven by a desire to avoid facing legal consequences, that ask is a crime. It is the combination of the act of interference with the intent to interfere and having that intent for the wrong reasons that constitutes one's criminality.

A person can be convicted under an obstruction of justice theory even for marrying a person. In *State v. Wilson*, a person who was charged with murder and was in custody awaiting his trial married a witness for the state's case "via telephone conversation with a pastor" eighteen days before the date of the trial in order to make it possible for the witness to refuse to testify by asserting spousal privilege.[71] The court held that "where a person marries a potential witness for the State with intent to have the witness invoke the spousal testimonial privilege at a criminal proceeding in order to prevent the witness from testifying at the proceeding, the evidence is sufficient to support convictions for witness tampering and obstruction of justice."[72] The court, in reaching this conclusion, cited the principle that "engaging in otherwise lawful conduct with the intent of trying to preclude a witness for the State from testifying at an upcoming criminal trial may constitute corrupt means."[73] Again, the idea is to refrain from acts that interfere with legal proceedings with a certain state of mind, even if the acts are otherwise lawful.

The obstruction of justice law can also ensnare those who delete items from their own computers, even if there is no ongoing legal proceeding that may have placed a "freeze" on such devices. *United States v. Kernell* is a case about a person who scrubbed information on his computer that contained traces of his successful hack into the email account of Sarah Palin, who was then Alaska governor and a vice presidential candidate. Gaining access to Sarah Palin's account without her permission was wrong, but what exactly was wrong with deleting files and applications from his own computer? It turns out his conduct was in violation of 18 U.S.C. § 1519, which prohibits destroying or altering "any record, document, or tangible object with the intent to impede, obstruct, or influence the investigation or proper administration of any matter within the jurisdiction of any department or agency of the United States . . . , or in relation to or contemplation of any such matter or case."[74] The defendant in the case gained access on September 16, 2008, and cleaned out his computer sometime before the evening of September 18, 2008. He "deleted everything" after he "panicked," worrying about what would happen if his conduct "ever got to the FBI" and then

[71] State v. Wilson, 240 A.3d 1140, 1144 (Md. 2020).
[72] Wilson, 240 A.3d at 1158.
[73] Wilson, 240 A.3d at 1158.
[74] 18 U.S.C. § 1519.

"unplugged [his] internet and just sat there in a comatose state."[75] From this account, the court concluded that his action was in "contemplation" of a federal investigation, which made the destruction of files on his computer a crime.[76]

It may not appear to be the case that obstruction of justice is an offense of disobedience. It seems uncontroversial to say that these are offenses of interference with the legal system, but that is different from the idea of disobeying. The reason obstruction of justice falls under the umbrella of disobedience offenses is, again, that whether one is potentially guilty of these offenses does not turn on the merits of the government's pursuit of "justice." The government may be wrong to pursue some of these cases, but a person's judgment that it is morally permissible to obstruct unjust proceedings does not give them a legal justification to engage in conduct that is considered to be obstruction of justice. A person who "obstructs justice" is going against the government's command not to interfere with certain official proceedings, and the fact that a person may disagree with the wisdom of those official proceedings is of no moment, even if the person may be correct on the question of the merits of the proceeding the person is obstructing, because it is the state that has the power to determine which courses to pursue. And that is the sense in which obstruction of justice offenses are disobedience offenses.

D. Perjury and False Statements

Offenses discussed thus far involve direct disobedience of a command by a legal institution or what the law characterizes as obstruction of official proceedings. There are other administration of justice crimes that are related in that they also tightly regulate conduct when closely interacting with the legal system. Perjury is defined in the US Code as a situation where a person "willfully and contrary to . . . oath states . . . any material matter which he does not believe to be true."[77] Since perjury law controls situations whenever one testifies under oath or makes a sworn declaration, the law covers both adjudication and investigation. But one need not be testifying or declaring under penalty of perjury to be prosecuted for lying to the government. It is a federal crime, for instance, "in any matter within the jurisdiction of the executive, legislative, or judicial branch of the Government . . . ," for a person to "knowingly and willfully . . . make[] any materially false,

[75] United States v. Kernell, 667 F.3d 746, 755 (6th Cir. 2012).

[76] Kernell, 667 F.3d at 755. In the case, there is a debate over when the FBI investigation started and what the defendant knew. But the point here is that his knowledge of an actual existence of an investigation was irrelevant, since the "in contemplation of" language was broad enough to cover his situation.

[77] 18 U.S.C. § 1621.

fictitious, or fraudulent statement or representation."[78] This crime, the crime of false statements, criminalizes lying to a federal government official conducting an investigation.[79]

The crime of false statements is less familiar than the crime of perjury. Here are some illustrative examples. In *United States v. Rodgers*, the US Supreme Court upheld the conviction of a person for lying to the FBI about his wife being kidnapped and lying to the Secret Service about her involvement in a (nonexistent) plot to kill the president.[80] The lies in that case started investigations that ended up diverting the government's resources to a made-up case, but the law also criminalizes lies that are told during existing investigations. So, in *Brogan v. United States*, a person was asked by Department of Labor and Internal Revenue Service agents investigating illegal gifts whether he had accepted any cash or gifts from a company while he was a union officer. He said "no," contrary to facts, and that lie was considered sufficient to give rise to criminal liability for false statements.[81]

Because of the broad wording of the false statements law, it need not be the case that the lies have to do with investigations of existent or nonexistent wrongdoing in order to be captured under the law. Lies that are told on government forms can also result in false statements charges. In *United States v. Yermian*, an employee of a private company that was also a defense contractor was convicted of lying on a Department of Defense security questionnaire that he had to fill out to receive security clearance to have access to classified material. The lies had to with his employment and criminal background.[82] And in *United States v. Moore*, there was a false statements conviction for failing to disclose a conflict of interest on a form filled out for the purposes of obtaining a grant from the Department of Housing and Urban Development.[83]

Perjury and false statements laws prohibit statements of falsehood in certain settings. One might argue that these are not offenses of disobedience because the core wrong of these offenses is lying, and lying is morally wrong. The reasons these offenses should nevertheless be considered offenses of disobedience are twofold. First, the question whether lying is a moral wrong does not have a simple answer, as it surely depends on the context.[84] Second, like the obstruction of justice offenses, perjury and false statements are legal wrongs whether

[78] 18 U.S.C. § 1001.

[79] See Lisa Kern Griffin, "Criminal Lying, Prosecutorial Power, and Social Meaning," *California Law Review* 97, no. 6 (2009): 1517–18.

[80] United States v. Rodgers, 466 U.S. 475, 476–77 (1984).

[81] Brogan v. United States, 522 U.S. 398, 400, 408 (1998).

[82] United States v. Yermian, 468 U.S. 63, 65–66 (1984).

[83] United States v. Moore, 446 F.3d 671, 673–74 (7th Cir. 2006).

[84] The literature on the morality of lying is extensive. For recent, illuminating discussions, see, e.g., Aditi Bagchi, "Lying and Cheating, or Self-Help and Civil Disobedience?," *Brooklyn Law Review* 85, no. 2 (2020): 363–67; Courtney M. Cox, "Legitimizing Lies," *George Washington Law Review* 90, no. 2 (2022): 304–43.

the government proceedings in which these falsehoods are told are just or not. The command is not to tell lies in certain settings, and the possibility of one disagreeing with the justice or wisdom of such proceedings does not change the content of the requirement.

III. Wrongness of Interference with Administration of Justice

The provisions discussed above criminalize interference with the legal system in certain situations. One might defend laws like these on the following grounds: the legal system needs to employ coercive devices like criminal law and punishment to ensure compliance with the law, because otherwise the rule of law could not become reality. Of course, the fact that the legal system needs the ability to punish people in order to administer justice is insufficient to show that those who interfere with law enforcement commit moral wrongs. At the same time, the observation that the legal system depends on the cooperation of those who are subject to it in order to function as a legal system can serve as the basis for a moral obligation on the part of the people. That is, as discussed in Chapter 2, persons have a moral duty to do their fair share by not interfering with workings of a legal system, and it is morally wrong for people to violate such duties by disobeying authoritative directives in these specified conditions.

This all seems pretty straightforward. So when a court releases a person charged with a crime from custody and then orders him to return so that he can be tried, a failure to appear without a good reason amounts to an interference with administration of justice.[85] Similarly, when there is an order by a court that prohibits a person from, say, contacting his ex-wife, it would be appropriate for a court to find him guilty of criminal contempt if he goes against the order and sends text messages to his ex-wife.[86] And when the government uses a grand jury to investigate tax evasion activities of an organization and subpoenas business and financial records, if the head of the organization, who is aware of the subpoena and has the ability to produce such records, fails to take appropriate actions, it is correct for the legal system to conclude that their disobedience interfered with administration of justice and treat them accordingly.[87] Or, when the government's grand jury investigation into a potential bribery case involving a public official subpoenas a witness to testify and the witness refuses to testify, that can lead to a conviction.[88]

Let's revisit the formula introduced in Chapter 2:

[85] Timmins v. State, 601 S.W.3d 345, 347 (Tex. Crim. App. 2020).
[86] Cogan v. State, 247 A.3d 229 (Del. 2021).
[87] United States v. Voss, 82 F.3d 1521, 1525–27, 1531–33 (10th Cir. 1996).
[88] Ex Parte Bruns, 58 P.2d 1318 (Cal. 1936).

$$C_t = C_d + C_a$$

Again, C_t is the "Total Culpability," C_a is culpability attributable to the badness of the prohibited act itself, and C_d is culpability attributable to the act of disobeying a prohibition. In these examples just mentioned, there is a clear order by a court, so the disobedience in that instance contributes to C_d. But what about C_a? It would depend on the merits of the underlying investigation or order in that whether an investigation or a protective order is meritorious would depend on the value of C_a. As a general matter, there may be a disagreement as to the value of C_a, but there may in fact be a right answer to the question of the value of C_a.

As we saw in Chapter 2, when applying the formula, $C_t = C_d + C_a$, we can have these four rough categories and reproduce them as shown in Table 3.1:

(1) $C_a > 0$ and $C_d > 0$
(2) $C_a > 0$ and $C_d = 0$
(3) $C_a = 0$ and $C_d > 0$
(4) $C_a = 0$ and $C_d = 0$

Under the first scenario (Quadrant I), there is culpability associated with the disobedience and with the underlying conduct. Under the second scenario (II), there is culpability associated with the underlying conduct but not with the disobedience. Under the third (III), the underlying conduct is not culpable, but there is culpability for the disobedience. Under the fourth, neither the underlying conduct nor the disobedience is culpable (IV).

Those who are skeptical about the idea of assigning culpability to a mere act of disobedience would be skeptical about Quadrants I and III. That is, whether there is a moral obligation to comply with the order would depend entirely on the underlying merits of the proceedings or processes from which the orders arise. In that case, Quadrants I and III do not exist, and C_t is entirely the function of C_a. But that would mean that there is no moral significance attached to the fact that it is a judge or a law enforcement officer making the order. Could that possibly be correct? Let's consider a few more examples.

Table 3.1 Conduct-Disobedience Culpability Matrix

	$C_d > 0$	$C_d = 0$
$C_a > 0$	I	II
$C_a = 0$	III	IV

Take a case like *Timmins v. State*, where a court released a defendant charged with manslaughter from confinement on the condition of not using drugs. When the defendant subsequently failed a drug test, the state wanted him to be confined to jail pending trial. The judge agreed with the state, but still let the defendant take his elderly mother home with a promise that he would report to jail afterward. The defendant never did report to jail, and was charged with the crime of "failure to appear."[89]

What is C_a in this case? Assuming that the government's manslaughter charge is warranted, the defendant ought to cooperate and appear for the trial and other court proceedings and orders, including this one. At the same time, the reason he was charged was not because he failed to show up for his trial but because he did not show up to be held in jail pending trial due to his violation of a condition of his release, which was not to use drugs. Perhaps he would have shown up to his manslaughter trial, and it may be the case that he should not have to wait for the trial in jail, and perhaps the fact that he was caught using drugs should not make a difference. All of these considerations would make a difference to the calculation of C_a, meaning that it is unclear whether the defendant did anything wrong if he would have shown up for his manslaughter trial anyway and jailing pending trial was unnecessary.

At the same time, there was an order by a judge, and assuming that the defendant knowingly defied the order when he could have complied with it, C_d for disobedience of the judge's order to report to jail would be some amount. Unless judges can operate their courtrooms and manage their cases backed up with power to penalize those who defy them, it would be difficult for the judicial system to function. If people routinely stopped respecting and obeying courts' orders, the judicial system would grind to a halt, and defying a court's order, even if it is unfair, unnecessary, or unreasonable, is wrong in that it can undermine the courts' authority in ways that are damaging to the robustness of the judicial system.

Or consider *State v. Wagar*, a case about events occurring after a pilot crashed a lightweight plane onto a runway. Law enforcement officers arrived on the scene shortly thereafter.[90] The pilot survived the crash but was "'very upset' and desired to move his plane." One of the officers repeatedly told him not to move the plane. The pilot "said he was going to move it any way" and "tied a rope to the plane in an attempt to move it." After repeated instructions not to move the plane, the pilot relented and dropped his efforts to move the plane. When the officer then made contact with the plane, the pilot asked the officer not to touch the plane. It appears that the officer lost her patience at that point and said that she

[89] Timmins, 601 S.W.3d at 347.
[90] State v. Wagar, 632 N.E.2d 546, 235 (Ohio App. 3d 1993).

was "tired of fucking around with him" and placed the pilot under arrest. The pilot was subsequently convicted of the crime of "misconduct at emergency."[91]

The facts in this case are simple, though they raise some questions. First, was the officer justified in ordering the pilot not to move the plane? The law prohibits "[h]amper[ing] the lawful operations of any law enforcement officer . . . engaged in the person's duties at the scene of a fire, accident, disaster, riot, or emergency of any kind" and also prohibits "[f]ail[ing] to obey the lawful order of any law enforcement officer engaged in the law enforcement officer's duties at the scene of or in connection with a fire, accident, disaster, riot, or emergency of any kind."[92] The law seems patently reasonable. And the court ruled in this case that the officer was "acting within the scope of her authority as a law enforcement officer" and also referred to "the myriad of potential activities that police and safety personnel may need to engage in at the scene of a plane crash."[93]

Given all that, perhaps the best way to proceed in that situation was to have the officer call the shots, in which case, under the formula, $C_t = C_d + C_a$, we had a situation where $C_a > 0$ and $C_d > 0$, or $C_a > 0$ and $C_d = 0$. But what if, for whatever reason, the pilot was correct in thinking that the best thing to do, all things considered, was for the pilot to move the plane to some other place? Those skeptical about assigning culpability to disobedience of government officials would say that we then have a situation where the culpability assigned to the pilot's conduct (C_t) should be zero.

On the other hand, for situations of ongoing emergency, it seems paramount to assign responsibility for dealing with them to entities who are trained to respond to such situations and for those present to support such efforts by following those entities' instructions, at least to a reasonable extent. This means that it is important for people to follow instructions given by law enforcement officers in situations of emergency, even if they disagree with the law enforcement officers, think they know better, and even if they do in fact know better. For a person to disobey in such situations would undermine the emergency-coping mechanisms that have been instituted. Such an undermining may happen in a variety of ways, even if in that particular case, not following the order may have been the better course of action. As a general matter, disobedience of authorities can contribute to an overall erosion of the respect for law enforcement that is necessary for emergency personnel to claim authority and rely on compliance. That is why it was sufficient for the court in this case to simply point out that the officer was "acting within the scope of her authority as a law enforcement officer" without going into the merits of the matter.

91 Wagar, 632 N.E.2d at 236.
92 Ohio Rev. Code § 2917.13 A(2), A(3).
93 Wagar, 632 N.E.2d at 238.

IV. Conclusion

Where does all this leave us? First, disobedience offenses can take the form of offenses that criminalize interference with administration of justice. Second, such offenses come in various guises, such as contempt of judicial and administrative proceedings, disobedience of law enforcement officers, obstruction of justice, perjury, and false statements. Third, one may identify the wrongness of committing these offenses as interfering with workings of governmental institutions without which the rule of law and effective governance cannot become a reality.

4

Administration of Justice Crimes II: Offenses of Failure to Assist

I. Introduction

The previous chapter examined laws that criminalize conduct that interferes with legal institutions and personnel such as disobedience of judges, legislative bodies, and government agencies; refusal to comply with orders from law enforcement officers; obstruction of justice; perjury; and false statements. Such laws draw their appeal from the intuition that it is wrong for people to interfere with the workings of institutions essential for the rule of law and effective governance. This chapter focuses on the ways in which the laws go further, beyond merely criminalizing interferences with the legal system, to also criminalizing failures to support and cooperate with law enforcement.

II. Types of Failure to Assist Law Enforcement Offenses

A. Accessory after the Fact and Hindering Prosecution

In the previous chapter, we looked at various obstruction of justice laws. Closely related is the crime of being an accessory after the fact, which is defined in the US Code as a person who, "knowing that an offense . . . has been committed, receives, relieves, comforts or assists the offender in order to hinder or prevent his apprehension, trial or punishment."[1] The same crime also goes by the name of "hindering prosecution" in many jurisdictions.[2]

In *United States v. Hill*, Charlie Hill, a man with child support obligations from his divorce in 1979, never made child support payments. He remarried in 1993, and shortly after, he and his new wife, Patricia King Hill, were informed

[1] 18 U.S.C. § 3.

[2] See Wayne R. LaFave, *Substantive Criminal Law*, vol. 2, 3rd ed. (Thomson West, 2017), § 13.6(a), 545–57. Troublingly, many of these cases involve women whose charges of accessory liability can be traced to their association with male intimate partners who commit crimes. For a general discussion of this phenomenon, see Sarah L. Swan, "Conjugal Liability," *UCLA Law Review* 64, no. 4 (2017).

Criminalizing Disobedience. Youngjae Lee, Oxford University Press. © Oxford University Press 2026.
DOI: 10.1093/9780197617175.003.0005

that he may face federal criminal charges for his failure to pay child support. Charlie then fled to Mexico, and Patricia listed her ranch in Oregon for sale and bought a similar one in Mexico. Charlie lived and worked on the ranch in Mexico while Patricia stayed behind and made money available for Charlie. A few months after, Charlie was indicted for failure to pay legal child support obligations and a felony arrest warrant was issued.[3] Patricia was subsequently apprehended, prosecuted, and convicted for being an accessory after the fact as well as for harboring a fugitive.

In *People v. Williams*, a woman was working at a Taco Bell when a man came in with his face covered and robbed the place at gunpoint. It turned out the person who committed the robbery was her boyfriend, though it is unclear if they were working together, and she denied prior knowledge of the robbery. When she spoke to the police about the robbery, however, she did not reveal the identity of the person who robbed the fast-food restaurant.[4] She was subsequently prosecuted for the crime of "hindering prosecution," which is defined in New York as, among other things, "[p]revent[ing] or obstruct[ing], by means of force, intimidation or deception, anyone from performing an act which might aid in the discovery or apprehension of [a] person" with "intent to prevent, hinder or delay the discovery or apprehension" of the person when she "knows or believes [that the person] has committed a crime or is being sought by law enforcement officials for the commission of a crime."[5] Her "deception" consisted only of failing to disclose to the police that she knew who the person who robbed the Taco Bell was and that he was her boyfriend (and it does not appear that she was asked if she knew who the robber was at the initial interview). However, the court reviewing the validity of the indictment against her said that "omitting her knowledge of the identity of the perpetrator" meant that she "actively deceived the police into thinking that the perpetrator's identity was unknown."[6]

Another closely related offense to hindering prosecution is the federal crime of misprision of felony.[7] Under the law, "[w]hoever, having knowledge of the

[3] See United States v. Hill, 279 F.3d 731, 734–36 (9th Cir. 2002); 18 U.S.C. § 228.

[4] See People v. Williams, 20 A.D.3d 72, 73–74 (N.Y. App. Div. 1st Dept. 2005).

[5] N.Y. Penal Law § 205.50; Williams, 20 A.D.3d at 73.

[6] Williams, 20 A.D.3d at 78.

[7] Commentaries on the crime of "misprision of felony," typically understood as a crime of failing to report known commissions of felonies, tend to be dismissive of the law as lacking in significance. See, e.g., Jens David Ohlin, *Wharton's Criminal Law*, 16th ed. (Thomson Reuters, 2021), § 40:13 ("At common law, a person was guilty of 'misprision of felony' when, knowing of the commission of a felony, he failed to report it to the authorities. The offense was given a less than warm 'reception' in America, it being wholly unsuited to American criminal law, and has come to be obsolete."); LaFave, *Substantive*; § 13.6(b) ("It is doubtful whether this offense ever had a meaningful existence beyond the textbook writers. The offense was said to be 'practically obsolete' in England almost a century ago, and the few prosecutions in that country in recent years have been limited to the most extreme situations. Doubt has been expressed as to whether this offense was ever inherited by the

actual commission of a [federal] felony . . . , conceals and does not as soon as possible make known the same to some judge or other person in civil or military authority" is guilty of the crime of misprision of felony.[8] The law makes it a failure to "make known" the commission of a federal felony "as soon as possible," so it looks like the law imposes a duty to report that a felony has been committed. Yet what prevents this crime from being a straightforward duty to report crime is the element of concealing. To prove that a person has committed the crime of misprision of felony, the person must have not only failed to report a felony but also concealed it.[9]

In *United States v. Brantley*, for instance, a woman was convicted of misprision of felony after her boyfriend shot two police officers during a traffic stop and ran away on foot because she parked the car in a place where she thought it was unlikely to be discovered by the police and kept the boyfriend informed of her actions as they coordinated their evasion effort over texts. She was convicted, and in upholding the conviction, the court said that "there is sufficient evidence of affirmative concealment of evidence—i.e., the removal and hiding of evidence related to a crime (the car)—to support the jury's finding of an affirmative act of concealment."[10]

United States as a part of the common law."). However, the version that is dismissed is the kind that does not have the concealment element. LaFave, *Substantive*, § 13.6(b) ("There is a misprision of felony statute in the United States Code, but it is not a true misprision statute in that it requires an act of concealment in addition to failure to disclose."). In addition, it would be a mistake to treat the federal crime of misprision of felony as irrelevant or unimportant, as the law continues to be used by federal prosecutors. For instance, misprision of felony is used as what Kyle Graham has called a "pleading crime," a type of offenses that "rarely (or never) provide[s] the basis for an initial arrest, and do[es] not often represent the most serious charge when a criminal case is filed (or even appear in the initial charging instrument)" but "frequently form[s] the basis for plea agreements in which other, more serious charges are dropped." Kyle Graham, "Facilitating Crimes: An Inquiry Into the Selective Invocation of Offenses Within the Continuum of Criminal Procedures," *Lewis & Clark Law Review* 15, no. 3 (2011): 695; see also Kyle Graham, "Crime, Widgets, and Plea Bargaining: An Analysis of Charge Content, Pleas and Trials," *California Law Review* 100, no. 6 (2012): 1573, 1605, 1608 n.186 (discussing misprision of felony as a pleading crime in federal prosecutions). Furthermore, convictions under the law are also used as a basis for deporting undocumented people and convicting individuals for being a felon in possession of a firearm. See, e.g., Alexandra Carl, "Misapprising Misprision: Why Misprision of a Felony Is Not a Crime Involving Moral Turpitude," *DePaul Law Review* 69, no. 1 (2020); Elyssa Klein, "Should Misprision of a Felony Be Considered a Crime Involving Moral Turpitude?," *Albany Law Review* 82, no. 1 (2018); Itani v. Ashcroft, 298 F.3d 1213, 1216 (11th Cir. 2022) (holding that misprision of a felony is a crime of moral turpitude that can provide the basis for deportation).

[8] 18 U.S.C. § 4.

[9] See Branzburg v. Hayes, 408 U.S. 665, n.36 (1972); Bratton v. United, 408 U.S. 665, 696–97 (1972); United States v. Brantley, 803 F.3d 1265, 1273 (11th Cir. 2015); United States v. Johnson, 546 F.2d 1225, 1227 (5th Cir. 1977).

[10] See Brantley, 803 F.3d at 1268–69.

B. Receiving or Possessing Stolen Property

Offenses of being an accessory after the fact, hindering prosecution, and misprision of felony implicate the behavior of a person in reaction to another person's commission of an offense. The crime of receiving or possessing stolen property takes the same form. Stealing from another person is a criminal offense, but it can also be a criminal offense to receive pieces of property that someone else has stolen. A typical formulation is that it is a crime to "receive, retain, or dispose of property of another knowing or having reasonable cause to believe that the property has been obtained through commission of a theft offense."[11] Even though this crime looks like it belongs in the family of theft crimes, it is better thought of not as a type of stealing but as a crime of making stealing profitable.[12] Seen this way, this crime has some resemblance to complicity and also seems analogous to certain possession offenses (to be discussed in Chapter 7), especially the kind prohibited by laws that exist in order to destroy markets that fuel undesirable activities.[13]

However, there is also an aspect to this crime that makes it an administration of justice crime. Sometimes stolen property is described as "hot." It may be thought of as "hot" in the sense of "hot" in the game of hot potatoes; it is not safe to hold onto "hot" items too long, and it is better to find some other place for them where they can safely cool.[14] Receiving stolen property then makes it possible for a person to dispose of potentially incriminating evidence and also facilitates movements of stolen goods through multiple hands, which makes it difficult to trace the current fate of stolen property. Such transactions make it

[11] Ohio Rev. Code § 2913.51.

[12] See Joseph P. Chamberlain, "Anti-Fence Legislation," *American Bar Association Journal* 14, no. 9 (1928): 517 ("The thief who takes a quantity of silk or a number of fur garments has no use for the articles themselves, and would have no temptation to take them except for the possibility of disposing them for cash."); Jerome Hall, *Theft, Law, and Society*, 2nd ed. (Bobbs-Merrill, 1952), 156 ("The professional receiver operates a business . . . For the prospective thief, he is a *reliable* market, known in advance to be available.").

[13] See, e.g., Stuart P. Green, "Thieving and Receiving: Overcriminalizing the Possession of Stolen Property," *New Criminal Law Review* 14, no. 1 (2011): 46 ("[W]ithout an efficient and profitable market in which stolen goods could be bought and sold, we would have a lot less thievery."); Anthony M. Dillof, "Possession, Child Pornography, and Proportionality: Criminal Liability for Aggregate Harm Offenses," *Florida State University Law Review* 44, no. 4 (2018): 1354 ("If, however, nobody bought stolen goods, undoubtedly far fewer items would be stolen."); People v. Myrick, 638 P.2d 34, 37 (Colo. 1981) (stating that "there is a legitimate governmental interest in seeking to interrupt the flow of stolen property" and that "it is not irrational for the legislature to attempt to accomplish this by making the receipt of non-stolen property, which is believed to be stolen, a crime").

[14] See Chamberlain, "Anti-Fence Legislation," 517 ("[I]t is important to a thief to be rid of the goods he has taken. Discovery of the property stolen in his room or upon his person makes conviction certain. . . . A 'salesman' . . . in whose room was found a considerable quantity of silk or a number of fur coats or diamonds, would be placed in a decidedly embarrassing situation. The fence with his store or warehouse ready to receive the stolen goods obviates this danger.").

easier for a person who has stolen to evade detection for theft, and this is the sense in which receiving stolen property is a type of administration of justice crime. The prohibited conduct helps legal wrongdoers avoid being apprehended by law enforcement.

C. Money Laundering and Currency Reporting

It is a federal crime in the United States to engage in "a monetary transaction in criminally derived property of a value greater than $10,000 [where the property] is derived from specified unlawful activity."[15] The term "specified unlawful activity" covers a variety of offenses such as drug offenses, bribery, human trafficking, and many other offenses associated with organized crime.[16] This is one of several rules that prohibit money laundering.[17] People who engage in these sorts of transactions tend not to be sympathetic figures. For instance, a person who uses his public office for personal gain by demanding payments from those eager to curry favor and funneling money into his personal accounts is corrupt and is in violation of his fiduciary obligations. Money laundering appears to be a way of completing whatever illicit activities one has engaged in by covering one's tracks after profiting from such activities. At the same time, money laundering can be a puzzling offense. Douglas Husak, for instance, has expressed some skepticism about the law by arguing that after persons commit a "first" wrong by, say, accepting bribes, "it is hard to see why persons who deposit or withdraw [criminally derived] funds from banks commit a *second* wrong," given that that such persons are presumably not guilty of money laundering if they simply hide the money "under a mattress."[18]

The above discussion of offenses of being an accessory after the fact, hindering prosecution, misprision of felony, and receiving or possessing stolen property is helpful in responding to Husak's objection. Money laundering, as conduct, is alleged to accomplish two things. First, the possibility of money laundering makes the prospect of committing crimes more attractive to potential perpetrators, and, in that sense, it encourages criminal activities.[19] Second, money laundering, by giving those who commit crimes a way to conceal proceeds from criminal activities, makes it easier for them to avoid detection by law enforcement

[15] 18 U.S.C. § 1957(a).

[16] 18 U.S.C. § 1956(c)(7).

[17] See also 18 U.S.C. § 1956.

[18] Douglas Husak, "*Malum Prohibitum* and Retributivism," in *Defining Crimes: Essays on the Special Part of the Criminal Law*, ed. R.A. Duff and Stuart Green (Oxford University Press, 2005), 67.

[19] See Peter Alldridge, *Money Laundering Law: Forfeiture, Confiscation, Civil Recovery, Criminal Laundering and Taxation of the Proceeds of Crime* (Hart Publishing, 2003), 65; Katie Benson, *Lawyers and the Proceeds of Crime: The Facilitation of Money Laundering and Its Control* (Routledge, 2020), 71.

authorities.[20] The first wrong, then, belongs to the family of wrongs having to do with complicity; the second wrong is a form of obstruction of justice. This combination of wrongs makes it closely analogous to the crime of receiving or possessing stolen goods.

If money laundering laws attempt to identify and criminalize tactics to conceal an underlying offense, efforts to evade *that* law enforcement tactic can also be a crime. It is a federal offense to "structure" any transaction with financial institutions "for the purpose of evading the reporting requirements" that apply to financial institutions.[21] So if a regulation requires banks to report financial transactions in the amounts of $10,000 or more, it is illegal to set up transactions so that each transaction is in the amount of less than $10,000 in order to avoid triggering the reporting obligations.[22] Financial institutions are also required to set up monitoring programs to catch potential instances of money laundering, and failure to do so can amount to criminal charges.[23] Individuals are subject to reporting requirements as well. For instance, a federal law requires persons to declare the amount of currency one is carrying abroad or bringing back to the United States if the amount is over $10,000.[24] One may, of course, just happen to be carrying that much in cash without having engaged in any illicit activities, and there is no law against moving one's own money around as long as the reporting obligations are met. But the point of such a law is clear; it is a way for the government to collect information about potentially suspect conduct.

All of these laws having to do with the reporting of movements of currency, money laundering, and transaction structuring prohibit conduct that may not amount to inherently harmful or wrongful acts. There are cases where simple depositing of criminally derived property has amounted to the crime of money laundering, which is not surprising given how broadly Section 1957 is worded.[25] And in one well-known case from 1989, a real estate agent named Ellen Campbell was convicted of money laundering for helping an apparent drug dealer purchase a house at the price of $182,500, with $60,000 in cash. It is true that the purchaser seemed to be somewhat unusual by a 1980s standard because he "drove new Porsches, . . . carried a cellular phone, flashed vast amounts of cash, and was able to be away from his purportedly legitimate business for long stretches of time during normal working hours."[26] It is also true that Campbell appears to

[20] See Peter Alldridge, *What Went Wrong with Money Laundering Law?* (Palgrave Macmillan, 2016), 34.

[21] 31 U.S.C. §§ 5324, 5313.

[22] See Ratzlaf v. United States, 510 U.S. 135, 136 (1994).

[23] See 31 U.S.C. §§ 5311 et seq. (establishing program, recordkeeping, and reporting requirements for financial institutions), 5322 (establishing criminal penalties for violations of Act). See also Consent Order Imposing Civil Money Penalty, In the Matter of TD Bank, N.A. and TD Bank USA, N.A. (2024) (No. 2024-02); Office of Public Affairs, "TD Bank Pleads Guilty to Bank Secrecy Act and Money Laundering Conspiracy Violations in $1.8B Resolution," news release, October 24, 2024.

[24] See 31 U.S.C. § 5316(a).

[25] See United States v. Johnson, 971 F.2d 562, 570 (10th Cir. 1992); United States v. Moore, 27 F.3d 969, 977 (4th Cir. 1994).

[26] See United States v. Campbell, 977 F.2d 854 (4th Cir. 1992).

have ignored all that and failed to inquire further about the purchaser's profession or the source of the funds. Still, in the end, the conduct that got Campbell in trouble was essentially facilitating a real estate transaction, which is what real estate agents do. Also, in *United States v. Bajakajian*, the Supreme Court treated a man attempting to take $357,144 in cash to Cyprus from the United States without filing a report to have done nothing wrong other than to fail to report as "[t]he money was the proceeds of legal activity and was to be used to repay a lawful debt."[27] Finally, in *Ratzlaf v. United States*, the Court noted that "currency structuring is not inevitably nefarious" given that "an individual . . . [may] mak[e] cash deposits in small doses, fearful that the bank's reports would increase the likelihood of burglary, or in an endeavor to keep a former spouse unaware of his wealth."[28]

All these supposedly innocent activities may still amount to offenses, and that is because these laws are attempts to discourage and detect other supposedly more harmful and wrongful conduct. Those who violate these laws are guilty of not playing along with the system of detection set in place by the government. The core wrongness of these crimes, then, is the wrong of failing to assist the state's effort to deal with what the state perceives to be undesirable activities.

D. Duty to Report Laws

While *obstructing* an ongoing process of "justice" seems different from *failing to report* something that might trigger a new process of "justice," the discussion in this chapter thus far has attempted to illustrate how the two types of offenses exist on a continuum. It is one of the highly misleading clichés of American criminal law that there is a presumption against punishing omissions.[29] And it is also often noted that "a private citizen has no legal duty to report serious crimes, even when that citizen is fully aware that a felony has been committed and knows the identity of the wrongdoer."[30] However, it is easy to exaggerate this point, given the proliferation of legal duties to report potential wrongdoing in specific circumstances.[31]

[27] United States v. Bajakajian, 524 U.S. 321, 338 (1998).

[28] *Ratzlaf*, 510 U.S. at 135.

[29] See generally Corey Rayburn Yung, "The Incredible Ordinariness of Federal Penalties for Inactivity," *Wisconsin Law Review* 2012, no. 3 (2012); Wayne A. Logan, "Citizen Searches and the Duty to Report," *Ohio State Law Journal* 83, no. 5 (2022); see also Zachary D. Kaufman, "Protectors of Predators or Prey: Bystanders and Upstanders amid Sexual Crimes," *Southern California Law Review* 92, no. 6 (2019): 1342–46.

[30] Gerard E. Lynch, "The Lawyer as Informer," *Duke Law Journal* 1986, no. 3 (1986): 520.

[31] There is a growing literature on this phenomenon. See, e.g., Sandra Guerra Thompson, "The White-Collar Police Force: 'Duty to Report' Statutes in Criminal Law Theory," *William & Mary Bill of Rights Journal* 11, no. 1 (2002): 5 ("[T]he typical substantive criminal law course in law school teaches students that common law countries do not punish for the failure to be a 'Good Samaritan' . . .

It is well known, for instance, that there are groups of people designated as mandated reporters, such as health care workers, educators, social workers, childcare providers, and therapists, who are required by the law to report instances of suspected child abuse.[32] Also well known are laws that require health care workers to report gunshot or other suspicious wounds.[33] However, it is not as well known that many reporting laws cut much more widely than that and implicate *anyone* who may become aware of or suspect child abuse. For instance, in Florida, a person who "knowingly and willfully fails to report to the central abuse hotline known or suspected child abuse, abandonment, or neglect . . . , commits a felony . . . ."[34] There are similar laws in Rhode Island,[35] Wyoming,[36] Tennessee,[37] Utah,[38] New Hampshire,[39] California,[40] and Nevada.[41]

What most criminal law courses fail to recognize, however, is that we have gradually increased the number of laws creating duties to assist the police (or, one might say, to assist the victim or society at large) by reporting situations in which a crime is being committed. These laws require reporting not only of crimes in progress, but also of past crimes."); see also generally Sungyong Kang, "In Defense of the 'Duty to Report' Crimes," *UMKC Law Review* 86, no. 2 (2017); Matthew R. Hall, "An Emerging Duty to Report Criminal Conduct: Banks, Money Laundering, and the Suspicious Activity Report," *Kentucky Law Journal* 84, no. 3 (1996); Christopher J. Wilkes, "A Case for Reforming the Anti-Money Laundering Regulatory Regime: How Financial Institutions' Criminal Reporting Duties Have Created an Unfunded Private Police Force," *Indiana Law Journal* 95, no. 2 (2020); Robert P. Mosteller, "Child Abuse Reporting Laws and Attorney-Client Confidences: The Reality and the Specter of Lawyer as Informant," *Duke Law Journal* 42, no. 2 (1992); Logan, "Citizen Searches"; Eldar Haber, "The Digital Samaritans," *Washington & Lee Law Review* 77, no. 4 (2020); Kaufman, "Bystanders and Upstanders."

[32] See, e.g., N.Y. Soc. Serv. Law §§ 413, 420 (designating certain groups of individuals as those "required to report . . . when they have reasonable cause to suspect that a child coming before them in their professional or official capacity is an abused or maltreated child" and outlining civil and criminal penalties for failure to report); Ga. Code § 19-7-5 (requiring individuals in certain specified groups who have "reasonable cause to believe that suspected child abuse has occurred" to report and designating knowing and willful failure to do so a misdemeanor); Mich. Comp. Laws § 722.623 (requiring individuals in certain specified groups who have "reasonable cause to suspect child abuse or child neglect" to "make an immediate report" and outlining civil and criminal penalties for failure to report); Minn. Stat. §§ 260E.06, 260E.08 (requiring individuals in certain specified groups who "know[] or ha[ve] reason to believe a child is being maltreated . . . or has been maltreated within the preceding three years" to "immediately report the information" and listing criminal penalties for failures to report); Tex. Fam. Code §§ 261.101, 261.109 (providing that "[i]f a professional has reasonable cause to believe that a child has been abused or neglected or may be abused or neglected . . . the professional shall make a report not later than the 24th hour after the hour the professional first has reasonable cause to believe that the child has been or may be abused or neglected" and outlining criminal penalties for failure to report).

[33] See, e.g., Minn. Stat. §§ 626.52, 626.55; Fla. Stat. § 790.24.

[34] Fla. Stat. § 39.205(1).

[35] See R.I. Gen. Laws. §§ 40-11-3, 6.1.

[36] See Wy. Stat. § 14-3-205.

[37] See Tenn. Code §§ 37-1-403, -412.

[38] See Utah Code §§ 80-2-602, -609.

[39] See N.H. Rev. Stat. §§ 169-C:29, C:39.

[40] See Cal. Penal Code § 152.3.

[41] See Nev. Rev. Stat. § 202.882.

That is not all. Some states require from every citizen reports of not just known or suspected cases of child abuse but of a wide range of offenses. In Kentucky, "[a]ny person," who has "reasonable cause to suspect that an adult has suffered abuse, neglect, or exploitation" is required to report, and failure to do so may be a misdemeanor.[42] In Florida, "[a] person who observes the commission of the crime of sexual battery and . . . [h]as reasonable grounds to believe that he or she has observed the commission of a sexual battery" is required to report.[43] In Massachusetts, "[w]hoever knows that another person is a victim of aggravated rape, rape, murder, manslaughter or armed robbery and is at the scene of said crime" is required to report the crime.[44] In Texas, any person who "observes the commission of a felony under circumstances in which a reasonable person would believe that an offense had been committed in which serious bodily injury or death may have resulted" is required to report.[45] In Washington, any person "who witnesses the actual commission of [a] violent offense . . . or preparations for the commission of such an offense" is required to report.[46] In Colorado, the law is even more broadly written as it imposes a duty on "every . . . person who has reasonable grounds to believe that a crime has been committed to report promptly the suspected crime to law enforcement authorities."[47] In Ohio, too, "no person, knowing that a felony has been or is being committed, shall knowingly fail to report such information to law enforcement authorities."[48] Prosecutions for these reporting laws, especially broadly worded ones, are rare,[49] but they are in the books nevertheless.[50]

The reporting laws require people to alert and involve state law enforcement officers when they come across certain legal violations, and to that extent they seem to be crimes of administration of justice. However, because at times these reports can interrupt and stop ongoing harmful activities and continuing victimization of individuals, they may simply be seen as legal recognition of moral obligations to prevent harm in certain situations. That is, if involving law enforcement is an effective way of stopping an ongoing rights violation without excessive negative side effects, then the law's reporting requirements may well mirror moral requirements. However, as we saw with obstruction of justice

42 Ky. Rev. Stat. §§ 209.030, 209.990(1).
43 Fla. Stat. § 794.027.
44 Mass. Gen Laws ch. 268, § 40.
45 Tex. Penal Code § 38.171.
46 Wash. Rev. Code § 9.69.100; see also Alaska Stat. § 11.56.767.
47 Colo. Rev. Stat. § 18-8-115.
48 Ohio Rev. Code § 2921.22.
49 Such prosecutions are rare in the sense that people are generally not charged with just the reporting crime violation. However, as mentioned above, these laws may still be used regularly as a pleading crime, a fallback charge often used as a compromise charge in plea negotiations.
50 See, e.g., Kaufman, "Bystanders and Upstanders," 1342–48; Wilkes, "Anti-Money Laundering," 660–64.

offenses in the previous chapter, these laws do not give people the option of deciding whether involving law enforcement is the most desirable avenue, all things considered. Once certain conditions are satisfied, the duty to report is peremptory, and the fact that a person may, correctly, see the law enforcement authorities as not the most helpful actors to involve in a given situation makes no difference from the legal perspective. This, plus the fact that the obligation to report is an offense created by the state to require assistance of the state in law enforcement, is the sense in which these reporting offenses are also offenses of disobedience.

E. Offender Registration Laws

The duty to report laws just discussed require people to alert law authorities about particular instances of known or suspected wrongdoing. Offender registry laws, on the other hand, require self-reports of presence by those who have a history of offending.[51] The most salient type of offender registries in current debates is the sex offender registry. For instance, a federal law in the United States requires every "sex offender" to "register, and keep the registration current, in each jurisdiction where the offender resides, where the offender is an employee, and where the offender is a student,"[52] and all fifty states in the United States, with a strong push by the federal government, now have similar registration laws.[53]

While sex offender registration laws consume all the attention, there are other offender registries throughout the United States.[54] In California, Louisiana, Ohio, and Illinois, those convicted of arson are required to register.[55] There are also registration requirements for those convicted of participation in a "criminal street gang" in California[56] and those convicted of "any offense against a peace officer or any terrorism offense" in Louisiana.[57] In Illinois, any "violent offender against youth" is required to register,[58] and in Hawaii, any "offender against minors" is required to register.[59] In Oklahoma, those convicted of certain

[51] For a history of offender registries, see Wayne A. Logan, *Knowledge as Power: Criminal Registration and Community Notification Laws in America* (Stanford University Press, 2009); Elizabeth Reiner Platt, "Gangsters to Greyhounds: The Past, Present, and Future of Offender Registration," *N.Y.U. Review of Law & Social Change* 37, no. 4 (2013): 729–42.

[52] 34 U.S.C. § 20913.

[53] For a discussion, see Logan, *Knowledge as Power*, 49–84.

[54] Much of this paragraph draws from Logan's book. Logan, *Knowledge as Power*.

[55] Cal. Code Regs. Tit. 15, § 3653; La. Rev. Stat. § 15:562.3; Ohio. Rev. Code § 2909.15; 730 Ill. Comp. Stat. 148/10, 148/65.

[56] Cal. Penal Code §§ 186.22, 186.30.

[57] La. Rev. Stat. § 15:643.

[58] 730 Ill. Comp. Stat. 154/10.

[59] Haw. Rev. Stat. §§ 846E-1, 846E-2.

listed violent offenses are required to register.[60] In Nevada, any person who has been convicted of a felony twice or more or of a felony that is considered the most serious in Nevada is required to register,[61] and in Alabama, any person who has been convicted of a felony more than twice is required to register.[62] And most broadly, in Florida, any person who has been convicted of a felony is required to register.[63]

The primary reason cited for these registry requirements is ease of law enforcement.[64] If the state can easily keep track of where people with these criminal histories live, then when they reoffend, they can be located and apprehended quickly.[65] And since the data collected under these laws are released to the public, which is a feature pushed by the federal government,[66] another purpose of these laws is to alert citizens about the presence of such individuals so that they can take appropriate preventive measures.[67] These two sources of scrutiny are supposed to deter individuals from reoffending.[68] These laws and policies have been examined and heavily criticized over the years for a variety reasons, but for now, we can at least conclude that given the purposes of these laws, we may classify them as offenses of administration of justice like the other laws discussed in this chapter. A person who is subject to the registration requirement is required to cooperate with law enforcement's efforts to keep track of individuals like themselves. A failure to register, then, amounts to a type of disobedience offense because the person is being told to cooperate with the government's policy in this particular way.

III. Wrongness of Failure to Support the Legal System

The previous chapter dealt with offenses of interfering with wheels of justice that are in motion. Once an order is out from a judge or from a law enforcement officer, and once an official proceeding or an investigation is on, *directly* interfering with such processes can amount to contempt, resisting arrest, obstruction

[60] Okla. Stat. Tit. 57, §§ 593, 594, 599.
[61] Nev. Rev. Stat. § 179C.100.
[62] Ala. Code § 13A-11-181.
[63] Fla. Stat. § 775.13.
[64] See Logan, *Knowledge as Power*, 109.
[65] See Logan, *Knowledge as Power*, 33, 51 ("[T]his state's policy is to assist local law enforcement agencies' efforts to protect their communities by regulating sex offenders by requiring sex offenders to register with local law enforcement agencies.") (quoting the Community Protection Act of 1990 from Washington); see also Logan, *Knowledge as Power*, 55–56.
[66] See Logan, *Knowledge as Power*, 56–61.
[67] See Logan, *Knowledge as Power*, 51–52, 57.
[68] See Logan, *Knowledge as Power*, 56.

of justice, perjury, and the like. Offenses discussed in this chapter deal with situations where people *indirectly* obstruct justice by increasing the distance between law enforcement and its actual or potential targets through, for instance, hiding a target or helping a target escape, withholding information that could start or facilitate a law enforcement investigation, helping lawbreakers hide or sanitize incriminating evidence, or not revealing whereabouts of those the law enforcement seeks to track and monitor.

There is an important question about what to criminalize, but let us for now focus on the question whether such indirect obstructions through failures to assist the law enforcement are morally wrong.[69] There will be times when alerting law enforcement may be the best way of stopping an ongoing victimization or helping a victim to recover financially, physically, or mentally, but many instances of indirect obstruction of justice would not have such features.[70] Is there an argument for the proposition that all or most instances of indirect obstruction of justice described in this chapter implicate a moral wrong?

Some have argued as much. Chief Justice John Marshall, for instance, wrote in *Marbury v. Brooks* that "[i]t may be the duty of a citizen to accuse every offender, and to proclaim every offense which comes to his knowledge," though he quickly also added that "the law which would punish him in every case for not performing this duty is too harsh for man."[71] Justice Lewis Powell has also noted in *Roberts v. United States* that "[c]oncealment of crime has been condemned throughout our history" and that "gross indifference to the duty to report known criminal behavior remains a badge of irresponsible citizenship," and added that "[t]his deeply rooted social obligation is not diminished when the witness to the crime is involved in illicit activities himself."[72]

Also, consider this remarkable passage in John Henry Wigmore's well-known treatise on evidence law, where he notes, "[f]or three hundred years it has now been recognized as a fundamental maxim that the public . . . has a right to every

[69] For some concerns raised about laws that criminalize failure to report, see, for example, Lynch, "Lawyer as Informer"; Mosteller, "Lawyer as Informant"; Thompson, "The White-Collar Police Force"; Miriam Gur-Arye, "Reflections," *Criminal Law and Philosophy* 18, no. 2 (2024): 647–54; Logan, "Citizen Searches"; Kaufman, "Bystanders and Upstanders"; Miriam Gur-Arye, "Human Dignity of 'Offenders': A Limitation on Substantive Criminal Law," *Criminal Law and Philosophy* 6, no. 2 (2012): 187.

[70] Cf. Miriam Gur-Arye, "A Failure to Prevent Crime—Should It Be Criminal?," *Criminal Justice Ethics* 20, no. 2 (2001): 6 (distinguishing between the duty to report a crime that has already occurred and the duty to report a crime that is about to occur); see also R.A. Duff and S.E. Marshall, "Reporting Crimes and Arresting Criminals: Citizens' Rights and Responsibilities Under Their Criminal Law," *Criminal Law and Philosophy* 18, no. 2 (2024): 558.

[71] Marbury v. Brooks, 20 U.S. 556, 575–76 (1822).

[72] Roberts v. United States, 445 U.S. 552, 558 (1980).

man's evidence."[73] He says that there is "a general duty to give what testimony one is capable of giving,"[74] and that this is a "sacrifice . . . due from every member of the community," bearing which is "a duty, not to be grudged or evaded."[75] In fact, as he sees it, civilization as we know it depends on it. He says that "[w]hether the achievements of the past shall be preserved, the energy of the present kept alive, and the ambitions of the future be realized, depends upon whether the daily business of regulating rights and redressing wrongs shall continue without a moment's abatement . . . ."[76] He sternly warns that "[w]hoever is impelled to evade or to resent it should retire from the society of organized and civilized communities, and become a hermit," as he is "not a desirable member of society."[77] Even though he appears to be talking mainly about courtroom testimony, the implications of his arguments go beyond the confines of a courtroom. His argument that we all have a duty to help uphold "justice as an institution[] and from law and order as indispensable elements of civilized life" seems to generate the conclusion that "the community as a whole" can rightly demand that citizens assist in increasing the legal system's knowledge of criminal wrongdoing.[78]

We will return to the question whether there is a duty to assist unjust law enforcement. But even assuming a state in which law enforcement is carried out in good faith for the common good in a reasonably just way, it is not clear whether laws, policies, or law enforcement activities should always be supported or assisted, as there may be good reasons not to in certain situations. Yet these laws do not demand obedience only in situations where relevant moral considerations call for assisting law enforcement; they demand obedience at all times. This is the sense in which offenses of failures to assist law enforcement are disobedience offenses.

IV. Conclusion

This chapter, continuing the discussion begun in the previous chapter, has argued that disobedience offenses can take the form of offenses of failures to assist law enforcement. Such offenses show up in many ways, such as hindering prosecution, receiving stolen property, money laundering, failure to report crimes,

[73] John Henry Wigmore, *Treatise on the System of Evidence in Trials at Common Law: Including the Statutes and Judicial Decisions of All Jurisdictions of the United States* (Little, Brown, and Company, 1905), 2965.
[74] Wigmore, *Treatise*, at 2965.
[75] Wigmore, *Treatise*, at 2967.
[76] Wigmore, *Treatise*, at 2968.
[77] Wigmore, *Treatise*, at 2967.
[78] Wigmore, *Treatise*, at 2967; cf. Duff and Marshall, "Reporting Crimes and Arresting Criminals," 559, 572–76.

and failure to register as someone with relevant criminal history. These are disobedience offenses because the commands do not generally invite individuals to make fine moral distinctions, and whatever the law demands may not be the best course to pursue all things considered. Yet the laws demand obedience and require assistance of law enforcement and punish certain failures to assist, and such demands may be considered a violation of the duty to support the state and the rule of law.

5
Regulatory Offenses

I. Introduction

What are regulatory offenses, and are they disobedience offenses? The state can create a criminal offense in any area it regulates, and since the state can regulate pretty much everything under the sun, the scope of the topic of regulatory offenses is virtually limitless. The phrase "regulatory offenses," if conceptualized this way, does not designate a category of offenses in an analytically useful way. This chapter examines regulatory offenses by first defining and describing them. This chapter then discusses examples from different areas of regulation to illustrate the ways in which regulatory offenses often punish disobedience.

II. Regulatory Offenses, Public Welfare Offenses, and *Mala in Se* Offenses

To define regulatory offenses, we can start by examining the idea of "public welfare offenses," often taken to be synonymous with regulatory offenses.[1] In the canonical 1952 case of *Morissette v. United States*, the US Supreme Court described public welfare offenses as follows:

> The industrial revolution multiplied the number of workmen exposed to injury from increasingly powerful and complex mechanisms, driven by freshly discovered sources of energy, requiring higher precautions by employers. Traffic of velocities, volumes and varieties unheard of came to subject the wayfarer to intolerable casualty risks if owners and drivers were not to observe new cares and uniformities of conduct. Congestion of cities and crowding of quarters called for health and welfare regulations undreamed of in simpler times. Wide distribution of goods became an instrument of wide distribution of harm when those who dispersed food, drink, drugs, and even securities, did not comply with reasonable standards of quality, integrity, disclosure and care. Such dangers have engendered increasingly numerous and detailed regulations

[1] See Darryl K. Brown, "Public Welfare Offenses," in *The Oxford Handbook of Criminal Law*, ed. Markus D. Dubber and Tatjana Hörnle (Oxford University Press, 2014), 862–83.

Criminalizing Disobedience. Youngjae Lee, Oxford University Press. © Oxford University Press 2026.
DOI: 10.1093/9780197617175.003.0006

> which heighten the duties of those in control of particular industries, trades, properties or activities that affect public health, safety or welfare.[2]

The Court continued: "While many of these duties are sanctioned by . . . civil liability, *lawmakers . . . have sought to make such regulations more effective by invoking criminal sanctions* to be applied by the familiar technique of criminal prosecutions and convictions."[3] Such prosecutions were based on "statutes or administrative regulations, for what been aptly called 'public welfare offenses.'"[4]

The basic idea expressed by the *Morissette* Court is that the modern society gave rise to a need for state regulation to control various risks of harm, and the state turned to criminal sanctions as one method of enforcement. A familiar example is a food and drug law that prohibits the "introduction or delivery for introduction into interstate commerce of any food, drug, device, tobacco product, or cosmetic that is adulterated or misbranded."[5] Most people are at least vaguely familiar with the fact that the state regulates products for human consumption such as animals, fruits, and vegetables.

But is there anything special about regulatory offenses? Criminal law and the types of sanctions it makes available belong to the state's toolbox used to promote various ends. The state faces many decisions as it attempts to address various social problems like food and drug safety, and for whatever reason, criminal law may sometimes be the favored tool to achieve the government's goals, among the many other policy options at its disposal. Since government regulations advance government ends, criminal law may be thought of simply as a means to pursue those ends.

The *Morissette* Court had an answer to this question, observing that many regulatory offenses "are not in the nature of positive aggressions or invasions, with which the common law so often dealt."[6] In regulatory offenses cases, the Court added, citing older cases *United States v. Balint*[7] and *United States v. Dotterweich*,[8] "the emphasis . . . is evidently upon achievement of some social betterment rather than the punishment of the crimes as in cases of *mala in se*," as "penalties serve as effective means of regulation."[9] But this distinction between social betterment and punishment seems to break down when we consider that social betterment is an end arguably sought by all laws, not just regulatory offenses. Moreover, regulatory offenses are fundamentally attempts to achieve

[2] Morissette v. United States, 342 U.S. 246, 253–54 (1952).
[3] Morissette, 342 U.S. at 254–55 (emphasis added).
[4] Morissette, 342 U.S. at 255.
[5] 21 U.S.C. § 331.
[6] Morissette, 342 U.S. at 255.
[7] United States v. Balint, 258 U.S. 250 (1922).
[8] United States v. Dotterweich, 320 U.S. 277 (1943).
[9] Morissette, 320 U.S. at 258–60 (citation and quotation omitted).

social betterment *through* punishment, as opposed to social betterment *instead of* punishment.

We may shed some light on the *Morissette* Court's analysis by juxtaposing regulatory offenses against the Displacement Thesis introduced in Chapter 1, according to which a core purpose of criminal law and punishment is to displace the system of private vengeance and thereby manage the punitive and retaliatory emotions that arise after serious acts of wrongdoing. James Fitzjames Stephen, similarly, described criminally sanctioned acts as "grosser forms of vice" which the law brands "with the deepest mark of infamy."[10] In Stephen's view, the point of criminal law is not just to prohibit certain acts in order to prevent them but "also [to] gratify[] the feeling of hatred—call it revenge, resentment, or what you will—which the contemplation of such conduct excites in healthily constituted minds."[11] Stephen's account seems to be incongruous with regulatory offenses; indeed, the *Morissette* Court noted that such public welfare offenses ought to be contrasted against "the earliest offenses known to the law," such as "[s]tealing, larceny, and its variants and equivalents," that involve "invasions of rights" and "arouse public demand for retribution."[12] And when a crime is serious enough to be considered a "felony," that would be "as bad a word as you can give to man or thing."[13] The idea behind regulatory offenses, then, is that they are different from those kinds of crimes that "arouse public demand retribution" but are rather mere instruments that aid the state's effort toward "social betterment."

These discussions of regulatory offenses roughly highlight two aspects of regulatory offenses, *what* the state does with these regulatory offenses and *why* the state turns to regulatory offenses. We can illuminate the category more by asking *how* the state enacts regulatory offenses.

III. Making of Regulatory Offense Laws

Regulatory offenses can be created the way other criminal offenses typically get created—through legislation. The food and drug safety laws already mentioned involving "adulterated or misbranded" food or drugs were created through legislation, and violations of such laws are regulatory offenses in that the laws are created in order to mitigate the risks inherent in commerce.[14] The management

[10] See James Fitzjames Stephen, *Liberty, Equality, Fraternity* (Holt & Williams, 1873), 149, 163.

[11] Stephen, *Liberty, Equality, Fraternity*, 149.

[12] Morissette, 342 U.S. at 260.

[13] Morissette, 342 U.S. at 260 (citation and quotation omitted).

[14] There are in fact two regimes when it comes to drug laws. There are laws that seek to guarantee the safety of drugs that are on the (legal) market, and there are laws that use criminal law to eliminate or severely limit circulation of certain drugs. The latter type of laws will be considered in Chapter 7. For a useful discussion, see David Herzberg, "Origins and Outcomes of the US Medicine-Drug Divide," in *The Oxford Handbook of Global Drug History*, ed. Paul Gootenberg (Oxford

of risk is one of the principal regulatory goals of the state, and regulatory offenses accomplish that goal through criminal penalties.

That criminal law is made through legislation seems like an obvious point to make. How else would you make criminal laws? Legislation is not the only way. Consider the Clean Water Act for instance. After declaring that the objective of the law is to "restore and maintain the chemical, physical, and biological integrity of the Nation's waters," the law places the administrator of the Environmental Protection Agency (EPA) in charge of administering the law.[15] The law prohibits "the discharge of any pollutant by any person" unless in compliance with the law, and "pollutant" is defined by a long list of things that can dirty the waters, such as "solid waste," "incinerator residue," "sewage," "garbage," "chemical wastes," "biological materials," "radioactive materials," and "industrial, municipal, and agricultural waste," while "discharge" is defined as "any addition of any pollutant to navigable waters," where "navigable waters" in turn is defined as "the waters of the United States."[16] One way in which one may discharge pollutants in compliance with the law is by obtaining a permit for discharge of pollutants, and the law authorizes the EPA Administrator to issue such a permit and attach conditions that "the Administrator determines are necessary to carry out" the law.[17]

The law then gives the administrator various enforcement powers, including seeking injunctive actions in a federal court. For our purposes, the most significant enforcement powers involve criminal liability. Under the section outlining criminal penalties, there are multiple provisions, and the law distinguishes between negligent and knowing violations. More specifically, the law provides, inter alia, that anyone who "negligently violates" various sections of the law or "any permit condition or limitation implementing" the law shall be punished by a fine up to $25,000 per day of violation or by imprisonment for up to one year, or both, with the penalties increasing for repeat offenders.[18] A knowing violation of the same law or permit conditions faces increased penalties, a fine of up to $50,000 per day of violation or by imprisonment for up to three years, or both. A repeat offender can be imprisoned for up to six years. And there are regulations that give a detailed explanation of the process of obtaining a permit with various conditions attached. In other words, Congress criminalized a number of provisions of the Clean Water Act but also gave the EPA Administrator authority to issue permits to discharge pollutants with various conditions as the

University Press, 2022) (discussing the two models of controlling harm from drugs—a consumer-regulatory model on one hand and a prohibit-and-punish model on the other).

15 33 U.S.C. § 1251.
16 33 U.S.C. §§ 1251, 1362.
17 33 U.S.C. § 1342.
18 33 U.S.C. § 1319.

administrator may see fit, and violations of such conditions could result in criminal convictions.[19]

Another example can be found in the related area of environmental conservation. The Endangered Species Act starts with a declaration of congressional findings and purposes and states that the purpose of the law is, among other things, "to provide a program for the conservation of . . . endangered species and threatened species."[20] "Endangered species" is defined as "any species which is in danger of extinction" (unless it is classified as a pest that "would present an overwhelming and overriding risk to man"), and "threatened species" means "any species which is likely to become an endangered species within the foreseeable future."[21] The law empowers the secretary of interior to designate a species as an endangered or threatened species and provides a number of factors to consider and the process to follow for the designation.[22] Once a species is designated as "endangered" by the secretary of interior, the law prohibits various acts having to do with the species, such as importing or exporting, killing, or selling.[23] In addition, the law prohibits violations of "any regulation pertaining to" endangered or threatened species.[24] The law then provides for civil penalties, which the secretary of interior may assess directly.[25] The law also says that "[a]ny person who knowingly violates any provision" of the law "or of any regulation" can be fined or imprisoned or both.[26] In short, like in the Clean Water Act, the Endangered Species Act gives the secretary of interior the power to criminalize by adding a species to the list of endangered or threatened species or by issuing a regulation under the law, or both.

Thus, regulatory offenses may be created in a manner distinct from ordinary offenses. In the United States, congressional legislation would authorize an agency to promulgate regulations to implement a statute and specify that certain violations of the statute or the regulations are crimes. Once the empowered agency issues regulations, those automatically become new crimes to which criminal penalties attach.[27]

19 33 U.S.C. § 1319; see also 33 U.S.C. § 1311(a); 42 U.S.C. §§ 6925(a), 7661a.
20 16 U.S.C. § 1531(b).
21 16 U.S.C. § 1532.
22 16 U.S.C. § 1533.
23 16 U.S.C. § 1538.
24 16 U.S.C. § 1538(a).
25 16 U.S.C. § 1540(a).
26 16 U.S.C. § 1540(b).
27 For a discussion, see Markus Dirk Dubber, "The Possession Paradigm: The Special Part and the Police Model of the Criminal Process," in *Defining Crimes*, ed. R.A. Duff and Stuart P. Green (Oxford University Press, 2005), 109–13.

IV. Do Regulatory Offense Laws Criminalize Disobedience?: Environmental Protection and Conservation

How should we evaluate the wrongfulness of committing a regulatory offense? Earlier we saw the example of the Endangered Species Act and its accompanying regulations, which prohibit killing of those animals considered endangered or threatened. Imagine a person who wants to kill a grizzly bear for sport and knows that he is not allowed to do so under the law. That person might also hold the view that the current law overprotects grizzly bears because, in his opinion, the grizzly bear population is large enough for it to be no longer considered endangered or threatened.[28] What would be wrong morally for him to kill a grizzly bear, assuming it is generally morally permissible to hunt animals for sport?

In order to answer that question, we would ask why the state protects certain species from being hunted, whether it is a good thing that there is a governmental institution that regulates this area, whether the rule it has promulgated is a good rule, and whether there are reasons to obey the rule even if the rule is not a good one. The statute says that endangered and threatened species "are of esthetic, ecological, educational, historical, recreational, and scientific value" and are thus to be conserved, and provides that the secretary of interior should determine whether a species belongs on the list of endangered or threatened species by considering the following factors:

(A) the present or threatened destruction, modification, or curtailment of its habitat or range;
(B) overutilization for commercial, recreational, scientific, or educational purposes;
(C) disease or predation;
(D) the inadequacy of existing regulatory mechanisms; [and]
(E) other natural or manmade factors affecting its continued existence.[29]

The law further provides that the secretary "shall make determinations required" "solely on the basis of" the following:

> the best scientific and commercial data available to [the secretary] after conducting a review of the status of the species and after taking into account those efforts, if any, being made by any State or foreign nation, or any political subdivision of a State or foreign nation, to protect such species, whether by

[28] Cf. Johnny Diaz, "U.S. Considers Lifting Protections for Grizzly Bears Near Two National Parks," *New York Times*, February 3, 2023.
[29] 16 U.S.C. §§ 1531, 1533(a)(1).

> predator control, protection of habitat and food supply, or other conservation practices, within any area under its jurisdiction; or on the high seas.[30]

This is only a partial list of the things that the secretary is to consider, as the secretary is also to "give consideration to species which have been designated as requiring protection from unrestricted commerce by any foreign nation, or pursuant to any international agreement; or identified as in danger of extinction, or likely to be become so within the foreseeable future, by any State agency or by any agency of a foreign nation" that focuses on conservation.[31] The secretary may even designate a species as "an endangered species or threatened species" even if it is not in fact endangered or threatened "if he finds that such species so closely resembles in appearance" an endangered or threatened species "that enforcement personnel would have substantial difficulty in attempting to differentiate" between them, "the effect of this substantial difficulty is an additional threat," and designating the non-endangered or non-threatened species as an endangered or threatened species "will substantially facilitate the enforcement and further" the relevant policy.[32]

To fully account for the ins and outs of the morality of killing a grizzly bear, we would need to understand the regulatory framework, why we have it, why it is set up the way it is, and so on. So, why is killing a grizzly bear wrong? One answer is that killing a grizzly bear is wrong because doing so could lead to the extinction of a species that is of "esthetic, ecological, educational, historical, recreational, and scientific value." But how would you know if that is actually the case, and is it obvious whether the loss of grizzly bears would be a net positive or a net negative in the long run?

Consider another example. *United States v. Leal* was a case about a man who collected some salt, "wood and wildlife bones," and "migratory bird parts, or feathers," from the Lower Rio Grande Valley National Wildlife Refuge.[33] He had a backpack and a digging tool, and said, when he was caught, that he was an artist collecting materials for his work. The defendant's behavior was found to be in violation of the relevant law, which prohibited removing certain items from the National Wildlife Refuge System, such as "any fish, bird, mammal, or other wild vertebrate or invertebrate animals or part or nest or egg thereof."[34] The law states that the purpose of the law is "restoration of the fish, wildlife, and plant resources and their habitats within the United States for the benefit of the present and future generations of Americans."[35] But did the defendant harm the Refuge

[30] 16 U.S.C. § 1533(b)(1)(A).
[31] 16 U.S.C. § 1533(b)(1)(B).
[32] 16 U.S.C. § 1533(e).
[33] United States v. Leal, 565 F. Supp. 3d 874, 867 (S.D. Tex. 2021).
[34] 16 U.S.C. § 688dd(c).
[35] 16 U.S.C. § 688dd(a)(2).

in any significant way by picking some salt, some bones, and feathers? The impact he had on the Refuge was likely minimal. When the government's witness was asked during trial if the defendant caused any harm to this cause, the witness testified that an action like the defendant's "could, in the aggregate, negatively impact the Refuge's status as a habitat for wildlife."[36]

The point here is not to question the importance of grizzly bears or wildlife refuges. Rather, the point for our purposes is to notice that the moral issues here are somewhat opaque from the perspective of an individual who may not be deeply familiar with the all the issues having to do with the question whether it is okay to kill a grizzly bear or to pick up salt and animal parts from a wildlife refuge. People are nevertheless expected to respect and obey the federal government's determination that the environment and its inhabitants are to be protected. That is, while we might say that a person who kills a grizzly bear is guilty of the crime of contributing to the extinction of a species (even if he kills an old one that is about to die soon anyway or a cub that would have been killed by another bear), it is more accurate to say that it is the very existence of a regulatory framework that protects and preserves the endangered species. The act of killing a grizzly bear is criminal because such acts interfere with that system of protection, not because it is inherently morally right or wrong.[37] Regardless of the individual's understanding of the issues, and regardless of whether they are correct on the merits in their decision to kill a particular grizzly bear, they would still be blameworthy for interfering with the government's regulatory framework, or at least for failing to do their fair share of supporting the framework. This is the sense in which regulatory offense laws punish disobedience.

We can extend this conclusion to conduct that may be more obviously harmful, such as pollution. Even here, it is no simple matter to determine the nature of legal violations, as some of the criminal violations involving something as harmful as pollution often do not have to do with endangering the public. The Clean Air Act,[38] for instance, provides that "[a]ny person who knowingly violates" any one of a broad array of commands given under various terms of the act can "be punished by a fine . . . or by imprisonment for not to exceed five years, or both."[39] To be sure, there are parts of the Clean Air Act that criminalize inherently dangerous acts, such as knowingly releasing a toxic substance and "know[ing] at the time that he thereby places another person in imminent danger of death or serious bodily injury."[40] But as a general matter, the law criminalizes

[36] Leal, 565 F. Supp. 3d at 877.

[37] Cf. Carmen E. Pavel, "A Legal Conventionalist Approach to Pollution," *Law and Philosophy* 35, no. 4 (2016): 342–46; Joel Feinberg, *The Moral Limits of the Criminal Law Volume 1: Harm to Others* (Oxford University Press, 1984), 229–32.

[38] 42 U.S.C. §§ 7401 et seq.

[39] 42 U.S.C. § 7413(c)(1).

[40] 42 U.S.C. § 7413(c)(5)(A).

knowing violations of the commands that are necessary to operate a regulatory scheme, some of which may have little to no direct bearing on the well-being of the public.[41] The regulatory scheme typically requires regular reports to the government, and such reporting requirements may be added as one of the conditions listed in a permit to operate a potentially polluting activity.[42] And a person can be punished for falsifying the report or "failing to . . . report as required" if the person does so knowingly.[43] Failing to pay fees as required is also criminalized.[44] The Clean Water Act[45] is similar to the Clean Air Act in that, in addition to a knowing endangerment crime like the discharge of hazardous substances,[46] there is a broad criminalization provision[47] that criminalizes violations of different provisions of the Clean Water Act "or any permit condition or limitation implementing" certain sections of the act.[48] Like the Clean Air Act, there are also crimes associated with reporting violations.[49]

Even when we look at polluting conduct, there are aspects having to do with disobedience and interference with an ongoing regulatory scheme, as opposed to endangering the public. The Clean Water Act does not prohibit releasing pollutants into the waters. Rather, it establishes a system to regulate the amount of discharge of pollutants into the waters, and it does so by creating a permit system where entities are given permits to discharge pollutants only up to a certain amount.[50] So, "[e]xcept as in compliance with" the law, "the discharge of any pollutant by any person [is] unlawful."[51] The law authorizes the EPA to "issue a permit for the discharge of any pollutant,"[52] and a person who negligently or knowingly violates "any permit condition or limitation . . . in a permit" can be held criminally liable.[53] In *United States v. Weitzenhoff*, for instance, the defendant had a permit authorizing discharge of 976 pounds per day over a thirty-day period of certain types of pollutants and was charged with the crime of knowingly discharging pollutants in an unauthorized manner and amount.[54]

[41] 42 U.S.C. § 7413(c)(1).
[42] 42 U.S.C. § 7414.
[43] 42 U.S.C. § 7413(c)(2). The law is broad as it covers "any notice, application, record, report, plan, or other document required . . . to be either filed or maintained." See also United States v. Louisiana Pacific Corporation, 908 F. Supp. 835 (D. Colo. 1995); Susan F. Mandiberg and Susan L. Smith, *Crimes Against the Environment* (Michie, 1997), §§ 4-2c3, 128–30.
[44] 42 U.S.C. § 7413(c)(1).
[45] 33 U.S.C. §§ 1251 et seq.
[46] 33 U.S.C. § 1319(c)(2); see also 33 U.S.C. § 1321(b)(3).
[47] 33 U.S.C. § 1319(c).
[48] 33 U.S.C. §§ 1319(c)(1)(A), (c)(2)(A), (c)(3)(A).
[49] 33 U.S.C. § 1319(c)(4).
[50] 33 U.S.C. §1342.
[51] 33 U.S.C. § 1311.
[52] 33 U.S.C. § 1342(a)(1).
[53] 33 U.S.C. §§ 1319(c)(1)(A), (c)(2)(A), (c)(3)(A).
[54] United States v. Weitzenhoff, 35 F.3d 1275, 1281 (9th Cir. 1993); see also United States v. Sinskey, 119 F.3d 712 (8th Cir. 1997).

Like the speed limit discussed in Chapter 2, these limitations are set by the government, and falling on one side of the permissible limitation on pollution as opposed to another turns a person into a criminal. Depending on the standards set by the EPA and conditions and limitations added to a permit by the EPA, then, one might be committing a *malum in se* or a *malum prohibitum* offense, but the expectation is for those who pollute to defer to and obey the government as a way of cooperating with the regulatory scheme. That is the sense in which even laws that control conduct as harmful as pollution may end up criminalizing disobedience.

V. Do Regulatory Offense Laws Criminalize Disobedience?: Drugs and Medical Devices

As mentioned above, it is a violation of the Food, Drug, and Cosmetic Act to introduce or deliver introduction into interstate commerce of "any food, drug, device, tobacco product, or cosmetic that is adulterated or misbranded."[55] When it comes to drugs and devices, the law defines "adulterated" as, among other things, "filthy," "prepared . . . under insanitary conditions," or "mixed . . . so as to reduce . . . quality or strength," and "misbranded" as having "labeling [that] is false or misleading," not labeled with "an accurate statement," not labeled with "adequate directions" and "adequate warnings," or giving directions following which would be "dangerous to health."[56] And any person who commits such a violation is to be "imprisoned for not more than one year or fined not more than $1,000, or both," and if the violation is committed "with the intent to defraud or mislead," the offending person is to be "imprisoned for not more than three years or fined not more than $10,000, or both."[57] Obviously, these crimes may be crimes of endangerment. People who buy misbranded or adulterated items and ingest or use them otherwise could hurt themselves and others, and those who are releasing such items to the stream of commerce may be endangering the public.

The definition of "adulterated" or "misbranded" includes other prongs. For instance, a drug or device is considered adulterated if an inspection of a place where such things have been "manufactured, processed, packed, or held" is delayed, denied, or limited.[58] A drug or device is considered misbranded, for instance, if it is produced in an unregistered facility or if it is promoted for

[55] 21 U.S.C. § 331(a); see generally Margaret P. Battin et al., *Drugs and Justice: Seeking a Consistent, Coherent, Comprehensive View* (Oxford University Press, 2007), 60–62.
[56] 21 U.S.C. §§ 351, 352.
[57] 21 U.S.C. § 333(a).
[58] 21 U.S.C. §351(j).

an off-label use.[59] A drug is also considered misbranded if, for instance, it is imported by an unregistered importer[60] or is dispensed without a prescription by a physician.[61] Certain types of devices are considered adulterated if they have not been approved by the Food and Drug Administration (FDA), and other types of devices are considered misbranded if they have been introduced into interstate commerce without obtaining clearance from the FDA.[62] (Clearance requires a demonstration that the device is substantially equivalent to a legally marketed device, whereas approval requires a much more stringent process.[63]) There are other prohibitions, such as introducing into commerce any drug that is not FDA-approved,[64] distributing drugs without a license,[65] distributing drugs without keeping track of their supply chain history,[66] and distributing human growth hormone when unauthorized.[67] These requirements of course are related to safety of drugs and devices, but they are essentially process requirements; they lay out the required processes to be followed before drugs or devices can be introduced to the market.

For instance, according to the indictment in *United States v. Stoll*, Stoll, a "regulatory affairs specialist" working for Aesculap, a medical devices company, created fake letters indicating that FDA has cleared a device called "ELAN-4 Air Drill," to be used for "cutting, sawing, and drilling of bone during surgical procedures."[68] According to the indictment, Stoll, who was responsible for seeking FDA clearance for sale of the device, never submitted the required paperwork for an FDA clearance but told his colleagues that he had done so and that the FDA cleared the device. He even produced counterfeit FDA documents and circulated them. The company then sold these devices over a three-month period in 2017 and received approximately $78,840 in revenue. According to the company, it notified the government once it discovered the fraud. Stoll was prosecuted and convicted, and the company released a statement saying that "[t]here have been no reports of patient harm related to the sale of those products."[69] The product ultimately received an FDA clearance.

[59] See United States v. Facteau, 89 F.4th 1 (1st Cir. 2023). This rule is especially controversial. See United States v. Caronia, 703 F.3d 149 (2d Cir. 2012); Lars Noah, "Banning Off-Label Drug Promotion Offends the U.S. Constitution: Making the Strongest Case," *Albany Law Review* 83, no. 1 (2020): 309–10.

[60] 21 U.S.C. § 352(o).

[61] 21 U.S.C. § 353(b).

[62] 21 U.S.C. § 351(f); 21 U.S.C. §§ 360c(f), 360e(a),(b),(k).

[63] 21 U.S.C. § 360c.

[64] 21 U.S.C. §§ 331(d), 355.

[65] 21 U.S.C. §§ 331(t); 353(e).

[66] 21 U.S.C. §§ 331(t), 360eee-1, 360eee-3.

[67] 21 U.S.C. § 333(e).

[68] United States v. Stoll, No. 5:23-cr-00089-EGS, at 1 (E.D. Pa. Mar. 6, 2023).

[69] Rudy Miller, "Ex-employee's Deception Led Lehigh Valley Company to Sell $139K in Unapproved Medical Devices, Feds Say," *Lehigh Valley Live*, March 8, 2023, https://www.lehighval

What was wrong with Stoll's behavior? Government attorneys argued that "[s]ubverting the FDA clearance process for medical devices can put patients' lives at risk" and that "impersonating FDA to cover up" the failure to receive clearance "is truly egregious and puts patients at risk."[70] But were any patients at risk in this case? The actual facts about the safety of the device may be what they are. For our purposes, let us assume that the device is safe enough to be cleared by the FDA. Let us also assume that Stoll understood the device well enough to know that the devices were safe but did not want to go through the FDA approval process. In that case, what was wrong with Stoll's behavior?[71] There is of course the fraud (to colleagues and to the market) aspect, which may be thought to turn every criminal violation of this law a *malum in se*, but, as mentioned in Chapter 3, the issue of wrongness of deception on its own is controversial as fraud is often harmless. A better answer to the question about wrongfulness of Stoll's behavior is that it is important to comply with the regulatory framework regarding drugs and devices even for safe devices because without some reassurance for the public that the items that they are purchasing have been cleared for sale by the government, people will be afraid to participate in the market. This would lead to people no longer being able to purchase items that they want or need, and ultimately the market for such goods would disappear. Therefore, the crime here consists of interference with the regulatory framework that is essential for the market for drugs and devices to function, and even if there was no risk to the public with a particular instance of dishonesty (or "misbranding"), punishing Stoll would be based on his failure to do his part to protect the integrity of the market for drugs and devices. That is the sense in which some regulatory offenses having to do with drugs and devices are also about disobedience.

VI. Conclusion

This chapter scratches the surface of the vast world of regulatory offenses. Regulatory offenses designate offenses that constitute violations of rules in existence in order to promote some regulatory scheme of the government. As we

leylive.com/news/2023/03/ex-employees-deception-led-lehigh-valley-company-to-sell-139k-in-unapproved-medical-devices-feds-says.html.

[70] Office of Public Affairs, "Former Employee of Medical Device Manufacturer Pleads Guilty to Forging Two FDA Clearance Letters for Medical Devices," Press Release, July 20, 2023, https://www.justice.gov/opa/pr/former-employee-medical-device-manufacturer-pleads-guilty-forging-two-fda-clearance-letters.

[71] Cf. James Edwards, "Criminalization without Punishment," *Legal Theory* 23, no. 2 (2017): 75–78.

can see in the contexts discussed in this chapter, many of these laws criminalize acts that endanger the public. However, those are not the only kinds of regulatory offenses. Regulatory offenses are more typically enacted by working backward from regulatory schemes. Once a regulatory scheme is set, the rules that need to be enforced in order to implement the regulatory scheme are created, and in some instances those rules are criminally enforced.[72] What this means is that rule violations in this context need not result in direct endangerment of the public but might merely interfere with a government-created regulatory scheme, consisting of government-created standards and commands to satisfy such standards. That is the sense in which regulatory offenses frequently turn out to be disobedience offenses.

[72] Some other examples are laws regarding the sale of securities and antitrust. See Securities Act of 1933, Pub L. No. 73-22, ch. 38, 48 Stat. 74 (codified as amended at 15 U.S.C. §§ 77a–77aa); Securities Exchange Act of 1934, Pub. L. No. 73-291, ch. 404, 48 Stat. 881 (codified as amended at 15 U.S.C. § 78a–nn); Sarbanes-Oxley Act of 2002, Pub. L. No. 107-204, 116 Stat. 745 (codified in scattered sections of 15 U.S.C., 18 U.S.C., and 29 U.S.C.); Sherman Antitrust Act of 1890, Pub. L. No. 51-647, ch. 647, 26 Stat. 209 (codified as amended at 15 U.S.C. §§ 1–7 (2012)).

6

Preventive Offenses I: Attempt

I. Introduction

Generally speaking, it is a crime for a person to beat up another person on purpose. Hitting another person harms that person, and it seems obvious that such an act should be classified as a crime. But criminal codes are filled with provisions that criminalize conduct that may not cause any harm. Injecting poison into an apple that your professor left on his desk while he is not looking and leaving it for him to consume may or may not cause any harm in the end, but it is a crime nevertheless.[1]

We might call criminal prohibitions that are created for the purposes of preventing harm "preventive offenses" and distinguish them from prohibitions that criminalize actual impositions of harm.[2] Of course, even laws that criminalize impositions of harm exist in large part to prevent harm. What is distinctive about preventive offenses is that, by design, an offense definition might criminalize something not necessarily because that thing is harmful in itself but because of its relationship, typically causal (direct or indirect), to harm.[3]

Are preventive offenses crimes of disobedience? That depends on the relationship of the thing that is criminalized to the harm that the law aims to prevent. Some acts, like leaving a poisoned apple on your professor's desk, may or may not cause harm but certainly risk harm and thereby exhibit a straightforward relationship between conduct and harm. But some acts that are criminalized in order to prevent harm may not bear that kind of direct relationship to harm. Lots of criminal prohibitions are enacted for the purposes of preventing harm, but the relationship of those offenses to harm is not always so clear. The topic of preventive offenses is vast and will be presented over two chapters. This chapter

[1] Cf. State v. Reeves, 916 S.W.2d. 909 (Tenn. 1996).

[2] See Andrew Ashworth and Lucia Zedner, *Preventive Justice* (Oxford University Press, 2014). Cf. Douglas N. Husak, "Is Drunk Driving a Serious Offense?," *Philosophy & Public Affairs* 23, no. 1 (1994): 66–70; Douglas N. Husak, "The Nature and Justifiability of Nonconsummate Offenses," *Arizona Law Review* 37, no. 1 (1995): 151.

[3] The category of preventive offenses, defined this way, is broader than what is covered in this chapter and the next. For instance, many laws discussed in Chapter 5 as regulatory offenses may be described as preventive offenses. But then, as we will see in this chapter and next, many preventive offenses also may be described as regulatory offenses. Not much turns on these labels as long as we understand the nature and function of these laws.

Criminalizing Disobedience. Youngjae Lee, Oxford University Press. © Oxford University Press 2026.
DOI: 10.1093/9780197617175.003.0007

focuses on attempt, specifically incomplete attempt. The next chapter addresses possession.

Criminalization of attempt is typically explained as a matter of prevention. Oliver Wendell Holmes, for instance, remarks in his discussion of attempt that "when [a] man has . . . cocked and aimed the pistol, . . . the danger becomes so great that the law steps in."[4] The Model Penal Code commentary on attempt says that "[w]hen a person is seriously dedicated to commission of a crime, a firm legal basis is needed for the intervention of the agencies of law enforcement to prevent its consummation" and also that "[t]here is a need . . . for a legal basis upon which the special danger that such individuals present may be assessed and dealt with."[5] A leading criminal law treatise also observes that "one important function served by the crime of attempt is to provide a basis whereby law enforcement officers may intervene in time to prevent a completed crime."[6] So these explain only the purpose of laws that prohibit incomplete attempts, but in what way are attempts blameworthy?

Attempt is one of the classic topics of substantive criminal law, like the act requirement, mens rea, causation, complicity, and justifications and excuses, and there is a substantial literature on attempt.[7] A feature of attempt liability that makes it seem like it is a *malum in se* is that it trades on an intuition that is wrong to attempt to commit a wrong. R. A. Duff, for instance, argues that "we must surely agree that if it is wrong to cause a harm intentionally . . . , it is also . . . wrong to attempt to cause such harm."[8] He adds, "A law that condemned and punished actually harm-causing conduct as wrong, but was utterly silent on attempts to cause such harms . . . would speak with a strange moral voice."[9] Gideon Yaffe also notes that there is "a deeply entrenched principle of moral thought: if you shouldn't do something, then you shouldn't try to do it either."[10] Yaffe endorses the following principle, which he calls the "Transfer Principle": "If a particular form of conduct is legitimately criminalized, then the attempt to engage in that form of conduct is also legitimately criminalized."[11] The idea here is that there is an independent moral significance to assign to the idea of "trying." If it is morally wrong to do *x*, then it is morally wrong to *try to do x*.

[4] Oliver Wendell Holmes Jr., *The Common Law* (Little, Brown, and Company, 1881), 69.
[5] American Law Institute, *Model Penal Code and Commentaries, Part I* (American Law Institute, 1985), 294.
[6] Wayne R. LaFave and Jens David Ohlin, *Criminal Law*, 7th ed. (West Academic Publishing, 2023), 759.
[7] See, e.g., R. A. Duff, *Criminal Attempts* (Oxford University Press, 1997); Gideon Yaffe, *Attempts: In the Philosophy of Action and the Criminal Law* (Oxford University Press, 2010).
[8] Duff, *Criminal Attempts*, 134.
[9] Duff, *Criminal Attempts*, 134.
[10] Yaffe, *Attempts*, 21.
[11] Yaffe, *Attempts*, 21 (emphasis omitted).

This chapter argues against this understanding, at least when it comes to incomplete attempts. The contention that it is wrong to try to do something if doing that thing is wrong might sound plausible if one is contemplating complete attempts, but, this chapter argues, the moral wrongfulness of incomplete attempt is not at all clear. This chapter also argues that we can improve our understanding of incomplete attempt if we start seeing it not as a traditional crime but more as a modern regulatory, or disobedience, offense. More specifically, incomplete attempt is a disobedience offense because the wrongfulness of committing an incomplete attempt does not consist in *trying* to engage in a wrongful act (such as harming others) but interfering with the government's program of managing risks. This chapter, unlike other chapters that discuss different ways in which laws criminalize disobedience, is more revisionist than interpretive.

II. Complete Attempt and Incomplete Attempt

Consider *People v. Smith* from California, a case in which a man with a handgun fired it once in the direction of a car with a woman and a baby, and the bullet came into the car but did not hit anyone.[12] The shooter was charged with and convicted of a number of crimes, including attempted murder of the woman and attempted murder of the baby. The court found that there was sufficient evidence to conclude that the defendant intended to kill the occupants in the car. And by shooting toward the car with the aim of killing the passengers, the defendant certainly imposed risks of harm. In fact, he was also charged with the crime of shooting at an occupied vehicle, which is not an attempt crime but a straightforward crime of risk imposition.

Another way in which behaviors like the one in the *Smith* case have been traditionally described is in terms of the "last act."[13] The act of pulling the trigger was the "last act" because that act marks the moment at which the actor's attempt to kill becomes complete, and the risk the actor creates is no longer within the actor's control. The attempt to kill in this case easily could have resulted in death. He could have killed them both by shooting in that direction, and the fact that he did not physically harm them does not change the fact that he put them in an extremely dangerous situation and that he could no longer control the amount of danger the victims were facing. These cases seem like cases of reckless endangerment, the wrongness of which is obvious. Therefore, assuming

[12] See People v. Smith, 124 P.3d 730 (Cal. 2005).
[13] LaFave and Ohlin, *Criminal Law*, 769–70.

the blameworthiness of the completed offense is clear, the moral issue is relatively straightforward for typical complete attempts.[14]

Attempt cases, however, are not all "last act" cases, as attempts may be "incomplete." A person may also be convicted of a crime of attempt before he has taken sufficient steps to complete his attempt to commit a crime. Different jurisdictions define "incomplete attempt" differently, and a perennially difficult question of definition for incomplete attempt has to do with the act requirement, and the issue has been framed as drawing a distinction between "preparation" and "attempt," where a person is not considered to have attempted until the person has crossed the line to go from mere preparation to attempt.[15]

The two most well-known tests in the United States to demarcate the line between preparation and attempt are the "substantial step" test and the "dangerous proximity" test.[16] These tests are formulated differently across jurisdictions in the United States, but a standard definition of the "dangerous proximity" test is that the act requirement of attempt liability is met if the defendant engages in "acts [that] . . . come or advance very near to the accomplishment of the intended crime."[17] Under the "substantial step" test, as defined in the influential Model Penal Code and adopted by many jurisdictions, a person has reached the threshold of attempt to commit a crime once the person has taken "a substantial step in a course of conduct planned to culminate" in the person's commission of the crime, as long as the step taken is "strongly corroborative of the actor's criminal purpose."[18]

[14] This is not to say that there are no difficult problems in attempt law when it comes to complete attempts. Even if we focus just on complete attempts, several puzzles remain. There is, for instance, the question over the role of moral luck in blameworthiness as shown in the debate over whether results matter. Also, attempts, even when complete, do not always impose risks of harm, in at least two categories of cases. The first is the category known in the law as "impossible attempts." To take an extreme example, a person who sticks needles into a voodoo doll in order to harm a person is not imposing any risks on that person or anyone else, even though that is a complete attempt. See, e.g., Larry Alexander and Kimberly Kessler Ferzan, *Crime and Culpability: A Theory of Criminal Law* (Cambridge University Press, 2009), 171–96. The second is the category known as "double inchoate crimes," where the offense a person is attempting to commit may be an inchoate offense, in which case even complete attempts are remote from the ultimate harm. See Ira P. Robbins, "Double Inchoate Crimes," *Harvard Journal of Legislation* 26, no. 1 (1989): 5–6.

[15] While there is some debate and variation in answers on this question, there is consensus, at least if we are talking about an attempt to harm a person, that an intent to harm is sufficient to satisfy the mental state requirement of the crime of attempt and that some high level of culpable mental state is necessary. See LaFave and Ohlin, *Criminal Law*, 803. For discussions from outside the United States, see Kai Ambos, *Treatise on International Criminal Law, Volume I: Foundations and General Part*, 2nd ed. (Oxford University Press, 2021), 339–41, 336–48; Markus D. Dubber and Tatjana Hörnle, *Criminal Law: A Comparative Approach* (Oxford University Press, 2016), 356–57.

[16] LaFave and Ohlin, *Criminal Law*, 769, 774.

[17] People v. Rizzo, 158 N.E. 888, 889 (N.Y. 1927).

[18] Model Penal Code § 5.01 (American Law Institute, 1985).

What do these tests mean in practice? To have a sense of what incomplete attempt cases look like, here are some examples of cases that have come out in different ways.

- In *State v. Smith* from Washington, the police noticed a car parked in a public park illegally after 1 a.m. and found three men in the car with fifteen 100 dollar bills, a pair of handcuffs, several knives and guns, ammunition, and a shovel, among other things. According to the police, the defendant Smith confessed that he and one other person in the car had planned to kill the third person, and the Supreme Court of Washington affirmed the trial court's finding that Smith had attempted to kill the intended victim.[19]
- In *People v. Walter* from Illinois, a 24-year-old man developed an online relationship with a 16-year-old girl, in which the man shared his fantasies of having sexual relations with the girl. They agreed to meet at a McDonald's one day, and the girl said she would come with a friend of hers. By that point, though, law enforcement had been alerted by the girl's father, and only a detective showed up to meet with the man. The detective found condoms in the man's car, and the man confirmed that he purchased them in case he and the girl ended up having sex. The man was convicted of attempted sexual conduct with an underage person, but the conviction was reversed on appeal. The appeals court stressed that the defendant merely showed up to a public place to meet a person and that is insufficient to constitute an attempted crime of sexual conduct with an underage person.[20]
- In *Stemple v. State* from Oklahoma, the defendant Stemple planned to kill his wife, and to put his plan into action, he hired a man to kill her. The plan was for Stemple to bring his wife to a designated location where the man he had hired was waiting to kill her, but the plan was foiled because she was ill and did not want to accompany Stemple. Stemple eventually succeeded in killing his wife on a different day, but the court found that he had merely prepared to kill his wife and had not attempted to kill her on that particular day when she failed to show.[21]

It is not obvious under existing doctrines whether these cases have been correctly decided, as the facts indicate that the cases could have gone either way, but they illustrate the kinds of line-drawing questions that arise in incomplete attempt cases. The next part addresses the normative question of wrongfulness of incomplete attempt.

19 State v. Smith, 801 P.2d 975 (Wash. 1990).
20 People v. Walter, 810 N.E.2d 626 (Ill. App. Ct. 2004).
21 Stemple v. State, 994 P.2d 61 (Cal. 2000).

III. Evaluating Incomplete Attempt

A. Crime of Risking Harm

To have a baseline with which to evaluate incomplete attempt, we should start with the idea of risking harm. In *Moulden v. Maryland*, a man robbed another man by sticking a "gun" against the man's face, but the "gun" turned out to be fake.[22] The perpetrator, who presumably knew that the gun was fake, was charged with the crime of reckless endangerment, defined as "recklessly . . . engag[ing] in conduct that creates a substantial risk of death or serious physical injury to another."[23] The court considered the question whether "wielding a 'fake', 'toy', or 'plastic' gun under the circumstances of the case could satisfy the necessary elements of reckless endangerment."[24] The court concluded that because "there is no evidence that the alleged weapon was either operable as a firearm or substantial enough to use as a bludgeoning instrument . . . there is no evidence to support a finding that appellant created a 'substantial risk of death or serious physical injury to another.'"[25]

In *Albrecht v. State*, another Maryland case, a police officer pointed a gun at a person near several other people, and the gun accidentally discharged, leading to the death of the person he was pointing his gun at.[26] The defendant was charged with manslaughter as well as with reckless endangerment of several bystanders.[27] When considering the issue of whether there was sufficient evidence to conclude that the defendant recklessly endangered one of the bystanders, the court asked whether one of the victims was "arguably within the line of fire so as to have been actually at risk" when the gun discharged[28] and concluded that he was.[29] However, when dealing with another bystander, the court held that the defendant did not recklessly endanger the bystander because the bystander was far from the line of fire.[30]

These are two cases where courts have found that in order for a person to commit the crime of reckless endangerment, the person has to *in fact* create a risk of harm to another person. One way of conceptualizing laws that criminalize these types of risk imposition is in terms of "unleash[ing] a risk of harm."[31]

22 Moulden v. State, 69 A.3d 36 (Md. Ct. Spec. App. 2013).
23 Moulden, 69 A.3d at 50.
24 Moulden, 69 A.3d at 51.
25 Moulden, 69 A.3d at 52.
26 Albrecht v. State, 658 A.2d 1122 (Md. Ct. Spec. App. 1995).
27 Albrecht, 658 A.2d at 1137.
28 Albrecht, 658 A.2d at 1138.
29 Albrecht, 658 A.2d at 1138.
30 Albrecht, 658 A.2d at 1140.
31 See, e.g., Alexander and Ferzan, *Crime and Culpability*, 197; see also Larry Alexander and Kimberly Kessler Ferzan, *Reflections on Crime and Culpability: Problems and Puzzles* (Cambridge University Press, 2018).

The formulation is associated with Larry Alexander and Kimberly Ferzan, but this is not the place to present the full version of their theory of criminal culpability and evaluate it. For now, we can focus on the proposition that unleashing unjustifiable risks of harm to others is blameworthy. Given that such acts are blameworthy on their own with or without laws that criminalize them, we can reasonably stipulate that laws that criminalize knowingly unleashing an unjustifiable risk of harm do not criminalize disobedience. We can then use that principle as the baseline to assess other offenses that are enacted to prevent harm by criminalizing conduct that stops short of unleashing risks.

B. Culpability of Incomplete Attempts

Above, we noted different formulations of incomplete attempt, but one way to generalize the idea is that attempt is the crime of taking steps toward commission of a crime with a culpable mental state. Of course, *People v. Smith*, the case of the man shooting in the direction of a car with a woman and a baby, was an attempt case that is easily assimilated into the category of crimes of risking harm (or unleashing a risk of harm), and such "complete" or "last act" attempt cases are not properly characterized as crimes of disobedience. But what about incomplete attempts? Are they crimes of disobedience or are they blameworthy on their own?

We need to start with the question whether incomplete attempts are morally wrong aside from the disobedience aspect (if any). It may be clear that taking the "last act" and trying to kill a person by shooting is morally wrong, but how about, say, the first act, when the first act is conceived of as a mental act of forming an intent to kill? Is that morally wrong, too? To be clear, the question here is not whether a jurisdiction may criminalize the "first act" of forming an intent to kill. The question that is most often raised about the act requirement in attempt law is, assuming *some* physical act toward actualizing a criminal intent is required for there to be an attempt, how much is enough? The reason the question of blameworthiness of mere thoughts is relevant to this question is that if forming an intention to kill is wrong, then taking *any* physical step toward implementing that intent also is wrong *a fortiori*.

High-profile examples of documented intent to harm are not difficult to find. Jared Lee Loughner, the man who shot and killed six people and injured thirteen, including US Representative Gabby Giffords, in 2011, reportedly wrote down his plan with words "I planned ahead," "My assassination," and "Giffords."[32]

[32] Chris McGreal, "Jared Lee Loughner Note Reveals Aim to Assassinate Gabrielle Giffords," *Guardian*, January 10, 2011.

Loughner did eventually shoot Giffords, but imagine that the law enforcement was alerted after he wrote these words but before he did much else. What had he done wrong by that point? Or consider Elliot Rodger, who, before he killed six people in 2014, spent years thinking about killing people as documented in a long, autobiographical essay he wrote.[33] Say his goal was discovered early on when he had the thought solidified in his mind but had not yet taken any steps toward implementing the plan other than thinking about killing and writing down his thoughts. Had Rodger done something wrong the moment he formed the intent to kill?

These are chilling examples, and because the facts of the actual cases are so horrific, we may be tempted to say that the initial thought itself is morally wrongful. But this is controversial. To think this issue through, perhaps we can start with the proposition that it is never morally wrong to have mere thoughts and see how it holds up to scrutiny. We can first get some bad arguments out of the way. A common argument given is that thoughts often occur to us, are involuntary, and are outside our control and that therefore we should not be held morally responsible for our thoughts.[34] Another common, related, argument is that when thoughts occur involuntarily, they do not always linger, as one may have all kinds of fleeting thoughts. Thoughts that have such short lives are incapable of causing harm, and it cannot be morally wrong to have thoughts that are that harmless.

These are not good arguments for the view that thoughts as a general matter cannot be morally wrongful since not all things that count as "thoughts" are involuntary, fleeting, or both.[35] When a thought occurs to us, one can dismiss

[33] Ian Lovett and Adam Nagourney, "Video Rant, Then Deadly Rampage in California Town," *New York Times*, May 24, 2014.

[34] By describing this argument, I am not endorsing it but am merely reporting a common reaction to the idea of punishing thoughts. It is not at all clear whether it is wrong to hold people morally responsible for involuntary thoughts, attitudes, and emotions. See, e.g., Angela M. Smith, "Responsibility for Attitudes: Activity and Passivity in Mental Life," *Ethics* 115, no. 2 (2005): 236–71.

[35] For a nice illustration of a variety of fleeting thoughts, see Daniel Ohana, "Desert and Punishment for Acts Preparatory to the Commission of a Crime," *Canadian Journal of Law and Jurisprudence* 20, no. 1 (2007): 115–16 ("The thought of perpetrating a crime may enter the mind of an actor as he entertains abstract and vague thoughts which are the product of sporadic emotional and mental states. These may include fantasizing, mischievous daydreaming, fuming resentment, lustful urges (for sexual gratification), cravings (for drugs), a fit of rage, despondency and disgust of life, moral outrage, religious or ideological zeal, prankish maliciousness, boredom or jadedness. Tantrums, ruminations and flights of the imagination of this sort can occasionally be followed by preliminary actions, like searching in an encyclopedia, surfing on the internet, casually inquiring by a close friend, setting aside tools which are easily within reach or taking a walk or quick drive by the site of the crime envisioned. Such actions, when performed in the immediate aftermath of the emergence of the criminal idea in the mind of the actor, primarily have the effect of temporarily releasing his aggression, satisfying his curiosity, or assuaging his mischievous drives. A genuine intention to carry out the offence, let alone a minimally structured plan, does not yet take form. At this incipient stage, the actor's project is still vague and the chances are relatively good that once the agitation subsides, he will not carry on further.").

it, disown it, or embrace it. A person may then, in a series of voluntary mental acts, keep a thought alive, entertain it, mull it over, embellish it, refine it, build plans around it, and so on.[36] Those who desire to harm other people often write those thoughts down or mention them to others. In other words, even if it is the case that there is no such thing as an involuntary immoral thought or a fleeting harmful thought, such observations do not extend to situations where a person consciously and voluntarily keeps a thought alive.[37]

We should therefore refine the question about morality of bad thoughts by focusing on thoughts that are voluntarily sustained by the one having the thoughts. We might single out, for instance, thoughts that are not mere thoughts but intentions as the kinds of thoughts (though not only ones) that can lead to harm, and think of "firm intentions," as Douglas Husak proposes, as something that could properly be condemned and perhaps even criminalized.[38] Alec Walen has similarly argued that "intentions are not mere thoughts," as "they are choices that one makes with regard to how one will behave" and has gone even further to say that "the fundamental basis for culpability is the *decision* to pursue a criminal aim."[39] Gabriel Mendlow seems to agree as well. He argues, for instance, that "[w]hen you form the intention to kill me, you . . . do something you have a conclusive moral reason not to do, you do something wrongful—even if all you do is form a mental state."[40]

Even when we narrow the issue down this way, one may still argue that thoughts cannot be immoral since many sustained thoughts are unattached from reality. Thoughts by themselves cannot make a difference in the world until they are acted upon, so we might conclude that thoughts are harmless and thus always morally permissible. But is that true? We certainly do not talk or behave as if thoughts make no difference in the world. For instance, Kwame Anthony Appiah, commenting on Benedict Anderson's idea of nations as "imagined communities," notes that "[i]magined . . . doesn't mean unreal," as "nothing could be more powerful than the human imagination."[41]

[36] Cf. Alexander and Ferzan, *Crime and Culpability*, 200–01 (discussing the view that intentions are acts); see also Stephen P. Garvey, "Are Attempts Like Treason?," *New Criminal Law Review* 14, no. 2 (2011): 202–03 ("[F]orming an intent is nothing at which to sneeze. Intentions are powerful and singular mental states. . . . Desires can come and go, but intentions stick around . . . .").

[37] Gabriel Mendlow, "Why Is It Wrong to Punish Thought?," *Yale Law Journal* 127, no. 8 (2018): 2342; Douglas Husak, "Does Criminal Liability Require an Act?," in *Philosophy and the Criminal Law: Principle and Critique*, ed. Antony Duff (Cambridge University Press, 1998), 87–88; Ohana, "Desert and Punishment," 116.

[38] Husak, "Does Criminal Liability Require an Act?," 89.

[39] Alec Walen, "Criminalizing Statements of Terrorist Intent: How to Understand the Law Governing Terrorist Threats, and Why It Should Be Used Instead of Long-Term Preventive Detention," *Journal of Criminal Law and Criminology* 101, no. 3 (2011): 835–36.

[40] Mendlow, "Why Is It Wrong to Punish Thought?," 2352.

[41] Kwame Anthony Appiah, *Ethics of Identity* (Princeton University Press, 2005), 242.

Couldn't one still insist that mere thoughts—even if they are intentions to harm—are categorically different from physical steps one may take to bring such thoughts to reality? That may be, and it is true that many thoughts may have no consequences. However, thoughts can be acted upon and make certain outcomes more likely in the same way some acts make certain outcomes more likely. Thoughts can have a causal relationship to harm in the same way certain acts that are harmless on their own have a causal relationship to harm. So, instead of then saying that thoughts, as a categorical matter, are harmless, we might focus on the kinds of thoughts that could give rise to harm.

What would such thoughts look like? In Donna Tartt's novel *The Secret History*, one character tries to work out mathematically how much poisonous mushroom his friend would have to ingest for him to die, as he explores the feasibility of that method of killing him, after a need to eliminate the friend from existence *somehow* becomes compelling enough to take him and his co-conspirator friends to the next step of coming up with a workable plan to do the deed.[42] The entire calculation, though, takes place at a desk with a pencil and a piece of paper. Is that wrongful enough? Possibly, but one worry about examples like this is the long distance between forming an intent to harm and actually harming, especially since a person may give up on the idea of killing a person after realizing that he has no good way of doing it. We may assuage this sense of unease by focusing on intentions that are accompanied by steps taken toward realizing such intentions.

And this brings us from "the first act" of forming an intent to harm to something that looks more like what the law designates as incomplete attempt. As discussed earlier, attempt law distinguishes between preparation and attempt and, when criminalizing attempt, leaves preparation outside the scope. The substantial step test draws the line at "a substantial step in a course of conduct planned to culminate" in the person's commission of the crime,[43] and the dangerous proximity test does the same at "acts [that] . . . that come or advance very near to the accomplishment of the intended crime."[44] So the question for us is, assuming we want to see some acts accompanying the intent in order to identify the moment at which a person's conduct turns "wrongful enough," where that moment of going over the threshold occurs.

Along these lines, Husak has suggested, when evaluating conduct that could lead to harm, that we focus on several criteria, such as whether the conduct "creates . . . the risk that a right will be violated," whether it is sufficiently "proximate" to harm, and whether it is "persisten[t]," that is, not abandoned.[45] In other

[42] See Donna Tartt, *The Secret History* (Alfred A. Knopf, 1992), 229–35.
[43] Model Penal Code § 5.01.
[44] Rizzo, 158 N.E. at 889.
[45] Husak, "Nonconsummate Offenses," 165–74.

words, one might believe that some steps taken toward harming others take the actor over a certain threshold of blameworthiness. Daniel Ohana, for instance, argues as follows:

> As the actor progresses, the probability rises that he will eventually complete his preparations and launch into the commission of the offense. The transitional awareness of this incremental accrual in the likelihood of harm adds to the blameworthiness of the actor, even if his (preparatory) conduct solely consists of putting a pre-conceived plan into action.[46]

Walen similarly has argued:

> [O]ne's culpability increases as one moves from mere intention formation, to starting to prepare, to commencing the commitment of the crime itself, to completing the last act needed to perform to complete the crime.[47]

Not everyone, though, agrees. Alexander and Ferzan argue that one is not culpable until and unless one "unleashes" the risk.[48] So for them, "[i]ntentions are guides to future actions that do not prevent our later reconsideration," and "an actor has committed a culpable act only at the point where the actor has truly relinquished control."[49] They elaborate as follows:

> [A]ctors can still change their minds, even after they have taken substantial steps. If actors have complete control over their future choices, then, no matter how firm their present resolve, they can always change their minds and refrain from imposing the risk. Often, when in the future they become fully aware of the risks their act will impose, they will cease intending to impose it.[50]

46 Ohana, "Desert and Punishment," 117.
47 Walen, "Criminalizing Statements of Terrorist Intent," 852.
48 Alexander and Ferzan, *Crime and Culpability*, 197.
49 Alexander and Ferzan, *Crime and Culpability*, 210.
50 Alexander and Ferzan, *Crime and Culpability*, 212–13. This view leads them to reject criminalization of incomplete attempts altogether. Alexander and Ferzan, *Crime and Culpability*, 216 ("[W]e believe it is only when the actor has committed the 'last act' that she has committed a culpable act."). Their view is controversial. For a criticism, see, e.g., Mitchell N. Berman, "Negligence and Culpability: Reflections on Alexander and Ferzan," *Criminal Law and Philosophy* 16, no. 3 (2022): 466 n.41; R. A. Duff, "Risks, Culpability and Criminal Liability," in *Seeking Security: Pre-Empting the Commission of Criminal Harms*, ed. G. R. Sullivan and Ian Dennis (Hart Publishing, 2012), 131 (concluding that while Alexander and Ferzan's criminal code "would not include a category of incomplete attempts as such," it could still "find room for a range of lesser offenses of risk-unleashing that are, taken together, not notably narrower in scope than our current laws of inchoate and precursor crimes").

Alexander and Ferzan's argument brings up the issue briefly alluded to above when discussing Husak's criteria: the significance of abandonment. Consider this example. The movie *The Shawshank Redemption* begins with a story of a man sitting in a car with a gun outside a building. Inside the building were his wife and her lover.[51] However, he does not go into the building and he does not kill them, but instead drives away and throws out the gun that night. It is unclear what his intent was,[52] but assuming that he had a firm intent to kill, it appears that he has likely crossed whatever threshold Ohana and Walen posit. At the same time, the fact that he has abandoned his plan also seems relevant to the moral analysis, which explains the existence of the voluntary abandonment defense in some jurisdictions.

Of course, not all instances of abandonment are the same. In the movie *Taxi Driver*, the main character plans to assassinate a political candidate during a campaign stop, but once he realizes that the security detail has noticed him, he abandons the plan and runs away.[53] The husband in *Shawshank Redemption*, on the other hand, abandons his plan without such an externally imposed interruption. Or consider the real case of John Lennon's killing. Hours before John Lennon was murdered, the future murderer interacted with Lennon and got his autograph. The killer had a gun with him then but did not kill Lennon at that moment.[54] By contrast, the *Shawshank Redemption* character's abandonment was complete.

For our purposes, the question is not whether there ought to be a voluntary abandonment defense to attempt or what its elements ought to be. The relevant question is what the voluntary abandonment defense says about the blameworthiness of those who take steps toward harming other people with an intent to do so. To the extent forming an intent or forming an intent and taking steps toward realizing the intent is blameworthy, the moral significance of abandonment seems to allow the person to erase all that and go back to living as if the wrongdoing never occurred. If no harm has been done, there is still an opportunity to renounce one's wrongful intentions and live as one should—at least in this one small way of not polluting one's life with that particular wrongdoing. The possibility of changing one's mind in this way highlights the appeal of Alexander and Ferzan's view that there is no culpability until "the last act" has been performed.

To summarize, the question we have been exploring is whether people who are guilty of incomplete attempts are morally blameworthy, and there are several

[51] *The Shawshank Redemption*, directed by Frank Darabont (Warner Bros. Entertainment Inc., 1994).

[52] In the movie, he says he was drunk and confused and thought maybe he would just scare them.

[53] *Taxi Driver*, directed by Martin Scorsese (Columbia Pictures, 1976).

[54] Jim Gold, "Chilling Details of John Lennon Shooting Recounted at Chapman Parole Hearing," *NBC News*, August 29, 2012.

possible answers. First, one might hold the view that a mere intention to, say, hurt another is sufficient to make a person blameworthy; therefore, attempting, or taking these steps to realize that intent, is also blameworthy. Second, one might hold the view that a person attempts and becomes blameworthy only when the person unleashes a risk of harm. Thus, the person is not blameworthy as long as they retain the ability to refrain from unleashing the risk, which means that only last acts are blameworthy and incomplete attempts are not.[55] And there are possibilities in between.

IV. Incomplete Attempt as Disobedience

Where does all this leave us? It seems that there is a range of answers to the question of blameworthiness of incomplete attempts. At the same time, even though the morality of such acts may not be clear, the state would be justified in intervening in some form, including prohibition of taking of such steps, instead of waiting for the moment of "unleashing" to occur. In fact, we may even assume that Alexander and Ferzan are correct and that incomplete attempts are not blameworthy and still affirm that the state has an interest, indeed a duty, to prevent harm posed by dangerous individuals who take preparatory steps with an intent to harm. And such interventions may take the form of criminalization.[56]

I suggest that a way out of this sea of uncertainty and conflicting intuitions is to reconceptualize criminal attempt as a crime of disobedience. If the state criminalizes incomplete attempt, that act of criminalization may be understood by the people in two different ways. First, criminalization of incomplete attempt is a form of paternalism. By criminalizing incomplete attempt, the state is warning people to not even go near criminality, as doing so would tempt or pull one to a place closer to completion of the crime and eventually lead to irreparable harm. Second, criminalization of incomplete attempt is a way of controlling the amount of risk of harm in a society by keeping people well away from harmful conduct, and in that sense, it is a form of regulatory offense similar to

[55] Of course, it will often be the case that those who start taking steps toward harming another person also pose danger to others and in that they "unleash" a risk of harm even before they take "the last act." Carrying a loaded weapon around other persons is dangerous no matter how far away the intended target of the next shooting may be. Such people then may be considered blameworthy for risking harm to others under the account that posits the moment a risk is unleashed as the moment a person becomes blameworthy. But such risk-taking activities would be considered crimes of endangerment as opposed to attempts. Cf. Duff, "Risks, Culpability, and Criminal Liability," 130–31.

[56] Cf. Kimberly Kessler Ferzan, "Inchoate Crimes at the Prevention/Punishment Divide," *San Diego Law Review* 48, no. 4 (2011): 1273–97; Kimberly Kessler Ferzan, "Beyond Crime and Commitment: Justifying Liberty Deprivations of the Dangerous and Responsible," *Minnesota Law Review* 96, no. 1 (2011): 141–93.

the public welfare offenses we saw in the chapter on regulatory offenses. This is the sense in which incomplete attempts can be a crime of disobedience.[57]

In other words, we may conceptualize incomplete attempts as *mala in se* or as *mala prohibita*. As noted above, when Duff says that "it is wrong to cause a harm intentionally . . . , it is also . . . wrong to attempt to cause such harm," he seems to see attempts as *mala in se* offenses, specifically related to causing harm.[58] Yaffe's endorsement of the idea that "if you shouldn't do something, then you shouldn't try to do it either,"[59] too, seems to rely on the intuition that it is morally wrong to try to engage in a moral wrong, meaning that attempts are *malum in se*. And I am suggesting that we think of incomplete attempts as *mala prohibita* offenses at least sometimes. Because the term "attempt" is both vague and possibly interpreted by the legal system in both under- and overinclusive ways, it is not always clear whether it is acting as a *malum in se* or a *malum prohibitum* offense. Sometimes it is clear that a person is attempting to harm another person and should be considered to have committed a *malum in se*, but it is not as clear in cases where one's "substantial steps" do not bring one to a situation where one can be uncontroversially described as having done something wrong. The legal system can capture those cases for the purpose of risk regulation and crime

[57] Stephen Garvey arrives at a conclusion that may look similar to mine but is quite different. Garvey, "Are Attempts Like Treason?" Garvey argues that "an actor who intends to cause or risk harm is akin to a traitor" and that "[t]he wrong of attempt consists in the formation of an intent to cause or risk harm to one's fellow citizens in violation of one's loyalty to them." Garvey, "Are Attempts Like Treason?," 173. Then he says that "treason . . . is a crime of disobedience." Garvey, "Are Attempts Like Treason?," 206 (emphasis omitted). His overall thesis, stated in this way, thus at least superficially resembles the position taken in this chapter, except that there are problems with his position. For one thing, he confuses the issues when he adds "as are all crimes" at the end of the sentence quoted so it reads, "treason . . . is a crime of disobedience, as are all crimes." Garvey, "Are Attempts Like Treason?," 206 (emphasis omitted). As to the idea that attempts are like treason, he explains as follows:

> Cast in this light, a would-be attempter should be punished, not because (and when) he is guilty of wrongdoing that causes or risks harm . . . . On the contrary, a would-be attempter should be punished because (and when) he forms an intent to cause or risk harm. The formation of such an intent is itself wrongful inasmuch as it constitutes a breach of the duty of loyalty that each citizen owes to his fellow citizens, and that breach becomes a crime when the state elects to bring it within the criminal law's reach. No harm needed: neither caused or risked. In other words, attempts are instances of harmless wrongdoing, and when the state elects to call such wrongs crimes, an actor who defies the state's authority to do so is properly subject to retributive punishment.

Garvey, "Are Attempts Like Treason?," 208. Explaining my disagreement with Garvey here would take up more space than warranted, though the first chapter touched on the disagreement a bit. I will just note that it seems to me that he is mistaken at least twice here. First, attempts are not like treason or about the duty of loyalty, as discussions of treason and disloyalty offenses in Chapters 8 and 9 should make clear. Second, as the rest of this book should also make clear, not all crimes are crimes of disobedience. In addition, as discussed in Chapter 1, there is a large gap philosophically between Garvey's view and the view presented in this book.

[58] Duff, *Criminal Attempts*, 134.

[59] Yaffe, *Attempts*, 21; see also Matthew Hanser, "Acting Wrongly by Trying," in *Oxford Studies in Normative Ethics: Volume 4*, ed. Mark Timmons (Oxford University Press, 2014), 138–39; Victor Tadros, *Wrongs and Crimes* (Oxford University Press, 2016), 313.

prevention, and may do so under the rubric of incomplete attempt. And those who engage in such conduct may be thought of as those who are committing the wrong of disobedience.

A theoretical advantage of this interpretation of incomplete attempt is that it leads us to think about incomplete attempt the way it is commonly understood—as a preventive offense. Scholars, especially philosophical scholars, have poured a lot of effort into the project of defining "attempt" as an abstract, philosophical matter, both as a metaphysical matter of what "attempt" is and the moral question of why "attempt" per se is bad. Such work is admirable and has yielded a lot of interesting insights. However, as indicated by quotes from Holmes and the Model Penal Code commentary mentioned above, the traditionally cited goals of criminalization of incomplete attempt are prevention, not retribution or condemnation of "trying" to do what is morally wrong.

That there is a not so insignificant intuition that voluntary abandonment should serve as a defense suggests as such as well. If retribution or condemnation of attempt drove criminalization of incomplete attempt, then the fact that a person has abandoned their attempt should not be able to cancel out the wrongdoing that has already been done.[60] It is more likely the case that voluntary abandonment is a possible defense because people who abandon are *preventing themselves* from committing offenses, in which case no legal intervention is necessary, since the very point of attempt liability is preventive. The approach proposed here, by conceptualizing incomplete attempt as a disobedience offense, highlights that the state lays down commands that prohibit incomplete attempt as a way of preventing harm, and the core moral wrong is that of disobeying such commands, not that of "trying" to commit a morally wrongful act.

Understanding incomplete attempt as a disobedience offense also brings potential for reform. For instance, we could begin the project of rewriting attempt laws in more specific ways to provide more notice instead of relying on vague words like "attempt" and various tests that have been invented to give it meaning.[61] As a general matter, at least in the United States, laws of attempt do

[60] See, e.g., Yaffe, *Attempts*, 291 ("Abandonment, of the sort that seems to have independent normative significance, happens after an attempt has already been committed."). But see Duff, *Criminal Attempts*, 395 (arguing that a person who abandons an attempt "turns what would otherwise have been a criminal attempt into something that is not after all a criminal attempt").

[61] It would take us too far afield to present a definition of "fair notice" and defend it here, but we may make the following generalizations about what individuals generally expect as they go about their daily lives. First, having certain thoughts, even if the thoughts are of harming others, may be frowned upon but generally belongs in the realm free from direct governmental interference through criminal law. Second, as far as the state is concerned, individuals are generally free to live as they choose as long as they do not harm others' interests and otherwise are not in violation of the law. Third, when the law does regulate an individual's life, it generally has to do with situations when an individual can have an adverse impact on another's interests in ways that properly concern the public. Fourth, the criminal law has numerous prohibitions that track common-sense expectations of how one is never to treat another, and such criminal prohibitions extend to cover situations where one tries to hurt another's interests but is unsuccessful. These ordinary expectations may be vague

not seem to have been designed with notice as a foremost concern. Rather, the laws seem most often to be rules designed for officials to sort people into different categories. Criminal codes define "attempt" vaguely. There is no general federal criminal "attempt" provision in the US Code, and when the word "attempt" shows up in definitions of specific offenses, the Code does not define the term and federal courts have generally adopted the substantial step test of the Model Penal Code, on a case-by-case basis.[62] Many state codes, similarly, just prohibit "attempt" without defining it,[63] and some states go a little further by prohibiting "any act" or any "overt act" toward the commission of an offense, but that does not give much more notice.[64]

The dangerous proximity test may give a little more information, but that phrase is judge-made in caselaw,[65] which tends to be obscure among the general population. Many state codes adopt the "substantial step" test, but do not define it further, and the phrase "substantial step" is hardly self-explanatory.[66] And when criminal codes add more to the definition in terms of corroborating evidence, that does not clarify much, either.[67] The command appears to be not in terms of attempt but in terms of appearance of attempt, and a legal command that tells you not to commit a crime while saying that what you are doing does not count as the crime as long as you do not look like you are committing the crime is very strange. So the primary manner in which the law

but carry sufficient capability to guide people's lives so that they can conduct their lives without being subject to criminal liability. A person who forms an intent to harm others may be of interest to law enforcement but should not be considered to have attempted. So, for example, being subject to criminal liability for trying to harm another person for merely forming an intent to harm would be contrary to these ordinary expectations and would be in violation of the principle of fair notice.

[62] Charles Doyle, "Attempt: An Overview of Federal Criminal Law, *Congressional Research Service*, April 11, 2015: 2; Michael R. Fishman, "Defining Attempts: *Mandujano*'s Error," *Duke Law Journal* 65, no. 2 (2015): 354; Avani Mehta Sood, "Attempted Justice: Misunderstanding and Bias in Psychological Constructions of Criminal Attempt," *Stanford Law Review* 71, no. 3 (2019): 602–05.

[63] Cal. Penal Code § 664; Idaho Code §§ 18-305, 18-306, 18-307; Nev. Rev. Stat. § 193.153; R.I. Gen. Laws § 12-17-14; S.C. Code § 16-1-80; Tex. Penal Code § 15.01; Vt. Stat. Tit. 13 § 9; VA. Code § 18.2-25; Wis. Stat. § 939.3.

[64] Ariz. Rev. Stat. § 13-1001; Fla. Stat. § 777.04; Kan. Stat. § 21-5301; LA. Rev. Stat. § 14:27; Mass. Gen. Laws Ch. 274 § 6; Mich. Comp. Laws § 750.92; Miss. Code § 97-1-7; Mont. Code § 45-4-103; N.M. Code Ann § 30-28-1; Ohio Rev. Code § 2923.02; Okla. Stat. Tit. 21 § 42; S.D. Codified Laws § 22-4-1.

[65] N.Y. Penal Law § 110.00; see Fishman, "Defining Attempts," 347–48 n.14; Jens David Ohlin, *Wharton's Criminal Law*, 16th ed. (Thomson Reuters, 2021), § 7:5; see also Hyde v. US, 225 U.S. 347, 388 (1912); Commonwealth v. Kennedy, 48 N.E. 770 (Mass. 1897).

[66] Alaska Stat. § 11.31.100; Ga. Code § 16-4-1, et seq.; Ill. Comp. Stat. Ch. 720 § 5/8-4; Ind. Code § 35-41-5-1; Minn. Stat. § 609.17; Ore. Rev. Stat. § 161.405; PA. Stat. Tit. 18, § 901; Wash. Rev. Code § 9A.28.020.

[67] Ark. Code § 5-3-201(a)(2)(c) ("strongly corroborative of the person's criminal purpose"); Del. Code 11 § 532 ("leaves no reasonable doubt as to the defendant's intention"); Hawaii Rev. Stat. §§ 705-500(3) ("strongly corroborative"); Ky. Rev. Stat. § 506.010(2) ("leaves no reasonable doubt"); Me. Rev. Stat. Tit. 17-A § 152(1); Mo. Stat. § 562.012; Neb. Rev. Stat. § 28-201; N.H. Rev. Stat. § 629.1; N.J. Stat. § 2C:5-1; N.D. Cent. Code § 12.1-06-01; Tenn. Code § 39-12-101; Utah Code § 76-4-101.

communicates to the public that it is a crime to attempt to commit a crime is by convicting people for attempting to commit a crime and attaching that label to convictions.

The vagueness of the term "attempt" is not necessarily a problem. Criminal codes frequently use vague terms, and many of them still give plenty of notice. The term can be problematic in enforcement, however, if the general public and legal decision makers, like the police, prosecutors, judges, and jurors, understand the term differently in a significant way.[68] That kind of discrepancy can occur if there are at least two types of legal materials in operation on the same idea. Criminal codes and notices of convictions may communicate the content of criminal prohibition in one way, with words like "attempt to commit a crime," but legal officials may apply another phrase, like "substantial steps." If the phrase substantial step is designed to offer a basis for early legal intervention by law enforcement and not necessarily to specify and clarify the meaning of attempt in a way that is faithful to how the term is generally understood by the lay audience, then there could be a gap between the law for the citizens and the law for officials.[69] And if the way the law of attempt is enforced by officials is broader than the way the law is understood by the citizens, there could be a problem of lack of fair notice. A potential way out of this predicament is by defining incomplete attempt more precisely, and seeing it as a disobedience offense would be a step in that right direction.

As an example, the Model Penal Code illustrates one possible way of defining attempt to mitigate the notice problem. We have been discussing the "substantial step" test as the contribution of the Model Penal Code, but the full definition is more extensive. It first defines the act requirement as "a substantial step in a course of conduct planned to culminate" that is "strongly corroborative of the actor's criminal purpose," and then it gives examples of what would *count* as a substantial step as follows, assuming the mental state requirement is satisfied:

a) lying in wait, searching for or following the contemplated victim of the crime;
b) enticing or seeking to entice the contemplated victim of the crime to go to the place contemplated for its commission;
c) reconnoitering the place contemplated for the commission of the crime;
d) unlawful entry of a structure, vehicle or enclosure in which it is contemplated that the crime will be committed;

[68] See generally Sood, "Attempted Justice."

[69] Cf. Meir Dan-Cohen, "Decision Rules and Conduct Rules: On Acoustic Separation in Criminal Law," *Harvard Law Review* 97, no. 3 (1984): 625–77.

e) possession of materials to be employed in the commission of the crime, that are specially designed for such unlawful use or that can serve no lawful purpose of the actor under the circumstances;
f) possession, collection or fabrication of materials to be employed in the commission of the crime, at or near the place contemplated for its commission, if such possession, collection or fabrication serves no lawful purpose of the actor under the circumstances;
g) soliciting an innocent agent to engage in conduct constituting an element of the crime.[70]

Once attempt laws are written like the Model Penal Code version, some of the aforementioned problems with attempt liability go away. That is, there would be no need to worry about whether a particular test for "attempt" picks out the conduct that would be accurately characterized as attempt since the more specific illustrations guide the general test. That is, the approach obviates the need to address the concern whether a definition comports with an ordinary understanding of the term "attempt" by giving a legal definition of attempt that announces itself as a distinct, legal concept with only superficial relationship to the term "attempt." Relatedly, the fair notice issue would no longer be an issue because it would be the rules not the word "attempt" doing all the work and giving people notice about what not to do. And thinking of these specific formulations as a list of what not to do is more plausible than thinking of them as illustrations that we can somehow derive from the single word "attempt."

V. Conclusion

This chapter is one of two chapters on preventive offenses, or offenses that criminalize conduct that may be harmless on its own but has a certain relationship to harm, which becomes the basis for its criminalization. The focus of this chapter has been on incomplete attempt, and this chapter has argued that moral blameworthiness of incomplete attempt is unclear and controversial but that we can get a better handle on longstanding problems with the crime of incomplete attempt by conceptualizing it as a disobedience offense where the purpose of the prohibition is paternalistic and regulatory.

[70] Model Penal Code § 5.01. There is at the moment one jurisdiction in the United States that follows the Model Penal Code method of listing examples of "substantial step," and it lists the Model Penal Code list of examples verbatim. Conn. Gen. Stat. § 53a-49.

7

Preventive Offenses II: Possession

I. Introduction

This chapter continues the discussion of preventive offenses by focusing on possession. Possession offenses may be classified as preventive offenses because possession by itself rarely causes harm. Criminalization of possession is not based on the view that possession itself is harmful but because of its relationship to harm.[1]

Possession is deceptively simple. Underneath the seeming simplicity are several reasons a state might invoke to criminalize and punish possession.[2] First, possession may be an inchoate offense akin to incomplete attempt. Second, possession may be a regulatory offense designed to keep the level of certain types of danger tolerably low by, for instance, keeping dangerous objects away from designated groups of people. Third, possession may be an offense because it constitutes participation in a market that the state seeks to eliminate. The first and third rationales for criminalizing possession bring possession offenses into the broader category of preventive offenses, whereas the second rationale highlights the similarity of some possession offenses to regulatory offenses, like the ones discussed in Chapter 5.[3]

[1] For some previous discussions, see R. A. Duff, "Perversions and Subversions of Criminal Law," in *The Boundaries of the Criminal Law*, ed. R. A. Duff et al. (Oxford University Press, 2010); R. A. Duff and S. E. Marshall, "'Abstract Endangerment,' Two Harm Principles, and Two Routes to Criminalisation," *Bergen Journal of Criminal Law and Criminal Justice* 3, no. 2 (2015): 149–57; Larry Alexander and Kimberly Kessler Ferzan, *Reflections on Crime and Culpability: Problems and Puzzles* (Cambridge University Press, 2018), 84 n.2; Larry Alexander and Kimberly Kessler Ferzan, *Crime and Culpability: A Theory of Criminal Law* (Cambridge University Press, 2009), 309–10; Douglas Husak, *Overcriminalization: The Limits of the Criminal Law* (Oxford University Press, 2008), 38.

[2] See generally Markus Dirk Dubber, "Policing Possession: The War on Crime and the End of Criminal Law," *Journal of Criminal Law and Criminology* 91, no. 4 (2001): 855–75; Markus Dirk Dubber, "The Possession Paradigm: The Special Part and the Police Model of the Criminal Process," in *Defining Crimes*, ed. R. A. Duff and Stuart P. Green (Oxford University Press, 2004); Andrew Ashworth, "The Unfairness of Risk-Based Possession Offenses," *Criminal Law and Philosophy* 5, no. 3 (2011): 237; see also Andrew Ashworth and Lucia Zedner, *Preventive Justice* (Oxford University Press, 2005), 99.

[3] Possession is also sometimes treated as a presumptive offense, where a person who is believed to have committed a more serious offense is charged with a mere possession offense, which may be generally easier to prove than the more serious offense. For instance, a person who is believed to have burglarized may be charged with possession of burglars' tools, not theft or burglary. See Dubber, "Possession Paradigm," 103; Frederick Schauer, *Profiles, Probabilities, and Stereotypes* (Harvard University Press, 2006), ch. 9. Seen this way, possession offenses facilitate the highly controversial practice of pretextual prosecution. See, e.g., Harry Litman, "Pretextual Prosecution," *Georgetown Law Journal* 92, no. 6: 1146–58 (2004); Daniel C. Richman and William J. Stuntz, "Al Capone's

Criminalizing Disobedience. Youngjae Lee, Oxford University Press. © Oxford University Press 2026.
DOI: 10.1093/9780197617175.003.0008

II. Possession as a Preparation to Commit a Crime with Intent

In the previous chapter, we saw that incomplete attempt may be generally characterized as the crime of taking steps toward the commission of a crime with a culpable mental state. There are possession laws with identical structures, except they are not crimes of attempting to commit some other crime but are self-standing inchoate offenses.[4] For instance, in New York, a person commits the crime of criminal possession of a weapon if the person possesses a weapon with "intent to use the same unlawfully against another."[5]

Such method of criminalization, where possessing a means of committing a crime with an intent to use the means to commit a crime is prohibited, can be and has been used to generate other criminal laws. A well-known example of a crime like this is the crime of possession of burglar's tools. A typical formulation criminally prohibits possession of "any tool, instrument or other article adapted, designed or commonly used for committing or facilitating offenses involving forcible entry into premises, with a purpose to use . . . the same in making an unlawful forcible entry into a building . . . ."[6] Because of phrases like "commonly used" for burglary, tools that have lawful uses may be considered "burglar's tools," and possessing such tools can lead to a criminal conviction once there is a finding of a criminal purpose accompanying the possession.[7]

Similarly, the Model Penal Code has a generic crime of "possessing instruments of crime," which criminalizes possession of "any instrument of crime with purpose to employ it criminally."[8] It further defines "instrument of crime" as "anything specially made or specially adapted for criminal use" or "anything commonly used for criminal purposes and possessed by the actor under circumstances which do not negative unlawful purpose."[9] Similar provisions can be found in states. For example, Pennsylvania prohibits "possess[ing] any instrument of crime with intent to employ it criminally,"[10] and Arkansas

Revenge: An Essay on the Political Economy of Pretextual Prosecution," *Columbia Law Review* 105, no. 2 (2005): 588–99; Erin Murphy, "Manufacturing Crime: Process, Pretext, and Criminal Justice," *Georgetown Law Journal* 97, no. 6 (2009): 1442–46.

[4] Cf. Douglas N. Husak, "The Nature and Justifiability of Nonconsummate Offenses," *Arizona Law Review* 37, no. 1 (1995): 168–69 (distinguishing between complex and simple nonconsummate offenses).

[5] N.Y. Penal Law § 265.03; see also Wyo. Stat. Ann. § 6-8-103; La. Stat. Ann. §14:95.

[6] Mo. Ann. Stat. § 569.180; see also Ala. Code § 13A-7-8.

[7] See, e.g., State v. Lake, 686 S.W.2d 19, 21 (Mo. Ct. App. 1984); McGlon v. State, 504 So.2d 745, 746 (Ala. Crim. App. 1987).

[8] Model Penal Code § 5.06 (American Law Institute, 1985).

[9] Model Penal Code § 5.06.

[10] 18 Pa. Stat. and Con. Stat. Ann. § 907. "Instrument of crime" is defined as "[a]nything specially made or specially adapted for criminal use" or "[a]nything used for criminal purposes and possessed by the actor under circumstances not manifestly appropriate for lawful uses it may have."

prohibits "possessing an instrument of crime . . . with a purpose to employ it criminally."[11]

Laws like this could cover cases like those of Jared Lee Loughner and Elliot Rodger, discussed in the previous chapter. Once they acquire weapons with intent to commit murder, law enforcement would not need to resort to the crime of attempted murder to apprehend them. As we saw in the previous chapter, a person who possesses a weapon, even if he has not "unleashed" a risk of harm, may still be considered blameworthy because taking steps toward harming a person with an intent to harm the person may be blameworthy, even in the absence of a law that prohibits such an act. In addition, that person may be blameworthy as a disobedient if he takes such steps with an intent to harm when there is a law against taking of such steps, a law that may be justified as a paternalistic measure to prevent people from being tempted to harm others or as a regulatory measure to control the amount of risk of harm at large. So there is conceptual continuity between incomplete attempt cases and possession with intent to harm cases, and the same normative considerations apply. However, possession with intent to harm is broader than incomplete attempt. In a typical incomplete attempt case, there is a specific offense that a person is supposedly attempting, so there may be an intended victim, or, if the crime is "victimless," there is some specific conduct that is contemplated as an end-point of the attempt.[12] However, in a case like possession of burglar's tools, that need not be the case.[13] A person could have an intent to harm that remains abstract and has not been specified but still be captured by possession with intent to harm laws.

III. Possession as an Offense of Defying a Regulatory Mandate

Another category of possession offenses is best illustrated with the example of guns. The world of gun laws is vast.[14] Some gun laws are akin to reckless endangerment offenses, discussed in the previous chapter. For instance, a law that provides for increased penalties for committing an offense while using, carrying, brandishing, or discharging a firearm may be rationalized to an extent as a law that punishes engaging in an activity in a particularly dangerous manner.[15]

[11] Ark. Code Ann. § 5-73-102.

[12] See Husak, "Nonconsummate Offenses," 161 (noting that "the claim that a right is violated by the commission of a criminal attempt" is tempting because "[u]sually it is possible to identify the person who would have been victimized had the attempted offense been successful").

[13] See Husak, "Nonconsummate Offenses," 162 ("Consider the possession of burglar's tools . . . [D]oes anyone have a right that [a person] not possess burglar's tools? If so, who?").

[14] For an overview, see Robert Spitzer, *Politics of Gun Control*, 7th ed. (Routledge, 2018), 227; James B. Jacobs, *Can Gun Control Work?* (Oxford University Press, 2002), 19–35.

[15] See 18 U.S.C. § 924(c); see also, e.g., Dean v. United States, 556 U.S. 568, 577 (2009) (holding that the ten-year mandatory minimum set forth in 18 U.S.C. § 924(c)(1)(A)(iii) applies if a gun is discharged in the course of a violent or drug trafficking crime whether on purpose or by accident).

Some gun laws having to do with manufacture, sale, and licensing regulate who can sell and buy, what can be sold and bought, and how. These laws look more like regulatory offenses that seek to regulate risks associated with various commercial activities, as discussed in Chapter 5 on regulatory offenses.[16] And then there are laws that criminalize behaviors that fall under the category of failing to help the state keep track of firearms, which may be classified as regulatory offenses or as offenses of failure to cooperate with law enforcement, which was covered in Chapter 4. And as just discussed, there are gun laws that resemble laws prohibiting incomplete attempts, if the laws prohibit possession of weapons with an intent to use them to harm others. This part focuses on laws that focus on restricting weapons possession by denying the ability to legally possess them to individuals that belong to certain groups.

In the United States, at the federal level, the primary legislation that controls possession of guns is the Gun Control Act of 1968,[17] which has been amended a few times since its enactment.[18] Under 18 U.S.C. § 922(g), a provision of the act, it is unlawful for a person who falls in one of many specified categories to possess a firearm.[19] Some of those categories are: a person who has been convicted of "a crime punishable by imprisonment for a term exceeding one year"; "an unlawful user of or [a person who is] addicted to any controlled substance"; a person "who has been adjudicated as a mental defective or who has been committed to a mental institution"; a person who is "unlawfully in the United States"; a person "who has been discharged from the Armed Forces under dishonorable conditions"; a person who has renounced his American citizenship; a person who is subject to a domestic violence restraining order;[20] and a person who has been convicted of a crime of domestic violence.

That this law singles out groups of people and designates them as those who are not eligible to possess guns has meant that a bulk of discussions about these laws has focused on whether the differential treatments are justifiable. The question is often framed in terms of whether there is a proper basis to conclude that people who belong to these categories are *especially* dangerous and should thus

[16] See Douglas N. Husak, "Guns and Drugs: Case Studies on the Principled Limited of the Criminal Sanction," *Law and Philosophy* 23, no. 5 (2004): 448; Spitzer, *Politics of Gun Control*, 81–87; Jacobs, *Can Gun Control Work?*, 3–14, 77–98.

[17] Pub. L. No. 90-618, 82 Stat. 1213 (1968).

[18] See Firearm Owners' Protection Act, Pub. L. No. 99-308, 100 Stat. 449 (1986) (codified as amended in scattered sections of 18 U.S.C.); Crime Control Act of 1990, Pub. L. No. 101-647, 104 Stat. 4789 (1990) (codified as amended, in pertinent parts, in scattered sections of 18 U.S.C.); Brady Handgun Violence Prevention Act, Pub. L. 103-159, 107 Stat. 1536 (1993); Violent Crime Control and Law Enforcement Act of 1994, Pub. L. No. 103-322, 108 Stat. 1796 (1994) (codified as amended, in pertinent part, at 18 U.S.C. § 922(g)(8)).

[19] 18 U.S.C. § 922(g).

[20] See also United States v. Rahimi, 602 U.S. 680 (2024).

be treated differently from others who are not classified as ineligible.[21] This issue of differential treatments often obscures the underlying issue of the potential wrongness of possession of guns as a general matter.

So why might it be wrong to possess a gun? Given that criminalization of gun possession is about controlling the risks of harm from gun violence,[22] an obvious question to ask is whether possessing a gun is a crime of risking harm, as discussed in the previous chapter. It is true that by possessing a gun, one increases the risk of harming others, but engaging in an act that increases the risk of harming others should not on its own be considered a wrong. There are two axes to consider: the amount of risk imposed and reasons to impose risks. As to the amount, it is the case that there are some objects, such as explosives, that one simply cannot possess *without* endangering others in ways that go beyond the threshold level of risk that people ordinarily expect from their everyday surroundings.[23] As a general matter, firearms such as long guns and handguns do not fall into this category.[24] And as to the reasons for risk impositions, even if there is some increased risk that accompanies owning guns, lots of things we do in life increase risks of harm to other people (like cooking, driving, playing sports) yet are not considered problematic as we have good reasons to engage in them. Similarly, people who defend individual ownership of guns argue that there are good reasons for people to possess guns—for self-defense, recreation, or tradition, depending on the type of firearm.[25]

Assuming, then, that we are talking about guns that can be possessed by individuals who intend to use them only for legitimate purposes and pose risks to others only up to a reasonable level (by taking appropriate safety precautions), we should not think of gun possession on its own as an act of unjustifiable risking of harm to other people. Gun possession translates into unacceptable danger, though, in cases where those who possess the guns seek to harm other people unjustifiably.[26] But this is the category of individuals already covered in the last part

[21] See, e.g., James B. Jacobs and Kimberley A. Potter, "Keeping Guns out of the Wrong Hands: The Brady Law and the Limits of Regulation," *Journal of Criminal Law & Criminology* 93, no. 1 (1995): 93–96; Husak, "Guns and Drugs," 447; William J. Vizzard, *Shots in the Dark* (Rowan & Littlefield Publishers, 2000), 36–52.

[22] Cf. Husak, "Guns and Drugs," 443–44.

[23] See, e.g., Ariz. Rev. Stat. Ann. § 13-3103 (prohibiting the knowing storage of more than fifty pounds of explosives); 42 U.S.C. § 2077 (prohibiting the unauthorized possession of special nuclear material); Ohio Rev. Code Ann. § 4163.02 (prohibiting the possession of "any special nuclear material, by-product material, production facility, or utilization facility" without the requisite license or permit); Alaska Stat. Ann. § 18.45.020 (same); NY Penal Law § 265.01(7) (prohibiting the knowing possession of a bullet containing an explosive substance designed to detonate upon impact).

[24] See Spitzer, *Politics of Gun Control*, 79–81; Jacobs, *Can Gun Control Work?*, 38–41; Gary Kleck, *Targeting Guns: Firearms and Their Control* (Aldine de Gruyter, 1997), 85–86.

[25] See Husak, "Guns and Drugs," 480–83; Spitzer, *Politics of Gun Control*, 87–88; Jacobs, *Can Gun Control Work?*, 14–15; Kleck, *Targeting Guns*, 74–75.

[26] See, e.g., Husak, "Guns and Drugs," 491 ("There would be no objection to criminal liability for gun . . . possession if persons could not be punished unless they intended to cause harm by using their guns . . . .").

when we considered the laws that prohibit possession of weapons with an intent to harm others. What we are considering now is different, as laws like 18 U.S.C. § 922(g) do not have an "intent to harm" element.[27] Rather, the laws presume that people who fall into certain categories are too dangerous to possess firearms.

These laws have been criticized extensively. Douglas Husak, for instance, points out that the categories of people who are not allowed to possess guns—such as "[f]elons, drug users or illegal aliens"[28]—generate prohibitions that are "almost certainly overinclusive,"[29] given that "[m]ost (and perhaps all) of the disqualified groups contain significant numbers of members who are *not* dangerous, and whose gun ownership would not create a substantial risk of harm—at least, no greater than that of the average person."[30] Husak concludes that "some individuals are punished for owning guns notwithstanding the fact that they are not dangerous."[31] Similar arguments have been made by many others recently.[32]

As we saw in the previous chapter, even those who are considered to be "dangerous," as in those who possess weapons with intent to harm others, may not be blameworthy enough to be considered criminally culpable. Husak's complaint about laws that prohibit possession of weapons by people with certain characteristics leads to the conclusion that such possession laws are even worse than the laws that target those who intend to harm because the possession laws sweep those who intend to harm others and those who do not into one category of suspect individuals who are not to be trusted with weapons. If it is not clear whether a person who possesses a weapon with intent to unjustifiably harm others is blameworthy, then a law that does not even attempt to distinguish between those who intend to harm others and those who do not is *a fortiori* overbroad. This means that the laws are likely to, at least at times, target those people who are not blameworthy at all. In fact, the categorical approach may be both over- and underinclusive in that the bans may cover those who can have weapons without unduly risking harm to others while failing to capture those who are too dangerous to have guns.

One reaction we might have to this state of affairs is that the laws should be redesigned so that only those who should not have guns because they cannot be trusted with them should be prohibited from possessing them, and we can then ask the further question of whether they are blameworthy. Another reaction is to ask why the laws look the way they do. One simple explanation may be the difficulty of more fine-grained determinations. For instance, one could imagine a law

27 18 U.S.C. § 922(g).
28 Husak, "Guns and Drugs," 479.
29 Husak, "Guns and Drugs," 477.
30 Husak, "Guns and Drugs," 478.
31 Husak, "Guns and Drugs," 479.
32 See Dru Stevenson, "In Defense of Felon-in-Possession Laws," *Cardozo Law Review* 43, no. 4 (2022): 1575–76 (collecting citations).

that prohibits people with felony convictions from possessing weapons but only those whose felony convictions are from violent offenses. Or the law could institute an individualized fact-finding to determine whether a person with a felony conviction is dangerous or not.

There are reasons to think that neither approach would work,[33] but for our purposes, let us assume that the laws are as broadly and crudely written as they are for reasons of controlling risks associated with guns.[34] The laws would cover those who are not dangerous,[35] and, as R. A. Duff explains, "[t]o justify creating such offences we must be able to say to the citizen that, even if she is wholly competent, careful, and reliable, she should accept such constraints on her own freedom because this is the only effective way of ensuring tolerably safe conduct by others who are less competent or reliable."[36] What does a thought like that suggest for the question of blameworthiness of offenders? We might say the following: because guns are dangerous, not only to those who are around the gun owners but also to the owners themselves, there are good reasons for the state to regulate the amount of risk that is associated with guns by instituting broad bans that are overinclusive. Once such bans are in place, then those who possess guns despite prohibitions that apply to them would be engaging in acts of disobedience.

But why is it wrong to disobey laws that take freedom away from the responsible and irresponsible alike? One answer is the same answer we have been giving: gun laws can be justified for reasons of risk regulation and perhaps even paternalism, and those who willfully violate such laws are undermining the effectiveness of such laws by introducing an element of risk into society, setting a bad example for others, and contributing to a push toward an arms race that would make everyone worse off.[37] Or, those who are in violation of laws prohibiting gun possession may be free riders. Say, plausibly, that the overall risk of harm from guns in a community can be brought down considerably if the state prohibits gun possession across the board. It means that once everyone gives up his or her gun, individuals in the community can move about more freely without fear of being gunned down. However, when an individual opts out of the

[33] See, e.g., Stevens, "In Defense of Felon-in-Possession Laws," 1605–29; cf. Samuel W. Buell, "The Upside of Overbreadth," *New York University Law Review* 83, no. 5 (2008): 1501–26.

[34] Cf. James Forman Jr., *Locking Up Our Own: Crime and Punishment in Black America* (Farra, Straus and Giroux, 2017), 47–77.

[35] Cf. A. P. Simester and Andreas von Hirsch, *Crimes, Harms, and Wrongs: On the Principles of Criminalisation* (Hart Publishing, 2014), 57 (describing "prohibitions of conduct which ordinary is not risky, but which is proscribed because *some* actors may endanger others").

[36] R. A. Duff, *Criminal Attempts* (Oxford University Press, 1997), 135.

[37] Cf. Spitzer, *Politics of Gun Control*, 81–82 (discussing the "weapon instrumentality effect," referring to the view that "the death rate and degree of injury associated with crimes involving guns is far higher than it would be if the guns were not involved."); see also Spitzer, *Politics of Gun Control*, 244–52.

system and comes into possession of a gun, that person would be having at their disposal an instrument of harm that others in the community do not hold, since only the gun possessor, except for law enforcement, would be armed. In such a case, that person enjoys a baseline level of safety thanks to the restraints others in the community have shown and an enhanced level of safety due to their gun possession, making the person a free rider on other people's efforts.[38] This is the sense in which possession offenses can be crimes of disobedience that are potentially blameworthy.

The argument given here does not justify the current categories of those who are not allowed to have guns.[39] The argument for now is only that one *could* justify having overbroad prohibitions on possession for public safety and that one *could* defend the idea that even non-dangerous individuals who go against such prohibitions are blameworthy, not necessarily for risking harm or posing danger to others, but for disobeying the law.

IV. Possession as a Market Participation Offense I: Child Pornography

Possession of child pornography, typically defined as visual depiction of an actual minor engaging in a sexually explicit act,[40] is a crime throughout the United States, both at the federal and state levels.[41] As the following headlines illustrate, child pornography possession often invites harsh punishments: "Justices Decline Case on a 200-Year Sentence for Man Who Possessed Child Pornography"; "Life

[38] For a similar argument, see Victor Tadros, "Wrongness and Criminalization," in *The Routledge Companion to Philosophy of Law*, ed. Andrei Marmor (Routledge, 2012), 168–69.

[39] We will return to the question of potential limiting principles to this logic in Chapters 10 through 12.

[40] See e.g., 18 U.S.C. § 2256; Del. Code. Ann. Tit. 11, § 1111; Tex. Penal Code § 43.26; S.D. Codified Laws § 22-24A-35. For some discussions of definitional issues, see Carissa Byrne Hessick, "Setting Definitional Limits for the Child Pornography Exception," in *Refining Child Pornography Law: Crime, Language, and Social Consequences*, ed. Carissa Byrne Hessick (University of Michigan Press, 2016), 57–58, 63–66; Amy Adler, "The '*Dost* Test' in Child Pornography Law: 'Trial by Rorschach Test,'" in *Refining Child Pornography Law: Crime, Language, and Social Consequences*, ed. Carissa Byrne Hessick (University of Michigan Press, 2016), 81–108; Mary Graw Leary, "The Language of Child Sexual Abuse and Exploitation," in *Refining Child Pornography Law: Crime, Language, and Social Consequences*, ed. Carissa Byrne Hessick (University of Michigan Press, 2016), 109–44; Audrey Rogers, "The Dignitary Harm of Child Pornography—From Producers to Possessors," in *Refining Child Pornography Law: Crime, Language, and Social Consequences*, ed. Carissa Byrne Hessick (University of Michigan Press, 2016), 172–73; Carissa Byrne Hessick, "The Limits of Child Pornography," *Indiana Law Journal* 89, no. 4 (2014): 1438–39, 1455–61; Amy Adler, "Inverting the First Amendment," *University of Pennsylvania Law Review* 149, no. 4 (2001): 936–61; Suzanne Ost, *Child Pornography and Sexual Grooming: Legal and Societal Responses* (Cambridge University Press, 2009), 123–30.

[41] See 18 U.S.C. § 2252(A)(a)(5); Del. Code. Ann. Tit. 11, § 1111; Tex. Penal Code § 43.26; S.D. Codified Laws § 22-24A-35; Wis. Stat. Ann. § 948.12; Va. Code Ann. § 18.2-374.1:1; Minn. Stat. Ann. § 617.247.

Sentence for Possession of Child Pornography Spurs Debate Over Severity"; "Ex-Headmaster Sentenced to 50 Years for Child Porn."[42] Such punishments are staggering, especially given that at one point the US Supreme Court said in *Stanley v. Georgia*, a 1969 case declaring an obscenity law unconstitutional, that "[i]f the First Amendment means anything, it means that a State has no business telling a man, sitting alone in his own house, what books he may read or what films he may watch" and that "[o]ur whole constitutional heritage rebels at the thought of giving government the power to control men's minds."[43]

The Court held later in 1990 in *Osborne v. Ohio* that despite its holding in *Stanley*, possession of child pornography, even in private, is not constitutionally protected.[44] Still, setting aside the constitutional issue addressed in the two cases, the question that the *Stanley* case highlights is this: What exactly is wrong with possession of child pornography if all that is done by a person is possession of objectionable materials? It is obvious that production of child pornography with a child (as opposed to using an adult posing as a child or computer-simulated images of a child[45]) physically and sexually abuses the child with long-term consequences and is thus a highly harmful and serious moral wrong.[46] It is also the case that a person who has images of children being sexually abused should not make them more available by distributing them to others, as doing so can exacerbate the harm that the production of images has done.[47] So production of child pornography is morally blameworthy, and so is its distribution, and that much is uncontroversial.

But what about possession by itself?[48] We may assume that the person who possesses child pornography downloaded it or received it from another person but that the possessor has no intention of distributing it to others.[49] On this issue,

[42] Linda Greenhouse, "Justices Decline Case on 200-Year Sentence for Man Who Possessed Child Pornography," *New York Times*, February 27, 2007; Erica Goode, "Life Sentence for Child Pornography Spurs Debate Over Severity," *New York Times*, November 4, 2011; Cris Barrish and Jessica Masulli Reyes, "Ex-Headmaster Sentenced to 50 Years for Child Porn," *USA Today*, April 24, 2025; see also Carissa Byrne Hessick, "Questioning the Modern Criminal Justice Focus on Child Pornography Possession," in *Refining Child Pornography Law: Crime, Language, and Social Consequences*, ed. Carissa Byrne Hessick (University of Michigan Press, 2016), 148–50; Carissa Byrne Hessick, "Disentangling Child Pornography from Child Sex Abuse," *Washington University Law Review* 88, no. 4 (2010): 856–64.

[43] Stanley v. Georgia, 394 U.S. 557, 565 (1969).

[44] See Osborne v. Ohio, 495 U.S. 103, 108–11 (1990).

[45] See Ashcroft v. Free Speech Coalition, 535 U.S. 234, 258 (2002).

[46] See Free Speech Coalition, 535 U.S. at 244 ("The sexual abuse of a child is a most serious crime and an act repugnant to the moral instincts of a decent people."); see also Ost, *Child Pornography*, 104–05; Rogers, "Dignitary Harm," 170–74; New York v. Ferber, 458 U.S. 747, 758 (1982); Osborne, 495 U.S. at 109.

[47] See Ost, *Child Pornography*, 107; Ferber, 458 U.S. at 759.

[48] For a discussion, see Hessick, "Disentangling Pornography from Abuse," 864–70.

[49] But see Rogers, "The Dignitary Harm," 168–69 (questioning the distinction between receipt and possession). It is easy for one to be a "distributor" even if one does nothing but receive and possess an image due to the nature of peer-to-peer networks, but there is a moral distinction to be made between receipt and possession and making it available to new individuals.

it has been argued that even if a child depicted in a pornographic way is unaware of the existence of the image, "those who . . . view child pornography harm the child's inherent right of human dignity not to be viewed in this fashion."[50] The idea is that a person who views (or possibly even just possesses) an image of a child being sexually abused wrongs the person depicted in that way. That is fair. When the actor Jennifer Lawrence's nude photographs were stolen from her phone and made public, she was angry not just at those who stole them and websites that spread them, but those who viewed them and said: "Anybody who looked at those pictures . . . should cower with shame. . . . I didn't tell you that you could look at my naked body."[51] The wrongness of possession of child pornography, then, is analogous to the wrongness of the voyeurism of a peeping tom.[52] Typically, instead of the violation taking place by peeking through a window, looking at child pornography violates the depicted person from a distance, but the core wrongdoing is the same. The long distance between the looker and the victim does not alter the moral significance of the act.

Perhaps an account like this explains the core moral wrongfulness of possession of child pornography, but it is woefully incomplete. The privacy account that analogizes possession of child pornography to being a peeping tom does not reflect the horror of being a victim of child pornography, as if it is only a matter of having someone creepily taking an illicit look. Because of the nature of the internet, an image of child pornography can be distributed to and viewed by millions of people and can stay on the internet forever or disappear and then reappear years later.[53] As the US Supreme Court said in *New York v. Ferber*, images of sexual abuse of children are "a permanent record" of the abuse and "the harm to the child is exacerbated by their circulation."[54] Similarly, the Court said in *Osborne* that the images' "continued existence causes the child victims continuing harm by haunting the children in years to come."[55] When victims of child pornography report harm to their lives from child pornography, the source of their distress has to do with the sense that people all over the world can view them and may even recognize the depicted persons in real life, affecting them

[50] Rogers, "The Dignitary Harm," 177.

[51] Sam Kashner, "Both Huntress and Prey," *Vanity Fair*, October 20, 2024.

[52] See 15 Cal. Penal Code 647(j); 16 Ga. Code 16-11-61; 16 S.C. Code Ann. 16-17-470; John Draeger, "What Peeping Tom Did Wrong," *Ethical Theory and Moral Practice* 14, no. 1 (2011): 48 ("[F]ew of us would want video cameras in our showers even if no harm was done to us and we remain unaware of another's peeping. It seems creepy."); Daniel O. Nathan, "Just looking: Voyeurism and the Grounds of Privacy," *Public Affairs Quarterly* 4, no. 4 (1990): 373–81; Stuart P. Green, "To See and Be Seen: Reconstructing the Law of Voyeurism and Exhibitionism," *American Criminal Law Review* 54, no. 2 (2018): 216–39.

[53] For some discussion of internet distribution, see Asaf Harduf, "Criminalization Downloads Evil: Reexamining the Approach to Electronic Possession When Child Pornography Goes International," *Boston University International Law Journal* 34, no. 2 (2016): 292–93.

[54] Ferber, 458 U.S. at 759.

[55] Osborne, 495 U.S. at 111.

both personally and professionally, and that the victims may never be able to fully escape the nightmare.[56] Such reasonable fears make it impossible for the victims to find closure, heal, and move on from the abuse.[57] The nature of the harm experienced by the victims of child pornography is then quite different from being violated when a person looks at you through a peephole. Erin Andrews, a victim of surreptitious recording of her in her hotel room, suffered from harm resulting not just from a person looking and recording but also making it widely available.[58]

There seems to be a mismatch, then, between the wrong that an individual viewing child pornography does to the depicted individual and the harm that is inflicted on the victim. Each individual plays a minuscule role in the overall harm from circulation of an image. The victim does not know who is viewing the images, when, and how many times, and a person may look at an image hundreds of times by himself in the privacy of his own home without adding to the amount of distress experienced by the victim.[59] However, the overall harm derived from the impact of the entire group of individuals acting more or less independently from one another can be profoundly and irreparably damaging to a person's life.[60] Because the amount of harm each person contributes to the overall harm is so small, the legal system has had trouble determining what sort of monetary damages to assign to each person who contributes to the harm in a scheme that seeks to compensate victims of child pornography by collecting from wrongdoers and distributing the funds to victims.[61] When we focus on the victim and the amount of harm done to the victim, not just through the production or distribution of child pornography, but from possession and viewing of the problematic images, the violation is unspeakably serious, but when we focus on each individual possessor, the wrong done seems almost trivial, negligible.

[56] Osborne, 495 U.S. at 111; Paul G. Cassell, "Not Just 'Kiddie Porn': The Significant Harms of Child Pornography Possession," in *The Routledge Companion to Philosophy of Law*, ed. Andrei Marmor (Routledge, 2012), 191–93; Audrey Rogers, "Child Pornography's Forgotten Victims," *Pace Law Review* 28, no. 4 (2008): 847, 853–54; Ferber, 458 U.S. at 760 n.10; Free Speech Coalition, 535 U.S. at 249–50.

[57] Paroline v. United States, 572 U.S. 434, 440 (2014); Ferber, 458 U.S. at 758–59. For a discussion, see Anthony M. Dillof, "Possession, Child Pornography, and Proportionality: Criminal Liability for Aggregate Harm Offenses," *Florida State University Law Review* 44, no. 4 (2017): 1356–57; Rogers, "The Dignitary Harm," 174–76.

[58] See Scott Stump, "Exclusive: Erin Andrews Gets Emotional Remembering When She Called Her Parents About Stalker Recording Her," *Today*, November 22, 2023 ("I used to walk in the stadiums where there's 70, 80,000 people, and I thought every single one of these people have seen me naked . . . And I was like, 'When am I going to stop feeling like that?'").

[59] See Hessick, "Limits of Child Pornography," 1463.

[60] See Rogers, "The Dignitary Harm," 174; cf. Joel Feinberg, *The Moral Limits of the Criminal Law Volume 1: Harm to Others* (Oxford University Press, 1984), 225–28 (discussing accumulative harms).

[61] See generally Paroline, 572 U.S. 434 (2014). For further discussion, see Dillof, "Aggregate Harm Offenses," 1362–66; Cassell, "Not Just 'Kiddie Porn,'" 196–203.

This is one of the reasons why the dominant narrative for justifying criminalizing possession of child pornography is not about an individual's act of looking at something he is not supposed to be looking at, but about the harm that the overall system of distribution of child pornography does to individual victims.[62] In *Osborne*, the US Supreme Court considered a law that prohibited possession or viewing of child pornography. The majority had no trouble finding the law to be constitutional. The Court said that the state enacted the laws "in order to protect the victims of child pornography" and noted the legislative judgment that "the use of children as subjects of pornographic materials is harmful to the physiological, emotional, and mental health of the child."[63] The Court *then* said that it is reasonable for the state "to conclude that it will decrease the production of child pornography if it penalizes those who possess and view the product, thereby decreasing demand."[64] To the defense's objection that the law's criminalization of mere possession and viewing of child pornography was overbroad, the Court responded that "much of the child pornography market has been driven underground" and "it is now difficult, if not impossible, to solve the child pornography problem by only attacking production and distribution."[65]

The law, in other words, does not have much to do with the ways in which possessing and viewing child pornography can directly harm a child. Rather, the law seeks to prevent sexual exploitation of children by destroying the market for child pornography,[66] especially because going after the problem by more directly targeting the site at which harm is inflicted, namely, at the production stage, is perceived to be insufficiently effective.[67] Understood this way, the wrongness of possession of child pornography acquires a new dimension. It is not just that a person violates another person's privacy by viewing a private record, as that understates the magnitude of the problem. The wrongdoing consists of the person's interference with the state's effort to shut down an entire industry that does grave damage. Child pornography possession is not just a criminal privacy violation but a crime of disobedience, where disobedience takes the form of interference with the state's attempt to deal with a serious problem.

[62] See Hessick, "Limits of Child Pornography," 1461–62; Ost, *Child Pornography*, 113–15.

[63] Osborne, 495 U.S. at 109.

[64] Osborne, 495 U.S. at 109.

[65] Osborne, 495 U.S. at 110. The Court also reasoned that the law criminalizing possession of child pornography encourages destruction of it, thereby eliminating the materials that "permanently record the victim's abuse." Osborne, 495 U.S. at 111.

[66] For criticism of the market theory, see Carissa Byrne Hessick, "The Expansion of Child Pornography Law," *New Criminal Law Review* 21, no. 3 (2018): 341; Ost, *Child Pornography*, 113–16; Dillof, "Aggregate Harm Offenses," 1354; Harduf, "Criminalization Downloads Evil," 296–97; Hessick, "Child Pornography Possession," 152.

[67] See Hessick, "Expansion of Child Pornography Law," 341–42; Ferber, 458 U.S. at 759 (stating that "the distribution network for child pornography must be closed if the production of material which requires the sexual exploitation of children is to be effectively controlled").

V. Possession as a Market Participation Offense II: Drugs

Another type of possession offense that is often justified in terms of the desirability of destroying harmful markets has to do with drugs. Drug laws, like gun laws, are of many different types. As we saw in Chapter 5, the Food, Drug, and Cosmetic Act[68] prohibits introduction into interstate commerce of "any food, drug, device, tobacco product, or cosmetic that is adulterated or misbranded"[69] or of any unapproved drug,[70] where drugs are defined as, among other things "articles intended for use in the diagnosis, cure, mitigation, treatment, or prevention of disease."[71] There are many other rules that regulate manufacturing and sale of drugs.[72] These laws, like some of the gun laws referred to above, are regulatory offenses that regulate risks associated with the distribution of drugs that people are legally allowed to possess and use so as to keep the risk of consumption of certain medical products at a tolerable level.[73]

In the United States, though, the law that looms large at the federal level when it comes to drugs is not the Food, Drug, and Cosmetic Act administered by the Food and Drug Administration but the Controlled Substances Act, which regulates "drugs and other substances" that are thought to carry risks of abuse or dependence, and is enforced by the Drug Enforcement Administration within the US Department of Justice.[74]

The Controlled Substances Act categorizes substances into different "schedules," from Schedules I through V, with Schedule I substances carrying a "high potential for abuse," with "no currently accepted medical use" and "a lack of accepted safety for use . . . under medical supervision,"[75] and Schedule

[68] 21 U.S.C. §§ 301 et seq.

[69] 21 U.S.C. § 331(a).

[70] 21 U.S.C. §§ 331(d), 355.

[71] 21 U.S.C. § 321(g). Defining "drugs" is not straightforward. For a discussion, see Margaret P. Battin et al., *Drugs and Justice: Seeking a Consistent, Coherent, Comprehensive View* (Oxford University Press, 2007), 14–18.

[72] For a summary, see Scott Bass and William McConagha, "FDA Enforcement Powers," in *Food and Drug Law and Regulation*, 3rd ed., ed. David G. Adams et al. (Food and Drugs Law Institute, 2015), 740–44; Battin et al., *Drugs and Justice*, 62–65.

[73] Cf. Battin et al., *Drugs and Justice*, 134 ("[D]rugs produce their effects by biochemical action on the body. In order to have a physiological effect . . . , drugs must be ingested, inhaled, injected, or otherwise absorbed . . . [I]n general, any drug with active ingredients can be innocuous or toxic depending on dose.").

[74] 21 U.S.C. § 811. The Controlled Substances Act is Title II of the Comprehensive Drug Abuse Prevention and Control Act. See Pub. L. No. 91-513, 84 Stat. 1236 (1970). See also Battin et al., *Drugs and Justice*, 56–58. For a discussion of problems with classification regarding what belongs to the ambit of the Controlled Substances Act, see *Drugs and Justice*, 84–88; 157–60.

[75] 21 U.S.C. § 812(b)(1). The most notorious scheduling decision made by the federal government is classification of marijuana as a Schedule I drug, though that may change with the new proposal to classify it as a Schedule III drug, which means that it "has a potential for abuse less than the drugs or other substances in schedules I and II," the drug "has a currently accepted medical use in treatment in the United States," and "[a]buse of the drug . . . may lead to moderate or low physical dependence or high psychological dependence." 21 U.S.C. § 812(b)(3); Eileen Sullivan, "The US Is

V substances with "a low potential for abuse" and "a currently accepted medical use" with some risk of "limited physical dependence or psychological dependence," and substances with characteristics in-between those poles.[76] Scheduling of drugs can be done by Congress legislatively[77] or by the Drug Enforcement Agency[78] in consultation with the Department of Health and Human Services.[79] There may also be international treaty obligations to regulate certain substances, and the law specifies how such treaty obligations are to be met through the provisions of the Controlled Substances Act.[80]

Once a substance is classified as a controlled substance and placed on a Schedule, numerous regulations, such as production quotas, registration, labeling, record-keeping, order form, and prescription requirements, kick in for those who manufacture, distribute, or dispense the substance,[81] and violations of such regulations may lead to civil and criminal penalties, similar to violations of regulatory offenses.[82] Substances listed on Schedule I, as they have no medical use, cannot be obtained by individuals, whereas substances on the rest of the Schedules may be dispensed as authorized.[83] The law prohibits manufacturing, distributing, and dispensing of controlled substances except as authorized.[84] The law also prohibits hiring minors for illicit trafficking of controlled substances,[85] investing proceeds from illicit drug trade,[86] and selling drug paraphernalia.[87] Possession is prohibited as well, whether it is done with or without intent to distribute, and it is this prohibition that is the focus of this discussion.[88] Many of these rules under the Controlled Substances Act—like those having to do with prescription, registration of vendors, record-keeping, and so on—are about managing risks associated with the manufacture and distribution of drugs. In this sense, they are like the regulatory offenses discussed in Chapter 5.

Easing Marijuana Restrictions. Here's How It Works," *New York Times*, May 16, 2024. For a discussion, see David Pozen, *The Constitution of the War on Drugs* (Oxford University Press, 2024), 50–63; Matthew B. Lawrence and David E. Pozen, "Drug Scheduling as Institutional Design," *Harvard Law Review*: 139 (forthcoming 2026). It is unclear at the moment, as the book goes to press, whether the rescheduling will in fact occur and, if so, when.

76 21 U.S.C. § 812(b).
77 21 U.S.C. § 812(c).
78 The Attorney General is given the authority to classify substances, but that authority has been delegated to the Drug Enforcement Agency. 21 U.S.C. § 811; 28 C.F.R. § 0.100(b).
79 21 U.S.C. § 811.
80 21 U.S.C. §§ 811, 801(a).
81 See, e.g., 21 U.S.C. §§ 822, 825–29.
82 21 U.S.C. §§ 842–43.
83 21 U.S.C. § 829.
84 21 U.S.C. § 841(a)(1).
85 21 U.S.C. § 861.
86 21 U.S.C. § 854.
87 21 U.S.C. § 863.
88 21 U.S.C. §§ 841(a)(1), 844(a); Forman, *Locking Up Our Own*, 164.

However, seeing laws like the Controlled Substances Act merely as a collection of regulatory rules would miss the big picture. As the historian David Herzberg has summarized, in the United States, there are "two different systems of drug control"—one "system set up to enable doctor-visiting consumers ('patients') to purchase desirable but dangerous goods as safely as possible" and another "to police and punish buyers and sellers in informal drug markets ('peddlers' and 'dope fiends')."[89] The first system contains regulatory offenses, whereas the second system is better known as the War on Drugs. The Controlled Substances Act is the law most associated with the War on Drugs.[90]

Possession of controlled substances is criminalized in two different provisions in the Controlled Substances Act. Under 21 U.S.C. § 841, it is "unlawful for any person knowingly or intentionally to manufacture, distribute, or dispense, or possess with intent to manufacture, distribute, or dispense, a controlled substance."[91] And under 21 U.S.C. § 844, it is "unlawful for any person knowingly or intentionally to possess a controlled substance unless such substance was obtained directly, or pursuant to a valid prescription or order, from a practitioner, while acting in the course of his professional practice, or except as otherwise authorized."[92] Section 841 crimes carry mandatory prison sentences, the length depending on the type and quantity of drugs and criminal history of the individual being sentenced.[93] Section 844 authorizes prison sentences and mandates prison sentences for repeat offenders.[94]

To understand what is supposedly wrong with committing these offenses, we might start by comparing possession of drugs to the other possession offenses we have discussed: guns and child pornography. Guns, even if they are acquired for self-defense purposes, are instruments that are designed to inflict harm on others. And even if a person plays no role in producing child pornography, just having it in one's possession can be a violation of another person's rights since

[89] David Herzberg, "Origins and Outcomes of the US Medicine–Drug Divide," in *The Oxford Handbook of Global Drug History* (Oxford University Press, 2022), 326. He adds: "It is important to recognize that both of these fledgling systems depended on, and helped to strengthen, social hierarchies of race, class, and gender. This is relatively easy to see in the case of informal markets, where Chinese, African American, and immigrant buyers and sellers were depicted in openly racist and sexually sensationalist terms." Herzberg, "Origins and Outcomes"; see also David Herzberg, *White Market Drugs: Big Pharma and the Hidden History of Addiction in America* (University of Chicago Press, 2020), 14–44; Pozen, *War on Drugs*, 12 ("[T]he war on drugs has been marked by a *punitive* and *prohibitive* approach to drug control rather than an approach that regulates potentially dangerous substances primarily through education, taxation, licensing, zoning, medical supervision, age requirements, or the like."); Battin et al., *Drugs and Justice*, 32–33, 77–80, 82–84; Kimani Paul-Emile, "Making Sense of Drug Regulation: A Theory of Law for Drug Control Policy," *Cornell Journal of Law and Public Policy* 19, no. 3 (2010): 703–11.

[90] See, e.g., Pozen, *War on Drugs*, 12.

[91] 21 U.S.C. § 841(a)(1).

[92] 21 U.S.C. § 844(a).

[93] 21 U.S.C. § 841(b).

[94] 21 U.S.C. § 844(a).

the victim depicted in it cannot have consented to the image being produced, distributed, or possessed. Drugs are different because, unlike guns, one could use drugs as they are intended to be used without harming another person and, unlike child pornography, there is no inherent rights violation that accompanies possession of drugs. The most likely "victim" of a person who possesses drugs for one's personal use is oneself because doing drugs may harm the person who uses them, and self-harm is generally not criminal, even if society may deem it important to reduce instances of it. And, furthermore, if one desires to use drugs and voluntarily chooses to do so, then even those who "manufacture, distribute, or dispense" drugs to the individual are not necessarily wrongdoers, either, as all they are doing is engaging in activities that facilitate another person's use of drugs.

Of course, there are limits to these propositions. If a person who is seeking a drug is addicted to it and is simply satisfying a craving without having a concrete plan for getting better, then giving more drugs to that person may be morally wrong, at least partly because the person who seeks the drugs may not be fully autonomous. If the person is not fully autonomous, giving a person who is addicted to drugs more drugs may be morally wrong unless, say, doing so is part of treatment for addiction.[95] Or if a person who is seeking a drug is doing so in order to commit suicide with it, then facilitating that transaction may also be morally wrong (except perhaps in cases of terminal illnesses under certain conditions) whether or not the person seeking the drug is fully autonomous.

However, the laws that prohibit possession of illicit substances with or without intent to distribute cut much more broadly and are not limited to situations where making drugs available to other people can foreseeably harm them. The law has just two categories—authorized and unauthorized conduct—and if a person engages in any unauthorized conduct with regard to controlled substances, the person has offended the law. The authorized/unauthorized distinction is articulated in terms of scheduling of drugs and those authorized to handle them as opposed to the question of when a particular conduct involving a controlled substance may be morally permissible all things considered.

Instead of letting these complications overwhelm the moral analysis, we can start by discussing recreational drug use in violation of the Controlled Substances Act, where "recreational use," as Husak defines it, means "consumption that is intended to promote the pleasure, happiness, or euphoria of the user."[96] In debates over legalization of marijuana, its potential use as pain reliever

[95] See, e.g., Bjarke Nielsen and Esben Houborg, "Addiction, Drugs, and Experimentation: Methadone Maintenance Treatment Between 'In Here' and 'Out There,'" *Contemporary Drug Problems* 42, no. 4 (2015): 280–84 (discussing use of substitution treatment in Denmark).
[96] Douglas N. Husak, *Drugs and Rights* (Cambridge University Press, 1992), 44.

for those with illnesses has received much attention.[97] But the problem with using medical marijuana as a paradigmatic instance of morally permissible drug use is that it is tempting to think of medical marijuana as an exception to a justifiable prohibition of marijuana as a general matter.[98] That is, asking what is wrong with possession of illicit drugs by using medical marijuana as a counterexample is akin to asking what is wrong with murder by using self-defense or assisted suicide as a counterexample. The possibility of justifiable self-defense or assisted suicide does not take away from wrongness of murder, and one might similarly endorse medical uses of marijuana as justifiable in ways that do not take away from wrongness of having and using marijuana. Therefore, focusing on medical marijuana obscures the issue of wrongness of use and possession of controlled substances. We should focus on recreational use of marijuana instead.

Recreational uses of drugs present relatively clean questions of wrongness of possession. The idea behind recreational use of drugs is enjoyment, so it does not immediately raise the question of the issue of serious self-harm and those who assist it; nor does it raise the question of potential permission to engage in a pro tanto wrong in situations of acute physical suffering from ailment. And when we contemplate the use of illicit drugs for recreational purposes, it is hard to see what is exactly morally wrong with such uses, and by implication, it is also hard to see what is wrong with possession of illicit substances, even with intent to distribute (or, for that matter, manufacturing, distributing, and dispensing of such).

One might respond by saying that drugs are dangerous, and that recreational uses of drugs are dangerous, but it is not so unrealistic to assume that responsible, well-informed adults have the ability to use such drugs without risking overdose or acquiring debilitating addictions.[99] Or, at least, responsible adults have such ability to the same extent we assume they do in consuming alcohol and tobacco and the same ability as those who engage in potentially harmful athletic and outdoor activities, like football, skiing, swimming, boating, and bicycling. And even if dangers of recreational uses of drugs are real and difficult to manage, drug users, assuming they are fully autonomous adults, would be right to object to paternalistic interference with their right to control what goes into their bodies, even if they may ultimately harm themselves in the process. After all, it is not a crime to possess and consume alcohol and tobacco, not to mention excessively sugary desserts and foods high in saturated fat, even if they are bad for people's health and are difficult for weak-willed individuals to resist on their own.

[97] See, e.g., Gonzales v. Raich, 545 U.S. 1 (2005) (affirming the constitutionality of applying the Controlled Substances Act to users and growers of marijuana for medical purposes).

[98] Cf. Pozen, *War on Drugs*, 65 (lamenting the focus on medical marijuana in the legalization of marijuana debate as the approach has "undersold the case for reform" by ignoring "the benefits that most users believe they derive" from the drug).

[99] For a compelling extended account making such a case, see Carl L. Hart, *Drug Use for Grown-Ups: Chasing Liberty in the Land of Fear* (Penguin Books, 2021).

If responsible recreational drug use is not morally wrong, then it appears that those who possess illicit substances with or without intent to distribute would be facing prosecution for innocent conduct. Is that true? James Forman points out that that is not how people have always seen things. He writes that while "drug users and sellers have become the paradigmatic 'non-violent offenders'" in today's conversation, such a characterization would have seemed "foreign . . . to many during the crack era"[100] because there was a common perception, at least among the prosecutors he encountered in the 1990s, that "anybody who participated in the distribution chain bore a moral responsibility for all the blood that had flowed" as a result of the illicit drug market.[101] Forman documents such rhetoric from the era, including: "There was not a single rock of crack anywhere in the District of Columbia that wasn't stained with the blood of some mother's child"; "[d]rug users, whether occasional or regular, are stockholders in an organized crime"; and "[drug] buyers are the financiers of the whole narcotics enterprise," as "drug trafficking would not exist" without them.[102]

The rhetoric is overheated, typical of political commentary from those in positions of power in the government, but statements that the illicit drug trade causes tremendous harm are not atypical. Here is a partial list describing "[t]he damage associated with illicit drugs" from an academic piece: "several million dependent users"; "an illicit industry generating tens of billions of dollars in revenue"; "recent cocaine or heroin use by nearly half of all those arrested for serious crimes in big cities"; "hundreds of thousands of people, many of them very young, regularly committing felony drug-selling offenses"; "enormous amounts of violence associated with drug transactions, or at least with weapons obtained for use in, and with proceeds of, drug selling"; "neighborhood disruption due to the disorder and violence of open illicit markets"; and "injection drug use as a strong second to sex in the transmission of HIV."[103]

[100] Forman, *Locking Up Our Own*, 175.
[101] Forman, *Locking Up Our Own*, 175.
[102] Forman, *Locking Up Our Own*, 174–75.
[103] Mark A. R. Kleiman, "Controlling Drug Use and Crime with Testing, Sanctions and Treatment," in *Drug Addiction and Drug Policy: The Struggle to Control Dependence*, ed. Philip B. Heymann and William N. Brownsberger (Harvard University Press, 2001), 169. For a similar list, see Bruce D. Johnson et al., "Drug Abuse in the Inner City: Impact on Hard-Drug Users and the Community," in *Crime and Justice, Vol. 13: Drugs and Crime*, ed. Michael Tonry and James Q. Wilson (University of Chicago Press, 1990), 56 (stating, for instance, that "[t]he economic importance of the drug trade has increased the systematic use of violence by dealers; drug-selling organizations can be found in most inner-city neighborhoods"; "[a]s drug sales have become particularly prominent in the inner city, criminality by users and dealers has increased, becoming more frequent and severe"; "[m]ost hard-drug abusers experience important declines in their economic well-being and typically live well below poverty levels"; "[d]rug abuse appears to be associated with a variety of morbidity and morbidity indicators"; "[s]haring needles is a primary cause of AIDS among heroin abusers"; "[f]amily formation, child rearing and responsible parenting are very difficult if not impossible during daily use of hard drugs"; and "[c]hildren of substance users are at high risk for similar outcomes as they grow up"). Even critics of the War on Drugs do not deny the harm associated with drug use and drug trade. See, e.g., Forman, *Locking Up Our Own*, 25–26 (on "the devastation heroin wrought in urban

It is of course much noted that it is the War on Drugs that helped create "a mass market that rivaled almost any other consumer sector of the American economy,"[104] with the implication being that ending the War on Drugs can undo much of the damage. Let us set that argument aside until later and assume that illicit drug trade harms individuals and society, since the answer to the question whether the illicit drug trade that is in existence harms or not does not change depending on what gave rise to the trade in the first place. What is still unclear is what the list of harms from illicit drugs has to do with recreational users who face prosecution for possession of such substances. Possession by itself does not cause harm to others, even if use can be inferred from possession. That is, those who, say, engage in violent drug trade are easily characterized as morally blameworthy as they intend to harm others, but how do those who simply possess and use drugs cause harm? It seems that the relationship between their conduct and ultimate harm to others is remote and their contributions to the problems of the drug trade are, if they exist at all, trivial.[105]

An answer to this challenge is that it is the consumer demand from drug users that maintains drug markets and accordingly brings about "the markets' violence."[106] The theory could be that by eliminating or shrinking the demand for illicit drugs from the market, we can reduce the size of the illicit market, thereby reducing the harm that the drug trade does.[107] Here is a list of four policy goals that might be used to justify attempts to squeeze the illicit market out of existence with every possible criminal enforcement tool available: "first, limit[] the number of persons who use various illicit drugs and the physical, psychological, behavioral, and moral damage they suffer as a result; second, reduc[e] the

America" in the 1960s); Forman, *Locking Up Our Own*, 156–64 (on "the crack epidemic"); Husak, "Guns and Drugs," 444–45 ("Drugs—both licit and illicit—cause tremendous harm.").

[104] David Farber, "Introduction," in *The War on Drugs: A History*, ed. David Farber (New York University Press, 2021), 5; see also Farber, "Introduction," 5 ("Illegal drug users in the US created a massive consumer demand that drug traffickers and their retail distributors have been more than pleased to service. The War on Drugs made supplying that demand dangerous in multiple ways, but it also made it extremely lucrative. It created an underground economy with its own global supply chain."); see also David Farber, "Drug Dealers," in *The War on Drugs: A History*, ed. David Farber (New York University Press, 2021), 56; Michael Polson, "Cultivating Cannabis, Excepting Cannabis," in *The War on Drugs: A History*, ed. David Farber (New York University Press, 2021), 102–05; Mark A. R. Kleiman and Kerry D. Smith, "State and Local Drug Enforcement: In Search of a Strategy," in *Crime and Justice, Vol. 13: Drugs and Crime*, ed. Michael Tonry and James Q. Wilson (University of Chicago Press, 1990), 72 (discussing research that suggests that drug enforcement raises prices of drugs and leads to more profit in selling drugs even if the amount of consumption drops). See generally David Michael Jaros, "Perfecting Criminal Markets," *Columbia Law Review* 112, no. 8 (2012): 1948–75.

[105] Cf. Husak, *Drugs and Rights*, 186–92.

[106] Forman, *Locking Up Our Own*, 175.

[107] See, e.g., Mark Moore, "Toward a Balanced Drug Prevention Strategy: A Conceptual Map," in *Drug Addiction and Drug Policy*, ed. Philip B. Heymann and William N. Brownsberger (Harvard University Press, 2001), 35–36 (sketching such a theory among many other theories).

violence connected with drug dealing and the property and violent crimes committed by users, whether to obtain money for drugs or as a result of intoxication; third, prevent[] the growth of stable, wealthy, powerful criminal organizations; and fourth, protect[] the civility of neighborhoods, and thus their attractiveness as places to live, work, shop, and raise children, from the disorder caused by open drug dealing."[108]

This list of goals is consistent with the congressional finding accompanying the Controlled Substances Act, which states as the law's premise that "[t]he illegal importation, manufacture, distribution, and possession and improper use of controlled substances have a substantial and detrimental effect on the health and general welfare of the American people."[109] And, as the US Supreme Court noted in *Gonzalez v. Raich*, "[t]he main objectives" of the law "were to conquer drug abuse and to control the legitimate and illegitimate traffic in controlled substances," and "Congress was particularly concerned with the need to prevent the diversion of drugs from legitimate to illicit channels."[110] Therefore, the law's criminal prohibition of simple possession, which makes it "unlawful for any person knowingly or intentionally to possess a controlled substance . . . except as . . . authorized,"[111] should be understood as part of a broader scheme to prevent the spread of potentially harmful drugs outside legally authorized channels. The theory behind prohibiting even simple possession is, then, that, by going after users, the law can help along the process of moving toward the goal of eliminating illicit markets of controlled substances.

Seen this way, we can see how the arguments in favor of criminalization of possession of illicit drugs are analogous to the arguments made in favor of criminalization of possession of child pornography. In both instances, harm from possession alone may be insignificant, and even individual contribution to the harm brought by the overall scheme of distribution of contraband might be insignificant, but we may still identify a person's interference with the government's policy of attacking the existence of a harmful market as the core of their wrongdoing. What is wrong with drug possession, in other words, is not harm to oneself or harm to others necessarily, but disobedience of the state as it issues commands in its attempt to deal with a serious problem. This is the sense in which possession of drugs is a disobedience offense.[112]

[108] Kleiman and Smith, "State and Local Drug Enforcement," 71.
[109] 21 U.S.C. § 801.
[110] Raich, 545 U.S. at 12–13.
[111] 21 U.S.C. § 844(a).
[112] Again, we will return to the issue of reasons to limit such arguments in Chapters 10 through 12.

VI. Conclusion

This chapter has made the following points. The crime of possession serves many different purposes. First, it is a way of identifying those who wrong by taking steps toward harming other people, especially when intent to harm is proven. Second, it is a regulatory mechanism that disallows some people to possess something in order to control the amount of risk from potentially harmful objects, like guns, in society. Third, it is a tool the government enlists to fight the existence of markets that harm society, such as those for child pornography or illicit drugs. Despite the variety, what possession offenses have in common is that they are best understood as disobedience offenses that are used to prevent harm. That is, the laws do not criminalize the wrong of harming others but rather criminalize the wrong of interfering with the government's attempt to reduce the overall amount of harm in society. These laws may or may not do the job well, but the government, through these laws, demands that the individuals follow the government-mandated ways of reducing harm. These laws are of course controversial, but by seeing them as disobedience offenses, we can be more precise about all the moral ins and outs of such laws, and a more complete picture will emerge once we discuss potential limiting principles in Chapters 10 through 12.

8

National Security Offenses I: Treason

I. Introduction

Offenses having to do with national security seem to be some of the most serious criminal offenses. To illustrate, in *Kennedy v. Louisiana*, the 2008 US Supreme Court case holding that the death penalty should not be available in cases "where the victim's life was not taken," the Court signaled that the matter may be different for "crimes defining and punishing treason, espionage, [and] terrorism, . . . which are offenses against the State."[1] The implication is that because these national security offenses are so serious that imposition of the capital punishment for them may be constitutionally permitted even if there is no death resulting from such an offense in a given situation.

It also seems to follow that, given such high stakes in the national security context, it is unlikely that criminal offenses of this kind are disobedience offenses. A person may end up causing an enormous amount of harm to one's own nation and fellow citizens by engaging in rogue behaviors or missteps in areas with sensitive national security implications, and it would be odd to characterize such harming or risking of harm as a case of the wrong of disobedience, as opposed to the wrong of harming or risking harm to others. However, there are many aspects of criminal offenses having to do with national security that are instances of criminalizing and punishing disobedience. This chapter focuses on treason and the next chapter on other national security laws, namely, laws regarding espionage, export controls, and sanctions.

II. Treason and Disloyalty

It is often said that treason is the most serious crime.[2] Treason is defined in the US Constitution as "levying War" against the United States" or "adhering to their

[1] Kennedy v. Louisiana, 554 U.S. 407, 437 (2008). The Court also mentioned "drug kingpin activity," as one of these offenses, which has been criticized as a puzzling addition. Kennedy, 554 U.S. at 437; Kennedy, 554 U.S. at 467 (Alito, J. dissenting) ("The Court takes pains to limit its holding to . . . to exclude 'offenses against the State,' a category that the Court stretches—without explanation—to include 'drug kingpin activity.'").

[2] See, e.g., Cécile Fabre, "The Morality of Treason," *Law and Philosophy* 39, no. 4 (2020): 428; Ex Parte Bollman, 8 U.S. 75, 125 (1807) ("[T]here is no crime which can more excite and agitate the

Criminalizing Disobedience. Youngjae Lee, Oxford University Press. © Oxford University Press 2026.
DOI: 10.1093/9780197617175.003.0009

Enemies, giving them Aid and Comfort."[3] Looking at this definition, we can see that there are two ways of committing the crime of treason: by "levying war" against the United States on one hand, and by "adhering" to the "enemies of the United States" and "giving them aid and comfort" on the other. On its face, one big difference between the two kinds of treason is that the crime of "adhering" to the enemies of the United States and "giving them aid and comfort" imagines the United States having "enemies," whereas it seems that one can "levy war" against the United States even in the absence of enemies, and those who "levy war" against the United States do not automatically turn themselves into enemies through the act, as a doctrinal matter.[4]

What this definition obscures, though, is the disloyalty aspect of the crime of treason. The word "treason" has its roots in the word "to betray,"[5] and while it seems that anyone can levy war or adhere to the enemies of the United States, not everyone can betray the United States. German soldiers during World War II participated in a war against the United States and adhered to the enemies of the United States, but they did not commit the crime of treason against the United States. The definition of treason in the US Code brings the disloyalty aspect out more clearly:

> Whoever, *owing allegiance to the United States*, levies war against them or adheres to their enemies, giving them aid and comfort within the United States or elsewhere, is guilty of treason . . . .[6]

The definition is essentially the same as the version in the US Constitution, except it adds the element "owing allegiance to the United States." But the Code's version is not to be thought of as different from the version in the Constitution. In the 1820 case of *United States v. Wiltberger*, Chief Justice John Marshall wrote:

> Treason is a breach of allegiance, and can be committed by him only who owes allegiance, either perpetual or temporary. The words, therefore, "owing allegiance to the United States," . . . are entirely surplus words, which do not, in the

passions of men than treason, no charge demands more from the tribunal before which it is made a deliberate and temperate inquiry. Whether this inquiry be directed to the fact or to the law, none can be more solemn, none more important to the citizen or to the government; none can more affect the safety of both."); Hanauer v. Doane, 79 U.S. 342, 347 (1870) ("No crime is greater than treason.").

[3] U.S. Const. art. III, § 3.

[4] See Carlton F. W. Larson, *On Treason: A Citizen's Guide to the Law* (Ecco, 2020), 134–35 ("[A]n enemy is always a foreign state, group, or person who owes no allegiance to the United States.").

[5] *Oxford English Dictionary*, s.v. "treason (*n*.)," https://www.oed.com/dictionary/treason_n.

[6] 18 U.S.C. § 2381 (emphasis added).

> slightest degree, affect its sense. The construction would be precisely the same were they omitted.[7]

That the crime of treason against the United States can be committed by only those who owe allegiance to the United States is consistent with the common understanding that in order for one to betray, the betrayer and the betrayed have to have a preexisting relationship.[8]

Moreover, a later case has also ruled that to commit the crime of treason, those who owe allegiance to the United States must not only levy war against the United States or adhere to the enemies of the United States but do so with an "intent to betray." In *Cramer v. United States*, the US Supreme Court drew out the "intent to betray" requirement from the phrase "adheres to their enemies" by stating as follows:

> [A] citizen may take actions, which do aid and comfort the enemy—making a speech critical of the government or opposing its measures, profiteering, striking in defense plants or essential work, and the hundred other things which impair our cohesion and diminish our strength—but if there is no adherence to the enemy in this, if there is no intent to betray, there is no treason.[9]

Therefore, treason is commonly understood to be a crime of disloyalty, and to understand the wrongness of treason, we first need to get a handle on the idea of disloyalty. One awkwardness with this conclusion, by the way, is that the idea of disloyalty fits the second way of committing treason—"adhering to the[] enemies, giving them aid and comfort"—well, but is not as illuminating on the first way of committing treason—"levying war" against the United States. An internal rebellion, which is what levying war would typically look like, need not be accompanied by an act of "adhering" to enemies, and while an internal rebellion can be as dangerous as helping an enemy, it is not obvious why disloyalty is the most relevant wrong implicated in the act, and if so, who the victim of disloyalty is. I will return to this complication later.

[7] United States v. Wiltberger, 18 U.S. 76, 97 (1820).

[8] That preexisting relationship, however, need not take the form of the accused traitor to the United States being a citizen of the United States. See Carlisle v. United States, 83 U.S. 147, 154–55 (1872); see also Larson, *On Treason*, 83–87, 90–92 (discussing the difference between permanent and temporary allegiance). For a philosophical, not legal or historical, discussion of who ought to be considered eligible to a treason charge, see generally Fabre, "Morality of Treason."

[9] Cramer v. United States, 325 U.S. 1, 29 (1945).

III. What Is Disloyalty?

What does it mean to be disloyal? We should start with the idea of partiality. When a person is called "disloyal" to their own country, the implication is that, contrary to expectations, they have failed to place the interests of their own country over that of other countries. Alasdair MacIntyre, for instance, has argued that patriotism, which he views as a kind of loyalty, entails that "I strive to further the interests of my community and you strive to further those of yours."[10] Samuel Scheffler, similarly, notes that loyalty requires "the assignment of priority to the interests of one's associates."[11] The relevant law reflects this idea of partiality. As noted above, one can be guilty of treason against the United States for "adhering to their enemies, giving them aid and comfort," which appears to be an instance of failing to prioritize the interests of the United States over those of others.[12]

A person may be said to be disloyal to the country they belong to, then, when they fail to prioritize the interests of their own country in an appropriate way. This by itself is too broad for our purposes, however, as a mere preference for other countries' interests can include something as trivial as cheering for foreign athletes when they are competing against one's own country.[13] Similarly, it seems clear that being "disloyal" to compatriots by buying only foreign-made products (German cars, French wines, Korean cellphones, and so on), donating only to charities that serve the needy overseas, vacationing only in foreign countries, living abroad for months at a time, and so on should not be within the scope of the kind of disloyalty at issue that is implicated in a crime like treason.[14]

[10] Alasdair MacIntyre, "Is Patriotism a Virtue?," in *Patriotism*, ed. Igor Primoratz (Humanity Books, 2002), 46.

[11] Samuel Scheffler, "Liberalism, Nationalism, and Egalitarianism," in *Boundaries and Allegiances: Problems of Justice and Responsibility in Liberal Thought* (Oxford University Press, 2001), 79; Kwame Anthony Appiah, *Ethics of Identity* (Princeton University Press, 2005), 221.

[12] See U.S. Const. art. III, § 3.

[13] See, e.g., Alan Schwarz, "Expatriate Enthusiasm on Display at Classic," *New York Times*, March 18, 2009; Mireya Navarro, "Latinos Still Call It Futbol," *New York Times*, July 10, 2002; Paul Zielbauer, "Soccer Upset in Korea, 500 Red Shirts in Flushing," *New York Times*, June 23, 2002; David M. Halbfinger and Paul Zielbauer, "SOCCER; Day for German Pride, and Worries," *New York Times*, June 22, 2002; Ford Fessenden et al., "Where You Watch Depends on Your Colors," *New York Times*, June 11, 2010 (showing where to watch the World Cup 2010 in New York City, organized by nationality). One potential distraction here with the example of "cheering" is that it seems to implicate the First Amendment. In order to avoid such distractions, one might think instead about volunteering to carry water bottles and towels for German soccer players about to play the American team or providing the French swim team a free use of your private gym so they can gain a critical edge against the American team. The point of these examples is to see that, even without the First Amendment problems, condemning such acts as disloyal would be a mistake.

[14] This is not to deny that the occasional misguided statements are out there. Dan Fisher, "Split Between Britain, U.S. Seen as 'Inevitable,'" *Los Angeles Times*, April 19, 1990 ("[Norman] Tebbit complained that 'a large proportion' of Britain's Asian population failed to pass what he called the 'cricket test'. 'Which side do they cheer for?' he said. 'It's an interesting test. Are you still harking back to where you came from, or where you are? And I think we've got real problems in that regard.'").

In order for an act to rise to the level of disloyalty against a country in a sense that is relevant to the idea of treason, it needs to be aimed at undermining the country's national security. The term "national security," of course, is a difficult phrase to unpack, though the phrase is commonly used and at least intuitively understood.[15] For the purposes of this chapter, I will treat "national security" as meaning "military security" and "political security," where military security involves armed forces and political security has to do with the stability of political institutions.[16] To elaborate on these two prongs, we can turn to Cécile Fabre's helpful analysis of the concept of security.[17] Fabre includes within her discussion two kinds of security goods, "goods which are part and parcel of [a state's] state and security apparatus" and "goods which are part of [a state's] ability to function as a political community."[18] For the former, Fabre lists "[m]ilitary hardware and installations, troops, intelligence and security services," and for the latter, "the resilience of the population, the shape of [the state's] territory, the stability of its political institutions and the robustness of its critical infrastructure."[19] In a democratic society, we would also include as part of the idea of the stability of political institutions what Fabre calls "the integrity of democratic procedures."[20]

From these considerations, we may arrive at the following definition of disloyalty when explaining what makes treason a crime of disloyalty:

> A person is disloyal to their country when they knowingly participate in efforts, either directly or by helping others engaged in such efforts, to directly undermine core institutional resources that their country requires to protect itself and to govern itself, and, in doing so, fails to prioritize the interests of their country's interests in an appropriate manner.

To see how this definition might illuminate the legal concept of treason, we can look at some treason cases.

Prosecutions for treason are rare in the United States. The last wave of prosecutions for treason in civilian courts was for conduct that took place during World War II,[21] though there were treason cases in military tribunals for acts during the Korean War,[22] and there were nonfrivolous allegations of treason

[15] See, e.g., Barry Buzan, *People, States and Fear: An Agenda for International Security Studies in the Post–Cold War Era*, 2nd ed. (Lynne Rienner Publishers, 1991), 16–23.
[16] See Buzan, *People, States and Fear*, 19.
[17] Cécile Fabre, *Spying Through a Glass Darkly: The Ethics of Espionage and Counter-Intelligence* (Oxford University Press, 2022), 44.
[18] Fabre, *Ethics of Espionage*, 44.
[19] Fabre, *Ethics of Espionage*, 45.
[20] Fabre, *Ethics of Espionage*, 48.
[21] For a summary, see Tom W. Bell, "Treason, Technology, and Freedom of Expression," *Arizona State Law Journal* 37, no. 4 (2005): 1003–04.
[22] See Bell, "Treason," 1003–04.

during the Vietnam War.[23] Most of the treason cases from the twentieth century can be classified as either helping enemy soldiers or saboteurs within the United States during a time of war or broadcasting propaganda for the enemy during a time of war.[24]

For instance, Max Stephan, a German-American who was born in Germany, served in the German military during World War I, moved to Detroit, became naturalized as a citizen in 1935, and was convicted of treason in 1942.[25] Stephan's treasonous acts consisted of helping a German prisoner of war escape by feeding him several times, lying about his identity to those nearby, helping him find a place to stay, giving him some spending money, and putting him on a bus from Detroit to Chicago, from which the escapee planned to find his way back to Germany.[26] In the same year, Hans Max Haupt, another German-born naturalized American citizen, was convicted of treason for helping a German saboteur, who happened to be his son, Herbert Haupt, carry out his mission in Chicago by letting him stay in his home, buying him a car that he could use for his work for the Germans, and helping him find a job at a factory where Herbert was to gather information and pass it on to the Germans.[27]

As to propaganda cases, there are several. Mildred Gillars, Douglas Chandler, and Robert Best were born in the United States and were US citizens, and all three were convicted of treason shortly after World War II for working as radio broadcasters in Berlin and making antisemitic, pro-Nazi propaganda broadcasts.[28] More recently, Adam Gadahn was indicted for treason for appearing in al-Qaeda propaganda videos.[29]

[23] See Henry Mark Holzer, "Why Not Call It Treason?: From Korea to Afghanistan," *Southern University Law Review* 29, no. 2 (2002): 199–220.

[24] Not all cases fit these two patterns. See, e.g., Kawatika v. United States, 343 U.S. 717, 745 (1952) (affirming a conviction of treason for mistreating American prisoners of war in Japan).

[25] Stephan v. United States, 133 F.2d 87 (6th Cir. 1943).

[26] See Gerald J. Senick, "The Odd and Curious Case of Max Stephan (part one)," *LegalNews.com*, April 17, 2013, https://legalnews.com/Home/Articles?DataId=1375022; John Sese with Gerald J. Senick, "Treason in Detroit—The Curious Case of Max Stephan (episode 22, part two)," *LegalNews.com*, March 19, 2021, https://legalnews.com/Home/Articles?DataId=1497500.

[27] See United States v. Haupt, 152 F.2d 771, 771–72 (7th Cir. 1946).

[28] See Best v. United States, 184 F.2d 131, 141 (1st Cir. 1950); Gillars v. United States, 182 F.2d 962, 984 (D.C. Cir. 1950); Chandler v. United States, 171 F.2d 921, 945 (1st Cir. 1949). There was also the case of Iva Toguri D'Aquino, who was accused of conducting wartime propaganda for Japan, but it is unclear if she did anything to warrant a conviction, and there were serious irregularities during the trial, including perjuries by the government's key witnesses. D'Aquino was pardoned after several stories questioning her trial came out, including on "60 Minutes." See D'Aquino v. United States, 192 F.2d 338 (9th Cir. 1951); Larson, *On Treason*, 149–61; Valerie J. Nelson, "Convicted as 'Tokyo Rose,' She Later Received Honors," *Los Angeles Times*, September 28, 2006; Kat Eschner, "Iva D'Aquino Toguri Remains the Only U.S. Citizen Convicted of Treason Who Has Ever Been Pardoned," *Smithsonian Magazine*, January 19, 2017.

[29] See Dan Eggen and Karen de Young, "U.S. Supporter of Al-Qaeda Is Indicted on Treason Charge," *Washington Post*, October 12, 2006; see also Larson, *On Treason*, 193–203.

These are straightforward cases of treason and disloyalty. True, there may be lingering line-drawing problems as to what counts as "adhering to the[] enemies, giving them aid and comfort"[30] and what counts as within one's free speech rights,[31] but the basic idea is clear. In a time of war, it is treason for those owing allegiance to the United States to help the enemy's war efforts against the United States in any way. And these activities fit the definition of disloyalty given above. The question we need to address now is what exactly is wrong with these acts.

IV. What's Wrong with Treason?

A. Cosmopolitan Challenge

The answer to this question may seem too obvious to be worth a discussion. It seems that a person should, of course, always take their own country's side when they are in an adversarial posture with those outside and those outsiders threaten their country's national security. However, consider the following before we readily accept this conclusion.

A number of moral philosophers—under the banner of "cosmopolitanism"—have questioned the view that national boundaries are morally significant.[32] Martha Nussbaum, for example, has argued that "[h]uman personhood . . . is the source of our moral worth, and this worth is equal."[33] This means that we should "recognize humanity wherever it occurs, and give its fundamental ingredients,

[30] See Cramer 325 U.S. at 1, 48 (holding that meeting, having drinks, and engaging in a long conversation with two people the defendant probably knew were German saboteurs is insufficient to satisfy the act element of the crime of treason); see also Cramer, 325 U.S. at 37 ("By direct testimony of two or more agents it was established that Cramer met Thiel and Kerling on the occasions and at the places charged and that they drank together and engaged long and earnestly in conversation. This is the sum of the overt acts as established by the testimony of two witnesses. There is no two-witness proof of what they said nor in what language they conversed. There is no showing that Cramer gave them any information whatever of value to their mission or indeed that he had any to give. No effort at secrecy is shown, for they met in public places. Cramer furnished them no shelter, nothing that can be called sustenance or supplies, and there is no evidence that he gave them encouragement or counsel, or even paid for their drinks.").

[31] Cf. Larson, *On Treason*, 184–91.

[32] There are many different kinds of cosmopolitanism, and different schemas abound. By cosmopolitanism, I am referring to a way of deliberating about morality, as opposed to a view about how international institutions for global governance ought to be designed or a view about the significance of culture for formation of individual identities. In other words, I am interested in "moral cosmopolitanism," not "cosmopolitanism about institutions" or "cosmopolitanism about culture." See Charles R. Beitz, *Political Theory and International Relations*, rev'd ed. (Princeton University Press, 1999), 199; Samuel Scheffler, "Conceptions of Cosmopolitanism," in *Boundaries and Allegiances: Problems of Justice and Responsibility in Liberal Thought* (Oxford University Press, 2001), 111–12; Cécile Fabre, *Cosmopolitan War* (Oxford University Press, 2012), 31–32.

[33] Martha C. Nussbaum, "Reply," in *For Love of Country: Debating the Limits of Patriotism*, ed. Joshua Cohen (Beacon Press, 1996), 133.

reason and moral capacity, our first allegiance and respect."[34] Giving national boundaries a significant role to play in one's moral deliberation would be indefensible, she argues, because the "accident of where one is born is just that, an accident; any human being might have been born in any nation."[35] In other words, one's nationality is "morally irrelevant"[36] and national boundaries, similarly, "morally arbitrary,"[37] and we cannot justify our differential treatment of individuals on such arbitrary grounds.[38]

Peter Singer also points out that "most of us unquestioningly support declarations proclaiming that all humans have certain rights, and that all human life is of equal worth" and that we "condemn those who say the life of a person of a different race or nationality is of less account than the life of a person of our own race or nation."[39] But if such a set of ideas is taken seriously, as Singer argues, it seems that we cannot also coherently maintain that "national boundaries carry moral weight."[40] And, if national boundaries do not carry moral weight, it is unclear whether there is a moral obligation to support your country or at least refrain from helping your country's enemy unless your country is on the morally correct side of every conflict.

Some philosophers have countered the cosmopolitan challenge by arguing that there is a legitimate place for partiality in our everyday lives and that one could not accept cosmopolitanism without threatening not only patriotism but also family ties and friendships.[41] For instance, the argument goes, if cosmopolitans are correct in thinking that all people are of equal worth, it seems illegitimate for a father to give special priority to the interests of his children over those of someone else's children just because his children are his.[42] This argument is fine as far as it goes, but only as far as it goes. Even if we grant that relationships matter to people, are valuable, and are important ingredients of moral lives, that does not show which relationships matter, which relationships are valuable, and which relationships are so valuable that we should treat the breach of responsibilities stemming from such relationships to be morally blameworthy. Therefore, we cannot easily argue in favor of a moral duty of loyalty to one's country by making general arguments about the importance of special relationships and special obligations in human lives.

[34] Martha C. Nussbaum, "Patriotism and Cosmopolitanism," in *For Love of Country*, 7.
[35] Nussbaum, "Patriotism," 7.
[36] Nussbaum, "Patriotism," 5.
[37] Nussbaum, "Patriotism," 14.
[38] See also Debra Satz, "Equality of What Among Whom?: Thoughts on Cosmopolitanism, Statism, and Nationalism," in *NOMOS, Vol. 41: Global Justice*, ed. Ian Shapiro and Lea Brilmayer (American Society for Political and Legal Philosophy, 1999), 67.
[39] Peter Singer, *One World: The Ethics of Globalization* (Yale University Press, 2002), 152.
[40] Singer, *One World*, 152.
[41] See Scheffler, "Conceptions of Cosmopolitanism," 118.
[42] See Scheffler, "Conceptions of Cosmopolitanism," 118.

In fact, there is a serious disanalogy between intimate relationships like family and friends and relationships among compatriots. Significant components of relationships among family members and (at least good) friends are the number, type, and scope of direct interpersonal interactions extending over significant periods of time. Obviously, we cannot say the same for relationships between an individual and the state or among compatriots. The state consists of large, impersonal organizations, and people live their lives having never met or otherwise interacted with most of their compatriots. Therefore, there is something prima facie dubious about arguments that justify loyalty to one's country by drawing attention to the importance of family relationships in one's life, and the force of the cosmopolitan challenge that national boundaries are not and, morally speaking, should not be significant does not diminish.

Another response to the cosmopolitan challenge is to point out the value of national membership and the value of states, and it is true that nations and states can and do serve a lot of important functions. In fact, this book has discussed many laws that seem to be premised on the view that it is wrong to undermine the state. However, that mode of argumentation does not work well in this context, as it is not easy to go from the importance of states (and nations for that matter) to the argument one should always take one's own country's side. Many have argued, for instance, that national membership can be valuable for individuals' well-being,[43] but even if that is true, such arguments do not specify which nations should be supported by individuals. Perhaps *every* existing nation should be protected and supported by *everyone*;[44] but that is not the same as saying that people ought to support *their own* nations. From the premise, "nations are great for individual well-being and should therefore be supported," the conclusion, "therefore, you should support your own nation," does not follow. Similarly, while, as noted in Chapter 2, the state is valuable for a variety of reasons, such as ensuring security, resolving disputes, and coordinating activities, such arguments cannot generate an argument in favor of an obligation to support your own state as opposed to another. In order to give a disloyalty-based

[43] See, e.g., Will Kymlicka, *Multicultural Citizenship: A Liberal Theory of Minority Rights* (Oxford University Press, 1995), 80–82, 87–90; Yael Tamir, *Liberal Nationalism* (Princeton University Press, 1993), 84; Avishai Margalit and Joseph Raz, "National Self-Determination," *Journal of Philosophy* 87, no. 9 (1990): 448–50; Neil MacCormick, "Nations and Nationalism," in *Theorizing Nationalism*, ed. Ronald Beiner (State University of New York Press, 1999), 193.

[44] In fact, the value of nations implies even less than that. First, there is the possibility of individuals converting from one nationality to another. As long as individuals belong to *some* cultures, individuals can take the benefits of belonging to a culture, which in turn means that not all existing nations even need to continue to exist in order for individuals to draw benefits of national membership. Of course, how far this argument can go depends on the ability of individuals to truly belong to different nations. Second, if nation *A* deems the existence of nation *B* to threaten its own well-being, then the arguments in favor of national membership would be pointing in two conflicting directions—toward eliminating *B* for the health of *A* and toward protecting *B* to protect its nationhood even if it means hurting *A*.

account of these crimes, we must have an explanation as to why harming one's own state as opposed to another is a distinct wrong, apart from and beyond the fact that it is wrong to produce harm.[45]

I do not mean to deny that many people do in fact value their nations in particular. And those who do indeed feel this way would feel guilt and would feel that they have betrayed the nation if they commit acts of disloyalty, and they will resent other compatriots who commit such acts.[46] There is no reason to disrespect or discount the validity of such sentiments, but acknowledging so need not involve the belief that that is how everyone should in fact feel. Judging people on the basis of the fact that they do not feel that they "belong" to their own nation to which they owe corresponding obligations essentially imposes on people an obligation to belong. Is there such an obligation? As a general matter, no, and the state cannot legitimately fault individuals for not identifying with the nation associated with it.[47]

Finally, while we might not be so sympathetic to those citizens of the United States who chose to take the side of Nazi Germany during World War II, there are those who betrayed their own countries to take the side of the Allied Powers during the war. Fritz Kolbe, for instance, was a German diplomat who delivered top-secret military documents to American officials.[48] Hotsumi Ozaki was a Japanese journalist who had access to discussions regarding Japan's war plans, and he passed on the information to Richard Sorge, a Soviet spy.[49] And then there are spies like Oleg Gordievsky and Oleg Penkovsky, who were Soviet officials who spied for the United States and the United Kingdom during the Cold War.[50] These individuals all committed acts that are disloyal to their own countries, but it is not unusual to see them described as heroes, not villains.

Maybe treason is wrong when *we* do it to *our own country*, but when *others* do it to *their own country* to take *our* side, it is not only okay but also sometimes imperative. This answer is unsatisfactory unless we can justify what appears to be a

[45] In the literature on political obligations, this problem has been called the "particularity" or "special allegiance" objection. See Christopher Heath Wellman, "Political Obligation and the Particularity Requirement," *Legal Theory* 10, no. 2 (2004): 98–100; Jeremy Waldron, "Special Ties and Natural Duties," *Philosophy & Public Affairs* 22, no. 1 (1993): 5–7.

[46] Joseph Raz, "The Obligation to Obey: Revision and Tradition," in *Ethics in the Public Domain: Essays in the Morality of Law and Politics* (Oxford University Press, 1994), 353–54 (noting "the possibility of one kind of obligation . . . which arises out of a sense of identifying with or belonging to the community").

[47] Raz, "Obligation to Obey," 354 ("One does not have a moral duty to feel a sense of belonging in a community; certainly there is no obligation to feel that one belongs to a country.").

[48] See Lucas Delattre, *A Spy at the Heart of the Third Reich: The Extraordinary Story of Fritz Kolbe, America's Most Important Spy in World War II* (Grove Press, 2006).

[49] See Charles Johnson, *An Instance of Treason: Ozaki Hotsumi and the Sorge Spy Ring* (Stanford University Press, 1964).

[50] See Gordon Corera, "Spy Game: A Familiar Tale Continues," *BBC News*, May 14, 2013, https://www.bbc.com/news/world-europe-22526793.

self-serving double standard. A better response to these examples is that saying that treason is *sometimes* justified is not the same as saying that treason is morally neutral and that these examples do not prove that cosmopolitans are correct to consider national boundaries to be morally arbitrary. That is fair enough, but for now the important point is that it is worth considering the question of morality of treason more carefully instead of condemning it outright.

B. Significance of Consent, Promise, and Oath

The question we are considering here is why it is morally wrong to be disloyal by, say, taking the side of one's country's enemy in a military conflict. One possible answer is that such a promise has been made. Now, an argument based on promising is an argument based on consent, and the problem with consent-based theories when it comes to an obligation to one's state is now familiar. A promise cannot be the ground to establish obligations that bind every member of the state simply because only a small percentage of people have made such explicit commitments, and there would be numerous problems with asking people to go through a process where they can give express consent.[51] This problem has led some consent theorists, including, most (in)famously, John Locke, to appeal to the idea of tacit consent.[52] The idea of tacit consent has been severely criticized for various reasons, mainly having to do with the conceit that mere residence or receipt of benefits can amount to an act of consent to be ruled.[53] But let's set that aside for now and focus on those who have expressly promised.

There are two groups of people who have taken explicit oaths of allegiance in the United States: public officers, including members of the military, and naturalized citizens. The wording of various oaths taken by federal office holders is different, but they all include languages of allegiance. Article II, Section 1 of the US Constitution, for instance, requires the following oath for the president:

[51] See George Klosko, *Political Obligations* (Oxford University Press, 2005), 122–40; George P. Fletcher, *Loyalty: An Essay on the Morality of Relationships* (Oxford University Press, 1993), 53–55.

[52] See John Locke, *Second Treatise of Government*, ed. C. B. MacPherson (Hackett Publishing 1980, originally published 1690). For a discussion, see Hanna Pitkin, "Obligation and Consent—I," *American Political Science Review* 59, no. 4 (1965): 990, 994–97; A. John Simmons, *Moral Principles and Political Obligations* (Princeton University Press, 1979), 83–95.

[53] See, e.g., David Hume, "Of the Original Contract," in *Essays: Moral, Political and Literary*. ed. Eugene F. Miller (Liberty Fund, 1985), 475 ("Can we seriously say, that a poor peasant or artisan has a free choice to leave his country, when he knows no foreign language or manners, and lives, from day to day, by the small wages which he acquires? We may as well assert that a man, by remaining in a vessel, freely consents to the dominion of the master; though he was carried on board while asleep, and must leap into the ocean and perish, the moment he leaves her."); Simmons, *Political Obligations*, 83–100; Leslie Green, "Law and Obligations," in *Oxford Handbook of Jurisprudence and Philosophy of Law*, ed. Jules Coleman and Scott Shapiro (Oxford University Press, 2002), 528.

> I do solemnly swear (or affirm) that I will faithfully execute the Office of President of the United States, and will to the best of my Ability, preserve, protect and defend the Constitution of the United States.

There are similar languages in oaths for various personnel, such as "support and defend the Constitution of the United States against all enemies, foreign and domestic," or "bear true faith and allegiance to [the United States]."[54] The citizenship oath taken by naturalized citizens is similar:

> I hereby declare, on oath, that I absolutely and entirely renounce and abjure all allegiance and fidelity to any foreign prince, potentate, state, or sovereignty, of whom or which I have heretofore been a subject or citizen; that I will support and defend the Constitution and laws of the United States of America against all enemies, foreign and domestic; that I will bear true faith and allegiance to the same; that I will bear arms on behalf of the United States when required by the law; that I will perform noncombatant service in the Armed Forces of the United States when required by the law; that I will perform work of national importance under civilian direction when required by the law; and that I take this obligation freely, without any mental reservation or purpose of evasion; so help me God.[55]

Such promises to defend the US Constitution against all enemies are easy to interpret to include a commitment not to betray the United States through acts of disloyalty like treason.[56]

But there is more to disloyalty than mere promise-breaking. Perhaps the existence of some kind of obligation not to be disloyal is secured through the oaths of allegiance; however, we have to ask the further question of what exactly the nature of the wrongdoing is when obligations of allegiance established through an oath are breached. When someone breaks a promise by performing an act, there are potentially two wrongs: the wrongness of promise breaking and the wrongness of the act itself. This is because when someone makes a promise to do *x*, it is understood that the promise creates a new obligation to do *x* over and above the

[54] 5 U.S.C. § 3331 (specifying the general oath of office for individuals "elected or appointed to an office of honor or profit in the civil service or uniformed services"); 10 U.S.C. § 502 (for each person enlisting in an armed force).

[55] 8 C.F.R. § 337.1. The part of the oath that requires renunciation of "all allegiance to fidelity to any foreign prince, potentate, state, or sovereignty of whom or which I have heretofore been a subject or citizen" has never been enforced and is looking outdated. See Peter J. Spiro, *Beyond Citizenship: American Identity after Globalization* (Oxford University Press, 2008), 72–73. The existence of this discrepancy probably hurts the credibility of the oath somewhat, but it does not damage the core substance involving loyalty, allegiance, and protection of the United States against all enemies.

[56] See Stephan, 133 F.2d at 91.

preexisting reasons to do *x*, and breaking the promise entails a violation of the promissory obligation as well as going against the reasons to do *x* that existed before the promise was made, if any existed.[57] Why breaking a promise is wrong is a topic that has been much debated, but it is unnecessary here to commit to any particular account of the nature of its wrongness.[58] The point being made is that there is an independent wrong associated with breaking a promise that is separate from the wrong of committing the conduct underlying the breach.

This means that when public officers or naturalized citizens commit acts of disloyalty, we may blame them for violating their oaths or for being disloyal, and the argument that those who have taken the oaths of allegiance have an obligation not to be disloyal is sufficient to establish the duty not to be disloyal but cannot establish further that we may blame them for the wrongness of betraying. In other words, the consent theory cannot justify the practice of taking people's acts of disloyalty to be blameworthy. At most, what we have established here is that public officers and naturalized citizens have duties not to be disloyal on the grounds that they have given their express consent to be under a duty not to be disloyal. Thus, when a naturalized citizen commits an act of disloyalty, we may blame them not only for being disloyal but also for breaking a promise. It is the blame for being disloyal part, however, that remains unexplained.

Furthermore, even when we condemn public officers and naturalized citizens for being disloyal, the part of our condemnation having to do with breaking the promise seems rather insignificant. Properly understood, the significance of the oath lies not in the fact that one is making a promise to undertake certain specific obligations; rather, what the oath does is express one's undertaking of a certain position or a role, which comes *with* certain obligations. The oath is thus different from signing a contract and promising to perform various terms of the contract; the oath, rather, is an expression of intent to enter a role and assume a set of responsibilities that comes with the role, as a public official or a citizen.[59]

The oath is, nevertheless, useful in that it expresses succinctly what is expected of those who occupy these positions. It cannot be used as a basis to condemn those who owe allegiance to the United States if they were natural born citizens, but the oath nevertheless spells out what it means to be an official and

[57] Cf. H. L. A. Hart, "Legal and Moral Obligation," in *Essays in Moral Philosophy*, ed. A. I. Melden (University of Washington Press, 1958), 102 ("Promises have pre-eminently the feature I have called independence of content: the obligation springs not from the nature of the promised action but from the use of the procedure by the appropriate person in the appropriate circumstances.").

[58] See, e.g., John Rawls, *A Theory of Justice*, rev. ed. (Harvard University Press, 1999), 303–08; T. M. Scanlon, *What We Owe to Each Other* (Harvard University Press, 1998), 295–327.

[59] But see Ethan J. Leib, "Contract as Vow or Oath," *Legal Theory* 30, no. 1 (2024): 23 (arguing that "vows and oaths furnish a surprisingly illuminating window into contract"). Also, the use of the word "citizen" is not meant to exclude others who may have a sufficiently thick relationship with a state to be considered members of the state, which may include permanent residents.

a citizen, even if the wrongfulness of disloyalty cannot be reduced to that of promise-breaking.

C. Treason as a Breach of Trust

Can we appeal to the idea of violation of trust to understand the wrongness of treason? That seems plausible. Violation of trust is closely related to betrayal—so closely related, in fact, that some would define disloyalty as violation of trust.[60] Here again, we may distinguish between naturalized citizens and public officers on one hand, and other members of society on the other hand. As we just saw, naturalized citizens and public officers appear different from other citizens because it may be argued that through a voluntary application and assumption of citizenship or public offices, these people have induced others' trust. If they behave disloyally, there is nothing wrong with describing them as having violated others' or the state's trust. Therefore, it seems that we have fairly clear instances of betrayal as a violation of trust in these cases, and we can analyze espionage cases involving those whose positions give them access to classified materials as violation of trust cases.[61] The cases of Aldrich Ames, a CIA agent, and Robert Hanssen, an FBI agent,[62] might fall into this category,[63] and we might also argue that naturalized citizens who transmit classified materials to other governments violate our trust from two sources, one stemming from the naturalization process and the other from his or her position of trust and access to classified information.[64]

The problem with the trust-based argument, however, is that a person may engage in acts of disloyalty even in the absence of trust. There may be officials in positions of access to secrets who manage not to lose their positions even

[60] See Nachman Ben-Yehuda, *Betrayals and Treason: Violations of Trust and Loyalty* (Westview Press, 2001), 107 (arguing that "[t]reason . . . consists of a behavior that is presumed to have betrayed trust and breached faith" and that "establishing an act of treason requires an a priori act of establishing a relationship of trust and loyalty").

[61] See Fabre, "Morality of Treason," 439.

[62] See, e.g., Richard Sale, *Traitors: The Worst Acts of Treason in American History from Benedict Arnold to Robert Hanssen* (Berkley Books, 2003); David Wise, *Spy: The Inside Story of How the FBI's Robert Hanssen Betrayed America* (Random House, 2002).

[63] Another person we might add to the category is Klaus Fuchs, who will be discussed in the next chapter, though his case is a bit more complicated. For a discussion, see the next chapter and Fabre, *Ethics of Espionage*, 116–17.

[64] As we will see more in detail in the next chapter, neither Hanssen nor Ames was convicted of treason. They were convicted rather of espionage offenses. See Ames v. United States, 155 F. Supp. 2d 525 (E.D. Va. 2000); "Aldrich Ames," Federal Bureau of Investigation: History, https://www.fbi.gov/history/famous-cases/aldrich-ames; "Robert Hanssen," Federal Bureau of Investigation: History, https://www.fbi.gov/history/famous-cases/robert-hanssen. However, that does not make their behaviors any less disloyal, which is what we are trying to explain as a way of understanding wrongness of treason.

though they have said enough things or behaved in such a way, or both, that people in that society generally do not trust them even if the people are having trouble keeping them away from their offices for whatever reason.[65] And the same goes for ordinary citizens. Max Stephan may have been naturalized as a citizen, but it is not clear whether it is accurate to say that he was a particularly trusted member of society. We expect the government to punish those who commit crimes because the government uses its coercive power to reassure the rest of us that we can play by the rules without fear of being taken advantage of or having our efforts be wasted. But it seems to me to be an exaggeration to say that we trust people not to commit acts of disloyalty. In fact, as a general matter, we do not trust one another, and that is why the state uses a variety of tools, some coercive, others less so, to induce desirable behavior from people.

Trust is also an inappropriate concept here because normally people can avoid being trusted to act in a certain way through the practice of full disclosure, but that is not an option in this context. For instance, imagine that Stephan, before he helped a German prisoner of war escape, regularly wrote antisemitic, pro-Nazi commentary and even expressed that he would have no trouble helping the German side win by committing acts of treason if given the opportunity.[66] None of that speech would be a crime, but if disloyalty is a violation of trust, then it seems that we would have no right to complain about Stephan's acts of betrayal since the trust placed in him would have been seriously misguided given his expressed views. Yet he still has the duty not to be disloyal.[67] The duty not to be disloyal against one's own country is not something that a person can free themselves of simply by asking people not to trust them.[68] Furthermore, given that it is difficult to justify the idea of trusting every naturalized citizen who has taken an oath to "support and defend the Constitution and laws of the United States of America against all enemies, foreign and domestic," the basis for trusting natural born citizens is even weaker, even though they, too, are under an obligation not to be disloyal. All in all, breach of trust does not work as an explanation of wrongness of disloyalty.

[65] This argument is similar to Cécile Fabre's point that explanations of wrongness of treason based on trust is limited because one could have a society in which there is general distrust but treason is still a possibility in such a trustless society. Fabre, "Morality of Treason," 439.

[66] In fact, it appears that he was well known as a Nazi sympathizer. See Senick, "The Odd and Curious Case."

[67] Again, for a similar argument, see Fabre, "Morality of Treason," 439–40.

[68] In fact, it is not easy to lose one's citizenship. For basic requirements, see 8 U.S.C. § 1481. See also Gillars, 182, F.2d at 981–82 (holding that a statement of allegiance to Germany typed on a piece of paper and signed by an American citizen and submitted to her work supervisor in Germany during World War II insufficient to cause a loss of citizenship). There is a separate issue here as to how difficult it should be for a person to lose one's duty of loyalty to their state.

D. Treason and Expectations

Despite all the problems with various arguments in favor of a duty to take your own country's side over another's, it is undeniable that there are powerful expectations that people not engage in acts of disloyalty. Once again, here's the definition of disloyalty we have been using:

> A person is disloyal to their country when they knowingly participate in efforts, either directly or by helping others engaged in such efforts, to directly undermine core institutional resources that their country requires to protect itself and to govern itself, and, in doing so, fails to prioritize the interests of their country's interests in an appropriate manner.

So, can we justify the expectation that people not engage in such acts? Here, we may draw a distinction between government officials and other individuals who are given access to state secrets or powers to deploy institutional resources, or both, on the one hand and ordinary individuals on the other. Robert Hanssen and Aldrich Ames, as FBI and CIA agents, respectively, had access to state secrets and passed them on to the Soviet Union and Russia, whereas Max Stephan and Hans Haupt were ordinary citizens who encountered an opportunity to help German war efforts. Both groups of individuals went against expectations not to be disloyal to the United States but were differently situated.

People like Hanssen and Ames are given access to sensitive information having to do with security of the state *so that* they can advance the interests of the United States. Prioritizing the interests of the United States over those of other nations is in their very job description. For the United States to protect itself from those who seek to undermine its core institutional resources that it needs to protect and govern itself, it needs personnel who are put in charge of carrying out the task of protecting it from various threats. For these people to do their job well, they need to be given access to state secrets that should be kept secret for national security reasons and to powers to deploy the state's security apparatus. Such acts of empowerment carry the risk of abuse and misuse but are necessary and are done with the understanding that those given the access to information and power to use it exercise their privileged position to prioritize and advance the interests of the United States. Their prescribed posture is not to treat every nation equally or to decide on their own which country's interests ought to be advanced; the job description clearly is that they are to prioritize the interests of the country that has hired them for the purposes of protecting itself from threats of various kinds.[69] And given the importance of the tasks assigned them, violations of such expectations are appropriately treated as a grave matter.[70]

Ordinary citizens are different because they are not given the kind of privileged access to information or power that raises the expectation of working to advance the interests of their country. At the same time, the expectation not to be disloyal is present with regard to ordinary citizens as well. Where does that come from? Perhaps the intuition is this: in order to have a state function as an effective entity, it needs not only cooperation from its members in terms of following the law but also loyal members who are committed to the long-term health and existence of it. People who are not loyal are free riders in the sense that not only are they deriving benefits from those who contribute more to the advancement of the common good but also are actively hurting the state that benefits them. Similarly, Fabre has argued that it is presumptively wrong for a person to "accept[] the benefits of membership" in a political community and "at the same time harm[] his fellow community members," and thus when a person is disloyal to their political community by, say, passing on state secrets to foreign adversaries, they "undermine[] the institutions which [their] fellow community members support, thanks to which [they] can enjoy the benefits of membership, and on which they too are dependent."[71]

This argument is not only plausible and powerful but goes a long way to explain the kind of resentment one may experience against fellow citizens who commit acts of disloyalty. However, there are a couple of problems and complications.

First, the kinds of benefits that political membership brings—such as physical security—tend to be the ones that an individual cannot easily opt out of without moving to a different country. So, for at least those who were born and raised in the United States and have benefited from their membership without ever seeking them out, there is a reason to at least hesitate about the idea of the state providing mandatory or practically mandatory benefits to them and giving them the following three choices: refrain from disloyal acts in return, be condemned as traitors, or leave the country to avoid receiving the benefits.

Second, people benefit from not just their own state but from other states and international bodies, and the logic of the benefits-based accounts sets us on a

[69] This is why, Aldrich Ames's self-serving statement that he spied in order "to even things out, to level the playing field" since the United States had more spies in Russia than the other way around does not help him. Walter Pincus, "Catch a Spy—And Look What Happens," *Washington Post*, March 25, 2001. His job description did not allow him to act for such reasons; if the playing field was uneven in favor of the United States, it was not his job to correct it.

[70] For a similar argument, see Fabre, "Morality of Treason," 440–41 (arguing in terms of "mutually understood and articulated expectations" among some, especially officials, that "they will not disclose sensitive intelligence to third parties in general, and foreign powers in particular").

[71] Fabre, "Morality of Treason," 441–42.

path of calculating who is providing benefits to whom. For one thing, we cannot ignore globalization as a phenomenon when we start looking for things to thank for giving our lives their current shape. International cooperation and international institutions are needed to address various issues that can affect individuals' day-to-day lives such as finance, trade, terrorism, climate, diseases, and nuclear proliferation.[72] And for individuals, how the benefits calculation works out is likely to vary greatly. Some Americans were born in other countries and raised there before they came to the United States. Some college students study abroad and are changed profoundly forever. Some build their careers on importing overseas cultural products and selling them to the American public. In short, if we can identify what benefits come to individuals and from where, then the sources of benefits would map out differently for different individuals, but the duty not to be disloyal does not vary depending on such variations. For example, before the moment of his treasonous acts, had Max Stephan benefited more from Germany or from the United States? It is not clear, yet the duty not to be disloyal to the United States as a US citizen was quite clear. The point is that the duty not to be disloyal against the state does not operate on a sliding scale that adjusts according to people's backgrounds, but benefits accounts do not have internal constraints to avoid such implications.

E. Treason and Disobedience

The resulting picture is thus complex but only in part. The task of spelling out the wrongness of treason is quite straightforward for those government officials who are given privileged access to information and power so that they can prioritize and advance the interests of a particular state. Traitors like Hanssen and Ames, therefore, are emblematic of straightforward cases of wrongful betrayal of those who have empowered and authorized them to be in their positions of power and are rightfully condemned as serious wrongdoers.

As to ordinary citizens, as just discussed, general moral considerations based on harm, promise, trust, and benefits do not conclusively and reliably establish an obligation not to commit acts of treason. Yet the law prohibits treason. To see what is at stake here, we might think of reasons why an ordinary citizen may be moved to commit acts of treason.

Consider the 2003 war between Iraq and the United States. During that war, it would have been treasonous for an American to help Iraqi war efforts by going to

[72] For a good snapshot of the state of global governance, see Joshua Cohen and Charles Sabel, "Extra Rempublicam Nulla Justitia?," *Philosophy and Public Affairs* 34, no. 2 (2006): 164–65. See also Martin Wolf, *Why Globalization Works* (Yale University Press, 2004), 61–73.

Iraq and working as a volunteer for the Iraqi military. An American might have gone to Iraq during that time for humanitarian reasons, to help Iraqi civilians whose lives have been adversely affected by war, to monitor potential human rights abuses and violations of laws of war, and so on. We can put such acts aside as not treasonous, even if they would incidentally have the effect of boosting the morale of the Iraqi army. But what if a US citizen believed that the right thing for him to do is to help the Iraqis with the goal of defeating America in the war because they believed that the United States was on the wrong side of this particular conflict, morally speaking, and that it was morally permissible to participate in the war on the side opposing the United States?[73] If the United States was engaging in an act of unjustified aggression, the Iraqis may have simply been innocent actors defending themselves, in which case helping the Iraqis defend against the US attack would have been a simple case of defense of others.

What would be wrong with this US citizen's behavior? One obvious response is that basing one's behavior on these sorts of arguments is unwise. Most of these behaviors carry the risk of doing more harm than good, and morally responsible individuals would probably refrain from engaging in them. But this way of thinking about what is wrong with such acts speaks in terms of what kinds of harms such acts would bring about and cannot well explain why we do not engage in case-by-case determinations to see whether individual disloyal acts undertaken are in fact harmful all things considered or whether the actor has in fact done the right thing. I mentioned the case of Hotsumi Ozaki earlier, and if we were to engage in a harm-based analysis, we might as well conclude that Ozaki, who passed on Japanese secrets to the Soviets, should escape the charge of treason because he may have accelerated the Allies' defeat of the Axis Powers during World War II.[74] Perhaps Ozaki did the right thing all things considered, but passing on Japanese war plans to the Soviets should still count as an act of treason.

A better response is simply that the state demands that you not take the enemy's side in situations like this even if you may have your own thoughts on the matter. Treason, in other words, is a crime of disobedience. Whether you think your country is on the right side or the wrong side of an international military conflict, you simply are not allowed to engage in certain acts that directly interfere with, say, your country's military efforts. Other acts of dissent may be permissible, but those that touch on the core institutional resources the state requires to protect itself, such as state secrets and the military, are not to be interfered

[73] For arguments that the 2003 war in Iraq was unjust, see Jeff McMahan, "Unjust War in Iraq," *The Pelican Record* 41, no. 5 (2004); Michael Walzer, "Regime Change and Just War," *Dissent* 53, no. 3 (2006): 103–08.

[74] See, e.g., Doug Tsuruoka, "Did a Forgotten Japanese Journalist Turn the Tide of World War II?," *Asia Times*, August 5, 2015.

with. That you are to avoid undermining your own country on matters of your national security with the underlying moral rights and wrongs to be set aside is what best reflects the logic of treason as an offense.

Now, this answer may strike one as unsatisfying as an answer to the cosmopolitan challenge with which we began this discussion. If the challenge is why one should always refrain from acts that could undermine core institutional resources that their country requires to protect itself and to govern itself when the country is in conflict with another country, the response, "Because the state said so" seems to beg the question. The response is to elaborate as follows. As we noted several times throughout this book, the state serves a number of valuable functions. The state goes about its business in the name of its people, and physical security is not only one of the main functions of the state but is a precondition of the cooperative activity of living together as members of a polity. This cooperative venture, in turn, cannot exist and continue unless it has physical security, and the state achieves this through a particular configuration of power between the state and the people, and one core feature of this configuration is the expectation that those who owe allegiance to the state not engage in acts of disloyalty. The relevant configuration of power effects a separation of powers between the state and its citizens and assigns different roles to each. The idea is that no matter what you think the right thing to do might be, and whether you are right or wrong about it, you must respect the political boundaries drawn by this particular allocation of power between you and the country that you owe allegiance to. When you commit an act of disloyalty, you breach the terms of the power-sharing arrangement that governs you, your country, and your fellow citizens. You must do your fair share by respecting the arrangement as handed to you, and that is the sense in which treason is an offense of disobedience.

F. Note on Levying War

In part I of this chapter, I noted that there are two different ways of committing the crime of treason: "levying war" against the United States, or "adhering to their enemies, giving them aid and comfort."[75] This chapter has proceeded on the proposition that treason is a crime of disloyalty and has thus focused on the second prong, after setting aside the first prong. How should we then make sense of the idea of "levying war" given the discussion thus far? The answer is that, just like the duty not to commit acts of disloyalty, which I have argued is ultimately based on the state's demand that the people take the state's side and not

[75] U.S. Const. art. III, § 3.

do anything that undermines its means of protecting itself, the prohibition on levying war is based on disobedience.

In fact, it is much easier to explain the prohibition on levying war against the state than the prohibition on adhering to the enemies. Throughout this book, we have discussed various ways in which the state prohibits disobedience of the state, and the prohibition on levying war can be understood as just another instance of criminalizing disobedience, as it is a particularly egregious form of disobeying. Now, one might attempt to justify levying war against the United States and overthrowing the government as a way of introducing a regime change and securing long-term benefits even if there are short-term costs due to the violence and disruption that are likely to be involved in such an effort. But no matter, according to the law. Levying war, too, is thus an offense of disobedience.

V. Conclusion

This chapter has argued that treason, while a crime of disloyalty, is also a crime of disobedience. Wrongness of treason, understood as a crime of disloyalty, is not entirely obvious, especially given the cosmopolitan challenge that urges that we treat national boundaries as morally arbitrary. This chapter has considered various arguments to identify the wrong of treason as a crime of disloyalty, such as arguments based on consent, trust, and expectations. This chapter has concluded that treason is morally wrong for government officials who are given access to power and information in exchange for their commitment to work on behalf of the political community that has given them such a privileged position. Wrongness of treason is a less straightforward matter for ordinary citizens without such special roles. For such people, the best account of the wrongness of treason is that they are going against the state's command not to engage in acts of disloyalty. Such commands stem from the expectation that those who owe allegiance to the state are not to engage in acts of disloyalty, where that expectation is a crucial part of the configuration of the power as devised by the state to ensure physical security of the state.

9

National Security Offenses II: Espionage, Export Control, and Sanctions

I. Introduction

The previous chapter examined treason. While often foremost in people's minds when thinking of offenses having to do with breach of national security, treason is only one of several in that category of offenses. This chapter focuses on crimes that are more commonly prosecuted than treason, such as espionage, engaging in unauthorized exports of items covered by export control laws, and sanctions violations.

II. Espionage

"Espionage" law comes in many guises. Here is one definition:

> Whoever, with intent or reason to believe that it is to be used to the injury of the United States or to the advantage of a foreign nation, communicates . . . to any foreign government . . . any . . . information relating to the national defense, shall be punished by death or by imprisonment for any term of years or for life . . . .[1]

This definition is consistent with the typical image of espionage as the passing of secrets from one country to another. The phrase "any information relating to the national defense" is quite broad but has been limited by courts to mean "information relating to the national defense" that is "closely held by the government" and is "the type of information that, if disclosed, could harm the United States."[2]

[1] 18 U.S.C. § 794.

[2] United States v. Rosen, 445 F. Supp. 2d 602, 611 n.5 (E.D. Va. 2006); see also Gorin v. United States, 312 U.S. 19, 28 (1941) (noting the term "national defense" has a "well understood connotation . . . referring to the military and naval establishments and related activities of national preparedness"); United States v. Heine, 151 F.2d 813, 816 (2d Cir. 1945) (noting that "information relating to the national defense" does not include information from publicly available sources); cf. United States v. Abu-Jihaad, 630 F.3d 102, 135 (2d Cir. 2010) (noting that defendant's possession of documents classified as "confidential" containing information about "anticipated movements of Navy ships

Criminalizing Disobedience. Youngjae Lee, Oxford University Press. © Oxford University Press 2026.
DOI: 10.1093/9780197617175.003.0010

But even with that narrowing, the law can be quite broad, as the law can cover situations that go beyond passing state secrets to foreigners.

For instance, it is a crime to "obtain[] . . . any . . . document . . . of anything connected with the national defense" "for the purpose of obtaining information respecting the national defense with intent or reason to believe that the information is to be used to the injury of the United States, or to the advantage of any foreign nation."[3] It is also a crime for a person who has "lawful[]" or "unauthorized" possession of "information relating to the national defense which information the possessor has reason to believe could be used to the injury of the United States or to the advantage of any foreign nation" to "willfully communicate[] . . . the same to any person not entitled to receive it."[4] And it is a crime to "receive[] . . . any document . . . of anything connected with the national defense" "for the purpose of obtaining information respecting the national defense," "knowing or having reason to believe . . . that it has been . . . obtained . . . by any person contrary to" these espionage laws.[5]

Unlike the first section quoted above, these latter provisions do not require passing of information to any foreign entity, so the term "espionage" is misleading, and these laws may be better understood as laws that criminalize certain handlings of state secrets. There is much debate about whether the laws are too broad, should be read more narrowly, should be amended, or are unconstitutional at least in part.[6] I will set those concerns aside for now.

Laws like these in the United States and elsewhere are often at the center of high drama and have produced a number of well-known prosecutions. Here are some high-profile cases from the United States and elsewhere (some of which were first mentioned in the previous chapter).

- Hotsumi Ozaki was an influential China expert in Japan during World War II and served as a consultant to the highest level of the Japanese government as part of a civilian advisory group. The Soviet Union sought information regarding Japan's war plans, more specifically whether it planned to attack the Soviet Union at any point, and Ozaki passed on what he learned about Japan's plans with regard to the Soviets to Richard Sorge, who was a Soviet spy working in Japan. Ozaki was communist, ant-imperialist, and anti-fascist, and he apparently hoped to bring about a communist revolution

into areas of heightened vulnerability to attack" constituted "information related to the national defense").

[3] 18 U.S.C. § 793(a), (b).
[4] 18 U.S.C. § 793(d), (e).
[5] 18 U.S.C. § 793(c).
[6] See generally Geoffrey R. Stone and Lee C. Bollinger, eds., *National Security, Leaks and Freedom of the Press: The Pentagon Papers Fifty Years On* (Oxford University Press, 2021).

throughout Asia, including in Japan, by working with Sorge. In 1943, Ozaki was convicted of violating, among other things, Japan's National Defense Security Law, which prohibited disclosure of state secrets to foreigners or to public, was sentenced to death, and was hanged in 1944.[7]

- Klaus Fuchs, from Germany, was a theoretical physicist who escaped the Nazis in 1933 due to his activism with and membership in the Communist Party of Germany. A talented mathematician and physicist, he went to the United Kingdom in 1933 and became a British citizen in 1942. In 1941, Fuchs was invited to join a team of scientists working on developing nuclear weapons in the United Kingdom, and the work led him to the Manhattan Project in Los Alamos, New Mexico. He stayed and worked there until 1946, at which point he returned to England and continued to work on nuclear weapons research. During the time period when he worked on the nuclear weapons projects, Fuchs clandestinely passed on massive amounts of information about the research to the Soviet Union. The espionage work lasted until 1949, and the work likely contributed to the speed with which the Soviets were able to develop their own nuclear weapon. Fuchs was arrested and convicted of violating Britain's Official Secrets Act in 1950. Fuchs's espionage appears to have been ideologically motivated, as he was a communist and sympathetic to the Soviet Union.[8]
- Julius Rosenberg was born in New York and grew up on the Lower East Side of Manhattan and graduated from City College of New York in the late 1930s with an engineering degree. Throughout the 1940s, he collected technical information of various kinds and passed it on to the Soviet Union, including documents collected from his wife Ethel's brother David Greenglass, who worked as an engineer on the Manhattan Project in Los Alamos, New Mexico. The Rosenbergs and Greenglass were, as communists, sympathetic to the Soviet Union. In 1950, all three were arrested and were convicted of conspiracy to commit espionage. The Rosenbergs were executed, and Greenglass was sentenced to fifteen years in prison.[9]
- Daniel Ellsberg, as an analyst for RAND Corporation, a think tank working closely with the US government, had access to the Pentagon Papers, a secret internal government study of the history of the US government's

[7] See generally Chalmers Johnson, *An Instance of Treason: Ozaki Hotsumi and the Sorge Spy Ring* (Stanford University Press, 1964).

[8] See generally Mike Rossiter, *The Spy Who Changed the World: Klaus Fuchs, Physicist and Soviet Double Agent* (Skyhorse, 2014); Nancy Thorndike Greenspan, *Atomic Spy: The Dark Lives of Klaus Fuchs* (Viking, 2020); Frank Close, *Trinity: The Treachery and Pursuit of the Most Dangerous Spy in History* (Allen Lane, 2019).

[9] See generally Ronald Radosh and Joyce Milton, *The Rosenberg File: A Search for the Truth*, 2nd ed. (Yale University Press, 1997).

decision-making with regard to the Vietnam War. Ellsberg made copies of the Pentagon Papers and tried to make them public through various avenues, with the hope of influencing the public debate over the war. In the end, he passed on parts of the Pentagon Papers to numerous newspapers, including the *New York Times* and the *Washington Post*, which published them, despite legal maneuvers from the White House to prevent their release. Ellsberg was indicted and tried for violating the Espionage Act, but the case was dismissed due to revelations of government misconduct relating to the prosecution.[10]

- Aldrich Ames, a CIA agent who was appointed the head of the counterintelligence branch of the Soviet division in 1983, started passing on secrets about the CIA's intelligence work in the Soviet Union to the Soviets and continued to do so for the Soviet Union and Russia—for hefty sums of money—until he was caught in 1994. The ranks of CIA agents working in the Soviet Union were decimated in the 1980s due to Ames's disclosure of their identities. Ames was convicted for his crimes and was sentenced to life in prison.[11]
- Robert Hanssen, an FBI agent working in counterintelligence, started selling state secrets to the Soviets in 1979 and sold state secrets to the Soviet Union and Russia until 2001, when he was caught. Hanssen gave up the name of a top agent working for the United States from the Soviet Union, revealed information about the United States' intelligence methods, military capability assessments, and war contingency plans. Hanssen was convicted for his crimes and was sentenced to life in prison.[12]
- Chelsea Manning, an army intelligence officer deployed in Iraq, released in 2010 troves of classified information about the US military activities in the Iraq and Afghanistan wars between 2004 and 2009 by sending the documents to WikiLeaks, a website founded and operated by Julian Assange with others, with a cover note remarking that "[t]his is possibly one of the more significant documents of our time, removing the fog of war, and revealing the true nature of 21st century asymmetric warfare."[13] She also sent to WikiLeaks a body of US State Department cables and documents regarding Guantánamo detainees. These documents were later published, in coordination with WikiLeaks, by the *Guardian*, the *New York Times*, *Der Spiegel*,

[10] See generally Daniel Ellsberg, *Secrets: A Memoir of Vietnam and the Pentagon Papers* (Penguin Books, 2002).

[11] See generally David Wise, *Nightmover: How Aldrich Ames Sold the CIA to the KGB for $4.6 Million* (HarperCollins, 1995); Tim Weiner et al., *Betrayal: The Story of Aldrich Ames, an American Spy* (Random House, 1995).

[12] See generally David Wise, *Spy: The Inside Story of How the FBI's Robert Hanssen Betrayed America* (Random House, 2002).

[13] Matthew Shaer, "The Long, Lonely Road of Chelsea Manning," *New York Times*, June 12, 2017.

Le Monde, and other media outlets. Manning later wrote that her conduct was "a direct action in the service of transparency"[14] and motivated by a desire for "the American people to know what was being done in their name."[15] Manning was convicted and sentenced to thirty-five years in prison, later commuted to expire after she served for nearly seven years.[16]

- Edward Snowden, who worked in various roles for the CIA and the National Security Agency between 2006 and 2013, leaked to several journalists documents showing that the US government had built a system of mass surveillance with capacity to collect, search, and examine everyone's activities without disclosing the full extent of the surveillance program to the lawmakers or to the public. Stories in the *Guardian* and the *Washington Post* followed.[17] Snowden was charged with violations of the Espionage Act and ended up in exile in Russia.[18]

In all of these examples, the underlying conduct, the bare minimum that amounts to lawbreaking, is the same—disclosure of state secrets to those who are not authorized to have them, whether the recipients of the information are foreign governments, journalists, or the public. Yet, as we can see from these examples, people who break espionage laws or laws like them are of many different types. Some cooperate with foreign governments for ideological reasons. Some cooperate with foreign governments for money. Some disclose state secrets to the public to bring attention to an issue. Some of these reasons are worse than others.

How should we think about the morality of these acts? As argued in the previous chapter, cases like Ozaki, Ames, and Hanssen suggest that the problem with espionage is disloyalty, and we may say the same about Fuchs, the Rosenbergs, and Greenglass. These were Japanese, British, and American citizens who gave up state secrets to the Soviet Union and Russia even though they owed allegiance to their countries of citizenship. It is true that owing allegiance is not necessarily an element of these crimes, but it is difficult to avoid at least a whiff of disloyalty

[14] Chelsea Manning, *README.txt: A Memoir* (Farrar, Straus and Giroux, 2022), 181.

[15] Manning, *README.txt*, 193.

[16] See Charlie Savage, "Chelsea Manning to Be Released Early as Obama Commutes Sentence," *New York Times*, January 17, 2017; Manning, *README.txt*, 250–58. Also, Julian Assange, after a prolonged negotiation, pleaded guilty for conspiracy to receive documents from Manning through his work in WikiLeaks. See Office of Public Affairs, "WikiLeaks Founder Pleads Guilty and Is Sentenced for Conspiring to Obtain and Disclose Classified National Defense Information," Department of Justice, Press Release, June 25, 2024, https://www.justice.gov/opa/pr/wikileaks-founder-pleads-guilty-and-sentenced-conspiring-obtain-and-disclose-classified.

[17] Glenn Greenwald et al., "Edward Snowden: The Whistleblower Behind the NSA Surveillance Revelations," *Guardian*, June 11, 2013; Barton Gellman and Laura Poitras, "U.S., British Intelligence Mining Data from Nine U.S. Internet Companies in Broad Secret Program," *Washington Post*, June 7, 2013.

[18] Edward Snowden, *Permanent Record* (Metropolitan Books, 2019).

when, say, an American commits the crime of delivering military secrets to a foreign government "with intent or reason to believe that it is to be used to the injury of the United States or to the advantage of a foreign nation."[19] The disloyalty story, however, does not work as well for cases of Ellsberg, Manning, and Snowden, who were whistleblowers and were likely not out to help another country compete against the United States. In fact, contrary to being disloyal to the United States, one might think of them as those who sought to protect and improve the United States—all three served in the military and report being disillusioned about the gap between the ideals the United States purportedly stood for, as well as official justifications given for state secrets, and reality.[20]

To sort through these issues, we might ask if there is ever a good argument for engaging in acts of espionage. Ames and Hanssen were financially motivated, but the Rosenbergs, Greenglass, and Fuchs appear to have thought that communism was morally superior and wanted to help the Soviet Union's nuclear weapons development during World War II and the Cold War. One can also imagine a non-communist with a cosmopolitan and universalist perspective engaging in similar acts with the thought that there are good reasons to pass along military secrets. For example, Fuchs is reported to have said while imprisoned that he spied because "knowledge of atomic research should not be the private property of any one country but should be shared with the rest of the world for the benefit of mankind."[21] Even Ames said at one point, self-servingly, that he wanted "to even things out, to level the playing field."[22]

Along these lines, one might think that national security is a good—it contributes to a sense of safety that enables people to pursue normal lives,[23] and a country's military power can enhance its ability to defend itself against potential aggressors. One might accordingly believe that some military secrets can be useful to some other country's national security, which in turn would benefit that country's inhabitants.[24] It might also be believed that if countries that worry

[19] 18 U.S.C. § 794.

[20] See Robert D. McFadden, "Daniel Ellsberg, Who Leaked the Pentagon Papers, Is Dead at 92," *New York Times*, June 16, 2023; Shaer, "Chelsea Manning"; The Editorial Board, "Edward Snowden, Whistle-Blower," *New York Times*, January 1, 2014.

[21] Greenspan, *Atomic Spy*, 276.

[22] Walter Pincus, "Catch a Spy—And Look What Happens," *Washington Post*, March 25, 2001.

[23] See, e.g., Ian Loader and Neil Walker, *Civilizing Security* (Cambridge University Press, 2007).

[24] For instance, Kok-Chor Tan supports the "right of nation state to self-determination and non-interference," which would presumably be a right that is more easily and freely exercised with a strong military force. Kok-Chor Tan, *Justice without Borders: Cosmopolitanism, Nationalism, and Patriotism* (Cambridge University Press, 2004), 114. Tan further argues that "differences in power relations between nations . . . obstruct the right to self-determination of the least advantaged" because "material inequalities will allow some nations to more easily exploit others, thereby compromising their right to self-determination." Tan, *Justice without Borders*, 116. It seems that this problem, too, can be alleviated if military knowledge from more powerful states can be redistributed to weaker states. Finally, he states that "the relative vulnerability of some nations with respect to others makes them susceptible to coercion and deception, which is clearly anathema to self-determination." Tan,

about another country's military interventions learn more about the military in that foreign country, these countries will better prepare themselves for a potential attack from that country. If military interventions in general or in particular instances are thought to be potentially an awful idea, then one might think that there is nothing wrong with preventing such interventions by weakening some militaries or strengthening the potential targets of military interventions.[25]

In addition, military power enhances a country's bargaining position in the world,[26] and to the extent that one country has an unfair advantage in this arena, one might think that revealing military secrets is a way of redistributing military-backed advantage. Moreover, to the extent that citizens in wealthy countries benefit from the current system of inequalities, one might say that they in fact have a moral duty to work toward undoing the system of inequality, perhaps by distributing military intelligence to other countries that may lack such resources and are thus in positions of vulnerability. Some might even argue that sending military secrets to some countries would mean those countries would be able to spend less on military and more on, say, social welfare, which would be a tremendous gain for the individuals living in those states.

These arguments would strike many people as, to say the least, highly problematic. Basing one's behavior on the sorts of arguments just laid out seems ill-advised. As noted with regard to treason in the previous chapter, these seem like the kinds of situations where individual citizens are unlikely to have superior knowledge as to what will endanger a nation's physical security, and individuals should not feel justified in acting contrary to the laws unless they are nearly certain that the government is wrong to think there is a risk of harm to national security from such acts.[27] But the risk of harm account does not accurately reflect how these laws work in that we do not generally engage in case-by-case determinations to see whether individual acts undertaken are in fact harmful all

Justice without Borders, 118. The argument is not that Tan would endorse acts of espionage; the only point here is that one way of addressing the kinds of relative vulnerabilities Tan points out may be through espionage.

[25] Cf. Barry Buzan, *People, States and Fear: An Agenda for International Security Studies in the Post–Cold War Era*, 2nd ed. (Lynne Rienner Publishers, 1991), 158 ("Would international security be better served by a more even distribution of power than by the huge inequalities, such as those between the United States and Burundi, that dominate the present system? It can be argued that more equal units might well provide a more manageable anarchy, because each would have difficulty mobilizing sufficient resources to threaten others seriously . . . .").

[26] Robert J. Art, "The Fungibility of Force," in *The Use of Force: Military Power and International Politics*, 6th ed., ed. Robert J. Art and Kenneth N. Waltz (Rowman & Littlefield, 2004), 7 (arguing that military power is "fungible" in the sense that it helps the state achieve various objectives, both military and non-military); Robert J. Art, "To What Ends Military Power?," in *America's Grand Strategy and World Politics* (Routledge, 2009); Alexander L. George, "Coercive Diplomacy," in *Use of Force*, 72–73; John Garnett, "The Role of Military Power," in *Perspectives on World Politics*, 2nd ed., ed. Richard Little and Michael Smith (Routledge, 1991), 74–82.

[27] Cf. Cécile Fabre, "The Morality of Treason," *Law and Philosophy* 39, no. 4 (2020): 446.

things considered before convicting, though such accounting may be relevant for sentencing.

In addition, there is a deeper problem with a harm-based account, as it leaves out an important feature of these crimes that one might call "usurpation" or "foreign relations vigilantism." In the previous chapter, I explained the duty not to be disloyal on the part of those who owe allegiance to the state as a fixed point in the way in which the state has configured power between the state and the people in order to guarantee physical security of the state. Another feature, one that is particularly relevant to this chapter, of this configuration of power is the idea that the state is to have exclusive control over matters of national security. Under this setup, individuals are to stay outside this domain of exclusive governmental power, and those who seek to take the matters into their own hands transgress the boundaries that delineate how the power is to be distributed within the polity for reasons of national security. In short, the relevant wrong here should be thought of as usurpation of state power.

An important difference between usurpation and disloyalty, which was discussed in the previous chapter and in this one, above, is that usurpation, unlike disloyalty, is not about prioritizing the interests of one's own community or associates. Rather, it is about respecting boundaries and the way in which power is allocated. Under this account, one may be a citizen of country *A*, believe that country *B*'s interests are more valuable overall, and work in ways to promote country *B*'s interests over those of country *A* every time but still avoid wronging through usurpation as long as he respects these political boundaries. Conversely, one may be a citizen of country *A* and promote country *A*'s interests over those of other countries at all times but can still wrong through usurpation if he transgresses the relevant boundaries. Therefore, under the proposed account, the idea of partiality in the sense of prioritizing one's own country's interests drops out.

The usurpation account has a number of advantages over the disloyalty account when it comes to explaining wrongness of espionage. For instance, consider an American who sells American state secrets to China but has no interest in how the competition between the two countries for global dominance shakes out. Here is someone whose heart does not belong to China or the United States but only to himself. It is debatable whether this is a genuine case of betrayal, but it is easy to assimilate the scenario as a case of usurpation.

The usurpation account also does a better job explaining why we do not see a distinction between disclosing state secrets to enemy nations and to allied nations in this area of the law, except in the case of treason.[28] If the real issue has to

[28] See, e.g., David M. Halbfinger and Isabel Kershner, "Jonathan Pollard, Spy for Israel, Gets Hero's Welcome From Netanyahu: 'You're Home,'" *New York Times*, December 30, 2020.

do with the idea of betrayal, then some distinction between friends and enemies seems plausible. Consider the way a person may reveal a friend's secret to their mutual friend with the belief that the mutual friend would not use the information against the friend with the secret. However, if a person commits the wrong of stepping into the government's exclusive territory, that in itself is wrong, and the concept of usurpation makes no distinction between spying for friends and spying for enemies.

Finally, a person may engage in acts that are in violation of the law but in order to protect the United States from a greater harm. As noted above, Daniel Ellsberg's leaking of the Pentagon Papers to the *New York Times* may have violated the law, yet it would be wrong to characterize his actions as disloyal. The same may be said for Manning and Snowden. That is, sometimes one's concern for the well-being of one's object of loyalty may lead one to commit criminal acts, such as revealing state secrets, but it would be inaccurate to characterize such acts as disloyal. If stealing state secrets were truly a crime of disloyalty, then the crimes of Ellsberg, Manning, and Snowden would fit awkwardly. By contrast, if we imagine their crimes as instances of usurpation, no such difficulty arises.

III. Export Controls and Sanctions

We can apply the same analysis to explain related laws that restrict international trade for national security reasons. For instance, take the Export Control Reform Act.[29] In the section of the law explaining the reasons for the law, it says that "[it] is the policy of the United States . . . to the extent necessary" to "restrict the export of items which would make a significant contribution to the military potential of any other country . . . which would prove detrimental to the national security of the United States."[30] The law lists a number of purposes of export controls by saying that exports are controlled to, among other things, "preserve the qualitative military superiority of the United States" and "carry out the foreign policy of the United States, including the protection of human rights and the promotion of democracy."[31] Under this law, some items are designated as "dual-use," meaning the items have "civilian applications and military, terrorism, weapons of mass destruction, or law-enforcement-related applications,"[32] and such items are regulated through the Export Administration Regulations,[33] which contain licensing requirements for exports, and the Commerce Control List,[34] which is

[29] Export Controls Act of 2018, Pub. L. 115–232, August 13, 2018, 132 Stat. 2208.
[30] 50 U.S.C. § 4811(1)(A).
[31] 50 U.S.C. § 4811(2)(B).
[32] 50 U.S.C. §4801(2).
[33] 15 C.F.R. Parts 730–74.
[34] 15 C.F.R. Part 774.

promulgated by the Commerce Department and spells out which items require a license to export.[35]

Similarly, under the Arms Export Control Act, the president of the United States is authorized to identify certain items as "defense articles and defense services," and such items cannot be exported without a license.[36] The policy rationale for the authorization is explained as being "[i]n furtherance of world peace and the security and foreign policy of the United States," and the president is to consider, when "issuing export licenses," "whether the export of an article would contribute to an arms race, aid in the development of weapons of mass destruction, support international terrorism, increase the possibility of outbreak or escalation of conflict, or prejudice the development of bilateral or multilateral arms control or nonproliferation agreements or other arrangements."[37] The State Department implements these provisions through the International Traffic in Arms Regulations[38] and the Munitions List.[39]

In addition, the International Emergency Economic Powers Act (IEEPA) grants authority to the president of the United States "to deal with any unusual and extraordinary threat . . . to the national security, foreign policy, or economy of the United States, if the President declares a national emergency with respect to such threat."[40] In such situations, the president is authorized to issue regulations that prohibit numerous types of transactions, including any "importation or exportation of . . . any property."[41]

All of these laws authorize criminal prosecutions,[42] and there have been prosecutions over the years for, for example, "attempting to export a controlled microwave amplifier to (then) West Germany without an export license,"[43] "exporting (and conspiring to export) a control panel for a large hot isostatic press . . . without the export license,"[44] and attempting to export encryption devices without a license.[45]

To test the limits of such laws, consider the following hypothetical of a person I will call "John."[46] John is a professor of engineering and an expert on plasma technology to control the flight of unmanned military drone aircrafts, and the project is being funded as a result of a contract awarded to him by the US Air

35 15 C.F.R. § 736.2.
36 22 U.S.C. § 2778(a)(1).
37 22 U.S.C. § 2778(a)(2).
38 22 C.F.R. Parts 120–30.
39 22 C.F.R. Part 121.
40 50 U.S.C. § 1701.
41 50 U.S.C. § 1702(a)(1)(B).
42 50 U.S.C. § 4819(b); 22 U.S.C. § 2778(c); 50 U.S.C. § 1705(c).
43 United States v. Shetterly, 971 F.2d 67, 68 (7th Cir. 1992).
44 United States v. Lachman, 521 F.3d 12, 15 (1st Cir. 2008).
45 United States v. Hsu, 364 F.3d 192, 197 (4th Cir. 2004).
46 The following description is based on United States v. Roth, 628 F.3d 827 (6th Cir. 2011).

Force. Like many professors in the United States, he has graduate students from overseas, and he has one student from China and one student from Iran. John lets those students have access to the data that the project has collected.

Under the regulations implementing the Arms Export Control Act, the Department of State has designated military drones as "defense articles,"[47] and technical data defined as information "required for the design, development, production, manufacture, assembly, operation, repair, testing, maintenance or modification of defense articles" to be "defense articles" as well.[48] The regulations also define "export" as, among other things, a "transmission out of the United States" or "[r]eleasing or otherwise transferring technical data to a foreign person in the United States."[49] Because the two graduate students are foreigners, John's giving of access to data from his project to his graduate students counts as an export of "defense articles."

Is John morally blameworthy in this case? It is unclear why someone like John would ignore the prohibition on making the data available to foreign students, but one can imagine that perhaps he relies on his graduate students in ways that would make giving them access to certain data useful for his work, seeks to hire the best graduate students he can find regardless of their nationality, does not think that his trust of his graduate students should vary depending on their nationality (giving the data to an American student would have been permitted, despite the purported sensitivity of the data), and thinks that the risk of benefiting Iranian and Chinese governments to the detriment of interests of the United States by giving his students access to the data is minimal to nonexistent. Perhaps he may be correct in his views and judgments with regard to these matters, which might in the end mean that it is not clear what he did wrong.

Or consider the case of a person I will call "Larry," a cryptocurrency expert and a US citizen.[50] One day, he travels to China and then from there goes into North Korea to give a talk at a conference on blockchain and cryptocurrency. But under the authority of IEEPA, presidents over time, including George W. Bush, Barack Obama, and Donald Trump, declared national emergencies with respect to North Korea through a series of executive orders,[51] and the Department of

[47] 22 C.F.R. § 121.1, Category VIII (a).

[48] 22 C.F.R. § 121.1, Category VIII (h)(29); 22 C.F.R. § 120.31(a); 22 C.F.R. § 120.33(a).

[49] 22 C.F.R. § 120.50(a).

[50] This description is based on United States v. Griffith, 515 F. Supp. 3d 106 (S.D.N.Y. 2021); United States v. Griffith, 19 Mag 10987 (S.D.N.Y. 2019).

[51] Exec. Order No. 13466, 3 C.F.R. 13466, "Continuing Certain Restrictions with Respect to North Korea and North Korea Nationals" (June 26, 2008); Exec. Order No. 13551, 3 C.F.R. 13551, "Blocking Property of Certain Persons with Respect to North Korea" (August 30, 2010); Exec. Order No. 13570, 3 C.F.R. 13570, "Prohibiting Certain Transactions with Respect to North Korea" (April 18, 2011); Exec. Order No. 13687, 3 C.F.R. 13687, "Imposing Additional Sanctions with Respect to North Korea" (January 2, 2015); Exec. Order No. 13722, 3 C.F.R. 13722, "Blocking Property of the Government of North Korea and the Workers' Party of Korea, and Prohibiting Certain Transactions

Treasury, after receiving authorizations from the presidents, issued regulations banning trading with North Korea. Under the act, it is "unlawful for a person to violate . . . any license, order, regulation, or prohibition" issued under the act,[52] and a person who willfully commits such an act may be imprisoned for not more than twenty years.[53]

Larry is arrested and prosecuted for violating Executive Order 13810, which commands that "[a]ll property and interests in property that are . . . within the possession or control of any United States person . . . are blocked and may not be transferred, paid, exported, withdrawn, or otherwise dealt in [a]ny person determined by the Secretary of the Treasury, in consultation with the Secretary of the State to be a North Korean person . . . ,"[54] and the regulation that prohibits "exportation . . . by a U.S. person, wherever located, of any goods, services, or technology to North Korea."[55]

This law is very similar to the Arms Export Control Act, with one difference being that the IEEPA requires a declaration of a national emergency by the president. Why would Larry think it is okay for him to do this? Larry may have thought it would be interesting to travel to North Korea and see it, as it is a society that is generally closed to foreign visitors. As to the content of his lecture, he may have thought it is not a big deal to give a generic talk on cryptocurrency at a conference (assuming that this is all he did) if the talk covers basic information that is easily available from various educational sources, and he may think that there is no harm in discussing an emerging technological tool like cryptocurrency with anyone, even if that person happens to be in North Korea. Again, he may be correct about all this, in which case perhaps there is nothing wrong with what he did.

However, in both of these cases, John and Larry acted in violation of the law, and the fact that they may have thought that they were not hurting the United States in any way or not doing anyone any harm as a general matter is irrelevant, even if they are correct. Again, as we saw above, these are examples of foreign relations vigilantism. In other words, we might think of violations of the Arms Export Control Act and the IEEPA as implicating the moral norm against usurpation of the state power, similar to violations of espionage laws. It follows that export control and sanctions violations, too, are disobedience offenses.

with Respect to Korea" (March 15, 2016); Exec. Order No. 13810, 3 C.F.R. 13810, "Imposing Additional Sanctions with Respect to North Korea" (September 20, 2017).

52 50 U.S.C. § 1705(a).
53 50 U.S.C. § 1705(c).
54 Exec. Order No. 13810.
55 31 C.F.R. § 510.206.

IV. Conclusion

This chapter has discussed crimes of national security such as espionage, export control, and sanctions violations. It is commonplace to think of the crime of espionage as a crime of disloyalty, akin to treason, or as a crime of harming one's country, given the high stakes. While such facets may be present in some instances of espionage, this chapter has argued, it is more theoretically sound to think of the wrong of espionage as involving not betrayal or risking harm, but usurpation. The relevant wrong here is rooted in the idea of separation of powers between individuals and the state, and we should conceive of national security crimes as crimes of usurpation or "foreign relations vigilantism." The crime of espionage is a crime of usurpation because the state is to have exclusive control over matters of national security, and individuals are to stay outside that domain. Those who seek to take the matters into their own hands transgress the boundaries that delineate how the power is to be distributed within the polity for reasons of national security. The same considerations explain, this chapter has argued, the wrongness of violations of export control laws and international sanctions.

10
Limits on Criminalization I: Rights and Liberty

I. Introduction

To summarize where we have been so far, a central thesis of this book is that criminal laws routinely and widely criminalize and punish mere disobedience. Chapter 2 has described what criminalizing and punishing disobedience means, especially in relation to legal moralism as described and defended in Chapter 1. Chapters 3 through 9 have given a detailed account of the ways in which the law criminalizes and punishes disobedience through discussing administration of justice crimes like contempt, obstruction of justice, perjury, and false statement; failure to assist crimes like hindering prosecution, receiving stolen property, money laundering, and failure to register as offenders or to report criminal activities; regulatory offenses in realms like environmental protection, environmental conservation, drugs, and medical devices; preventive offenses like attempt and possession offenses; and national security offenses like treason, espionage, and export control and sanctions violations.

A question that has repeatedly come up throughout these chapters is whether criminalization and punishment of disobedience in each context is normatively justifiable and desirable. In Chapter 2, we gave an account of how we might conceive of the wrongfulness of disobedience: the wrongfulness of disobedience can come from an understanding of the value of the state, which is also the source of the criminal laws and the institutions that support the laws. That is, it may be thought to be morally wrongful to fail to do one's fair share to support the institutions of the state that make it possible for individuals to live normal lives as we understand normalcy today.

But even if we are convinced of the wrongfulness of disobedience, should there be any principled limits on criminalization and punishment of disobedience? If yes, where do such limits come from? The rest of this chapter and the next two chapters consider answers to these questions.

Criminalizing Disobedience. Youngjae Lee, Oxford University Press. © Oxford University Press 2026.
DOI: 10.1093/9780197617175.003.0011

II. Rights and Duties in Conflict?

A. How the Duty to Support the State Can Conflict with Rights

We should start by exploring the outer limits of the idea that disobedience is wrong given each individual's duty to support the state. In Chapters 3 and 4, to explain the wrongfulness of crimes like obstruction of justice, hindering prosecution, or failure to report criminal activities, we introduced the idea that there is a duty to assist law enforcement.

To start with a stark example, consider the plot of *Unfaithful*, a movie about an extramarital affair, where a husband whose wife has an affair kills her lover, destroys all evidence of the crime, hides the dead body, and lies to the police when the officers, following a lead, come to the couple's house to investigate.[1] At the end of the movie, the married couple drive to a police station and pause in front of it, though the audience never finds out if the husband goes in or flees. Should he or should he not go in? According to Justice Antonin Scalia of the US Supreme Court, the answer is clear. Dissenting in *Minnick v. Mississippi*, a case reinforcing certain constitutional restrictions on police interrogations, Justice Scalia wrote that "[w]hile every person is entitled to stand silent, it is more virtuous for the wrongdoer to admit his offense and accept the punishment he deserves" and that "to design our laws on premises contrary" to that view is "to abandon belief in either personal responsibility or the moral claim of just government to obedience." Furthermore, he added that investigators should be allowed "to urge, or even ask, a person in custody to do what is right."[2]

Similarly, Sandra Marshall and R. A. Duff have argued in favor of "a civic responsibility" for a person who has committed a crime to "admit her crimes and to submit herself to the judgment of her peers through the criminal process."[3] Duff has also written that a defendant has a "civic duty" to play "an active, and honest, role in the process," which "must encompass admitting, confessing, one's guilt if one knows it—which is to plead 'Guilty.'"[4] Not only that, Duff even says a responsible citizen should also "be ready to give evidence and undergo cross-examination at her trial."[5]

Justice Scalia was not talking about criminalizing a failure to cooperate, and neither are Marshall and Duff.[6] However, if there is a moral duty to assist law enforcement, would it mean that the government could criminalize individuals'

[1] See *Unfaithful*, directed by Adrian Lyne (20th Century Fox, 2002).
[2] Minnick v. Mississippi, 498 U.S. 1146, 167 (1990).
[3] Sandra Marshall and R. A. Duff, "Civic Punishment," in *Democratic Theory and Mass Incarceration*, ed. Albert W. Dzur et al. (Oxford University Press, 2016), 43.
[4] R. A. Duff, *The Realm of Criminal Law* (Oxford University Press, 2018), 134.
[5] Duff, *The Realm of Criminal Law*, 134.
[6] See Marshall and Duff, "Civic Punishment," 42.

failures to turn themselves in after committing crimes without violating the wrongfulness constraint? Given the laws we saw in Chapters 3 and 4, it is not so far-fetched to imagine such a crime. We saw cases there involving a woman convicted for harboring a fugitive for making arrangements for her husband to avoid federal law enforcement by financing his stay in Mexico (*United States v. Hill*[7]), a woman convicted for hindering prosecution for failing to tell the police that the person who robbed a restaurant she was working in was her boyfriend (*People v. Williams*[8]), and a man convicted for obstruction of justice for marrying a woman so she would not be required to testify in his criminal trial for murder (*State v. Wilson*[9]). More generally, the Model Penal Code lists as an offense "hindering apprehension or prosecution," which provides in part that "[a] person commits an offense if, with purpose to hinder the apprehension, prosecution, conviction or punishment of another for crime, he . . . conceals or destroys evidence of the crime."[10]

It is true that both the *Hill* and *Williams* cases involved not failing to turn oneself in but interfering with the government's pursuit of another person, and the Model Penal Code provision is also worded in terms of interfering with "apprehension, prosecution, or conviction or punishment of *another*." It is also true that the offense involved in the *Wilson* case, where a person attempted to avoid being convicted by marrying another person, may be thought of as a type of witness tampering, which is not the same as failing to turn oneself in. All the same, the logic of an obligation to support the state's pursuit of a potential offender applies even if the target of the pursuit is oneself.

And there are more examples of instances that come close to criminalizing evading law enforcement. In the US Code, there is a crime of "flight to avoid prosecution," which makes it a crime for anyone to "move[] or travel[] in interstate or foreign commerce with intent . . . to avoid prosecution."[11] The language of the statute does not specify the meaning of "prosecution," and it could be construed quite broadly to cover situations where one simply goes from one state to another after committing a crime with intent to avoid being apprehended and prosecuted. Indeed, there is language in the caselaw that suggests as much. In *United States v. Bando*, for instance, defendants were charged with a conspiracy to injure a witness in a pending investigation in New York and to remove one of the co-conspirators from the state in order to prevent his prosecution.[12] The alleged co-conspirator was driven to Youngstown, Ohio, from New York, and

[7] United States v. Hill, 279 F.3d 731 (9th Cir. 2002).
[8] People v. Williams, 20 A.D.3d 72 (App. Div. 1st Dept. 2005).
[9] State v. Wilson, 240 A.3d 1140 (MD. App. 2020).
[10] Model Penal Code § 242.3(3) (American Law Institute, 1985).
[11] 18 U.S.C. § 1073.
[12] United States v. Bando, 244 F.2d 833, 835–36 (2d Cir. 1957).

the court noted that "[i]t does not appear that at the time [he] was driven to Youngstown, the police knew who had committed the crime," and "[n]o formal charge had been filed against anyone for the attack" on the witness.[13] Rejecting the defendants' challenge that there was no conspiracy to violate the flight to avoid prosecution law because no one had been "formally charged," the court held that "[t]he words 'to avoid prosecution' mean 'to avoid being prosecuted'" and that "[t]he statute does not say 'to avoid a *pending* prosecution.'"[14]

Another case that comes close to punishing evasion of law enforcement is the case of Jeffrey Gafoor from the United Kingdom.[15] Gafoor was convicted in 2003 for killing Lynette White in 1988. This was not an ordinary murder case because three men known as the "Cardiff Three" were initially convicted of the same killing in 1992, but the convictions were thrown out in the same year because of the coercive nature of the police interrogations. The case was reopened in 2000, and DNA evidence linked the killing to Gafoor. For our purposes, the interesting part of the case is what the judge sentencing him noted as "the most serious aggravating factor in this case, namely, allowing innocent men to be convicted of the murder."[16] The judge added that it was a "very serious aggravating factor . . . that Gafoor was content to allow innocent men to be arrested, to stand their trial and be convicted of a murder he knew had committed."[17] The idea seems to be that failing to turn oneself in to prevent a wrongful conviction is criminally wrongful and a basis for increasing one's punishment.[18]

It seems we may posit a general obligation to support the state and to adopt the view that the state can not only command people to make the state's job of apprehending criminal wrongdoers easier, but can criminalize failures to do so, including a failure to turn oneself in. But at the same time, such a broad statement can generate some strange outcomes. Say a person stabs a person to death and throws the victim in a car trunk where the victim bleeds to death. The killer buries the body in the woods that night, and the next morning he cleans the blood from his car. Or a person scores a big heist and then "lies low" and avoids major purchases in order to avoid detection. Would both of them be committing a second wrong of interfering with law enforcement after the first wrongs of murder and theft? Or say a person simply goes about one's ordinary and normal routine on a day-to-day basis after committing a crime. If "hindering prosecution" were a genuine moral wrong that can be criminalized, then a person who commits a crime and does not immediately turn himself in may be in continuing

[13] Bando, 244 F.2d at 837.
[14] Bando, 244 F.2d at 843 (emphasis in original).
[15] See Satish Sekar, *The Cardiff Five: Innocent Beyond Any Doubt*, 2nd ed. (Waterside Press, 2017).
[16] See Sekar, *The Cardiff Five*, 137.
[17] See Sekar, *The Cardiff Five*, 129.
[18] See Sekar, *The Cardiff Five*, 130.

violation of the obligation from the moment the crime is committed.[19] This means that everyone who commits a criminal act and fails to turn themselves in could be guilty of at least two crimes.

The point here is not to argue in favor of criminalizing a failure to turn oneself in, but to spell out the implications of positing a duty to support the state's law enforcement and using the duty as a basis to support criminalization of hindering prosecution. To put the point more sharply in different terms, the idea of a general duty to cooperate with law enforcement is troubling because it directly comes into conflict with the idea of asserting one's rights—that is, the privilege against self-incrimination—where rights-assertions interfere with law enforcement. The obvious problem with such laws is that the privilege against self-incrimination generally prohibits criminalization of a failure to confess to a crime that one has committed.[20] As such, we may take the position that one way of limiting the state's ability to criminalize failures to support law enforcement is by exploring when such criminalizations exceed limits defined in constitutional law.

In fact, many constitutional rights that people may assert against the government can be characterized as vehicles for obstruction of justice—a form of interfering with or failing to support the state—yet asserting such rights cannot serve as a basis for criminalization. Refusing to consent to a warrantless search,[21] insisting on the presumption of innocence and making the government prove one's guilt beyond a reasonable doubt,[22] exercising one's right to a speedy trial,[23] exercising one's right to a jury trial,[24] invoking the prohibition against double jeopardy,[25] asserting the privilege against self-incrimination,[26] refusing to answer questions without a lawyer present,[27] and demanding not only assistance of counsel but also *effective* assistance of counsel throughout the criminal process[28] are all exercises of rights guaranteed in the US Constitution that can "obstruct" the state's attempt to enforce the law, even though, as we saw in Chapter 4, obstruction of justice has been criminalized in many different ways.

To be sure, not all constitutional rights guaranteed in the Constitution that may slow down the criminal process may be accurately characterized as a failure

[19] It is, after all, the case that when a convicted person in the middle of a prison sentence escapes, he may be committing a continuing offense of failing to return as well as the initial crime of escape. See United States v. Bailey, 444 U.S. 394, 413 (1980); 18 U.S.C. § 751(a).

[20] See U.S. Const. amend. V.

[21] See U.S. Const. amend. IV.

[22] See In re Winship, 387 U.S. 358 (1970).

[23] See U.S. Const. amend. VI.

[24] See U.S. Const. amend. VI.

[25] See U.S. Const. amend. V.

[26] See U.S. Const. amend. V.

[27] See Miranda v. Arizona, 384 U.S. 436 (1996).

[28] See U.S. Const. amend. VI.

to assist law enforcement or support the state,[29] as assertions of these rights do different things. Consider *Powell v. Alabama*, a 1932 US Supreme Court case arising from one of the most notorious American legal disasters, also known as the Scottsboro Boys case, where, despite substantial evidence indicating their innocence, nine young Black males, ages ranging from thirteen to twenty, were convicted of the crime of raping two White women, after not having been given a fair, deliberate trial, not having received adequate legal representation, and having been tried by an all-White jury.[30] The *Powell* Court, after listing various procedural failures in the case, held that the defendants' convictions were unconstitutional because they were denied adequate legal representation.[31] Rulings in cases like these show that what may appear to be "resistance" of law enforcement—in the form of invoking one's constitutional rights—in fact aids law enforcement writ large by preventing or rectifying false convictions. And that is how an adversarial system is supposed to work. The system is set up to produce optimal outcomes through contestation.

This feature of rights is not limited to unjust prosecutions. Even assuming that law enforcement officers work in good faith within a reasonably just state, government actors may be misguided in any number of ways: they can make mistakes, may be working with limited information that leads them astray, may have on institutional blinders that prevent them from seeing the full picture clearly, or may be pursuing prosecutions on the basis of a legal interpretation that is wrong or may be proven to be ultimately incorrect or unwise. Given these possibilities, some assertions of rights are not correctly characterized as "obstruction of justice." Though the empirics are obviously controversial, the right to effective assistance of counsel, presumption of innocence, and the proof beyond a reasonable doubt requirement can keep the government disciplined about how it selects cases to prosecute.[32] Further, the right to trial by jury is often defended as a form of epistemic democracy that has a better chance of arriving at correct answers than an adjudication system run by professionals and experts.[33]

[29] Some, especially those who are unfamiliar with the legal phrase "obstruction of justice," might object to my terminology. Given that the Constitution may enshrine a notion of justice through individual rights provisions, one might say that a constitutional right that prevents a criminal conviction is an instance of justice being done, not an obstruction of it. However, I am using the term "obstruction of justice" in a narrower sense of obstructing the state's attempt to enforce its criminal laws by apprehending those who have committed criminal offenses. Given that, by design, the Constitution places a number of procedural roadblocks for the state to clear during the criminal process, such roadblocks may be fairly described as a form of obstruction of "justice."

[30] See Powell v. Alabama, 287 U.S. 45 (1952).

[31] See Powell, 287 U.S. at 52–72.

[32] See Larry Laudan, *Truth, Error, and Criminal Law: An Essay in Legal Epistemology* (Cambridge University Press, 2006), 218.

[33] See Youngjae Lee, "The Criminal Jury, Moral Judgments, and Political Representation," *University of Illinois Law Review* 2018, no. 4 (2018): 1285–87; Melissa Schwartzberg, "Justifying the Jury: Reconciling Justice, Equality and Democracy," *American Political Science Review* 112, no. 3

So if we define "justice" as apprehending the guilty, then asserting these rights may be vehicles of *assisting*, not obstructing, justice.

But not all rights are like that, as some do get in the way of apprehending the guilty and are more appropriately characterized as obstructionist, even though they may also serve other valuable purposes like protecting privacy or dignity of individuals. The right to refuse a search and the right against self-incrimination are both ways of denying the government access to potentially highly probative evidence. In these cases, at least, there does seem to be direct conflict between law enforcement and individual rights. And when there is such a genuine conflict, the idea of having individual rights is precisely to block certain laws from coming into existence or being applied in certain ways. Of course, the issue is complicated. Rights may be defined or narrowed in ways that take into account the government's need for effective law enforcement, in which case the situation may not be described as conflicting. That is, rights have limits and need to be specified in particular circumstances with conflicting considerations. As a general matter, though, what we seek to prevent with the concept of rights or constraints are situations where important interests are given up without special justification, and that is the sense in which there can be genuine conflicts.[34]

B. What Are These Rights For?

Can we say anything more theoretically about this conflict? Some might draw a distinction between the guilty and the innocent here. It is, after all, one of the clichés about rights that just because one has a right does not mean that one is right to exercise it. Maybe some criminal procedural rights are like that and should not be exercised when dealing with the state's effort to enforce the law against the guilty. That is, one might argue, a person who knows he is innocent would be right in exercising these rights to protect himself from misguided searches or interrogations, but a guilty person would be simply obstructing justice.

(2018): 447–48; Hélène Landemore, *Democratic Reason: Politics, Collective Intelligence, and the Rule of the Many* (Princeton University Press, 2012).

[34] For some discussions about these features of rights, see, e.g., Ronald Dworkin, *Taking Rights Seriously* (Harvard University Press, 1977), 90–100; James Griffin, *Well-Being: Its Meaning, Measurement, and Moral Importance* (Oxford University Press, 1986), 242–45; Joseph Raz, *The Morality of Freedom* (Oxford University Press, 1986), 183–86; Jeremy Waldron, "Rights in Conflict," in *Liberal Rights: Collected Papers 1981–1991* (Cambridge University Press, 1993), 203, 208–11; David Lyons, "Utility and Rights," in *Theories of Rights*, ed. Jeremy Waldron (Oxford University Press, 1984), 115, 117–18; Frederick Schauer, "A Comment on the Structure of Rights," *Georgia Law Review* 27, no. 2 (1993): 428–31.

Is this right? Consider here an interesting theoretical path taken by Alice Ristroph.[35] Ristroph has suggested in her Hobbes-inspired account that criminal procedure rights may be more specific instantiations of a general, more fundamental right to resist that both the innocent and the guilty retain. Ristroph says that under a Hobbesian account, "punishment is so great an intrusion on human freedom, dignity, and self-preservation that the only way to respect the humanity of those we punish is to acknowledge their right to resist" and to "refuse[] to blame humans for acting on the fundamental and rational drive for self-preservation."[36] This need not mean "anything goes" as long as one is seeking to resist punishment since some ways of resisting punishment are more harmful than others. But what we can do, according to Ristroph, is rationalize "constitutional and statutory rights of the accused and the already-convicted as forms of legitimate, nonviolent resistance to punishment"[37] and as "weaker relatives of the right to resist punishment."[38] Because Ristroph's suggestion does not depend on the right to resist *injustice* but rather depends on a person's right of self-preservation, this right to resist account would apply to everyone who is facing prosecution, even the guilty and even in a just society.

Yet while it certainly is theoretically convenient to have the right to resist manifest itself as a variety of rights that defendants already have, say, under the Constitution, there is no reason to expect the scope of the so-called right to resist to stay within the confines of various procedural guarantees, as the right to resist stemming from the right of self-preservation seems quite blunt as a concept. For instance, if there were such a right, it seems that various crimes against law enforcement should not exist as prohibitions. As we have seen, obstruction of justice is a crime. Disobedience of law enforcement officers can be a crime. It is also a crime to disobey commands of courts, for instance, to appear to face one's own prosecution. Perhaps many of these crimes are overbroad and should be appropriately limited by invoking the right to resist,[39] but it is still not clear how impositions of such duties, as a general matter, can coexist with the right to resist.[40]

[35] See Alice Ristroph, "Respect and Resistance in Punishment Theory," *California Law Review* 97, no. 2 (2009): 622–30.

[36] Ristroph, "Respect and Resistance," 628.

[37] Ristroph, "Respect and Resistance," 629.

[38] Ristroph, "Respect and Resistance," 623.

[39] See Lisa Kern Griffin, "Criminal Lying, Prosecutorial Power, and Social Meaning," *California Law Review* 97, no. 6 (2009): 1556–69; Stuart P. Green, "Lying, Misleading, and Falsely Denying: How Moral Concepts Inform the Law of Perjury, Fraud, and False Statements," *Hastings Law Journal* 53, no. 1 (2001): 168–73, 198–201.

[40] Ristroph acknowledges all this when she says, "American law does not endorse violence against police officers, prosecutors, judges, or corrections officials," and "in various ways the law does impose duties to submit to specific exercises of state force," as "it is a crime to resist arrest, or flee from prosecution ('jump bail'), or escape from custody." Alice Ristroph, "Regulation or Resistance?: A Counter-Narrative of Constitutional Criminal Procedure," *Boston University Law Review* 95, no. 5 (2015): 1596. However, the issue of reconciling these laws with a right to resist remains.

In sum, the problem with the idea of a "right to resist" is its seemingly peremptory nature, and Ristroph's explanation does not help us understand how such a right is to be limited.[41] That is, the concept of the right to resist does not offer a way of taking into account the idea of a duty to cooperate with the government. How else, then, should we think about the examples of "hindering prosecution" by committing crimes and then engaging in apprehension-avoidance acts—some relatively passive like not making flashy purchases from a big heist, some more active like moving to a different state to avoid apprehension after committing a crime, and some even more active like engaging in money laundering by investing criminally derived funds in various ways?

It seems to me that instead of thinking of these acts as justified exercises of the right to resist, we should see some of them, though not all, as free movements of individuals within a realm that the legal system ought to protect from state intrusion. While individuals do not have a general right to resist after committing crimes, their decision not to turn themselves in or otherwise make prosecutions easier, even if at times morally wrong, should be considered their privilege as free persons. And in order to preserve a sphere of autonomous living for individuals, there ought to be an understanding as to what sorts of detection avoidance behaviors are within the acceptable "rules of the game" for all the participants.

What would such "rules of the game" look like? We can start, as a general matter, with the proposition that citizens have a duty to cooperate with the government in a reasonably just society. As we have seen throughout the book, it would be difficult to give a moral justification for various disobedience offenses without positing such a duty. At the same time, such duties of citizenship do not necessarily justify legally requiring individuals to assist the state carry out its activities. Situations where such lack of cooperation or even resistance should not be legally required are not limited to situations characterized by injustice or to situations involving laws that are misguided for any number of reasons. Even when the state appropriately requests that citizens serve the common good by cooperating with the state, there are times when the state should still not go so far as to turn such requests into legal requirements that can be criminally enforced. The state has the power to set down all kinds of rules to make the project of living together possible, but that power can easily lead to oppression, and the oppression can take the form of the state requiring cooperation with law enforcement and criminalizing failures to do so. Therefore, while the state may correctly claim that there is an obligation to support the state's law enforcement efforts, it should

[41] In fact, Ristroph says that the Hobbesian right to resist is not even meant to be understood as a "legally enforceable claim" as the right has "no correlative duties." Ristroph, "Respect and Resistance," 617–18. If that is so, then the implications of the right to resist account for rights of criminal defendants are obscure.

at times refrain from using criminal law tools to ensure such support when doing so would be unduly intrusive.

As to what it all means in concrete terms, it is difficult to say, as case-by-case assessments need to be made. The state may be well-intentioned and even competent enough to know which policies to pursue to do its job of protecting the people's physical security and promoting general welfare. It may sometimes and appropriately carry out its functions with the help of criminal law. When the criminal law appears to overreach, our focus should not just be on whether the government is on the right track as it tackles social problems but also on the costs that are imposed on persons when legal requirements are introduced, even if such requirements come simply from the seemingly reasonable proposition that people should assist or at least not interfere with the government's core functions. And in order to understand what sorts of costs are too burdensome, we need to have a baseline understanding of the realm of autonomy that needs to be protected, next to the question of what sorts of duties to support the state exist, can be legally prescribed, and can be criminally enforced.

In other words, individual rights ought to be considered with an eye toward specifying the proper terms of interaction between citizens and the state even in a just state and with the goal of preserving a sphere of autonomy in which individuals can move freely and pursue their ordinary lives free from the state's coercive interference. In fact, while we have been focusing on detection-avoidance activities and their relationship to the duties to support the state, we can generalize from this model as a way of thinking about all other individual rights that may conflict with criminal laws, including those that criminalize disobedience.

III. Constitutional Rights and Disobedience Offenses

What kinds of limitations, derived from the principles articulated in the previous part, should be placed on criminalizations of disobedience? Which criminal laws discussed throughout this book are either invalid or should be limited due to their conflict with individual rights? Unfortunately, a detailed discussion of the constitutional implications of each crime definition we have encountered thus far will take us too far afield. Constitutional rulings are often line-drawing exercises, and lines may be drawn arbitrarily or irrationally by any given court, and locations of such lines shift back and forth over time. However, the fact that it is difficult to locate a line that stays fixed over time need not preclude us from at least highlighting areas of tension between constitutional rights and criminalization of disobedience.

Let us discuss several examples, mostly drawn from cases we have already seen. The law prohibiting disobedience of law enforcement officers, covered in Chapter 3, may be limited to allow, for instance, recording of law enforcement officers at work on freedom of speech grounds, so long as the act of recording does not interfere with the law enforcement.[42] And a law that criminalizes refusals to follow an officer's orders may be unconstitutional if the legal basis for such an order is so vaguely defined as to create a problem of fair notice, as the US Supreme Court held in *City of Chicago v. Morales*, which will be discussed in more detail later.[43] We also saw an obstruction of justice case of a person who attempted to persuade another to invoke her privilege against self-incrimination and refuse to testify in a case where he was the target of an investigation (*United States v. Baker*[44]). That case may not have produced a violation of the Fifth Amendment, but there is a fine line between that case and a case like *Maness v. Meyers*, where the Court limited a judge's ability to hold a person in contempt by holding that a judge may not hold an attorney in contempt for advising his client that he has a right not to testify in court when the privilege against self-incrimination is implicated.[45] In *Brogan v. United States*, the Court held that the law prohibiting making false statements to federal government officials covers situations where a person denies their involvement in a crime when asked by a federal government agent.[46] It is true that the Court in that case said that "neither the text nor the spirit" of the Constitution "confers a privilege to lie,"[47] but as Stuart Green points out, for over three decades, it was common to read the false statements law to include an exception for denials of guilt, and its persistence had to do with the intuition that there was a deep relationship between lying to deny one's guilt and the privilege against self-incrimination.[48]

Even the *Hill* case, in which a woman was convicted of helping her husband escape the authorities, potentially implicated a constitutional right. The defendant argued that the prosecution was unconstitutional because the laws as applied to her "impermissibly infringe upon her rights of association, marriage, [and] privacy."[49] While the court rejected her claim, it acknowledged that the laws prohibiting being an accessory after the fact and harboring a fugitive "could conceivably operate directly on an intimate relation of a marriage

[42] Rodeny A. Smolla, *Smolla and Nimmer on Freedom of Speech*, vol. 1 (Clark Boardman Callaghan, 2025), § 8:53 ("There is essential consensus . . . on the underlying proposition that citizens do have a First Amendment right to record police activity, subject only to reasonable time, place, and manner restrictions.").

[43] City of Chicago v. Morales, 527 U.S. 41 (1999).

[44] United States v. Baker, 611 F.2d 964 (4th Cir. 1979).

[45] Mannes v. Myers, 419 U.S. 449, 464–65 (1975).

[46] Brogan v. United States, 522 U.S. 398, 400–01 (1998).

[47] Brogan, 522 U.S. at 404.

[48] See Green, "Lying, Misleading," 50–54, 200–201.

[49] Hill, 279 F.3d at 736.

and exert a maximum destructive impact upon it."[50] The court did not specify "where lies the line between conduct that is normal spousal support . . . and conduct that demonstrates an intent to frustrate law enforcement," but in saying so it highlighted the need to "fully reconcile the harboring and accessory statutes" with constitutional law.[51]

The right of association or to choose a marriage partner could also theoretically impact obstruction of justice cases like the one we saw in *Wilson*, where a man was convicted of obstruction of justice for marrying a woman, while being incarcerated awaiting trial for murder, for the purpose of preventing her from testifying.[52] The state prosecuted the defendant for witness tampering and obstruction of justice, and the Supreme Court of Maryland upheld the conviction with the rationale that "otherwise lawful" conduct of "entering into a marriage" can amount to obstruction if done "with the intent to preclude another person from testifying at a criminal proceeding."[53] There are strong reasons to suspect that the marriage in *Wilson* was not in good faith, in which case one could carve out a "sham marriage" exception to the spousal privilege to require the spouse to testify. It seems, though, that the right to marry would be more troublingly implicated if a person marries another person in good faith *but also* with a desire to avoid having to testify, and is prosecuted for doing so.

Registration requirements for those who have been convicted of certain types of offenses, especially sex offenses, also burden important constitutional interests to problematic extents. Sex offender registration laws have been extensively discussed and criticized over time.[54] Under the federal version in the United States, a "sex offender" is to "register, and keep the registration current, in each jurisdiction where the offender resides, where the offender is an employee, and where the offender is a student."[55] Those subject to the law also have to "appear in person" within "3 business days after each change of name, residence, employment, or student status" to keep the registration current.[56] And, even with no changes, those affected must verify the information in the registry on a regular basis, as often as every three months and at least every year, depending on how the offense is classified.[57] Also depending on how each offense is classified,

[50] Hill, 279 F.3d at 737.
[51] Hill, 279 F.3d at 737.
[52] Wilson, 240 A.3d at 1140.
[53] Wilson, 240 A.3d at 1158.
[54] See, e.g., Wayne A. Logan, *Knowledge as Power: Criminal Registration and Community Notification Laws in America* (Stanford University Press, 2009); Emily Horowitz, *From Rage to Reason: Why We Need Sex Crime Laws Based on Facts, Not Fear* (Bloomsbury Publishing, 2023); Michael L. Perlin and Heather Ellis Cucolo, *Shaming the Constitution: The Detrimental Results of Sexual Violent Predator Legislation* (Temple University Press, 2017).
[55] 34 U.S.C. § 20913(a).
[56] 34 U.S.C. § 20913(c).
[57] 34 U.S.C.§ 20918.

the registration requirement can last from fifteen years to life.[58] In addition, state versions of sex offender registry laws impose residency requirements that limit where those who have been convicted of sex offenses can live, at some distance (typically between one hundred feet and two thousand feet) from schools, parks, playgrounds, and so on.[59]

There have been some successful challenges against these laws. For instance, in *In re Taylor*, decided in 2015, the Supreme Court of California declared unconstitutional "blanket enforcement" of a law making it "unlawful for any person for whom registration is required" under the sex offender registration law to "reside within 2000 feet of any public or private school, or park where children regularly gather."[60] The court based its holding upon the finding that the law "barred . . . access to approximately 97 percent of the multifamily rental housing units in San Diego County that would otherwise be available" to those impacted by the residency restriction and that the law made it unlawful for them to reside in "large areas of the county." Such restrictions also impacted "the ability . . . to live and associate with family members" and to have access to "[m]edical treatment, psychological counseling, drug and alcohol dependency services, and other rehabilitative social services," and also "led to greatly increased homelessness among registered sex offenders . . . ."[61] The court concluded that enforcement of the restrictions "has imposed harsh and severe restrictions and disability on . . . liberty and privacy rights" and "has infringed on . . . basic constitutional right to be free of official action that is unreasonable, arbitrary, and oppressive."[62]

Similarly, in 2016, the US Court of Appeals for the Sixth Circuit noted that the sex offender registration law in the state of Michigan imposed "geographical restrictions [that] are . . . very burdensome," as those impacted by the law "often have great difficulty in finding a place where they may legally live or work," including those "jobs that require traveling from jobsite to jobsite . . . since work will surely take place within a school zone at some point."[63] The court concluded that "these restrictions put . . . direct restraints on personal conduct."[64] The court's analysis was to justify the ultimate holding that the restriction amounted to punishment, as opposed to just regulation, but its observation that significant restrictions are being placed on people's liberty interests by the application of these laws is still relevant for our discussion.

[58] 34 U.S.C.§ 20915.
[59] See "Residency Restriction by State (For Persons Required to Register as Sex Offenders)," Florida Action Committee, July 11, 2019, https://floridaactioncommittee.org/residency-restrictions-by-state-for-persons-required-to-register-as-sex-offenders [https://perma.cc/CR4M-DBYX]; Perlin and Cucolo, *Shaming the Constitution*, 56–57.
[60] In re Taylor, 343 P.3d 867 (2015); Cal. Penal Code § 3003.5(b).
[61] In re Taylor, 343 P.3d at 880–81.
[62] In re Taylor, 343 P.3d at 879.
[63] Doe #1-5 v. Snyder, 834 F.3d 696, 701–02 (6th Cir. 2016).
[64] Doe #1-5, 834 F.3d at 703.

Preventive offenses discussed in Chapters 6 and 7 also have constitutional implications. As we saw in Chapter 6, incomplete attempt is often defined as having an intent to commit a crime and taking substantial steps toward committing the crime.[65] The law is designed to catch people before they cause any harm to others if they are in the process of implementing a thought or a plan. As we saw, there is the risk of drawing the line in the space between having harmful thoughts and causing a harm in a way that comes too close to punishing people for their thoughts or at least for conduct that is far from harm just because the conduct is accompanied by thoughts that society deems threatening.

A notorious example of such a danger is the case of Gilberto Valle, a New York police officer who was "an active member of an Internet sex fetish community called Dark Fetish Network."[66] The government accused Valle of conspiracy to commit kidnapping and provided as evidence chat transcripts of Valle talking with others on the Network about "kidnapping, torturing, cooking, raping, murdering, and cannibalizing various women."[67] The discussion was quite detailed as the chats included "Facebook photographs of women Valle knows; dates for planned kidnappings; prices Valle will charge for kidnapping these women; surveillance Valle has allegedly conducted of these women; the use of chloroform to incapacitate victims; acts of sexual violence that will be perpetrated on these women; and fantastical elements such as human-size ovens and rotisseries, and the construction of soundproofed basements and pulley apparatuses that will be used for purposes of torture."[68] The government also produced evidence showing that "Valle performed Internet searches for how to kidnap people, how to make chloroform, and how to restrain and cannibalize people."[69] Valle also discussed with another person on the network the possibility of kidnapping, butchering, and eating a woman he knew, went into specific details about how they would go about doing so, and wrote up the steps into a document he called a "blueprint."[70] Valle met with the intended victim for a seemingly ordinary lunch, and continued the discussion with the person on the Network.

The trial court ruled and the appeals court agreed that Valle's discussions and writings did not amount to a crime. The appeals court stated that "mere indulgence of fantasy, even of the repugnant and unsettling kind here, is not, without more, criminal."[71] The court emphasized that "a person's inclinations and fantasies are his own and beyond the reach of the government"[72] and that it

[65] See Model Penal Code § 5.01 (American Law Institute, 1985).
[66] United States v. Valle, 807 F.3d 508, 512 (2d Cir. 2015).
[67] Valle, 807 F.3d at 512.
[68] Valle, 807 F.3d at 514.
[69] Valle, 807 F.3d at 519.
[70] Valle, 807 F.3d at 521.
[71] Valle, 807 F.3d at 523.
[72] Valle, 807 F.3d at 511 (quoting Jacobson v. United States, 503 U.S. 540, 551–52 (1992)).

was "loath to give the government the power to punish us for our thoughts and not our actions," including "the power to criminalize an individual's expression of sexual fantasies."[73] Much of the court's discussion in Valle's case turned on the court's conclusion that Valle's thoughts were fantasies and not actual plans because the details of the "plan" often were fabrications about what equipment he owned and involved an unrealistic timeline of "kidnapping three different women in three different places spanning thousands of miles on the same day."[74] But, as the prosecution of this case shows, even fantasies can have an adverse impact on a person in an inchoate offense case, which can raise free speech concerns.

Another example is *United States v. Curtin*, in which the US Court of Appeals for the Ninth Circuit addressed an evidentiary issue in a case about a man named Curtin who was convicted for "traveling across state lines with intent to engage in a sexual act with a minor" and "using an interstate facility to attempt to persuade a minor to engage in sexual acts."[75] Curtin had been chatting in a sexually explicit manner with an undercover agent pretending to be a fourteen-year-old girl, and they planned to meet up. He was arrested when he showed up for the meeting but claimed that he expected to meet an adult pretending to be a child. Since traveling across state lines and using an interstate facility are otherwise lawful acts, and since doing such things with intent to engage in a sexual act with an adult or to persuade an adult to engage in sexual acts is also lawful, the case turned on Curtin's intent to have sex with a minor. To demonstrate such an intent, the prosecutor introduced into evidence "over 140 stories about adults having sex with children" that were found "in the form of text" in a digital device that he had on him.[76] Inclusion of this evidence was ultimately upheld over a dissent arguing that "[t]here is no avoiding the First Amendment implications of using what people read as evidence of what they did" and that the evidence should have been excluded to "protect [Curtin] from being convicted for his excreable taste in reading material and repulsive fantasies."[77] While the relevant laws did not directly "criminalize thoughts," they clearly aimed to prevent, via criminalization, conduct that has the potential to harm. What turned otherwise innocent conduct into a criminal act was the content of the defendant's mind, proven by the government using records of Curtin's reading materials. The laws' reach could thus have been limited by a more stringent enforcement of the right to free speech.

[73] Valle, 807 F.3d at 511.
[74] Valle, 807 F.3d at 514.
[75] United States v. Curtin, 489 F.3d 935, 937 (9th Cir. 2007).
[76] Curtin, 489 F.3d at 938.
[77] Curtin, 489 F.3d at 959–60 (Kleinfeld, J., concurring).

As foreshadowed in Chapter 7's mention of *Stanley v. Georgia*, possession offenses pose similar constitutional concerns. In *Stanley*, the US Supreme Court held that an obscenity law prohibiting "mere private possession of obscene matter" was in violation of the Constitution because "a State has no business telling a man, sitting alone in his own house, what books he may read or what films he may watch."[78] Taken to its logical extreme, the same principle, one would think, should apply even if the possessed material is child pornography, but as we have seen, courts have distinguished possession of child pornography from the facts in *Stanley*. Yet it remains the case that free speech considerations are impacted in such cases.

There are constitutional concerns having to do with guns and drug possession cases as well. There are a lot of open questions in the area of gun regulation in the United States after the Supreme Court interpreted the Constitution to include an individual right to guns, such as whether it is constitutionally permissible to prohibit those with felony convictions from owning guns.[79] As to drugs, it is instructive that the Constitutional Court of Colombia held in 1994, on grounds of "the right to free development of personality," that criminalization of personal use of narcotics was unconstitutional.[80] David Pozen has persuasively expanded upon such a rationale as follows:

> People use psychoactive substances for a wide range of reasons, including social lubrication, creative stimulation, spiritual and psychological exploration, mental and physical relaxation, pain relief, escapism, energy, sleep, sex—for ends of great moral seriousness, frivolous fun, and everything in between. The decision to use such substances implicates a correspondingly wide range of civil libertarian interests, including the ability to govern one's body and brain, the freedom to make self-defining ethical and aesthetic choices, and [the] right to be let alone. Laws that criminalize drug taking are thus inherently suspect from a liberal perspective.
>
> . . . .
>
> The U.S. Constitution contains various provisions that can be read to protect liberty, privacy, and the pursuit of happiness, a set of values that helped motivate the entire constitutional project. Punitive drug laws imperil those same values . . . .[81]

[78] Stanley v. Georgia, 394 U.S. 557, 565 (1969).

[79] See Dave S. Sidhu, "Courts Disagree as to Whether the Federal Felon in Possession Firearm Prohibition Violates the Second Amendment," *Congressional Research Service*, May 28, 2024.

[80] Manuel José Cepeda Espinosa and David Landau, *Colombian Constitutional Law: Leading Cases* (Oxford University Press, 2017), 52–59 (discussing Corte Constitucional [C.C.], mayo 5, 1994, Sentencia C-221/94 (Colom.)).

[81] David Pozen, *The Constitution of the War on Drugs* (Oxford University Press, 2024), 20 (quotation omitted); see also generally Carl L. Hart, *Drug Use for Grown-Ups: Chasing Liberty in the Land of Fear* (Penguin Books, 2021).

The story Pozen tells is the story of how such arguments have had only limited success in US courts over time. Courts' restrictive reading of the Constitution has not eliminated the tension between the general right to liberty and criminal prohibitions of possession of drugs.

There are also obvious constitutional implications having to do with national security offenses. Recall that many treason cases are propaganda cases, and as one court said, there is a need to distinguish between "[t]he speech [that] may tend to weaken our country in its war effort . . . and in that sense may be of aid and comfort to the enemy" yet is "the expression of honest criticism and sincere conviction as to what is best for the country" on one hand, and "traffick[ing] with the enemy and . . . collaborat[ing] in the execution of a program of psychological warfare designed by the enemy to weaken the power of the United States" on the other.[82] In fact, it appears to be the case that Jane Fonda, who went to Vietnam during the Vietnam War and committed acts that resembled those of individuals convicted of treason during World War II, escaped prosecution partly because of the view that her right to free expression was at stake.[83] As to espionage, given that the law covers not only the passing of state secrets to foreign governments but also the leaking of such information to the public or to journalists, like in cases of Daniel Ellsberg, Chelsea Manning, and Edward Snowden, there are, to say the least, clear conflicts between national security interests and valid freedom of speech concerns that require careful and nuanced resolution.[84]

IV. Individual Liberty and Disobedience Offenses

The constitutional rights just discussed—freedom of thought, freedom of speech and expression, freedom of association, right to privacy, privilege against self-incrimination, and so on—are typically labeled as fundamental rights. But fundamental rights do not exhaust the world of rights and liberty interests that the law ought to protect.

First, what people generally mean when they talk about individual constitutional rights that can limit government actions are constitutional rights the contours of which have been determined by courts as a result of constitutional challenges brought and litigated in courts. However, that is not the only way to

[82] Chandler v. United States, 171 F.2d 921, 929 (1st Cir. 1948).

[83] See Carlton F. W. Larson, *On Treason: A Citizen's Guide to the Law* (Ecco, 2020), 186.

[84] For discussions, see, e.g., Mary-Rose Papandrea, "Leaker Traitor Whistleblower Spy: National Security Leaks and the First Amendment," *Boston University Law Review* 94, no. 2 (2014): 512–44; Heidi Kitrosser and David Schultz, "House Built on Sand: The Constitutional Infirmity of Espionage Act Prosecutions for Leaking to the Press," *First Amendment Law Review* 19 (2021): 185–211; see also generally Geoffrey R. Stone and Lee C. Bollinger, eds., *National Security, Leaks and Freedom of the Press: The Pentagon Papers Fifty Years On* (Oxford University Press, 2021).

think about protecting constitutional rights. The way courts enforce rights is informed at least in part by various pragmatic and institutional implications. For instance, even if a constitutional norm guarantees an individual right to leak what may have been classified as a state secret, the courts may decide not to intervene to protect such a right in favor of institutional deference.[85] In such situations, it might make sense for one of the other branches of the government, like the executive branch, to interpret rights more broadly than the courts do and decline to enforce the law at times for that reason, even if enforcement may be allowed by the courts.

Second, some liberty interests may not be considered important or "fundamental" enough to receive special protection by the Constitution or the courts, but that does not mean they are not important. The US Constitution currently constrains criminal law in two ways: (1) it takes certain things off the list of things that the government may criminalize, and (2) it imposes various restrictions on how the government may go about enforcing the criminal law. One might summarize the current state of constitutional restrictions on criminal law in the United States in the following way:

1. Do not criminalize *A*, *B*, or *C*... (*A*, *B*, and *C*... being exercises of fundamental rights).
2. So long as fundamental rights are not inhibited, the government may criminalize any conduct—from speeding to murder—as the government sees fit.
3. When the government enforces criminal law (enacted within constraints 1 and 2), it must do so without violating constraints *X*, *Y*, *Z*... (i.e., constraints relating to established constitutional criminal procedures such as search and seizure, right to counsel, trial by jury, confrontation of witnesses, cruel and unusual punishments, etc.).

Under this framework, things that lie outside the scope of fundamental rights (those covered under constraint 2) receive no protection from being criminalized. If a government passes a law that prohibits selling ice cream near elementary schools as a way of dealing with obesity, as long as the crime is defined in a way that does not interfere with constitutionally recognized fundamental rights, the government is free to punish a person after proving beyond a reasonable doubt to a jury that the person sold ice cream in front of an elementary school.[86]

[85] For a general discussion, see, e.g., Richard H. Fallon Jr., *Implementing the Constitution* (Harvard University Press, 2001).

[86] For similar arguments involving different food items, see Douglas Husak, "The Criminal Law as Last Resort," *Oxford Journal of Legal Studies* 24, no. 2 (2008): 210–11 (criminalizing eating sausage);

As a general matter, we should start by assuming that there is a loss whenever the state criminalizes something. By criminalizing something, the state makes the option of doing that thing unavailable, and thus reduces freedom. The general interest one has in one's liberty does not disappear just because "fundamental rights" are not implicated. We discussed above, for instance, that possession of drugs may implicate a fundamental right, but even if there is no fundamental right to use drugs for recreational purposes, taking away the option of using drugs recreationally is a restriction of liberty.[87] And this point generalizes. Even in cases where no fundamental rights are at stake, the liberty interest remains, so there is a loss if the option to engage in the prohibited conduct is taken away. And this is a cost that is borne by everyone, not just those who are interested in engaging in the prohibited activities.[88]

How criminalization of disobedience can intrude upon and restrict liberty is most starkly visible in laws that prohibit disobedience of law enforcement officers, which were discussed in Chapter 3. Such laws contemplate individualized commands given by law enforcement officers and criminalize disobedience of such commands. These laws restrict liberty as one may be going about one's business and suddenly find oneself subject to a binding legal order. A law that prohibits disobedience may seem reasonable on its face if it refers to an ongoing emergency, which we discussed in connection with *State v. Wagar*, a case about a pilot's act of disobedience at the scene of a plane crash. But laws authorizing law enforcement officers to dispense orders can cut much more broadly than that.

Consider, for example, the law at issue in *City of Chicago v. Morales* (mentioned briefly above), which made it a crime to disobey an order by a police officer to "disperse and remove themselves from the area" given after "a police officer observes a person whom he reasonably believes to be a criminal street gang member loitering in any public place with one or more persons."[89] The

Douglas Husak, *Overcriminalization* (Oxford University Press, 2007), 102, 124 (criminalizing eating doughnuts).

[87] See Douglas Husak and Peter De Marneff, *The Legalization of Drugs* (Cambridge University Press, 2005), 41–53.

[88] See, e.g., Joel Feinberg, *The Moral Limits of the Criminal Law Volume 1: Harm to Others* (Oxford University Press, 1984), 210 (defending the idea that a person "who *can* do what he wants most to do, but nothing else, *lacks* something in value" and a person "who *cannot* do what he wants most to do but can do everything else, *possesses* something of value (his liberty)"); Joseph Raz, "Rights and Individual Well-Being," in *Ethics in the Public Domain* (1994), 54–55 ("If I were to choose between living in a society which enjoys freedom of expression, but not having the right myself, or enjoying the right in a society which does not have it, I would have no hesitation in judging that my own personal interest is better served by the first option . . . Th[e] real value [of civil and political rights] is in their contribution to a common liberal culture. That culture serves the interests of members of the community.").

[89] Morales, 527 U.S. at 47 n.2.

law defined "loitering" as "remain[ing] in any one place with no apparent purpose."[90] The US Supreme Court, when it struck down the law, pointed out that the law "applies to everyone in the city who may remain in one place with one suspected gang member as long as their purpose is not apparent to an officer observing them."[91] If there is a duty to support law enforcement, then it appears that disobeying such an order would be wrongful, and that would supply the basis for the proposition that disobedience is wrongful and can be punished in a way that is consistent with the principle of punishing only the morally blameworthy. There are obvious concerns with laws like this having to do individual police officers' discretion to apply the law, but the point here is different. Even if we assume that the police officer would dispense orders to disperse reasonably and in good faith, the fact that the law authorizes police officers to give binding commands in reaction to "loitering" with certain people empowers them to create new legal obligations that restrict people's ability to be where they choose to be. This is the sense in which criminalizing disobedience has potential to restrict liberty in troubling ways.

There is another level at which the laws requiring cooperation with law enforcement limit freedom. In Chapter 4, we looked at laws that criminalize failure to cooperate with law enforcement. The case of Ellen Campbell, the real estate agent who was convicted of money laundering for helping a drug dealer buy a house, showed how money laundering laws required her to investigate the source of another person's money or pass on a business opportunity altogether.[92] We also saw laws imposing reporting obligations on those who come across evidence of criminal wrongdoing by others.[93] Unlike laws that criminally prohibit harming other people or even failing to prevent harm to those to whom one owes a preexisting legal or moral obligation, some of these laws trigger obligations to report when one happens to come across indicators of criminal violations by others. When those obligations kick in, failure to report is a crime, and the person subject to such obligations now must direct their efforts toward assisting law enforcement instead of continuing to pursue their chosen life projects and preexisting commitments. And, as discussed above, there are also offender registration laws that burden those who have already completed their sentences with reporting obligations and prolonged contact with the criminal justice system, such as verification in person every three months for the rest of the person's life.[94]

Now, the observation that every criminal prohibition restricts liberty does not mean that the prohibition is not justified. Taking away the option of killing

90 Morales, 527 U.S. at 47 n.2.
91 Morales, 527 U.S. at 62–63.
92 United States v. Campbell, 977 F.2d 854 (4th Cir. 1992).
93 See, e.g., 18 U.S.C. § 4.
94 34 U.S.C. §§ 201915, 20918.

another person for no good reason restricts liberty, but there are good reasons to restrict liberty in that way. At the same time, it is certainly not the case that just because there is a criminal prohibition of something in place, one should not complain about the inability to do that thing. Such a view might be more plausible for *mala in se* offenses, where harming another person unjustifiably should not be on that person's menu of available options to begin with, but in *mala prohibita* offenses—or the kinds of laws that I have described throughout this book as instances of criminalization of disobedience—the nature of the wrong necessarily refers back to the power of the state to devise rules of behavior as it sees fit, even when the behavior being criminalized does not involve a moral wrong other than the failure to support the state. In such cases, criminalization and the loss of liberty it imposes ought to receive more scrutiny as a general matter, as the state can easily end up overreaching when it enlists whatever help it decides to get for it to advance its objectives. The need to place limitations on the state's ability to criminalize is particularly pressing in this realm due to its potential to restrict liberty, and that is the significance of the fact that mere disobedience is being criminalized in disobedience offenses.

V. Conclusion

This is the first of three chapters addressing potential principled limitations on the state's power to criminalize disobedience. The focus of this chapter has been on individual rights and liberties. The state may devise and implement various rules to make it possible for people to live together, and without denying the ways in which the state may legitimately criminalize disobedience and without denying the moral wrongfulness of disobedience, we ought to recognize the ways in which giving the state such powers can lead to infringements of constitutional rights and individual liberty. This chapter has argued that when the state considers limiting liberty via criminalization of disobedience, such limitations should consider the importance of preserving a sphere of autonomy in which people can move about and pursue their ordinary life projects free from state interference. This chapter then has identified areas where such limitations might need to be introduced in order to protect that sphere of autonomy from state intrusions through various criminal prohibitions.

11
Limits on Criminalization II: Proportionalities

I. Introduction

This chapter continues our exploration of potential ways to limit criminalization of disobedience by focusing on the principle of proportionality—or, to be more accurate, *principles* of proportionality as the term refers to different ideas. The idea that the punishment should be proportional to the crime is familiar in criminal law and has a lengthy history. But that idea is not the only place where one encounters the concept of proportionality in law and ethics. Proportionality is also important in the self-defense context where the right to defend oneself with force extends only to what is considered proportional. Proportionality plays a role in the context of war too, especially in the idea that military advantages must not be achieved at the disproportionate expense of civilian lives. Finally, constitutional theorists around the world have worked for decades on the principle of proportionality as a constitutional principle. This chapter first discusses various ways in which the idea of proportionality is used in law and legal theory and then suggests ways to use such concepts to limit criminalization of disobedience.

II. Proportionality in Punishment, Self-Defense, War, and Constitutional Law

A. Proportionality in Punishment

The idea of proportionality in punishment may be put succinctly like this: "[T]he punishment . . . should be in proportion to the crime."[1] This idea has been interpreted and concretized in many different ways. H. L. A. Hart describes the idea as the "requirement that the punishment should in some way 'match' the crime."[2] Oliver Wendell Holmes restates it as the principle that "the punishment

[1] John Gardner, "Crime: In Proportion and in Perspective," in *Offences and Defences: Selected Essays in the Philosophy of Criminal Law* (Oxford University Press, 2007), 221.

[2] H. L. A. Hart, *Punishment and Responsibility: Essays in the Philosophy of Criminal Law* (Clarendon Press, 1968), 233.

Criminalizing Disobedience. Youngjae Lee, Oxford University Press. © Oxford University Press 2026.
DOI: 10.1093/9780197617175.003.0012

must be equal, in the sense of proportionate to the crime."[3] These statements harken back to the way Kant and Hegel have invoked the notion of "equality" to describe the proper relationship between crime and punishment and to the Biblical maxim of *lex talionis*.[4]

As discussed in Chapter 1, this book assumes the legal moralist perspective, and this idea of proportionality in punishment is frequently associated with legal moralism, though it has shown up under different theories as well. Among contemporary punishment theorists, the idea of proportionality is often explained in terms of desert or retributivism. For instance, Victor Tadros explains that "[p]unishment is regarded as proportionate if the suffering imposed on the offender bears the appropriate relationship to the gravity of his crime."[5] Douglas Husak also says that "[i]njustice occurs when punishments are disproportionate, exceeding what the offender deserves."[6]

Some theorists emphasize censure, as opposed to desert. Andrew von Hirsch and Andrew Ashworth, the leading proponents of the principle of proportionality as the guiding principle of sentencing, argue that "[t]he principle of proportionality . . . is grounded . . . on the blaming character of punishment" and that "[o]nce one has created an institution with the condemnatory implications that punishment has, then it is a requirement of justice . . . to punish offenders according to the degree of reprehensibleness of their conduct."[7] They further explain: "Disproportionate punishments are unjust . . . because they purport to condemn the actor for his conduct and yet visit more or less censure on him than the degree of blameworthiness of that conduct would warrant."[8]

The basic idea is, then, to look at the crime that is to be punished and ask what punishment "matches," "fits," or is "appropriate" for that crime. This idea of fittingness operates on both comparative and noncomparative dimensions.[9] The noncomparative dimension evaluates an appropriate punishment in a

[3] Oliver Wendell Holmes Jr., *The Common Law* (Little, Brown, and Company, 1881), 42.

[4] See Immanuel Kant, *The Metaphysics of Morals*, trans. and ed. Mary Gregor (Cambridge University Press, 1996; originally published 1797), 105; G. W. F. Hegel, *Philosophy of Right*, trans. T. M. Knox (Oxford University Press, 1967; originally published 1821), § 101 (Remark); Exodus 21:23–5; Marvin Henberg, *Retribution: Evil for Evil in Ethics, Law, and Literature* (Temple University Press, 1990), 68–74.

[5] Victor Tadros, *The Ends of Harm: The Moral Foundations of Criminal Law* (Oxford University Press, 2011), 332.

[6] Douglas Husak, *Overcriminalization: The Limits of the Criminal Law* (Oxford University Press, 2008), 14. I myself discussed proportionality in these ways when I argued that the US Constitution's Cruel and Unusual Punishments Clause's ban on excessive punishment should be understood in terms of "the retributivist principle that the harshness of punishment should not exceed the gravity of the crime—one should not be punished more harshly than one deserves." Youngjae Lee, "The Constitutional Right Against Excessive Punishment," *Virginia Law Review* 91, no. 3 (2005): 683.

[7] Andrew von Hirsch and Andrew Ashworth, *Proportionate Sentencing: Exploring the Principles* (Oxford University Press, 2005), 134.

[8] von Hirsch and Ashworth, *Proportionate Sentencing*, 134.

[9] See Joel Feinberg, "Noncomparative Justice," *Philosophical Review* 83, no. 3 (1974): 298.

particular instance based on the seriousness of the crime, irrespective of how others are treated. In contrast, the comparative dimension considers how others are punished. For example, if a person is sentenced to five years in prison for car theft, the noncomparative inquiry asks whether the act justifies the state's response, regardless of how similarly or differently situated individuals are being treated.[10] On the other hand, the comparative inquiry examines whether the individual who stole the car is receiving equitable treatment compared to others who committed more or less serious crimes.[11]

B. Proportionality in Self-Defense

In the context of self-defense, proportionality means something quite different from proportionality in punishment. As we saw above, proportionality in punishment has to do with the *desert* or *blameworthiness* of the person being punished. By contrast, in self-defense, proportionality has to do with the idea of *liability*.[12] The idea of liability is used in the self-defense context to explain why it is morally permissible to attack a person. If *A* tries to kill *B*, and *B* kills *A* in self-defense, why is it morally permissible for *B* to kill *A*? The answer is that *A* has made himself *liable* to being killed in that situation because *A*, who would normally have a right not to be killed, has lost that right by his act of aggression. Since *A* no longer retains the right not to be killed in this situation, it is permissible for *B* to kill *A*. An intuitive way of explaining the concept of being liable to

[10] See Youngjae Lee, "Proportionality in Punishment," in *The Palgrave Handbook of Applied Ethics and the Criminal Law*, ed. Larry Alexander and Kimberly Kessler Ferzan (Palgrave Macmillan, 2019), 552–53.

[11] There is a way of thinking about proportionality in punishment that is different from the account I have given here, and that is the kind of proportionality principle one might derive from the utilitarian theory of punishment. One can work out a theory of proportionate punishment from the core idea, as stated by Jeremy Bentham, that "all punishment is mischief: all punishment in itself is evil," and that punishment should be allowed only "as far as it promises to exclude some greater evil," Jeremy Bentham, *An Introduction to the Principles of Morals and Legislation* (first edition published 1789, reis., Clarendon Press, 1832), 179. However, because the primary concern of the utilitarian theory is to minimize the social loss associated with criminal activities, as opposed to attaining the correct relationship between the gravity of crime and the harshness of punishment, this version of proportionality departs too much from the idea of "proportionality in punishment" as it is generally understood. Therefore, I will set aside the utilitarian notion of proportionality here. For further discussion, see Lee, "Proportionality in Punishment," 737–41; Youngjae Lee, "Problem of Proportional Punishment," in *The Routledge Handbook of the Philosophy and Science of Punishment*, ed. Farah Focquaert et al. (Routledge, 2021), 126–28.

[12] See, e.g., Jonathan Quong, "The Morality of Defensive Force: Replies to Otsuka, Frowe, Fabre, and Burri," *Criminal Law & Philosophy* 16, no. 3 (2022): 555; Kimberly Kessler Ferzan, "Forfeiture and Self-Defense," in *The Ethics of Self-Defense*, ed. Christian Coons and Michael Weber (Oxford University Press, 2016), 233; Helen Frowe, "The Role of Necessity in Liability to Defensive Harm," in *The Ethics of Self-Defense*, 152.

harm is in terms of *forfeiture*.[13] By trying to kill *B*, *A* has forfeited his right not to be killed.

However, the degree of forfeiture is limited by the proportionality constraint, which in turn sets a limit to the amount of force *B* is morally permitted to use to repel *A*'s attack. As Tadros explains, the principle of proportionality means that "one may not use the force necessary to avert a threat if that force is out of all proportion to the magnitude of the threat that one faces."[14] So, for example, if instead of *A* trying to kill *B*, we had a situation where *A* is trying to tickle *B* and *B* does not want to be tickled, *B* may protest and prevent the unwanted touching by pushing *A* away with minimal harm, if any, but not by killing *A*. In the tickle situation, *A* may have made himself liable to be pushed away against his will, but he has not made himself liable to be killed.

Another distinct idea, separate from proportionality but proximate to it, is *necessity*. In the original hypothetical, while *A* may have made himself *liable* to be killed by trying to kill *B*, it may still be morally impermissible for *B* to kill *A*, if it is possible for *B* to avoid being harmed by *A* merely by breaking *A*'s arm. If *B* is able to neutralize the threat of *A* in some other way besides lethal force, but nevertheless kills *A*, *B*'s response may have been *proportionate*, but it was not *necessary*, and therefore may still be morally impermissible.[15] This distinction between *necessity* and *proportionality* means that the word *excessive* is ambiguous in this context. *B*'s response to *A* may be *excessive* in the sense of being *disproportionate* or in the sense of being *unnecessary*.

As this quick discussion shows, concepts surrounding the idea of self-defense can become complex in combination, but for our purposes the important point is that the idea of proportionality in self-defense should not be confused with the idea of proportionality in punishment, as the two ideas track distinct moral features. It is true that because one may make oneself *liable* to harm by attacking another, the question of *culpability*, which the idea of *desert* or *blameworthiness* tracks, sometimes appears to play an important role in self-defense analysis. However, that one's moral *desert* sometimes correlates with one's *liability* does not mean they are one and the same;[16] accordingly, it does not render proportionality in self-defense equivalent to proportionality in punishment.[17]

[13] See generally Quong, "The Morality of Defensive Force"; Ferzan, "Forfeiture."

[14] Tadros, *The Ends of Harm*, 331.

[15] See, e.g., Quong, "Morality of Defensive Force," 557; Frowe, "The Role of Necessity," 152; Ferzan, "Forfeiture and Self-Defense," 153.

[16] For a discussion about the difference between proportionality in punishment and proportionality in self-defense, see Tadros, *The Ends of Harm*, 332; Jeff McMahan, "Proportionate Defense," *Journal of Transnational Law & Policy* 23, no. 1 (2014): 22; Jonathan Quong, "Proportionality, Liability, and Defensive Harm," *Philosophy & Public Affairs* 43, no. 2 (2015): 146–47.

[17] For a discussion of the possibility of limiting amounts of punishment with the self-defense principle of proportionality rather than the traditional punishment principle of proportionality, see Tadros, *The Ends of Harm*, 332.

C. Proportionality in War

Another place where the idea of proportionality plays an important role is in the context of war. As Thomas Hurka explains, "a war . . . is wrong if the destruction it causes is excessive, or out of proportion to, [its] benefits," and "an act in war is wrong if the harm it causes, especially to civilians, is out of proportion to its military benefits."[18] Unlike proportionality in punishment, which is about whether a punishment appropriately reflects the blameworthiness of a crime, and unlike proportionality in self-defense, which is about assessing permissibility of one's defensive action according to the extent to which the attacker the defender is defending against has made himself liable, proportionality in war is about weighing various consequences and asking if the benefits of a war or a particular act in war outweigh the costs.

This statement, however, needs to be qualified. While proportionality in war is typically discussed in terms of weighing costs and benefits against one another, an influential discussion by Jeff McMahan has made it commonplace for theorists of war to distinguish between *narrow proportionality* and *wide proportionality*.[19] Under this account, *narrow proportionality* deploys the considerations we saw above in the self-defense context. In war, targets of a potential military attack may have made themselves *liable* to be attacked by, for instance, engaging in an act of aggression. The proportionality analysis would be similar to one in the context of self-defense: To what extent did the aggressors make themselves liable to the potential attack? In the process of that attack, however, if, say, civilian bystanders who have not made themselves liable to be attacked are to be harmed, then the attack can also be assessed in part by asking whether the benefits of the attack outweigh the costs the attack is likely to impose overall. This latter type of proportionality is termed *wide proportionality*.

There are two more parallels to draw to the self-defense framework. As in the self-defense context, the concept of *necessity* plays a role in the context of war as well in the sense that even if a military attack is proportionate (in both senses), it may still be morally problematic if a less harmful attack could have achieved the same objective. Also, even in the self-defense context, one may draw a distinction between *narrow* and *wide* proportionality, though such discussions are not common. Specifically, if a person attacks an aggressor in self-defense, the narrow proportionality analysis would focus on the aggressor's liability (to what extent have they forfeited their right to be free from harm?), and the wide

[18] Thomas Hurka, "Proportionality and Necessity," in *War: Essays in Political Philosophy*, ed. Larry May (Cambridge University Press, 2008), 127–28.

[19] See McMahan, "Proportionate Defense," 7–8.

proportionality analysis would consider the overall costs of the defensive attack (might innocent bystanders be harmed?).

Proportionality in self-defense and proportionality in war are thus analogous: in both contexts, one may employ the ideas of narrow proportionality, wide proportionality, and necessity. Proportionality in punishment is distinct from these ideas.

D. Proportionality in Constitutional Law

Proportionality is also central in constitutional law. As Moshe Cohen-Eliya and Iddo Porat observe, "European constitutional lawyers are concerned predominantly with one thing—proportionality!"[20] They continue: "Whether you are a German constitutional lawyer, an Italian, a French or an English one, you will invariably have been debating and talking about the proportionality doctrine as part of your work."[21] And it is not only European constitutional lawyers who use the idea of proportionality; it is important also "if you [are] a Canadian, Australian, Indian, Israeli, or a Chinese lawyer."[22] A large literature on the constitutional doctrine of proportionality has developed over time, mostly by work of legal academics outside the United States.[23]

Proportionality in constitutional law concerns conflicts between rights and societal interests, which may sometimes necessitate placing limitations on the scope of rights. Proportionality in constitutional law formalizes this analytic process of placing limitations on rights in light of competing considerations with the following set of steps, as summarized by Cohen-Eliya and Porat:

> [W]henever the government infringes upon a constitutionally protected right, the proportionality principle requires that the government show, first, that its objective is legitimate and important; second, that the means chosen were rationally connected to achieve that objective . . . ; third, that no less drastic means were available . . . ; and fourth, that the benefit from realizing the objective exceeds the harm to the right . . . .[24]

[20] Moshe Cohen-Eliya and Iddo Porat, *Proportionality and Constitutional Culture* (Cambridge University Press, 2013), 2.
[21] Cohen-Eliya and Porat, *Proportionality*, 2.
[22] Cohen-Eliya and Porat, *Proportionality*, 2.
[23] See, e.g., Robert Alexy, *A Theory of Constitutional Rights* (Oxford University Press, 2002); Jacco Bomhoff, *Balancing Constitutional Rights: The Origins and Meanings of Postwar Legal Discourse* (Cambridge University Press, 2013); Cohen-Eliya and Porat, *Proportionality*; Grant Huscroft et al., *Proportionality and the Rule of Law: Rights, Justification, Reasoning* (Cambridge University Press, 2014).
[24] Cohen-Eliya and Porat, *Proportionality*, 2.

As Cohen-Eliya and Porat also point out, the United States has its own version of the proportionality doctrine in constitutional law—balancing, which can specify how constitutional rights may be limited in particular instances in light of important governmental interests.[25] There is an extensive debate about similarities and differences between balancing and proportionality, but the core idea of comparing costs and benefits of a government action infringing on an individual right is present in both balancing and proportionality. Additionally, to the extent that the proportionality doctrine involves a weighing of costs and benefits, it also bears some similarity to the idea of *wide* proportionality, discussed above in the context of war and self-defense. Proportionality in punishment, however, is not about weighing and balancing costs and benefits against one another, so it is distinct, not just from proportionality in self-defense and war but also from proportionality in constitutional law.

III. Proportionality in Punishment and Disobedience Offenses

A. Basic Idea

The question I want to raise is how to use the idea of proportionality in punishment to place limitations on punishment of disobedience. In Chapter 2, I introduced the following formula:

$$C_t = C_d + C_a$$

Again, C_t is the "Total Culpability," C_a is culpability attributable to the badness of the prohibited act itself, and C_d is culpability attributable to the act of disobeying a prohibition. I also discussed how this formula would apply to two drivers, both driving over the speed limit, but one of them is driving dangerously and the other driving safely. What would be the proportionate sanctions for these two?

The value of C_a for the one who is driving safely is zero, so C_t for the person who is driving safely despite driving over the speed limit has to do exclusively with C_d from his disobedience. On the contrary, the value of C_a is some amount more than zero for the person who drives dangerously. So while both drivers are culpable, the dangerous driver is more culpable than the safe driver since the value of C_t is larger for the dangerous driver than that of the safe driver, and the difference in culpability should be taken into account when considering appropriate sanctions for the two, according to the principle of proportionality in punishment.

[25] Cohen-Eliya and Porat, *Proportionality*, 3.

The significance of analysis like this is that it gives us a way of thinking about seriousness of various disobedience offenses. For example, consider regulatory offenses we discussed in Chapter 5. The seriousness of environmental crimes, like pollution or killing of endangered species, would depend on how much harm one is causing or how much risk of harm one is imposing plus the blameworthiness associated with interfering with the relevant regulatory scheme. The same goes for regulatory offenses having to do with drugs and medical devices. Possession and distribution of illicit drugs sometimes may impose risks of harm on other people, but at other times may be wrong primarily because such acts interfere with the government's program of shutting down an undesirable market or controlling the amount of risk that exists in society. Because so many of these offenses have some relationship to prevention of harm, it is easy to condemn those who commit them as those who unwarrantedly harm or risk harm to others, when in fact they may not be doing so but are merely disobeying, and that difference ought to be recognized when assessing the seriousness of each offense.

Difficulties of proportionality analysis—such as its indeterminacy and manipulability—are, of course, well known.[26] I do not pretend to have solved its various problems, and understanding the nature of disobedience offenses does not make the longstanding problems go away. What it does, however, is give us a better understanding of what these laws are about, what exactly is wrong with committing these crimes, and how bad the conduct is. Without such understandings, we cannot get a proportionality analysis going. There are, however, some special problems with proportionality analyses of disobedience offenses.

B. The Problem of Identifying the Relevant Wrongs

Sometimes, because of the way laws are drafted, it is difficult to identify the exact wrong that a law targets. This is a general problem, but it is most acute with disobedience offenses.[27] Take drunk driving for instance. In New York, it is unlawful for a person to "operate a motor vehicle while such person has .08 of one percentum or more by weight of alcohol in the person's blood."[28] This offense is "driving while intoxicated," and the standard this law refers to in terms of weight of alcohol in a person's blood is "blood alcohol concentration," commonly known

[26] For a discussion, see Lee, "Problem of Proportional Punishment," 131–34.

[27] Cf. Gabriel S. Mendlow, "The Elusive Object of Punishment," *Legal Theory* 25, no. 2 (2019): 117–25.

[28] N.Y. Vehicle & Traffic Laws § 1192.2.

as BAC.[29] Driving while intoxicated (DWI) is a misdemeanor, and a person can be imprisoned for up to one year for committing this offense.[30]

Driving is always a potentially dangerous activity, and those engaged in it should ensure that they are and will stay mentally alert and physically able while conducting the activity. Driving while drunk puts oneself and others on the road at great danger, and DWI is thus rightly considered morally wrongful.[31] However, consider the way in which New York's DWI law is defined. The crime is not defined in terms of reckless driving but in terms of BAC.

There are several issues here. First, some people may be able to drive safely—or as safely as we generally demand from one another—with a BAC of 0.08, especially if they are driving a short, familiar route, in good driving conditions.[32] Second, people simply do not know what their BAC at a given moment is. A subjective sensation of feeling drunk or impaired is a highly unreliable guide to one's BAC level, as people with high tolerance may not feel particularly drunk.[33] Third, the method of estimating one's BAC level through counting the "number

[29] N.Y. Vehicle & Traffic Laws § 1192.

[30] N.Y. Vehicle & Traffic Laws § 1193. Moreover, if a person drives while intoxicated with a child under the age of fifteen in the vehicle as a passenger, then the person is guilty of a felony, and can be imprisoned for up to four years. See N.Y. Vehicle & Traffic Laws § 1192.2-a(b); N.Y. Penal Law § 70(2)(e).

[31] But see Douglas N. Husak, "Is Drunk Driving a Serious Offense?," *Philosophy & Public Affairs* 23, no. 1 (1994): 61–73.

[32] In a study designed to test the effects of alcohol on driving ability, "parameters differed distinctly between the BAC conditions depending on the underlying scenario." Ramona Kenntner-Mabiala et al., "Driving Performance Under Alcohol in Simulated Representative Driving Tasks," *Journal of Clinical Psychopharmacology* 35, no. 2 (2015): 140. The test subjects "drove slightly faster under alcohol than under placebo only in the difficult tracking scenario." Kenntner-Mabiala et al., "Driving Performance," 139. Difficult roads resulted in the number of lane departures increasing for those under the influence of alcohol, "whereas in easy tracking scenarios, no lane departure was observed at all." Kenntner-Mabiala et al., "Driving Performance," 140. Difficult scenarios testing the standard deviation of lane position—which refers to swaying from the middle of the road—resulted in a ceiling effect, as sober test subjects had just as much trouble driving in such conditions as drunk subjects. See also Arne Helland et al., "Comparison of Driving Simulator Performance with Real Driving After Alcohol Intake: A Randomised, Single Blind, Placebo-Controlled, Cross-Over Trial," *Accident Analysis & Prevention* 53 (2013): 13 (showing that while increasing BAC increased drivers' tendency to "weave" on the road overall, the effect increased as the difficulty of the test track increased). Circadian sleep propensity can also affect the riskiness of driving after alcohol consumption. See Sergio Garbarino et al., "Circadian Sleep Propensity and Alcohol Interaction at the Wheel," *Journal of Clinical Sleep Medicine* 12, no. 7 (2016): 1011 (finding that increased sleep propensity led to a higher likelihood of motor vehicle crashes when drunk driving). How unsafe a driver with a high BAC is seems to vary depending on the age and sex of the driver, too. See Paul L. Zador et al., "Alcohol-Related Relative Risk of Driver Fatalities and Driver Involvement in Fatal Crashes in Relation to Driver Age and Gender: An Update Using 1996 Data," *Journal of Studies on Alcohol* 61, no. 3 (2000): 393 (finding that "the relative risk decrease[s] with increasing driver age at every BAC level, for both men and women" and that for the 16–20 age group, "women had lower relative risk than men at every BAC").

[33] One study reported that "more than one third of participants legally intoxicated for driving purposes (37%) reported feeling no buzz or slightly buzzed . . . ," and "16% of participants who reported no buzz were legally impaired for driving purposes. . . ." Matthew E. Rossheim et al., "Feeling No Buzz or a Slight Buzz Is Common When Legally Drunk," *American Journal of Public Health* 106, no. 10 (2016): 1761.

of drinks" one has had is unreliable given that one's BAC level depends on a number of different factors.[34] As a result, a person who drives despite their BAC being 0.08 may not be aware of or *feel* any impairment, may not be aware that their BAC is above the legally permitted limit for driving, and may not in fact be impaired at all.

Now consider a driver whose BAC is above 0.08. What exactly is he doing wrong? Let us set aside the strict liability aspect of the offense.[35] Is the offense driving while knowing (or taking a risk) that he is not a safe driver due to intoxication? Perhaps this is the correct description of the relevant wrong, but it is much narrower than what the law covers, given that the law prohibits driving with a certain BAC level and people frequently underestimate their drunkenness.

Is the wrong of drunk driving, then, driving *knowing* that one's BAC is above the legal limit? This is closer to the mark. Say a person knows that his BAC is 0.08. What would be wrong with driving in such a situation? Is it wrongful for such a person to drive? It would be wrongful in two different senses. At that point, if he drives, he would be taking a risk (say, substantial) of being an unacceptably dangerous driver, and that might make him blameworthy (for taking on a substantial and unjustifiable risk). What if he is confident that he can drive safely? He might still be taking the same risk, given that he (let us assume) is aware that his judgment may be too impaired to make a correct assessment of his own driving ability. (So, in other words, there is a heightened risk that his assessment of his own driving ability is incorrect, and to act in reliance on such assessment is to take the risk of being an unacceptably dangerous driver.) It is also possible that, despite the elevated BAC level, he is correct to think that he can drive safely, in which case his behavior may not be wrongful at all.

[34] The "number of drinks" consumed is hardly the only relevant factor to BAC; how quickly the drinks were consumed, the amount of water consumed, whether food was consumed, and the type of alcohol consumed all affect the BAC and the time to peak BAC. See Steven M. Teutsch et al., *Getting to Zero Alcohol-Impaired Driving Fatalities: A Comprehensive Approach to a Persistent Problem* (The National Academies Press, 2018), 177. In fact, the amount of fluid intake consumed with alcohol had a higher impact on BAC than the amount of alcohol intake. See Julian E. Dilley et al., "Alcohol Drinking and Blood Alcohol Concentration Revisited," *Alcoholism: Clinical and Experimental Research* 42, no. 2 (2018): 260. BAC increased with the concentration of alcohol, rather than the number of doses of alcohol, effectively proving "that alcohol concentration can influence BAC independent of alcohol dose." Dilley et al., "Alcohol Drinking and Blood Alcohol Concentration Revisited," 269. Individualized factors were also relevant. See, e.g., Shunji Oshima, "Individual Differences in Blood Alcohol Concentrations After Moderate Drinking Are Mainly Regulated by Gastric Emptying Rate Together with Ethanol Distribution Volume," *Food and Nutrition Sciences* 3, no. 6 (2012): 732 (identifying individual differences in "gastric emptying rate" as a significant factor in explaining individual differences in BAC after consuming alcohol). There also appears to be a male–female difference in the rate at which alcohol consumption impacts the BAC. See Martin S. Mumenthaler et al., "Gender Differences in Moderate Drinking Effects," *Alcohol Research & Health* 23, no. 1(1999): 55.

[35] See Mendlow, "The Elusive Object of Punishment," 124.

Of course, people do not generally know what their BAC is (though that could change with technological advances over time through devices like smart watches), and, as noted above, it is difficult for an individual to know on the basis of drinks one has consumed. Perhaps then the relevant wrong is the wrong of driving after drinking. The wrongs analysis would be similar, except, instead of BAC, it is the fact of driving knowing that one has had a few drinks that makes a driver potentially blameworthy. If he starts driving after a few drinks, it may be the case that he is behaving dangerously. But what if he believes that he is "good to drive" because, say, he is large, has been drinking while eating food, has been drinking while rehydrating himself plenty, and has stopped drinking an hour ago? The answer may have to be partly that he cannot rely on his own judgment after having had a few drinks, which makes him potentially blameworthy when he drives in that state, but, at the same time, again, he might reasonably think that he is as safe as an ordinary sober driver, in which case it is unclear why his behavior is wrongful.

And all of this is just about C_a. What about C_d? What exactly is the directive from the state? This, too, is less than crystal clear. The law simply says "[n]o person shall operate a motor vehicle while such person has .08 of one percentum or more by weight of alcohol in the person's blood as shown by chemical analysis of such person's blood, breath, urine or saliva . . . ."[36] Because people are not expected to know their BAC, it would be odd to see this law as directly articulating a command that is to be obeyed, though if a person happens to know his or her BAC, then that person would be under a duty to obey the law written in terms of BAC. But if "Do not drive when your BAC is .08" is not the command, then what is the command? The command cannot simply be, "Don't drive when you believe you are not safe to drive," as the law cuts more broadly than that. It seems, then, that the most likely command is, "Do not drink and drive."[37]

In sum, here, in Table 11.1, are some possible descriptions of the relevant wrongs in a drunk driving case.

The point of this example is to show that the wrongs of even seemingly simple crimes like drunk driving can be described in different ways, and it is not always easy to read a crime definition and discern what wrongs are targeted by a given statute. And depending on what wrongs are targeted, we could arrive at different understandings about the correct culpability level. Namely, it seems that:

$$c_a(1) > c_a(2) > c_a(3) \text{ and } c_d(1) > c_d(2) > c_d(3)$$

[36] N.Y. Vehicle and Traffic Law § 1192(2).

[37] In this way, this law is similar to statutory rape laws, the message of which may not be, "Do not have sexual relations with someone under the age of consent as legally specified," but rather, "Do not have sexual relations with a youngish looking person."

Table 11.1 Culpability Possibilities for Driving while Intoxicated

	C_a	C_d
1	Driving when intoxicated and thus dangerous.	Disobeying the command, "Do not drive when you may be intoxicated and thus dangerous as a driver."
2	Driving knowing one's BAC is 0.08 or above.	Disobeying the command, "Do not drive when your BAC is 0.08 or above."
3	Driving after having consumed one or more alcoholic drinks.	Disobeying the command, "Do not drink and drive."

In other words, the wrong of driving while knowing that one is unsafe is worse than that of driving while knowing that one's BAC is above the legal limit, which, in turn, is worse than that of driving while knowing that one has had some number of alcoholic drinks. Similarly, going against the state command not to drive as an intoxicated driver seems worse than going against the command not to drive when the BAC is 0.08 or above, which is in turn worse than going against the command not to drive after drinking.

And visually, we may represent the upshot as shown in Figure 11.1.

Amounts of culpability are obviously made up, but the basic idea should be clear enough. The wrong of driving after having had some drinks by itself (3) may not be very blameworthy, certainly less blameworthy than the wrong of driving

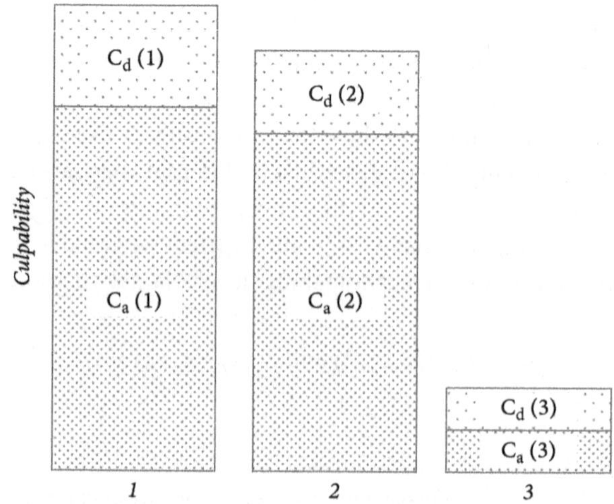

Figure 11.1 Culpability Possibilities for Driving while Intoxicated

Table 11.2 Conduct-Disobedience Culpability Matrix

	$C_d > 0$	$C_d = 0$
$C_a > 0$	I	II
$C_a = 0$	III	IV

knowing that one's BAC is at 0.08 or above (2), which is less blameworthy than the wrong of driving while too intoxicated to drive safely (1). Given the disparate outcomes as represented here, a challenge to overcome when devising proportionate punishments for an offense like drunk driving is knowing which wrongs are implicated.

C. The Problem of Labeling

The problem of identifying the relevant wrongs could lead to the following problem of labeling. Let's revisit the four quadrants (Table 11.2).

What should we do in a situation where two offenders break the same law, but the level of blameworthiness is different for the two because C_a is different? Let's assume that in that situation $C_d > 0$, so there is some blameworthiness in disobeying. In that case, we might have two situations, Quadrants I and III, from the possibilities. The two cases might look the same from the legal perspective because they break the same law, but C_t would be different for the two individuals.

This possibility was alluded to earlier with examples of drunk driving and of two speeding drivers, one safe and one dangerous, but consider a starker example. Take two statutory rape cases, where two defendants are guilty of the crime of having sexual relations with a sixteen-year-old. Say that both of them know that they are going against the law that prohibits sexual relations with someone under the age of seventeen, but one of them is careful about assessing the maturity level of the particular sixteen-year-old and correctly concludes that the teenager is mature enough to consent whereas the other one disregards, and even takes advantage of, the fact that the particular teenager is not mature enough to consent. Both defendants would be guilty of "the same crime," but C_t would be different for the two, since in the situation where $C_a = 0$, the only culpability would be C_d.

This is a familiar problem, something that can occur where there is an overbroad crime definition or a person engages in conduct that may be morally permissible or even desirable but cannot meet the requirements for a justification defense. But is it also a serious problem? It is possible that the problem can be minimized through the use of various discretionary devices so that the person caught in Quadrant III can be treated with leniency. The police and the prosecutor can decline to pursue such a case, a plea negotiation or a judge's discretion can lead to a mild sentence, or a jury can even nullify. At the same time, it is not clear whether the expressive dimension associated with words like "rape" and "homicide" is sensitive and fine-tuned enough to distinguish between offenders once there is a conviction, if there is a conviction. We theorists may expend a lot of effort to justify convicting offenders in situations where $C_a = 0$ by articulating what is wrong with disobeying, but the problem of treating two offenders of different levels of culpability the same way despite differences in C_t remains.[38]

D. The Problem of Undercompliance

Sometimes the answer to the question whether disobedience of a law is a wrong depends on whether enough people comply with the law in question. That proposition sounds odd when it comes to *mala in se* offenses. As a general matter, whether one's act of battery is wrong should not depend on whether other people are committing battery.[39]

But take, for instance, the crime of transnational bribery. Bob is a commercial real estate agent living and working in the United States. Bob's father owns a major commercial building and is looking for a potential buyer for the building. Bob

[38] Stuart Green has discussed this problem and has called it "the problem of wrongfulness conflation." Stuart P. Green, "Legal Moralism, Overinclusive Offenses, and the Problem of Wrongfulness Conflation," *Criminal Law & Philosophy* 14, no. 3 (2020): 417. In the statutory rape context, a solution Green suggests is to separate out the two kinds of offenders by convicting them under different statutes, both of which criminalize sex with a juvenile, but one of them has the element "exploitative sex" and the other one does not. Green, "Wrongfulness Conflation," 418. The more serious charge would be then "exploitative sex with a juvenile," and either "non-exploitative sex with a juvenile" or simply "sex with a juvenile" would be the less serious charge. Green, "Wrongfulness Conflation," 427–28.

[39] For a discussion of this set of issues, see Douglas Husak, "The 'But Everyone Does That!' Defense," *Public Affairs Quarterly* 10, no. 4 (1996): 313 ("The wrongfulness of many acts—most intentional killings, for example—does not depend on a convention . . . ."); Gideon Yaffe, "Revisiting the 'But Everyone Does That!' Defense," *Law and Philosophy* 41, no. 2 (2022): 422 ("Finding out that a lot of your neighbors beat their partners is a reason to despair of one's community not a reason to disapprove less of the neighbor who does that."); see also Yaffe, "'But Everyone Does That!' Defense," 430 ("Every rape is wrongful no matter how many or few there are; the more there are, the more wrongful acts there are."); Joseph Raz, "The Obligation to Obey: Revision and Tradition," in *Ethics in the Public Domain: Essays in the Morality of Law and Politics* (Oxford University Press, 1994), 349 (observing that in some cases "the reasons for acting in accord with the law apply with the same stringency in each case regardless of the degree of general conformity with the law," whereas in other cases "existence of reasons for the action, and their weight, depend on general conformity or the likelihood of it").

happens to know, from his social circles, Ken, the person in charge of the sovereign wealth fund of country *X*. Bob asks Ken if the fund he manages would be interested in purchasing the building, and Ken tells him that the purchase can be arranged if he gets a payment in the amount of $500,000. Bob and his father arrange for the money to be given to Ken.[40] Bob is subsequently prosecuted and convicted for violating the Foreign Corrupt Practices Act (FCPA), which prohibits, among other things:

> an offer, payment, promise to pay, or authorization of the payment of any money, or offer, gift, promise to give, or authorization of the giving of anything of value to any foreign official for purposes of influencing any act or decision of such foreign official in his official capacity . . . in order to . . . obtain[] or retain[] business . . . .[41]

What is Bob's blameworthiness in this? That is, why is bribery wrong? The basic transaction seems like any other transaction; there is an exchange of things of value between two or more parties, and, as an abstract matter, it is unclear what is problematic about it.[42] In order, then, to articulate what is wrong with bribery, we need an account of the proper way of conducting such exchanges, and what is at stake in conducting such exchanges in the proper way.

Deborah Hellman defines bribery "as an exchange . . . prohibited by the relevant decision-maker," and says that precisely which wrong is implicated in an act of bribery depends on why the exchange is prohibited.[43] Kevin Davis explains that "[t]he most obvious problem with bribery is that it undermines state policies," where "[t]he harm will depend on the policy being undermined."[44] Under either account, if the state sets up a system where a state official wields power in a domain, and the way in which the official exercises his or her power

[40] This description is roughly based on United States v. Joo Hyun Bahn, 16 Cr. 831 (S.D.N.Y. 2018), but with many modifications. In the actual case, there was a "middle man" between the defendant and the sovereign wealth fund, and it turned out the "middle man" did not know anyone at the fund and was defrauding the defendant. The defendant nevertheless was convicted for violating the Foreign Corrupt Practices Act after pleading guilty and was sentenced to six months in prison.

[41] 15 U.S.C. § 78dd-2(a)(1)(A)(i).

[42] For some interesting suggestions about the relationship between criminal law and the idea of "market integrity," see Lindsey Farmer, "The 'Market' in Criminal Law Theory," *The Modern Law Review* 85, no. 2 (2022): 439–40.

[43] The full formulation by Hellman is "an exchange across boundaries prohibited by the relevant decision-maker" where "an exchange across boundaries" is defined as an exchange of "values . . . of different types," such as an "exchange of money for a vote." Deborah Hellman, "Understanding Bribery," in *The Palgrave Handbook of Applied Ethics and the Criminal Law*, 147–48. In the hypothetical being discussed here, a monetary payment is being made in order for a sovereign fund to make a monetary payment to purchase a building, so it is not clear whether this is "an exchange across boundaries" in Hellman's terms. I will set that complication aside here.

[44] Kevin E. Davis, *Between Impunity and Imperialism: The Regulation of Transnational Bribery* (Oxford University Press, 2019), 60.

is improperly directed by, say, a monetary payment, then whatever policy goal this official's power is supposed to serve is likely undermined. In that sense, the wrong of bribery seems to be analogous to the wrong of committing a regulatory offense, where the specific nature of the wrong will depend on the nature and purpose of the regulation.

So, in the case of the sovereign fund, we would have to know more about how investment decisions of that particular fund are supposed to be made to answer the question fully, but the basics are straightforward. Public officials who manage the sovereign wealth fund have a fiduciary duty to citizens to make decisions that are based on the merits or are at least consistent with the purpose of having such a sovereign wealth fund in the first place. In Bob's case, since the attempt to influence the official to buy Bob's father's building is an attempt to short-circuit the investment decision process, he would be inducing the official to stray from his obligation to follow a process that is designed to maximize the overall value of the fund from the perspective of the people the fund is to serve. And to the extent that Bob is seeking to have his father benefit from such a short-circuiting of the process, then he and his father would be benefiting from the fund's activities at the expense of the intended beneficiaries of the fund, namely, citizens of country *X*.

Put in terms of C_a and C_d, we might think of the bribery in this case as a form of stealing from beneficiaries of the fund if the idea is that the sovereign fund could have invested in some other property which would have yielded a better return,[45] and that would constitute C_a. As to C_d, the culpability arises from Bob's using a prohibited method of inducing a sovereign wealth fund to purchase his father's building. A difficulty arises, though, if the "proper way" of investing the funds is in theory only, but not in practice. What if, for instance, it is well known to everyone that it is quite commonplace for an official in a particular foreign country to accept bribes when it directs the government's actions in different ways? That is, if only a minority of participants in the relevant market follows the rules of the game as written down, is it so obvious for us to conclude that a person who bribes officials because of the unwritten rule that "bribery" is business as usual is culpable?

It seems unseemly to be making an argument defending corruption, but it is easy to remind ourselves of situations where we know what the law says, but we also know that the compliance rate is low, and we feel like we alone are the ones burdening ourselves and doing more than our fair share as law-abiding citizens. For example, there may be a particular street in a neighborhood where everyone

[45] Davis, *Between Impunity and Imperialism*, 236 (describing the harm of a bribery scheme in Haiti to consist of "the Haitian government . . . receiv[ing] less money than it should have" and calling it a form of stealing from ordinary Haitians).

parks illegally, and the chances of detection are low for whatever reason.[46] Or you may live in a society where people generally do not pay taxes that they owe.[47] Or perhaps you are in an industry that heavily depends on government contracts, and you know that surviving as a business in that competitive environment requires paying off the right government officials since that is how "everyone does it."[48] In such a situation, is disobedience blameworthy?

Perhaps an argument could be made that at that point C_d is zero because bribery appears to be lawful, and there is in fact no disobedience. The FCPA does provide as an affirmative defense the argument that "the payment, gift, offer, or promise of anything of value that was made, was lawful under the written laws and regulations of the foreign official's . . . country."[49] The key term there, however, is lawfulness "under the *written* laws," and, since bribery like the one described here is generally not explicitly permitted, this defense is rarely applicable. In other words, there is disobedience here, and the problem is what culpability to assign to disobedience when there is widespread disobedience.

Another argument one might make is that undercompliance signals an ineffective state, and an ineffective state may lack standing to demand obedience, which would mean that there cannot be a just punishment for disobedience of an ineffective state. That may be, and we will focus on arguments like that in the next chapter, but the FCPA is a peculiar law in that it is a US law that seeks to control behaviors of entities doing business in countries other than the United States, since the core of the crime is to bribe a foreign official. So if corruption is a way of life in a country, that is not because the United States is an ineffective state, yet the law a briber violates would be a US law. Because the United States lacks jurisdiction to control the general amount of corruption in a country and has jurisdiction only over those entities that the United States has power over, those entities still owe the United States a duty to obey, even if they may not have a duty to obey the state where corruption takes place.

One might respond by saying that if it is the case that corruption is a problem, then the only way to eliminate corruption is by each individual doing their part, even if the compliance rate may be low today. That is fair enough, but if the expected compliance rate remains low, then an obligation for one to "play by the rules" seems to amount to an obligation to do more than one's share and sacrifice business opportunities today so that the world overall can improve in the long run. We seem to have crossed the line between a duty of doing one's fair share

[46] I noticed, when I lived in Florence some years ago, that the locals interpreted the "24-hour no parking" sign as "free parking" (as in there were no meters to feed) in certain spots, and it was important to know where that was the case and where that was not.

[47] Cf. Yaffe, "Revisiting," 419–20 (discussing "minor tax evasion" and reporting on a study showing that perception of its wrongfulness seems to depend on its prevalence).

[48] Cf. generally Husak, "The 'But-Everyone-Does-That!' Defense."

[49] 15 U.S.C. § 78dd-1(c)(1).

to the supererogatory duty of beneficence, and failing to do more than one's fair share for the greater common good does not seem as blameworthy as failing to do one's fair share.[50]

At the same time, if it is the case that corruption is a problem, and the reason it is so difficult to combat is the dynamic of the collective action problem just noted, then it is understandable why government-imposed sanctions are necessary to make any progress on the problem of corruption. If the United States enacts the FCPA, then, to take a stand against transnational corruption and attempt to jumpstart efforts to eliminate it (in other countries—even if in a given country corruption is a way of life), individuals to whom the law applies have a duty to obey, and the disobedience seems blameworthy, a violation of the duty to support the state.[51]

The point here is not to settle the question of what is wrong with bribery or transnational bribery once and for all. Rather, the point is that disobedience offenses are often enacted as a way of setting down the "rules of the road" as the government attempts to coordinate the behavior of individuals to pursue a common good, and there is a real question as to how blameworthy a person's disobedience of such rules might be in situations of undercompliance.

E. Conclusion

It may seem deflating to propose the principle of proportionality in punishment as a source of limiting disobedience offenses and then list several problems with the application. The point of this part is not to argue that the principle of proportionality is unworkable but to highlight some challenges that are particularly pressing for disobedience offenses. The idea that the harshness of punishment should not exceed the seriousness of the offense remains an important ideal not to be given up, despite its messiness in application.

[50] Cf. Laura Valentini, "The Natural Duty of Justice in Non-Ideal Circumstances: On the Moral Demands of Institution Building and Reform," *European Journal of Political Theory* 20, no. 1 (2017): 7–17 (considering citizens' obligations in situations of "moderate expected non-compliance" and "pervasive expected non-compliance").

[51] Cf. Joseph Raz, "The Obligation to Obey," 347 ("[W]e all have reason to preserve the countryside. In areas visited by many people, this would be enhanced if no one had barbecues. In fact everyone had barbecues in those areas. The damage is done, and my refraining from a barbecue will not help. The situation is so bad that my having a barbecue will not make even a small difference. At long last the government . . . forbids having barbecues . . . Because the regulation might reverse the trend, I have an obligation to obey this law."); see also Joseph Raz, "The Obligation to Obey the Law," in *The Authority of Law: Essays on Law and Morality* (Oxford University Press, 1979), 247 ("[I]f most people pollute [the rivers] and they are badly polluted there is normally no reason why I should refrain from polluting them myself.").

IV. Proportionality in Self-Defense, War, and Constitutional Law and Disobedience Offenses

A. Basic Idea

The principle of proportionality in punishment, while a source of limitations on the state's power to criminalize and punish, hardly guarantees justice. Even if every punishment is "proportionate" in the sense of proportionality in punishment, we still need to curb the criminal justice system because of its coercive and violent nature.

Such an aspect of the criminal justice system is most salient in the process of apprehending and punishing offenders. There is no need to rehash here the mindboggling numbers associated with populations of persons held in prisons and jails in the United States,[52] as even a criminal justice system without such numbers can still be coercive and violent. Criminal justice systems routinely send people to prisons for years. For most people, even spending just a three-month period in prison away from their work, friends, and families, would be a highly traumatizing, disruptive experience. Sentences significantly longer than that are nothing less than personal catastrophes for those convicted. Yet criminal justice systems bring about such catastrophes on purpose, as a matter of routine, and in the name of upholding the rule of law. In addition, as argued in Chapter 1, punishment is harsh also because it is *judgmental* in the sense that when the state punishes, it also blames the offenders and condemns and censures the offending behavior.

Furthermore, when we resort to criminal law, we authorize the state not only to prohibit certain behaviors but also to use violent means to enforce the prohibitions. Criminalization means, at least, more stops and more searches, even when the law enforcement is working in good faith and in a nondiscriminatory fashion, as well as other intrusive forms of interference in people's lives.[53] In addition, we will likely have those who are singled out and repeatedly scrutinized by law enforcement in ways that are discriminatory, oppressive, and dignity-stripping. Law enforcement may focus on certain groups of individuals not necessarily because of what those individuals have done but for the purpose of "managing people" and for "social control." A broad criminal code enables such projects of surveillance and control.[54]

[52] John Pfaff, *Locked In: The True Causes of Mass Incarceration and How to Achieve Real Reform* (Basic Books, 2018); Michelle Alexander, *The New Jim Crow: Mass Incarceration in the Age of Colorblindness* (The New Press, 2010); Douglas Husak, *Overcriminalization* (Oxford University Press, 2007), 3–5.

[53] Cf. Victor Tadros, "Crime and Security," *The Modern Law Review* 71, no. 6 (2008): 949–51; Husak, *Overcriminalization*, 12.

[54] See Issa Kohler-Hausmann, "Managerial Justice and Mass Misdemeanors," *Stanford Law Review* 66, no. 3 (2014): 614.

Those are some common features of the criminal justice system, at least as we know it. It is certainly the case that we ought to work on addressing such excesses and injustices directly. But assuming that the nature of the criminal justice system is such that it will likely remain coercive and intrusive, ethics of self-defense and war provides a potentially fruitful source of ideas about limiting such a system, as one thing that self-defense, war, and the criminal justice system have in common is that they are sites of legally permissible, intentional infliction of violence.[55] To think through the analogy, we may start by borrowing the concepts of narrow and wide proportionality discussed in the context of self-defense and war. Adapted to the context of criminal law, narrow proportionality may refer to proportionality in punishment and wide proportionality can be a way of weighing the costs and benefits of using criminal law to deal with a social problem.[56] Another idea that we can borrow from these contexts is necessity: even if a punishment imposed on a person for a crime that the person has committed is not disproportionate, it may still be *unnecessary* in that a less intrusive option may be available. In sum, we can consider not just whether a punishment is disproportionate but also whether the punishment is necessary and whether the benefits of resorting to criminal law outweigh the costs. It is at this stage that we can ask questions like whether the burdens criminal law places on marginalized groups and on society overall are justified by its benefits.

To operationalize this, let us revisit the current state of limits on criminalization that I introduced and criticized in the previous chapter and vary it slightly to focus on the proportionality question:

1. Do not criminalize *A*, *B*, and *C*... (*A*, *B*, and *C*... being exercises of fundamental rights).
2. So long as fundamental rights are not inhibited, the government may criminalize any conduct—from speeding to murder—as the government sees fit.
3. When the government enforces criminal law (enacted within constraints 1 and 2), it must do so without violating the principle of proportionality in punishment (*narrow* proportionality).

[55] For a good discussion of the war and punishment parallel, see Alice Ristroph, "Just Violence," *Arizona Law Review* 56, no. 4 (2014): 1022–28. Cf. Husak, *Overcriminalization*, 91–95 (discussing the right not to be punished).

[56] Ristroph has made a suggestion in this direction. See Ristroph, "Just Violence," 1059–60. Tadros has also developed something similar. See Tadros, *The Ends of Harm*, 331–59. However, because they both reject proportionality in punishment as an idea, their approaches are very different from what is proposed here.

A society that applies this framework, however, might still be overly carceral as noted above. A system of criminal law and punishment activates involvement of public actors who are equipped with and authorized to use powerful and destructive tools, and such tools can be wielded in abusive and dehumanizing ways and further bring about disrespect of and alienation from the law, even if very few people are punished and even if those who are punished are punished relatively mildly. To address this issue, we might bring in the concept of *wide* proportionality to produce a proposal that looks like this:

1. Do not criminalize *A*, *B*, and *C* . . . (*A*, *B*, and *C* . . . being exercises of fundamental rights).
2. When regulating behaviors that do not fall within the scope of exercises of fundamental rights, use criminal law only when the costs of using criminal law are outweighed by its benefits (*wide* proportionality).
3. When the government enforces criminal law (enacted within constraints 1 and 2), it must do so without violating the principle of proportionality in punishment (*narrow* proportionality).

This framework could be more sensible than the first because it calls for an analysis of both the costs and benefits of using criminal law, while respecting the constraint of proportionality in punishment. This, too, however, may not go far enough because it may entail more sacrifice for society (or certain segments of society) than is necessary. So, to all this, we can incorporate the concept of necessity as follows:

1. Do not criminalize *A*, *B*, and *C* . . . (*A*, *B*, and *C* . . . being exercises of fundamental rights).
2. When regulating behaviors that do not fall within the scope of exercises of fundamental rights, use criminal law only when the costs of using criminal law are outweighed by its benefits *and* only when *necessary*, given all other regulatory tools the government has at its disposal (*wide* proportionality and necessity).
3. When the government enforces criminal law (enacted within constraints 1 and 2), it must do so without violating the principle of proportionality in punishment (*narrow* proportionality).

This analysis has some relationship to the idea of proportionality in constitutional law. If we revisit Cohen-Eliya and Porat's summary, the proportionality test says:

> [W]henever the government infringes upon a constitutionally protected right, the proportionality principle requires that the government show, first, that its objective is legitimate and important; second, that the means chosen were rationally connected to achieve that objective . . . ; third, that no less drastic means were available . . . ; and fourth, that the benefit from realizing the objective exceeds the harm to the right . . . .[57]

We can see that my proposed framework of combining different kinds of proportionality and necessity has a strong resemblance to the framework of proportionality in constitutional law. The concept of wide proportionality is similar to the first, second, and fourth factors of proportionality in constitutional law, and the concept of necessity is similar to the third factor. It is important, though, to notice what is missing from the idea of proportionality in constitutional law: *narrow proportionality* or proportionality in punishment. The problem with collapsing the idea of proportionality in punishment with the idea of proportionality in constitutional law is the real possibility of eliminating the concept of proportionality in punishment as a constraint with a structure that provides for stringency or resistance to trade-offs. Therefore, while I am proposing that we use proportionality in constitutional law (and self-defense and war) to think about crime and punishment, it is important not to lose sight of proportionality in punishment as a source of limits that are inviolable or close to inviolable.

B. Application

So, assuming that the idea of proportionality (in self-defense and war) and the related idea of necessity can be used to restrict the scope of disobedience offenses, how would the framework apply in practice? We are now entering an area that has received much attention by those who have sought to devise a general comprehensive theory of criminalization and limits to place on it, and that is not the task of this book.[58] But I can at least make some suggestions by discussing some relevant ideas.

The first such idea is that of *de minimis* infractions, sometimes expressed as the legal maxim, "*De minimis non curat lex*," or "The Law does not concern itself with trifles."[59] The Model Penal Code has a specific *de minimis* provision, which

[57] Cohen-Eliya and Porat, *Proportionality*, 2.

[58] See, e.g., Husak, *Overcriminalization*; R. A. Duff, *The Realm of Criminal Law* (Oxford University Press, 2018).

[59] Joel Feinberg, *The Moral Limits of the Criminal Law Volume 1: Harm to Others* (Oxford University Press, 1984), 189; Douglas Husak, "The De Minimis 'Defence' to Criminal Liability," in *Philosophical Foundations of Criminal Law*, ed. R. A. Duff and Stuart Green (Oxford University

says in part that "[t]he Court shall dismiss a prosecution if . . . it finds that the defendant's conduct . . . did not actually cause or threaten the harm or evil sought to be prevented by the law defining the offense or did so only to an extent too trivial to warrant the condemnation of conviction."[60]

It is unclear how useful this idea can be in practice. For the kinds of crimes we have discussed throughout this book especially, often the very point of the law seems to be to outlaw undesirable behaviors which may not in individual cases cause significant harm or impose risks of harm, yet in the aggregate can burden individuals and society. Regulatory offenses, like the environmental crimes we saw in Chapter 5, had this feature, and preventive offenses like incomplete attempt and various possession offenses regarding drugs, guns, and child pornography that we saw in Chapters 6 and 7 were similar in these respects as well. Even some of the national security offenses involving espionage and export controls where basic or useless information may have been given to foreigners or other unauthorized parties can seem trivial in isolation yet dangerous in the aggregate. At the same time, it is hard to deny the idea that criminal law should not be used in situations where the harm or wrongfulness of a person's conduct has not crossed a certain threshold.[61] Therefore, even if it may be difficult to work out the precise contours of such a "defense," the idea of *de minimis* can still serve as a useful resource.

The second idea is that "criminalization is the legislator's *ultima ratio*" or that "[c]riminalization should be used as a last resort."[62] There are many questions as to how to understand, interpret, and apply such a principle.[63] To get the idea of a "last resort" going, let us start with a list of alternatives since the principle seems to assume that other options ought to be considered first. As we first discussed in Chapter 1, there are different types of alternatives to criminal law. Some alternatives to criminal law resemble criminal law in that they incapacitate those who are likely to harm others by segregating them from others. Quarantine facilities and mental institutions are obvious examples. Of course, if the idea behind the last resort principle is to reduce reliance on deprivation of liberty, then

Press, 2011); R. A. Duff, "'De Minimis' and the Structure of the Criminal Trial," *Law and Philosophy* 42, no. 1 (2023): 57–86.

[60] Model Penal Code § 2.12 (American Law Institute, 1985).

[61] Husak, "The De Minimis 'Defence,'" 349–50; Duff, "'De Minimis,'" 69–72.

[62] Nils Jareborg, "Criminalization as Last Resort (*Ultima Ratio*)," *Ohio State Journal of Criminal Law* 2, no. 2 (2005): 523; see also Máximo Langer, "Penal Abolitionism and Criminal Law Minimalism: Here and There, Now and Then," *Harvard Law Review Forum* 133, no. 9 (2020): 72–76.

[63] Douglas Husak, "The Criminal Law as Last Resort," *Oxford Journal of Legal Studies* 24, no. 2 (2004): 207–35; Douglas Husak, "Applying *Ultima Ratio*: A Skeptical Assessment," *Ohio State Journal of Criminal Law* 2 (2005): 535–45; Kaarlo Tuori "Ultima Ratio as a Constitutional Principle," *Oñati Socio-Legal Series* 3, no. 1 (2013): 6–20; Langer, "Penal Abolitionism," 42–77.

these are hardly attractive alternatives, so merely moving people from one type of carceral facility to another type of carceral facility would not constitute a satisfactory application of the last resort principle.[64]

What other alternatives should we consider, then? There are three different types of alternatives to consider. First, there are alternatives to criminal law as a way of preventing harm. If the goal is to prevent harm, we can devote resources to measures that prevent harmful activities in the first place, such as education, health care—including treatments for substance abuse and for mental illness—job training and employment, child care and welfare benefits, universal basic income, and so on. These options call for taking a wide, long-term perspective on the general problem of harm in society and what tools one should employ to address it. So taking such a perspective can be thought of as one manifestation of the last resort principle.

Second, there are criminal law alternatives to imprisonment as a way of responding to violations of laws. The most familiar examples are fines, community service, house arrest, revocation of licenses, and electronic monitoring. Given that these modes of punishment are likely less intrusive and less burdensome than incarceration, relying on these alternatives when they are available and workable for different types of offenses can be an outgrowth of the last resort principle. And then there are more ambitious programs like reparative and restorative justice.[65] Some of these victim-centered approaches might be good alternatives in some situations, though they are not generally applicable to the kinds of disobedience offenses covered in this book where often the state or society at large is the only "victim."

Third, there are noncriminal law alternatives as a way of responding to violations of laws. One possibility might be private lawsuits, though, again, such solutions are more appropriate when there are identifiable individual victims, and do not work well for the kinds of offenses discussed in this book. A more appropriate alternative is suggested in James Whitman's observation of an "ongoing European drive to downgrade offenses" and adding "more and more offenses" to a lower category of offenses in contrast to the "American drive toward 'zero tolerance.'"[66] An example that is perhaps particularly applicable to the subject matter of this book is *Ordnungswidrigkeiten*, a German legal category that has received some notice by Anglo-American legal scholars

[64] Cf. Youngjae Lee, "Is Prison Abolitionism Self-Defeating?" *Criminal Law and Philosophy* 19, no. 3 (2024): 500–02.

[65] For discussions, see, e.g., Tommie Shelby, *The Idea of Prison Abolition* (Princeton University Press, 2022), 171; *see also* Duff, *The Realm of Criminal Law*, 282–83.

[66] James Q. Whitman, *Harsh Justice: Criminal Punishment and the Widening Divide between America and Europe* (Oxford University Press, 2005), 83.

and is translated as "violations of good order,"[67] "violations of order,"[68] "regulatory violations,"[69] "petty infractions,"[70] or "administrative penalties."[71] These violations generally carry monetary penalties only, imprisonment is not available as a response to them, and stigma is low.[72] Andrew Ashworth and Lucia Zedner, for example, citing the *Ordnungswidrigkeiten* system as guidance, argue that there should be "an initial decision about whether the conduct constitutes a serious wrong that merits criminalization, with public censure and sentencing to follow, or whether the conduct is a minor wrong that can properly be dealt with in this non-stigmatic way by a financial penalty."[73] Such an alternative seems appropriate to consider for regulatory offenses discussed in Chapter 5 as well as some of the preventive offenses we saw in Chapters 6 and 7, and perhaps even some of the export controls violations discussed in Chapter 9.[74]

So that is one way to give some content to the last resort principle. It does seem that the idea of "last resort" may be a misnomer in that it clearly should not be taken literally. The principle certainly would be unworkable if lawmakers had to demonstrate that *every* other option has been tried and proven unworkable and therefore we have no option but to resort to criminal law.[75] A more sensible interpretation is to establish a heavy presumption against criminalization that would need to be overcome in order for an act of criminalization to be justified.[76] That is, instead of treating the principle of criminal law as a resort as a rule of exhaustion of other possibilities, we should think of it as an ethos that calls for seriously considering alternatives to criminal law before reaching for this particularly blunt instrument.

[67] Whitman, *Harsh Justice*, 83; John H. Langbein, "Controlling Prosecutorial Discretion in Germany," *University of Chicago Law Review* 41, no. 3 (1974): 439.

[68] Langbein, "Controlling Prosecutorial Discretion," 451.

[69] R. A. Duff, "Two Models of Criminal Fault," *Criminal Law and Philosophy* 13, no. 4 (2019): 643.

[70] Langbein, "Controlling Prosecutorial Discretion," 451.

[71] Daniel Ohana, "Administrative Penalties in the *Rechtsstaat*: On the Emergence of the *Ordnungswidrigkeit* sanctioning System in Post-War Germany," *University of Toronto Law Journal* 64, no. 2 (2014): 243.

[72] Ohana, "Administrative Penalties," 243–44 n.1; Langbein, "Controlling Prosecutorial Discretion," 451.

[73] Andrew Ashworth and Lucia Zedner. "Prevention and Criminalization: Justifications and Limits," *New Criminal Law Review* 15, no. 4 (2012): 568.

[74] For a discussion of some concerns about taking certain violations outside the realm of criminal law, see Duff, *The Realm of Criminal Law*, 282–83, 286; Douglas Husak, "The Price of Criminal Law Skepticism: Ten Functions of the Criminal Law," *New Criminal Law Review* 23, no. 1 (2020): 36–38, 50–51.

[75] Husak, "The Criminal Law as Last Resort," 215, 220.

[76] See Husak, *Overcriminalization*, 121–32.

V. Conclusion

This chapter has argued that the label "proportionality" applies to many different aspects of criminal and other law: proportionality in punishment, narrow proportionality in self-defense and war, wide proportionality in self-defense and war, and proportionality in constitutional law. This chapter has also argued that the principles of proportionality can serve as sources of limits on the state's ability to criminalize and punish. This chapter has outlined some special difficulties of applying the principle of proportionality in the context of disobedience offenses and sketched what it would mean to apply other principles of proportionality to the question of criminalization in the context of disobedience offenses, especially as they may manifest in the ideas of the *de minimis* defense and "criminal law as a last resort."

12

Limits on Criminalization III: Standing to Command and Punish

I. Introduction

Throughout the book, I have argued that many laws in criminal codes criminalize disobedience, and that the wrongfulness of committing such offenses can be traced to disobeying the state. The last two chapters discussed some limiting principles that should serve to constrain criminalization and punishment of disobedience, namely, individual rights and liberties and principles of proportionality. This chapter focuses on the question of whether and when the state can lose its status as an entity worthy of being obeyed, in which case disobedience is not wrongful and punishment of disobedience accordingly unjustifiable.

II. Some Preliminaries

The question of whether the state is worthy of being obeyed brings us into an area of legal and political philosophy on which there is already a large and ever-growing literature.[1] It is not my task here to relitigate old theoretical debates about the relationships among authority, legitimacy, and the duty to obey the law. Rather, I will assume that the question whether a state is owed obedience

[1] See, e.g., Arthur Isak Applbaum, *Legitimacy: The Right to Rule in a Wanton World* (Harvard University Press, 2019); Thomas Christiano, *The Constitution of Equality: Democratic Authority and Its Limits* (Oxford University Press, 2008); William A. Edmundson, *Three Anarchical Fallacies: An Essay on Political Authority* (Cambridge University Press, 1998); David M. Estlund, *Democratic Authority: A Philosophical Framework* (Princeton University Press, 2007); Leslie Green, *The Authority of the State* (Oxford University Press, 1988); Fabienne Peter, *The Grounds of Political Legitimacy* (Oxford University Press, 2023); Abner S. Greene, *Against Obligation: The Multiple Sources of Authority in a Liberal Democracy* (Harvard University Press, 2012); Joseph Raz, *The Morality of Freedom* (Oxford University Press, 1986); A. John Simmons, *Moral Principles and Political Obligations* (Princeton University Press, 1979); A. John Simmons, *Justification and Legitimacy: Essays on Rights and Obligations* (Cambridge University Press, 2000); Anna Stilz, *Liberal Loyalty: Freedom, Obligation, and the State* (Princeton University Press, 2009); Robert Paul Wolff, *In Defense of Anarchism* (Harper and Row, 1970).

Criminalizing Disobedience. Youngjae Lee, Oxford University Press. © Oxford University Press 2026.
DOI: 10.1093/9780197617175.003.0013

is not something that has only one answer. Whether the state may reasonably expect obedience from those over whom they have jurisdiction may depend on specific factors that apply to the laws, behaviors, and situations in question. Even the most morally bankrupt state might have traffic rules that people have an obligation to obey,[2] and even an exemplary state may make mistakes in a particular area that are bad enough for it to lose its standing to demand obedience of relevant laws.

For our purposes, the most important point is that unlike *mala in se* offenses that involve violating others' rights, the duty to obey the kinds of laws discussed in this book—that is, laws criminalizing disobedience in various ways—turns on whether the state is worthy of being obeyed in regard to relevant matters. That is, unlike laws prohibiting, say, murder, whether a person can be said to have done a moral wrong by committing a disobedience offense is closely related to the question of whether the state is worthy of being obeyed.[3] One conclusion that we can draw right away, then, is that a state that seeks to criminalize disobedience in various ways needs to have—and to continually work to maintain—what I will call its "cooperation-worthiness" as it sets rules, demands obedience, and punishes people for disobedience.

I should clarify here that, as I indicated in Chapter 2, I do not think the state loses its cooperation-worthiness every time it makes a mistake. The state is fallible, and its laws are fallible, but that does not mean the duty to obey disappears every time the law gets things wrong. I am thus in agreement with John Rawls when he expresses his skepticism of the idea that "any deviation from justice, however small, nullifies the duty to comply with existing rules."[4] The task of the rest of this chapter is to give specific examples of the kinds of situations in which a state may have acted in a way that is grave enough to undermine its status as an entity that is worthy of being obeyed as it criminalizes and punishes disobedience. I should admit at the outset that the suggestions I will make here are controversial, and readers may walk away unpersuaded. I hope, however, to highlight some factors that, to say the least, place the state in an uncomfortable position from which to demand obedience, and to advance the thesis that the state should seek to avoid placing itself in such positions.

[2] Cf. Tommie Shelby, *Dark Ghettos: Injustice, Dissent, and Reform* (Harvard University Press, 2016), 229 ("The duty to comply with [some] laws arises . . . from the contingent fact that the existing state is best positioned to maintain order and safety.").

[3] Cf. Shelby, *Dark Ghettos*, 229, 232–34.

[4] John Rawls, *A Theory of Justice*, rev. ed. (Harvard University Press, 1999), 310.

III. Loss of Standing to Demand Obedience: Some Examples

A. Disobeying and Failing to Support Law Enforcement

In Chapters 3 and 4, we saw that some of the disobedience offenses involve law enforcement. In Chapter 10, we discussed how these laws might conflict with constitutional rights and infringe on the liberty of movement. But here I want to focus on the ways in which law enforcement may not have standing to demand obedience or support.

Consider *People v. Seck*, a case in which a person was convicted of "disorderly conduct" for "recklessly creat[ing] a risk of public inconvenience, annoyance, or alarm by obstructing pedestrian traffic" and "congregating with other persons in a public place and refusing to comply with a lawful order of the police to disperse."[5] According to the facts as recounted by the court, the defendant was standing on a sidewalk "obstructing pedestrian traffic," and when an officer ordered them to disperse, "the defendant repeatedly refused, and pushed the officer," and "[w]hen the officer attempted to place defendant in handcuffs, defendant began yelling, and grabbed the officer's pepper spray and radio."[6]

A similar case is *People v. Knoedler*. Brent Knoedler was holding an open can of beer in public, and when a law enforcement officer asked for his name or his identification so the officer could issue him a ticket for the open can of beer, Knoedler did not identify himself, though he did throw away the can. When he continued to refuse to identify himself, the officer and another officer tried to get him to identify himself again. When that did not work, they tried to arrest him, at which point Knoedler broke free, hit an officer, and ran away. Knoedler was eventually charged with and convicted for "resisting, obstructing, or delaying a peace officer who was lawfully performing his or her duties."[7]

These are only two stories among many, and many of them have endings that are much worse.[8] What we think of *Seck* and *Knoedler* depends, obviously, on whether we can trust the law enforcement officers involved. And it is unfortunately the case that there are good reasons to think that many encounters like those in *Seck* and *Knoedler* are instances of police abuse of power and harassment rather than legitimate law enforcement activities.[9] The idea that disobedience of the state is blameworthy is most defensible when it is rooted in the

[5] People v. Seck, 4 N.Y.S.3d 209, 210 (N.Y. App. Div. 1st Dept. 2015); N.Y. Penal Law § 240.20.

[6] Seck, 4 N.Y.S.3d at 210–11.

[7] People v. Knoedler, 44 Cal. App. 5th Supp. 1, 3 (Cal. App. Dep't Super. Ct. 2019); see also Rodgers v. State, 620 S.W.3d 869 (Tex. App. 2021) for similar facts and a conviction for the crime of failure to identify.

[8] See, e.g., Mike Baker et al., "Three Words. 70 Cases. The Tragic History of 'I Can't Breathe,'" *New York Times*, June 29, 2020.

[9] See generally Alex S. Vitale, *The End of Policing* (Verso Books, 2017).

idea that supporting just institutions includes not interfering with their work. That is, a person who disobeys commands issued by legal officials fails to accord proper normative significance to the legal system and to the actors empowered by it to serve the common good. This framing seems to imply that when such actors are not, for instance, acting in good faith or genuinely serving the common good, the obligation to obey their commands may be nullified. In such cases, even though there may be clear lawbreaking through disobedience, there should be no conviction or punishment.

The same considerations apply when we focus on not just the duty to *obey* law enforcement but the duty to *assist* law enforcement. *Saturday Night Live* has a recurring segment called "Black Jeopardy!," which uses the format of the quiz show "Jeopardy!" to illustrate, in a comically exaggerated way, the different worlds that people of different races—Blacks and Whites, mostly—inhabit in the United States. One of the most well-known episodes is the one featuring Chadwick Boseman as King T'Challa of the fictional state of Wakanda in *Black Panther*. The question posed is "[what one does when] [t]he policeman says there's been some robberies in your neighborhood and asks if you have 'any information.'" T'Challa answers: "[N]ot only do I tell this man what I know, but I also assist him in tracking down the offender. After all, our ministers of law enforcement are only here to protect us. Is this correct?" The quiz show host responds with a chuckle, implying not only "no" as an answer to the question but also with an immediate dismissive ridicule. He then adds: "I mean, it should be. But I'm thinking you haven't spent much time in America."[10]

That response to T'Challa's suggestion is of course emblematic of a deep animosity between the police and the Black community.[11] There may be good reasons not to assist law enforcement even in situations where the law enforcement works for the common good in good faith, such as times where the state actors' law enforcement actions are misguided for whatever reason. Where law enforcement uses its coercive power in a systematically unjust and racially discriminatory manner, this problem is compounded. In sum, the proposition that there is a moral obligation to assist law enforcement seems more questionable in a state with a significant history and practice of injustice—in the form of harassment, brutality, and surveillance doled out in racially discriminatory manners—within law enforcement.[12]

[10] "Black Jeopardy with Chadwick Boseman—SNL," posted April 8, 2018, by Saturday Night Live, YouTube, https://www.youtube.com/watch?v=hzMzFGgmQOc (relevant clip at 4:01–4:33).

[11] Cf. Monica C. Bell, "Police Reform and the Dismantling of Legal Estrangement," *Yale Law Journal* 126, no. 7 (2017): 2068–72.

[12] Cf. I. Bennett Capers, "Criminal Procedure and the Good Citizen," *Columbia Law Review* 118, no. 2 (2018): 653; Trevor George Gardner, "Police Violence and the African American Procedural

B. Possessing Drugs and Guns

In Chapter 7, we saw that possessing drugs and guns may be criminalized as part of the government's program of eliminating unauthorized markets of dangerous substances and instruments. The idea is to reduce the harm these items impose on society by making it difficult to traffic in them. As such, the ban on possession should be understood not as grounded in the immorality of using drugs or having guns, but in interfering with the government's program of destroying harmful markets. At least that is the theory. Both guns and drugs are topics with vast literatures, and there is no room here for comprehensive discussions of histories and policy issues regarding them.[13] But let me highlight some things about these laws that make them particularly problematic as sites in which the state can demand obedience.

Take drugs first. It is fair to say, though, that the drug law is one of the most maligned aspects of our criminal justice system.[14] Statements like the following are common: "It is hard to think of a contemporary public policy regime more discredited than the 'war on drugs'";[15] "[e]ssentially every drug policy researcher agrees that the war has been an abject failure, the cause of far greater harm than the problem it was meant to solve";[16] "[d]ozens of commentators have argued that our system of drug prohibition has been a colossal failure";[17] "[m]any commentators have made an impressive case that prohibition has caused greater harm both to users and to society than drug use itself";[18] "[t]oday, . . . Americans are fast losing their faith that a 'War on Drugs' is fair, moral, or

Habitus," *Boston University Law Review* 100, no. 3 (2020): 849; Ekow N. Yankah, "Whose Burden to Bear?: Privilege, Lawbreaking and Race," *Criminal Law and Philosophy* 16, no. 1 (2022): 13; Shelby, *Dark Ghettos*, 218–19.

[13] See, e.g., David F. Musto, *The American Disease: Origins of Narcotic Control*, 3rd ed. (Oxford University Press, 1999); David Farber, ed., *The War on Drugs: A History* (NYU Press, 2021); Paul Gootenberg, ed., *The Oxford Handbook of Global Drug History* (Oxford University Press, 2022); Robert Spitzer, *Politics of Gun Control*, 7th ed. (Routledge, 2018); Gary Kleck, *Targeting Guns: Firearms and Their Control* (Routledge, 1997).

[14] It is important, however, not to forget that the current consensus is of relatively recent vintage. See, e.g., David Farber, "Introduction," in *The War on Drugs: A History*, ed. David Farber (NYU Press, 2021), 3 ("When President Nixon launched the modern War on Drugs in 1971, few Americans believed that cannabis . . . should be legal or even 'decriminalized' in the US. In 1969, 84 percent of Americans said that they believed anyone caught with even the smallest amount of marijuana should go to jail. . . . For decades, a broad political consensus that included liberal democrats and conservative Republicans championed a mercilessly punitive War on Drugs."); David Farber, "Drug Dealers," in *The War on Drugs: A History*, ed. David Farber (NYU Press, 2021), 54–55; James Forman Jr., *Locking Up Our Own: Crime and Punishment in Black America* (Farrar, Straus and Giroux, 2017).

[15] David Pozen, *The Constitution of the War on Drugs* (Oxford University Press, 2024), 1.

[16] Pozen, *War on Drugs*, 1 (quotation omitted).

[17] Douglas N. Husak, "Guns and Drugs: Case Studies on the Principled Limited of the Criminal Sanction," *Law and Philosophy* 23, no. 5 (2004): 451.

[18] Husak, "Guns and Drugs," 452.

sensible, let alone winnable";[19] "the consensus has been that, at a minimum, the war on drugs has been ineffective";[20] "the drug war has not only been ineffectual, it has caused significant additional and needless harm both in the United States and around the world."[21] It is also a widely held notion that "the war on drugs is synonymous with racial injustice."[22]

If it is the case that drug possession laws criminalize and punish disobedience, it is fair to say that there are serious problems with punishing individuals for failing to support a bankrupt policy. We might say several things in terms of such a conclusion, and let's examine them more closely. First, if the War on Drugs has failed to deliver on its goal of reducing harm done to society from illicit substances, then it is an *ineffective* policy that is not worthy of support. Second, the War on Drugs may have its origins and even its continued existence in policies driven by racism, in which case the state may be punishing people for disobeying laws that fuel *racist* policies conducted in *bad faith*. Third, if the War on Drugs has made the problem of harm to society worse because it is the policy that created the harmful market, then the policy itself is the problem, and the state is *complicit* in whatever drug crimes it seeks to punish.[23]

From these considerations, could we conclude that, given that possession of drugs is a crime of disobedience, such problems make the drug laws associated with the War on Drugs highly suspect, and the duty to obey such laws thus particularly weak? That seems compelling, but it is not a simple issue.

First, just because a policy is *ineffective* does not mean the laws that implement the flawed policy are not worthy of people's support. It is possible that the law is ineffective because it does not go far enough. Perhaps an ineffective set of laws needs more support, not less, if the laws represent steps in the right direction. It may be the case that the War on Drugs is a particularly catastrophic policy, but the point here is that mere ineffectiveness is not enough to destroy the state's standing to demand obedience.

[19] Farber, "Introduction," 1.

[20] Samuel Roberts, "The Impact of the US Drug War on People of Color," in *The Oxford Handbook of Global Drug History*, ed. Paul Gootenberg (Oxford University Press, 2022), 474.

[21] Matthew Pembleton, "The Globalization of US Drug Enforcement," in *The Oxford Handbook of Global Drug History*, ed. Paul Gootenberg (Oxford University Press, 2022), 434.

[22] Pozen, *War on Drugs*, 67; see also Michelle Alexander, *The New Jim Crow: Mass Incarceration in the Age of Colorblindness* (The New Press, 2010); Roberts, "The Impact of the US Drug War," 474 ("More critical assessments—including those launched in the first years of the war on drugs, and since 2010 increasingly mainstream in social science and political thinking—have made the case that the war on drugs was launched on spurious grounds, capitalized on racist fear, and has been detrimental to the most vulnerable groups in American society."); David A. Sklansky, "Cocaine, Race, and Equal Protection," *Stanford Law Review* 47, no. 6 (1995): 1283–1302.

[23] See, e.g., Matthew B. Lawrence and David E. Pozen, "Drug Scheduling as Institutional Design," *Harvard Law Review*: 139 (forthcoming 2026).

Second, as to the issue of bad faith policymaking, it is certainly the case that an intentionally racist policy does not deserve the society's respect. The complication here is that sometimes a good policy may be motivated by illicit preferences, in which case the solution is to change the attitude of the public and the lawmakers so that the illicit preferences do not contaminate good policies, as opposed to undermining the policies themselves. For instance, statutory rape law may have patriarchal roots,[24] but that does not mean the law itself is suspect, as it can be supported by a different rationale that is less problematic. There are many other examples like this.[25] Similarly, national security laws may look the way they do because of some combination of national security concerns and prejudice against certain groups, but it is not obvious whether that means laws in existence for national security are entirely meritless in terms of protecting national security.

Third, the fact that it was the state's terrible policy that made the War on Drugs even more intractable and the fact that the state's interventions made the problems worse does not necessarily mean that the law loses its standing to demand obedience. If the market for illicit drugs harms the public, then it is wrong to participate in it, no matter who created the market. The argument that without the government's intervention, we would not have the problems to begin with is not obviously relevant to the question of a person's individual culpability in making the problem worse by disobeying the law.

These three defenses of the duty to obey unwise drug laws have the feel of bending over backward to preserve the state's standing to demand obedience, and at some point, all that bending over becomes unsustainable. The War on Drugs may be one of those areas where the combination of ineffectiveness, racial prejudice, and the state's responsibility for the problems has reached the point where the state no longer has standing to demand obedience and punish disobedience. The fact that these criticisms have been well known for years yet the state has not been proactive in responding to such problems exacerbates the erosion of the state's standing to expect obedience.[26]

[24] See, e.g., Frances Olsen, "Statutory Rape: A Feminist Critique of Rights Analysis," *Texas Law Review* 63, no. 3 (1984): 387–432.

[25] See, e.g., Adam Winkler, "Racist Gun Laws and the Second Amendment," *Harvard Law Review* 135, no. 8 (2022): 543 ("While the racism of past gun laws does and should give one pause, we might nonetheless recognize that many areas of law have historically been used to perpetuate racial discrimination but that courts don't approach every law in those areas as inherently suspect. Property laws were used to enforce racially restrictive covenants, but that doesn't mean that all laws regulating property should be presumptively unconstitutional. Zoning laws were used to create and maintain racial segregation, but courts do not automatically review zoning laws with strict scrutiny. Marriage laws were explicitly racially discriminatory, as were criminal laws and laws regulating voting. Yet in all of these areas we still recognize that some forms of regulation are necessary and lawmakers are given wide leeway, more or less, to devise regulatory reforms absent the explicit use of race.").

[26] I thank David Pozen for this point.

Similar arguments have been made about guns.[27] Like drug laws, gun laws can be criticized for: being ineffective,[28] drawing nonsensical distinctions,[29] and serving as instruments of oppression applied in a racially motivated[30] and discriminatory way.[31] And without repeating the same discussion, we might say similar responses can be made to these criticisms. However, demanding that citizens obey laws with such features carries the danger of being ignored, which would make the law a self-undermining directive. The state's complicity in creating the need for individuals, especially those in marginalized communities who feel both overpoliced *and* underprotected, to arm themselves for reasons of self-protection, makes the state's standing to demand obedience to its gun laws particularly weak.[32] The argument here is not that there is a fundamental right to possess guns that should override state efforts to regulate them—which is the

[27] Benjamin Levin draws the link in a particularly salient way by arguing that the usual criticisms of the War on Drugs, such as "(1) the disparate impact of criminalization and criminal enforcement on low-income communities of color; (2) the expansion in police powers and prosecutorial discretion that drug statutes and judicial opinions have facilitated; and (3) the social and economic costs that have resulted from the mass incarceration of drug offenders," can be applied to gun laws to "highlight[] similar pathologies." Benjamin Levin, "Guns and Drugs," *Fordham Law Review* 84, no. 5 (2016): 2176.

[28] Nicholas J. Johnson, "The Modern Orthodoxy Is a Failed Experiment: Toward a Race Sensitive, Hard Look at Firearms Policy and the Black Community," *UC Irvine Law Review* 14, no. 4 (2024): 1247–49.

[29] Husak, "Guns and Drugs," 479.

[30] Emma Luttrell Shreefter, "Federal Felon-in-Possession Gun Laws: Criminalizing a Status, Disparately Affecting Black Defendants, and Continuing the Nation's Century-Old Methods to Disarm Black Communities," *City University of New York Law Review* 21, no. 2 (2018).

[31] Zach Sherwood, "Time to Reload: The Harms of the Federal Felon-in-Possession Ban in a Post-*Heller* World," *Duke Law Journal* 70, no. 6 (2021): 1463–66; Levin, "Guns and Drugs," 2193–98; Jacob D. Charles and Brandon L. Garrett, "The Trajectory of Federal Gun Crimes," *University of Pennsylvania Law Review* 170, no. 3 (2021): 695–97; Avinash Samarth et al. "Second Class," *Inquest*, November 5, 2021, https://inquest.org/nyc-public-defenders-amicus-second-class/. For an overview, see Danny Y. Li, "Antisubordinating the Second Amendment," *Yale Law Journal* 132, no. 6 (2023): 1856–64.

[32] See, e.g., Brief of Black Attorneys of Legal Aid, at 32, *New York State Rifle & Pistol Ass'n, Inc. v. Bruen*, 597 U.S. 1 (2022) ("It is not safe to be approached by police on suspicion that you possess a gun without a license. It is not safe to have a search warrant executed on your home. It is not safe to be caged pretrial at Rikers Island. It is not safe to lose your job. It is not safe to lose your children. It is not safe to be sentenced to prison.") (references omitted); Brief of Black Guns Matter, at 11–13, *New York State Rifle & Pistol Ass'n, Inc. v. Bruen*, 597 U.S. 1 (2022) ("The need for armed self-defense is most critical when the local, state and federal government fails to offer assistance. . . . [There is] a realization by African Americans that reliance upon the government is inadequate to address the challenges they face in their own communities and shows the current, modern importance of armed self-defense to the African American community."); Johnson, "The Modern Orthodoxy," 1215 ("For most of the Black experience in America, the idea of disarming and just trusting the state was laughable. The rich Black tradition of arms was an outgrowth of deep-seated and longstanding reasons for Black distrust of the state"); Johnson, "The Modern Orthodoxy," 1245 ("Government failure and overt malice . . . are reasons Black folk might choose the option for self-help that guns promise. The killings of George Floyd, Michael Brown, Philando Castille, and others underscore the continuing case for Black distrust of police. In recent polling, 48% of Blacks have very little or no confidence that police will treat Black and white people equally. This compares with twelve percent of whites who have the same view.").

way the discourse is often framed in the United States because of the Second Amendment of the Constitution[33]—rather, the idea is that because gun laws often criminalize disobedience, a state that loses its standing to demand obedience of gun laws from some people creates a situation in which such people are not blameworthy for violating the gun laws.

C. Whistleblowing

In Chapter 9, we discussed the cases of Daniel Ellsberg, Chelsea Manning, and Edward Snowden, all of whom were charged with the crime of disclosing state secrets to unauthorized parties. We should of course not discount the possibility of the damage that the disclosures may have done to the United States, and the extent to which each person may have compromised or risked compromising national security may impact our assessment of their culpability. But setting that aside, if we understand violations of the Espionage Act as disobedience offenses, we can see how the government's behaviors might undermine its standing to demand obedience, in which case it is unclear whether each individual's disobedience was blameworthy.

As noted above, each of the three cases tells the story of an individual working for the government, presumably to help the United States, and then learning details of government activity that each thought should be exposed. Ellsberg exposed an internal assessment of the trajectory of the US involvement in Vietnam that differed starkly from what was being told to the American public.[34] In Manning's case, the documents disclosed involved potential US military activities in Iraq, Afghanistan, and Guantánamo and the disclosure was prompted at least in part by Manning's realization that the United States was committing war crimes and covering them up.[35] Manning also tells the story of how she learned that the classification system that the military was using to keep information from being released to the public was used primarily as a way of painting a favorable portrait of the US military through overclassification and selective disclosure to the public rather than for national security.[36] In Snowden's case, the objectionable practice was the system of mass surveillance that the National Security Agency of the US government had built while lying to Congress about its surveillance activities.[37] These are all claims that the US government was

[33] U.S. Const. amend. II.

[34] Daniel Ellsberg, *Secrets: A Memoir of Vietnam and the Pentagon Papers* (Penguin Books, 2002).

[35] Chelsea Manning, *README.txt* (Farrar, Straus and Giroux, 2022), 181 (noting that her action was "a direct action in the service of transparency").

[36] Manning, *README.txt*, 10–12.

[37] Edward Snowden, *Permanent Record* (Metropolitan Books, 2019), 231.

engaging in acts that undermined its own standing as an entity capable of demanding obedience. Once that loss of trust occurs, it is not clear whether we could conclude that disobedience in these contexts is actually blameworthy, though the individuals may still be held criminally accountable for the damage to national security they may have caused through their acts of disclosure.

D. Draft Resistance

The most well-known cases of draft resistance in US history come from the Vietnam War. Like other national security crimes we saw in Chapters 8 and 9, there is a good case for draft resistance to be considered a disobedience offense given that whether one agrees with the wisdom of the war does not change what people owe the state, unless the war is an obviously unjust one and those who are being asked to enlist are being enlisted for the wrong side. But given the kind of deception about the progress of the war in Vietnam the US government engaged in, there is a good reason to believe that at one point those who were called upon to serve in the war did not have a duty to obey and enlist.[38]

A less well-known instance of draft resistance is the case of Heart Mountain draft resisters.[39] After Japan's attack on Pearl Harbor, Japanese-Americans were rounded up and placed in concentration camps in the United States by the federal government. One of those concentration camps was Heart Mountain Relocation Center in Wyoming, and when the US government tried to draft those eligible to serve among those who had been interned, a movement to resist the draft developed there. Those who resisted were prosecuted as a group for violation of the Selective Training and Service Act of 1940.[40] Each of the sixty-three defendants made the argument that "his removal from his home and his confinement behind barbed wire in the relocation center without being charged with any crime deprived him of his liberty and property without due process of law, and that therefore he ought not to be required to render military service until his rights were restored."[41] However, all of them were convicted and the appeals court upheld the convictions.[42] Whether the case was correctly decided or not according to the prevailing legal standards, the defendants in the case made a compelling argument—namely, that if the government seeks to get individuals to report for military service and enter a relationship in which they are expected

[38] See, e.g., Elizabeth Becker, "The Secrets and Lies of the Vietnam War, Exposed in One Epic Document," *New York Times*, June 9, 2021.
[39] See Eric L. Muller: *Free to Die for Their Country: The Story of the Japanese American Draft Resisters in World War II* (University of Chicago Press, 2001).
[40] United States v. Fujii, 55 F. Supp. 928 (D. Wyo. 1944).
[41] Fujii v. United States, 148 F.2d 298, 299 (10th Cir. 1945).
[42] Fujii, 148 F.2d at 300.

to follow orders whether they agree with them or not, they ought to first receive fair treatment as citizens and not be taken away from their homes on the basis of nothing but their ethnicity.[43] Through the government's unjust treatment of the Japanese-American citizens, it may have lost its standing to demand compliance to its order for eligible Japanese-American men to report for military service.[44]

E. Exporting Illegally

We saw in Chapter 10 how export controls lists get constructed. The Export Control Reform Act authorizes the Commerce Department to determine what items cannot be exported without a license.[45] The Arms Export Control Act authorizes the president to do the same, and the authority has been delegated to the State Department.[46] Similarly, the International Emergency Economic Powers Act grants authority to the president of the United States "to deal with any unusual and extraordinary threat . . . to the national security, foreign policy, or economy of the United States, if the president declares a national emergency with respect to such threat."[47] In such situations, the president is authorized to issue regulations that prohibit certain transactions.[48]

These offenses all involve national security, and since private individuals are poorly situated to undertake their own assessment of the necessity or wisdom of specific regulations, it would make sense, as a general matter, to defer to and cooperate with the government. At the same time, despite all such good reasons not to commit these acts, whether a person can be considered blameworthy or not seems to turn at least partly on whether the US government is entitled to this sort of respect in these matters. And the judgment that these individuals are blameworthy for their conduct is most plausible when the political leaders are credible actors whose judgments are entitled to deference. The question all of this raises, though, is what to think of situations where the case can be made that disobeying the law in a particular situation is not blameworthy because, for instance, the president cannot be trusted to have acted with the best interests of the United States in these matters or to have acted within the scope of the law. In such situations, it is not clear whether there is still a duty to obey.

[43] See Muller, *Free to Die for Their Country*, 181–82.

[44] For more on these cases, see Denny Chin and Kathy Hirata Chin, "Asian Americans and the Law," *Judicial Notice*, no. 11 (2016): 7–21; Eric L. Muller, "The Japanese American Cases—A Bigger Disaster than We Realized," *Howard Law Journal* 49, no. 2 (2006): 436–43.

[45] 50 U.S.C. § 4801(2); 50 U.S.C. § 4801(10); 50 U.S.C. § 4813(a)(1); 50 U.S.C. § 4801(c)(1).

[46] 22 U.S.C. § 2778; 22 C.F.R. § 120.1(a).

[47] 50 U.S.C. § 1701.

[48] 50 U.S.C. § 1702.

IV. Legal System's Response to Its Own Lack of Cooperation-Worthiness

These are just some examples where the state's standing to demand obedience and punish people for disobedience seems precarious. Let's revisit the formula and the four quadrants (Table 12.1):

$$C_t = C_d + C_a$$

Situations where the state's standing to demand obedience is compromised would be in the "$C_d = 0$" column, or Quadrants II and IV. This shows that even in situations where culpability associated with disobedience is zero, those who break the law may still be punished because $C_a > 0$, or the act is blameworthy for reasons other than disobedience.

What about, then, situations where neither the conduct nor the person's mere disobedience is blameworthy? In such situations, it appears that C_t is zero, in which case the person has not done anything wrong and should not be punished even though the person has broken a law. We seem to be in a place, then, where the state may end up punishing a blameless individual, which would be unjust. But is there a legal mechanism for recognizing such a situation?

Currently, we do not have a lot of options if a situation like this arises. It is possible that discretionary devices held by certain legal actors like the prosecutor (declining to prosecute) or the executive branch or the judge (sentencing mitigation or narrowing construction of laws) or the jury (nullifying) or executive pardons and commutations could take care of these problems. But those are unreliable, unpredictable, and uncalibrated devices that do not yield consistent results over time. It seems that what we may need is a defense or a venue in which a defendant could make the case that the government has failed to maintain its standing to demand obedience, and that therefore there is no duty to obey and thus he or she should not be convicted. It appears that draft resisters at Heart Mountain made such an argument, though the argument did not carry the day. As a general matter, a proceeding where the government openly acknowledges

Table 12.1 Conduct-Disobedience Culpability Matrix

	$C_d > 0$	$C_d = 0$
$C_a > 0$	I	II
$C_a = 0$	III	IV

(even if only through a judicial ruling) that there may be good reasons not to obey the law seems unlikely.[49]

To say the least, then, the practice of criminalizing and punishing disobedience comes under severe strain in untrustworthy states, and even in well-functioning states, the legal system's inability or reluctance to accommodate a forum in which the state can acknowledge the ways in which it is not worthy of its citizens' deference presents a problem from the perspective of the principle that the state should not be able to demand obedience and punish disobedience when it does not have a standing to do so. The ultimate upshot is that the state, if it seeks to continue to set rules for people to follow and punish those who break the law, should strive to earn and maintain its cooperation-worthiness.

V. Conclusion

In this book, I have discussed the myriad ways in which the state criminalizes and punishes disobedience. I have argued that it can at times be blameworthy for people to fail to support the state, that this failure can take the form of disobedience, and that such disobedience is the wrong that the state may criminalize and punish.

In the last three chapters, I have outlined several principles that ought to be applied to limit the scope of criminalization and punishment of disobedience. First, laws creating disobedience offenses may conflict with certain constitutional rights, which should not be easily sacrificed for the sake of having disobedience offenses. Second, these laws may suppress peoples' liberty in unwarranted ways, and the state needs to refrain from restricting liberties unnecessarily.

[49] One indicator of such reluctance is the legal system's conflicted stance on the practice of jury nullification, which is recognized as a feature, not a bug, in the system yet is unmentionable through official channels during a trial. See Duncan v. Louisiana, 391 U.S. 145, 187 (1968) (Harlan, J., dissenting) ("A jury may, at times, afford a higher justice by refusing to enforce harsh laws."); United States v. Thomas, 116 F.3d 606, 614 (1997) ("We categorically reject the idea that, in a society committed to the rule of law, jury nullification is desirable or that courts may permit it to occur when it is within their authority to prevent."). However, there can be exceptions. See, e.g., Commonwealth v. Warren, 58 N.E.3d 333, 342 (Mass. 2016) ("[W]here the suspect is a black male stopped by the police on the streets of Boston, the analysis of flight as a factor in the reasonable suspicion calculus cannot be divorced from the findings in a recent Boston Police Department . . . report documenting a pattern of racial profiling of black males in the city of Boston. . . . We do not eliminate flight as a factor in the reasonable suspicion analysis whenever a black male is the subject of an investigatory stop. However, in such circumstances, flight is not necessarily probative of a suspect's state of mind or consciousness of guilt. Rather, the finding that black males in Boston are disproportionately and repeatedly targeted for [police] encounters suggests a reason for flight totally unrelated to consciousness of guilt. Such an individual, when approached by the police, might just as easily be motivated by the desire to avoid the recurring indignity of being racially profiled as by the desire to hide criminal activity. Given this reality for black males in the city of Boston, a judge should, in appropriate cases, consider the report's findings in weighing flight as a factor in the reasonable suspicion calculus.").

Third, punishments for disobedience should be constrained by the principle of proportionality in punishment. Fourth, the use of criminal law and punishment should be limited by the principles of proportionality and necessity found in self-defense law and laws of war. Fifth, the state needs to refrain from punishing individuals for mere disobedience when it lacks standing to demand obedience. Finally, to avoid the corrosive situation where a law may be broken but the state does not have the standing to demand obedience from the lawbreaker, the state must work continually to earn and maintain its cooperation-worthiness. We cannot live without a state that mandates obedience, but a state that is not cooperation-worthy does not deserve our support.

Bibliography

Adler, Amy. "Inverting the First Amendment." *University of Pennsylvania Law Review* 149, no. 4 (2001): 921–1002.

Adler, Amy. "The '*Dost* Test' in Child Pornography Law: 'Trial by Rorschach Test.'" In *Refining Child Pornography Law: Crime, Language, and Social Consequences*, edited by Carissa Byrne Hessick. University of Michigan Press, 2016.

Alexander, Larry. "The Gap." *Harvard Journal of Law and Public Policy* 14, no. 3 (1991): 695–702.

Alexander, Larry. "Can Law Survive the Asymmetry of Authority?" *Quinnipiac Law Review* 19, no. 3 (2000): 463–82.

Alexander, Larry and Kimberly Kessler Ferzan. *Crime and Culpability: A Theory of Criminal Law*. Cambridge University Press, 2009.

Alexander, Larry and Kimberly Kessler Ferzan. *Reflections on Crime and Culpability: Problems and Puzzles*. Cambridge University Press, 2018.

Alexander, Michelle. *The New Jim Crow: Mass Incarceration in the Age of Colorblindness*. The New Press, 2010.

Alexy, Robert. *A Theory of Constitutional Rights*. Oxford University Press, 2002.

Alldridge, Peter. *Money Laundering Law: Forfeiture, Confiscation, Civil Recovery, Criminal Laundering and Taxation of the Proceeds of Crime*. Hart Publishing, 2003.

Alldridge, Peter. *What Went Wrong with Money Laundering Law?* Palgrave Macmillan, 2016.

Ambos, Kai. *Treatise on International Criminal Law, Volume I: Foundations and General Part*, 2nd ed. Oxford University Press, 2021.

American Law Institute. *Model Penal Code and Commentaries, Part I*. American Law Institute, 1985.

Appiah, Kwame Anthony. *Ethics of Identity*. Princeton University Press, 2005.

Applbaum, Arthur Isak. *Legitimacy: The Right to Rule in a Wanton World*. Harvard University Press, 2019.

Arendt, Hannah. "Civil Disobedience." In *Crises of the Republic*. Harcourt Brace Jovanovich, 1972.

Art, Robert J. "The Fungibility of Force." In *The Use of Force: Military Power and International Politics*, 6th ed., edited by Robert J. Art and Kenneth N. Waltz. Rowman & Littlefield, 2004.

Art, Robert J. "To What Ends Military Power?" In *America's Grand Strategy and World Politics*. Routledge, 2009.

Ashworth, Andrew. "The Unfairness of Risk-Based Possession Offenses." *Criminal Law and Philosophy* 5, no. 3 (2011): 237–57.

Ashworth, Andrew and Andrew von Hirsch. *Proportionate Sentencing: Exploring the Principles*. Oxford University Press, 2005.

Ashworth, Andrew and Lucia Zedner. "Prevention and Criminalization: Justifications and Limits." *New Criminal Law Review* 15, no. 4 (2012): 542–71.

Ashworth, Andrew and Lucia Zedner. *Preventive Justice*. Oxford University Press, 2014.

Bagchi, Aditi. "Lying and Cheating, or Self-Help and Civil Disobedience?" *Brooklyn Law Review* 85, no. 2 (2020): 355–92.

Baker, Mike et al. "Three Words. 70 Cases. The Tragic History of 'I Can't Breathe.'" *New York Times*, June 29, 2020.

Barrish, Cris and Jessica Masulli Reyes. "Ex-Headmaster Sentenced to 50 Years for Child Porn." *USA Today*, April 24, 2025.

Bass, Scott and William McConagha. "FDA Enforcement Powers." In *Food and Drug Law and Regulation*, 3rd ed., edited by David G. Adams et al. Food and Drugs Law Institute, 2015.

Battin, Margaret P. et al. *Drugs and Justice: Seeking a Consistent, Coherent, Comprehensive View*. Oxford University Press, 2007.

Bayles, Michael. "Character, Purpose, and Criminal Responsibility." *Law and Philosophy* 1, no. 1 (1982): 5–20.

Becker, Elizabeth. "The Secrets and Lies of the Vietnam War, Exposed in One Epic Document." *New York Times*, June 9, 2021.

Bedau, H. A., ed. "Civil Disobedience and Personal Responsibility for Injustice." In *Civil Disobedience in Focus*. Routledge, 1991.

Beitz, Charles R. *Political Theory and International Relations*, rev'd ed. Princeton University Press, 1999.

Bell, Monica C. "Police Reform and the Dismantling of Legal Estrangement." *Yale Law Journal* 126, no. 7 (2017): 2054–2150.

Bell, Tom W. "Treason, Technology, and Freedom of Expression." *Arizona State Law Journal* 37, no. 4 (2005): 999–1045.

Ben-Yehuda, Nachman. *Betrayals and Treason: Violations of Trust and Loyalty*. Westview Press, 2001.

Benson, Katie. *Lawyers and the Proceeds of Crime: The Facilitation of Money Laundering and Its Control*. Routledge, 2020.

Bentham, Jeremy. *An Introduction to the Principles of Morals and Legislation*. First edition published 1789. Claredon Press, 1832.

Berman, Mitchell N. "Negligence and Culpability: Reflections on Alexander and Ferzan." *Criminal Law and Philosophy* 16, no. 3 (2022): 1–17.

Bomhoff, Jacco. *Balancing Constitutional Rights: The Origins and Meanings of Postwar Legal Discourse*. Cambridge University Press, 2013.

Brown, Darryl K. "Public Welfare Offenses." In *The Oxford Handbook of Criminal Law*, edited by Markus D. Dubber and Tatjana Hörnle. Oxford University Press, 2014.

Brownlee, Kimberly. *Conscience and Conviction: The Case for Disobedience*. Oxford University Press, 2012.

Buell, Samuel W. "The Upside of Overbreadth." *New York University Law Review* 83, no. 5 (2008): 1491–1564.

Buzan, Barry. *People, States and Fear: An Agenda for International Security Studies in the Post-Cold War Era*, 2nd ed. Lynne Rienner Publishers, 1991.

Campell, Beatrix. "'Our Silence Permits Perpetrators to Continue': One Woman's Fight to Expose a Father's Abuse." *Guardian*, July 25, 2021. https://www.theguardian.com/uk-news/2021/jul/25/our-silence-permits-perpetrators-to-continue-one-womans-fight-to-expose-a-fathers-abuse.

Capers, I. Bennett. "Criminal Procedure and the Good Citizen." *Columbia Law Review* 118, no. 2 (2018): 653–712.

Carl, Alexandra. "Misapprising Misprison: Why Misprison of a Felony Is Not a Crime Involving Moral Turpitude." *DePaul Law Review* 69, no. 1 (2020): 143–70.

Carlson, Amber Rose. "Is There a Rational Punishment for My Rapist?" *New York Times*, October 23, 2017.

Cassell, Paul G. "Not Just 'Kiddie Porn': The Significant Harms of Child Pornography Possession." In *The Routledge Companion to Philosophy of Law*, edited by Andrei Marmor. Routledge, 2012.

Chafetz, Josh. *Congress's Constitution*. Yale University Press, 2017.

Chamberlain, Joseph P. "Anti-Fence Legislation." *American Bar Association Journal* 14, no. 9 (1928): 517–20.

Charles, Jacob D. and Brandon L. Garrett. "The Trajectory of Federal Gun Crimes." *University of Pennsylvania Law Review* 170, no. 3 (2021): 637–715.

Chiao, Vincent. "Two Conceptions of the Criminal Law." In *The New Philosophy of Criminal Law*, edited by Chad Flanders and Zachary Hoskins. Rowman & Littlefield International, 2016.
Chiao, Vincent. *Criminal Law in the Age of the Administrative State*. Oxford University Press, 2018.
Chin, Denny and Kathy Hirata Chin. "Asian Americans and the Law." *Judicial Notice*, no. 11 (2016): 6–21.
Christiano, Thomas. *The Constitution of Equality: Democratic Authority and Its Limits*. Oxford University Press, 2008.
Cohen, Joshua and Charles Sabel. "Extra Rempublicam Nulla Justitia?" *Philosophy and Public Affairs* 34, no. 2 (2006): 147–75.
Cohen-Eliya, Moshe and Iddo Porat. *Proportionality and Constitutional Culture*. Cambridge University Press, 2013.
Close, Frank. *Trinity: The Treachery and Pursuit of the Most Dangerous Spy in History*. Allen Lane, 2019.
Corera, Gordon. "Spy Game: A Familiar Tale Continues." *BBC News*, May 14, 2013. https://www.bbc.com/news/world-europe-22526793.
Cox, Courtney M. "Legitimizing Lies." *George Washington Law Review* 90, no. 2 (2020): 297–375.
Dan-Cohen, Meir. "Decision Rules and Conduct Rules: On Acoustic Separation in Criminal Law." *Harvard Law Review* 97, no. 3 (1984): 625–77.
Darabont, Frank, dir. *The Shawshank Redemption*. Warner Bros. Entertainment Inc., 1994.
Davis, Angela Y. *Are Prisons Obsolete?* Seven Stories Press, 2003.
Davis, Kevin E. *Between Impunity and Imperialism: The Regulation of Transnational Bribery*. Oxford University Press, 2019.
Delattre, Lucas. *A Spy at the Heart of the Third Reich: The Extraordinary Story of Fritz Kolbe, America's Most Important Spy in World War II*. Grove Press, 2006.
Delmas, Candice. *A Duty to Resist: When Disobedience Should Be Uncivil*. Oxford University Press, 2018.
Dempsey, Michelle Madden. "Authority, Obedience, and Justification." *University of Cincinnati Law Review* 90, no. 2 (2021): 559–615.
Devlin, Patrick. *The Enforcement of Morals*. Oxford University Press, 1965.
Diaz, Johnny. "U.S. Considers Lifting Protections for Grizzly Bears Near Two National Parks." *New York Times*, February 3, 2023.
Dilley, Julian E. et al. "Alcohol Drinking and Blood Alcohol Concentration Revisited." *Alcoholism: Clinical and Experimental Research* 42, no. 2 (2018): 260–69.
Dillof, Anthony M. "Possession, Child Pornography, and Proportionality: Criminal Liability for Aggregate Harm Offenses." *Florida State University Law Review* 44, no. 4 (2017): 1331–78.
Doyle, Charles. "Attempt: An Overview of Federal Criminal Law." *Congressional Research Service*, April 11, 2015.
Draeger, John. "What Peeping Tom Did Wrong." *Ethical Theory and Moral Practice* 14, no. 1 (2011): 41–49.
Dubber, Markus Dirk. "Policing Possession: The War on Crime and the End of Criminal Law." *Journal of Criminal Law and Criminology* 91, no. 4 (2001): 829–996.
Dubber, Markus Dirk. "The Possession Paradigm: The Special Part and the Police Model of the Criminal Process." In *Defining Crimes*, edited by R. A. Duff and Stuart P. Green. Oxford University Press, 2005.
Dubber, Markus D. and Tatjana Hörnle, *Criminal Law: A Comparative Approach*. Oxford University Press, 2016.
Duff, R. A. "Choice, Character, and Criminal Liability." *Law and Philosophy* 12, no. 4 (1993): 345–83.
Duff, R. A. *Criminal Attempts*. Oxford University Press, 1997.

Duff, R. A. "Crime, Prohibition, and Punishment." *Journal of Applied Philosophy* 19, no. 2 (2002): 97–108.

Duff, R. A. "Rule-Violations and Wrongdoing." In *Criminal Law Theory: Doctrines of the General Part*, edited by Stephen Shute and A. P. Simester. Oxford University Press, 2002.

Duff, R. A. "Virtue, Vice, and Criminal Liability: Do We Want an Aristotelian Criminal Law?" *Buffalo Criminal Law Review* 6, no. 1 (2002): 147–84.

Duff, R. A. "Perversions and Subversions of Criminal Law." In *The Boundaries of the Criminal Law*, edited by R. A. Duff et al. Oxford University Press, 2010.

Duff, R. A. "Risks, Culpability and Criminal Liability." In *Seeking Security: Pre-Empting the Commission of Criminal Harms*, edited by G. R. Sullivan and Ian Dennis. Hart Publishing, 2012.

Duff, R. A. *The Realm of Criminal Law*. Oxford University Press, 2018.

Duff, R. A. "Two Models of Criminal Fault." *Criminal Law and Philosophy* 13, no. 4 (2019): 643–65.

Duff, R. A. "'De Minimis' and the Structure of the Criminal Trial." *Law and Philosophy* 42, no. 1 (2023): 57–86.

Duff, R. A. and S. E. Marshall. "'Abstract Endangerment,' Two Harm Principles, and Two Routes to Criminalisation." *Bergen Journal of Criminal Law and Criminal Justice* 3, no. 2 (2015): 132–61.

Duff, R. A. and S. E. Marshall. "Reporting Crimes and Arresting Criminals: Citizens' Rights and Responsibilities Under Their Criminal Law." *Criminal Law and Philosophy* 18, no. 2 (2024): 557–77.

Duus-Otterström, Göran. "Do Offenders Deserve Proportionate Punishments?" *Criminal Law and Philosophy* 15, no. 3 (2021): 463–80.

Dworkin, Ronald. *Taking Rights Seriously*. Harvard University Press, 1977.

Dworkin, Ronald. *A Matter of Principle*. Harvard University Press, 1985.

Edmundson, William A. *Three Anarchical Fallacies: An Essay on Political Authority*. Cambridge University Press, 1998.

Edmundson, William A. "State of the Art: The Duty to Obey the Law." *Legal Theory* 10, no. 4 (2004): 215–59.

Edwards, James. "Criminalization without Punishment." *Legal Theory* 23, no. 2 (2017): 69–95.

Edwards, James and Tarek Yusari. "The Internal Morality of Criminal Law." *Oxford Journal of Legal Studies* 43, no. 3 (2023): 475–96.

Eggen, Dan and Karen DeYoung. "U.S. Supporter of Al-Qaeda Is Indicted on Treason Charge." *Washington Post*, October 12, 2006.

Eldar, Shachar. "Criminal Law, Parental Authority, and the State." *Criminal law and Philosophy* 12, no. 4 (2017): 695–705.

Ellsberg, Daniel. *Secrets: A Memoir of Vietnam and the Pentagon Papers*. Penguin Books, 2002.

Enoch, David. "Intending, Foreseeing, and the State." *Legal Theory* 13, no. 2, (2007): 69–99.

Eschner, Kat. "Iva D'Aquino Toguri Remains the Only U.S. Citizen Convicted of Treason Who Has Ever Been Pardoned." *Smithsonian Magazine*, January 19, 2017.

Espinosa, Manuel José Cepeda and David Landau. *Colombian Constitutional Law: Leading Cases*. Oxford University Press, 2017.

Estlund, David M. *Democratic Authority: A Philosophical Framework*. Princeton University Press, 2007.

Fabre, Cécile. *Cosmopolitan War*. Oxford University Press, 2012.

Fabre, Cécile. "The Morality of Treason." *Law and Philosophy* 39, no. 4 (2020): 427–61.

Fabre, Cécile. *Spying Through a Glass Darkly: The Ethics of Espionage and Counter-Intelligence*. Oxford University Press, 2022.

Fallon Jr., Richard H. *Implementing the Constitution*. Harvard University Press, 2001.

Farber, David. "Introduction." In *The War on Drugs: A History*, edited by David Farber. New York University Press, 2021.

Farmer, Lindsey. "The 'Market' in Criminal Law Theory." *The Modern Law Review* 85, no. 2 (2022): 435–60.

Federal Bureau of Investigation. "Aldrich Ames." *Federal Bureau of Investigation: History*. https://www.fbi.gov/history/famous-cases/aldrich-ames.

Federal Bureau of Investigation. "Robert Hanssen." *Federal Bureau of Investigation: History*. https://www.fbi.gov/history/famous-cases/robert-hanssen.

Feinberg, Joel. "The Expressive Function of Punishment." *The Monist* 49, no. 3, (1965): 397–423.

Feinberg, Joel. "Justice and Personal Desert." In *Doing and Deserving*. Princeton University Press, 1970.

Feinberg, Joel. "Noncomparative Justice." *Philosophical Review* 83, no. 3 (1974): 297–338.

Feinberg, Joel. *The Moral Limits of the Criminal Law Volume 1: Harm to Others*. Oxford University Press, 1984.

Feinberg, Joel. "Some Unswept Debris from the Hart-Devlin Debate." *Synthese* 72, no. 2 (1987): 249–75.

Ferzan, Kimberly Kessler. "Defending Imminence: From Battered Women to Iraq." *Arizona Law Review* 46, no. 2 (2004): 213–62.

Ferzan, Kimberly Kessler. "Beyond Crime and Commitment: Justifying Liberty Deprivations of the Dangerous and Responsible." *Minnesota Law Review* 96, no. 1 (2011): 141–93.

Ferzan, Kimberly Kessler. "Inchoate Crimes at the Prevention/Punishment Divide." *San Diego Law Review* 48, no. 4 (2011): 1273–98.

Ferzan, Kimberly Kessler. "Forfeiture and Self-Defense." In *The Ethics of Self-Defense*, edited by Christian Coons and Michael Weber. Oxford University Press, 2016.

Fessenden, Ford et al. "Where You Watch Depends on Your Colors." *New York Times*, June 11, 2010.

Fisher, Dan. "Split Between Britain, U.S. Seen as 'Inevitable.'" *Los Angeles Times*, April 19, 1990.

Fletcher, George P. *Loyalty: An Essay on the Morality of Relationships*. Oxford University Press, 1993.

Florida Action Committee, "Residency Restriction by State (For Persons Required to Register as Sex Offenders)." July 11, 2019. https://floridaactioncommittee.org/residency-restrictions-by-state-for-persons-required-to-register-as-sex-offenders [https://perma.cc/CR4M-DBYX].

Forman Jr., James. *Locking Up Our Own: Crime and Punishment in Black America*. Farrar, Straus and Giroux, 2017.

Frowe, Helen. "The Role of Necessity in Liability to Defensive Harm." In *The Ethics of Self-Defense*, edited by Christian Coons and Michael Weber. Oxford University Press, 2016.

Garbarino, Sergio et al. "Circadian Sleep Propensity and Alcohol Interaction at the Wheel." *Journal of Clinical Sleep Medicine* 12, no. 7 (2016): 1011–17.

Gardner, John. "On the General Part of the Criminal Law." In *Philosophy and the Criminal Law: Principle and Critique*, edited by Antony Duff. Cambridge University Press, 1998.

Gardner, John. "Crime: In Proportion and in Perspective." In *Offences and Defences: Selected Essays in the Philosophy of Criminal Law*. Oxford University Press, 2007.

Gardner, John. "Reply to Critics." In *Offences and Defences: Selected Essays in the Philosophy of Criminal Law*. Oxford University Press, 2007.

Gardner, John and Stephen Shute. "The Wrongness of Rape." In *Oxford Essays in Jurisprudence: Fourth Series*, edited by Jeremy Horder. Oxford University Press, 2000.

Gardner, Trevor George. "Police Violence and the African American Procedural Habitus." *Boston University Law Review* 100, no. 3 (2020): 849–93.

Garnett, John. "The Role of Military Power." In *Perspectives on World Politics*, 2nd ed., edited by Richard Little and Michael Smith. Routledge, 1991.

Garvey, Stephen P. "Are Attempts Like Treason?" *New Criminal Law Review* 14, no. 2 (2011): 173–212.

Garvey, Stephen P. "Was Ellen Wronged?" *Criminal Law and Philosophy* 7, no. 2 (2013): 185–216.

Gellman, Barton and Laura Poitras. "U.S., British Intelligence Mining Data from Nine U.S. Internet Companies in Broad Secret Program." *Washington Post*, June 7, 2013.

George, Alexander L. "Coercive Diplomacy." In *The Use of Force: Military Power and International Politics*, 6th ed., edited by Robert J. Art and Kenneth N. Waltz. Rowman & Littlefield, 2004.

Gold, Jim. "Chilling Details of John Lennon Shooting Recounted at Chapman Parole Hearing." *NBC News*, August 29, 2012.

Goode, Erica. "Life Sentence for Child Pornography Spurs Debate Over Severity." *New York Times*, November 4, 2011.

Gootenberg, Paul, ed. *The Oxford Handbook of Global Drug History*. Oxford University Press, 2022.

Graham, Kyle. "Crime, Widgets, and Plea Bargaining: An Analysis of Charge Content, Pleas and Trials." *California Law Review* 100, no. 6 (2012): 1–58.

Graham, Kyle. "Facilitating Crimes: An Inquiry into the Selective Invocation of Offenses Within the Continuum of Criminal Procedures." *Lewis & Clark Law Review* 15, no. 3 (2011): 665–714.

Green, Leslie. *The Authority of the State*. Oxford University Press, 1988.

Green, Leslie. "Law and Obligations." In *Oxford Handbook of Jurisprudence and Philosophy of Law*, edited by Jules Coleman and Scott Shapiro. Oxford University Press, 2002.

Green, Stuart P. "Lying, Misleading, and Falsely Denying: How Moral Concepts Inform the Law of Perjury, Fraud, and False Statements." *Hastings Law Journal* 53, no. 1 (2001): 157–212.

Green, Stuart P. *Lying, Cheating, and Stealing: A Moral Theory of White-Collar Crime*. Oxford University Press, 2006.

Green, Stuart P. "Thieving and Receiving: Overcriminalizing the Possession of Stolen Property," *New Criminal Law Review* 14, no. 1 (2011): 35–54.

Green, Stuart P. "To See and Be Seen: Reconstructing the Law of Voyeurism and Exhibitionism." *American Criminal Law Review* 54, no. 2 (2018): 203–58.

Green, Stuart P. "Legal Moralism, Overinclusive Offenses, and the Problem of Wrongfulness Conflation." *Criminal Law & Philosophy* 14, no. 3 (2020): 417–30.

Greenawalt, Kent. *Conflicts of Law and Morality*. Oxford University Press, 1989.

Greene, Abner S. *Against Obligation: The Multiple Sources of Authority in a Liberal Democracy*. Harvard University Press, 2012.

Greenhouse, Linda. "Justices Decline Case on 200-Year Sentence for Man Who Possessed Child Pornography." *New York Times*, February 27, 2007.

Greenspan, Nancy Thorndike. *Atomic Spy: The Dark Lives of Klaus Fuchs*. Viking, 2020.

Greenwald, Glenn et al. "Edward Snowden: The Whistleblower Behind the NSA Surveillance Revelations." *Guardian*, June 11, 2013.

Griffin, James. *Well-Being: Its Meaning, Measurement, and Moral Importance*. Oxford University Press, 1986.

Griffin, Lisa Kern. "Criminal Lying, Prosecutorial Power, and Social Meaning." *California Law Review* 97, no. 6 (2009): 1515–70.

Gur-Arye, Miriam. "A Failure to Prevent Crime—Should It Be Criminal?" *Criminal Justice Ethics* 20, no. 2 (2001): 3–30.

Gur-Arye, Miriam. "Human Dignity of 'Offenders': A Limitation on Substantive Criminal Law." *Criminal Law and Philosophy* 6, no. 2 (2012): 187–205.

Gur-Arye, Miriam. "Reflections." *Criminal Law and Philosophy* 18, no. 2 (2024): 631–61.

Haber, Eldar. "The Digital Samaritans." *Washington & Lee Law Review* 77, no. 4 (2020): 1559–1645.

Halbfinger, David M. and Isabel Kershner. "Jonathan Pollard, Spy for Israel, Gets Hero's Welcome From Netanyahu: 'You're Home.'" *New York Times*, December 30, 2020.

Halbfinger, David M. and Paul Zielbauer. "Day for German Pride, and Worries." *New York Times*, June 22, 2002.
Hall, Matthew R. "An Emerging Duty to Report Criminal Conduct: Banks, Money Laundering, and the Suspicious Activity Report." *Kentucky Law Journal* 84, no. 3 (1996): 643–83.
Hanser, Matthew. "Acting Wrongly by Trying." In *Oxford Studies in Normative Ethics: Volume 4*, edited by Mark Timmons. Oxford University Press, 2014.
Harduf, Asaf. "Criminalization Downloads Evil: Reexamining the Approach to Electronic Possession When Child Pornography Goes International." *Boston University International Law Journal* 34, no. 2 (2016): 279–318.
Hart, Carl L. *Drug Use for Grown-Ups: Chasing Liberty in the Land of Fear*. Penguin Books, 2021.
Hart, H. L. A. "Legal and Moral Obligation." In *Essays in Moral Philosophy*, edited by A. I. Melden. University of Washington Press, 1958.
Hart, H. L. A. *Law, Liberty, and Morality*. Stanford University Press, 1963.
Hart, H. L. A. *Punishment and Responsibility: Essays in the Philosophy of Law*. Clarendon Press, 1968.
Hart, Henry M. "The Aims of the Criminal Law." *Law and Contemporary Problems* 23, no. 3 (1958): 401–41.
Hegel, G. W. F. *Philosophy of Right*. Translated by T.M. Knox. Oxford University Press 1967. Originally published 1821.
Helland, Arne et al. "Comparison of Driving Simulator Performance with Real Driving After Alcohol Intake: A Randomised, Single Blind, Placebo-Controlled, Cross-Over Trial." *Accident Analysis & Prevention* 53 (2013): 9–16.
Hellman, Deborah. "Understanding Bribery." In *The Palgrave Handbook of Applied Ethics and the Criminal Law*, edited by Larry Alexander and Kimberly Kessler Ferzan. Palgrave Macmillan, 2019.
Henberg, Marvin. *Retribution: Evil for Evil in Ethics, Law, and Literature*. Temple University Press, 1990.
Hershovitz, Scott. "The Authority of Law." In *The Routledge Companion to Philosophy of Law*, edited by Andrei Marmor. Routledge, 2012.
Hershovitz, Scott. "Vindicating Criminal Law." In *From Morality to Law and Back Again: A Liber Amicorum for John Gardner*, edited by Michelle Madden Dempsey and Francois Tanguay-Renaud. Oxford University Press, 2023.
Herzberg, David. "Origins and Outcomes of the US Medicine-Drug Divide." In *The Oxford Handbook of Global Drug History*, edited by Paul Gootenberg. Oxford University Press, 2022.
Herzberg, David. *White Market Drugs: Big Pharma and the Hidden History of Addiction in America*. University of Chicago Press, 2020.
Hessick, Carissa Byrne. "Disentangling Child Pornography from Child Sex Abuse." *Washington University Law Review* 88, no. 4 (2010): 853–902.
Hessick, Carissa Byrne. "The Limits of Child Pornography." *Indiana Law Journal* 89, no. 4 (2014): 1437–84.
Hessick, Carissa Byrne. "Questioning the Modern Criminal Justice Focus on Child Pornography Possession." In *Refining Child Pornography Law: Crime, Language, and Social Consequences*, edited by Carissa Byrne Hessick. University of Michigan Press, 2016.
Hessick, Carissa Byrne. "Setting Definitional Limits for the Child Pornography Exception." In *Refining Child Pornography Law: Crime, Language, and Social Consequences*, edited by Carissa Byrne Hessick. University of Michigan Press, 2016.
Hessick, Carissa Byrne. "The Expansion of Child Pornography Law." *New Criminal Law Review* 21, no. 3 (2018): 321–44.
Holmes Jr., Oliver Wendell. *The Common Law*. Little, Brown, and Company, 1881.
Holmes Jr., Oliver Wendell. "The Path of the Law." *Harvard Law Review* 10, no. 8 (1897): 457–78.

Holzer, Henry Mark. "Why Not Call It Treason?: From Korea to Afghanistan." *Southern University Law Review* 29, no. 2 (2002): 181–224.

Horder, Jeremy. "Criminal Culpability: The Possibility of a General Theory." *Law and Philosophy* 12, no. 2 (1993): 193–215.

Horowitz, Emily. *From Rage to Reason: Why We Need Sex Crime Laws Based on Facts, Not Fear.* Bloomsbury Publishing, 2023.

Hume, David. *A Treatise of Human Nature.* 1739; Reis. ed. Oxford University Press, 1978.

Hume, David. "Of the Original Contract." In *Essays: Moral, Political and Literary*, edited by Eugene F. Miller. Liberty Fund, 1985.

Hurd, Heidi M. "Justifiably Punishing the Justified." *Michigan Law Review* 90, no. 8 (1992): 2203–324.

Hurka, Thomas. "Proportionality and Necessity." In *War: Essays in Political Philosophy*, edited by Larry May. Cambridge University Press, 2008.

Husak, Douglas N. "Already Punished Enough." *Philosophical Topics* 18, no. 1 (1990): 79–99.

Husak, Douglas N. *Drugs and Rights.* Cambridge University Press, 1992.

Husak, Douglas N. "Why Punish the Deserving?" *Noûs* 26, no. 4 (1992): 447–64.

Husak, Douglas N. "Is Drunk Driving a Serious Offense?" *Philosophy & Public Affairs* 23, no. 1 (1994): 52–73.

Husak, Douglas N. "The Nature and Justifiability of Nonconsummate Offenses." *Arizona Law Review* 37, no. 1 (1995): 151–83.

Husak, Douglas. "The 'But Everyone Does That!' Defense." *Public Affairs Quarterly* 10, no. 4 (1996): 307–34.

Husak, Douglas. "Does Criminal Liability Require an Act?" In *Philosophy and the Criminal Law: Principle and Critique*, edited by Antony Duff. Cambridge University Press, 1998.

Husak, Douglas N. "Guns and Drugs: Case Studies on the Principled Limited of the Criminal Sanction." *Law and Philosophy* 23, no. 5 (2004): 437–93.

Husak, Douglas. "Applying *Ultima Ratio*: A Skeptical Assessment." *Ohio State Journal of Criminal Law* 2, no. 2. (2005): 535–45.

Husak, Douglas. *Overcriminalization: The Limits of the Criminal Law.* Oxford University Press, 2008.

Husak, Douglas. "The Criminal Law as Last Resort." *Oxford Journal of Legal Studies* 24, no. 2 (2008): 207–35.

Husak, Douglas. "*Malum Prohibitum* and Retributivism." In *Defining Crimes: Essays on the Special Part of the Criminal Law*, edited by R. A. Duff and Stuart P. Green. Oxford University Press, 2010.

Husak, Douglas. "The De Minimis 'Defence' to Criminal Liability." In *Philosophical Foundations of Criminal Law*, edited by R. A. Duff and Stuart Green. Oxford University Press, 2011.

Husak, Douglas. *Ignorance of Law: A Philosophical Inquiry.* Oxford University Press, 2016.

Husak, Douglas. "The Price of Criminal Law Skepticism: Ten Functions of the Criminal Law." *New Criminal Law Review* 23, no. 1 (2020): 27–59.

Husak, Douglas and Peter De Marneff. *The Legalization of Drugs.* Cambridge University Press, 2005.

Huscroft, Grant et al. *Proportionality and the Rule of Law: Rights, Justification, Reasoning.* Cambridge University Press, 2014.

Jacobs, James B. *Can Gun Control Work?* Oxford University Press, 2002.

Jacobs, James B. and Kimberley A. Potter. "Keeping Guns out of the Wrong Hands: The Brady Law and the Limits of Regulation." *Journal of Criminal Law & Criminology* 86, no. 1 (1995): 93–120.

Jareborg, Nils. "Criminalization as Last Resort (*Ultima Ratio*)." *Ohio State Journal of Criminal Law* 2, no. 2 (2005): 521–34.

Jaros, David Michael. "Perfecting Criminal Markets." *Columbia Law Review* 112, no. 8 (2012): 1947–91.

Johnson, Bruce D. et al. "Drug Abuse in the Inner City: Impact on Hard-Drug Users and the Community." *Crime and Justice, Vol. 13: Drugs and Crime*, edited by Michael Tonry and James Q. Wilson. University of Chicago Press, 1990.

Johnson, Charles. *An Instance of Treason: Ozaki Hotsumi and the Sorge Spy Ring.* Stanford University Press, 1964.

Johnson, Nicholas J. "The Modern Orthodoxy Is a Failed Experiment: Toward a Race Sensitive, Hard Look at Firearms Policy and the Black Community." *UC Irvine Law Review* 14, no. 4 (2024): 1208–63.

Kang, Sungyong. "In Defense of the 'Duty to Report' Crimes." *UMKC Law Review* 86, no. 2 (2017): 361–403.

Kant, Immanuel. *The Metaphysics of Morals.* Translated and edited by Mary Gregor. Cambridge University Press, 1996. Originally published 1797.

Kashner, Sam. "Both Huntress and Prey." *Vanity Fair*, October 20, 2024.

Katz, Leora Dahan. "Criminal Law: Political or Moral? Defending a Complementary Conception of Criminal Law in the Age of the Administrative State." *Jerusalem Review of Legal Studies* 17, no. 1 (2018): 111–27.

Kaufman, Zachary D. "Protectors of Predators or Prey: Bystanders and Upstanders Amid Sexual Crimes." *Southern California Law Review* 92, no. 6 (2019): 1317–406.

Kelly, Erin I. *The Limits of Blame: Rethinking Punishment and Responsibility.* Harvard University Press, 2018.

Kenntner-Mabiala, Ramona et al. "Driving Performance Under Alcohol in Simulated Representative Driving Tasks." *Journal of Clinical Psychopharmacology* 35, no. 2 (2015): 134–42.

Kitrosser, Heidi and David Schultz. "House Built on Sand: The Constitutional Infirmity of Espionage Act Prosecutions for Leaking to the Press." *First Amendment Law Review* 19, no. (2021): 153–212.

Kleck, Gary. *Targeting Guns: Firearms and Their Control.* Aldine de Gruyter, 1997.

Kleiman, Mark A. R. "Controlling Drug Use and Crime with Testing, Sanctions and Treatment." In *Drug Addiction and Drug Policy: The Struggle to Control Dependence*, edited by Philip B. Heymann and William N. Brownsberger. Harvard University Press, 2001.

Kleiman, Mark A. R. and Kerry D. Smith. "State and Local Drug Enforcement: In Search of a Strategy." In *Crime and Justice, Vol. 13: Drugs and Crime*, edited by Michael Tonry and James Q. Wilson. University of Chicago Press, 1990.

Klein, Elyssa. "Should Misprison of a Felony Be Considered a Crime Involving Moral Turpitude?" *Albany Law Review* 82, no. 1 (2018): 299–322.

Klein, Susan R. and Ingrid B. Grobey. "Debunking Claims of Over-Federalization of Criminal Law." *Emory Law Journal* 62, no.1 (2012): 1–120.

Klosko, George. *Political Obligations.* Oxford University Press, 2005.

Kohler-Hausmann, Issa. "Managerial Justice and Mass Misdemeanors." *Stanford Law Review* 66, no. 3 (2014): 611–94.

Kymlicka, Will. *Multicultural Citizenship: A Liberal Theory of Minority Rights.* Oxford University Press, 1995.

Lacey, Nicola. *State Punishment: Political Principles and Community Values.* Routledge, 1988.

Lacey, Nicola and Hanna Pickard. "From the Consulting Room to the Court Room? Taking the Clinical Model of Responsibility without Blame into the Legal Realm." *Oxford Journal of Legal Studies* 33, no. 1 (2013): 1–29.

LaFave, Wayne R. *Substantive Criminal Law*, vol. 2, 3rd ed. Thomson West, 2017.

LaFave, Wayne R. and Jens David Ohlin. *Criminal Law*, 7th ed. West Academic Publishing, 2023.

Landemore, Hélène. *Democratic Reason: Politics, Collective Intelligence, and the Rule of the Many.* Princeton University Press, 2012.

Langbein, John H. "Controlling Prosecutorial Discretion in Germany." *The University of Chicago Law Review* 41, no. 3 (1974): 439–67.

Langer, Máximo. "Penal Abolitionism and Criminal Law Minimalism: Here and There, Now and Then." *Harvard Law Review Forum* 133, no. 9 (2020): 42–77.
Larson, Carlton F. W. *On Treason: A Citizen's Guide to the Law*. Ecco, 2020.
Laudan, Larry. *Truth, Error, and Criminal Law: An Essay in Legal Epistemology*. Cambridge University Press, 2006.
Lawrence, Matthew B. and David E. Pozen. "Drug Scheduling as Institutional Design." *Harvard Law Review* 139 (forthcoming 2026).
Lazarus, Richard J. "Meeting the Demands of Integration in the Evolution of Environmental Law: Reforming Environmental Criminal Law." *Georgetown Law Journal* 83, no. 7 (1995): 2407–529.
Leary, Mary Graw. "The Language of Child Sexual Abuse and Exploitation." In *Refining Child Pornography Law: Crime, Language, and Social Consequences*, edited by Carissa Byrne Hessick. University of Michigan Press, 2016.
Lee, Ambrose Y. K. and Alexander F. Sarch. *The Moral Prerequisites of the Criminal Law: Legal Moralism and the Problem of Mala Prohibita*. Cambridge University Press, 2023.
Lee, Youngjae. "The Constitutional Right Against Excessive Punishment." *Virginia Law Review* 91, no. 3 (2005): 677–745.
Lee, Youngjae. "The Criminal Jury, Moral Judgments, and Political Representation." *University of Illinois Law Review* 2018, no. 4 (2018): 1255–292.
Lee, Youngjae. "Is Prison Abolitionism Self-Defeating?" *Criminal Law and Philosophy* 19 (2024): 497–510.
Lee, Youngjae. "Problem of Proportional Punishment." In *The Routledge Handbook of the Philosophy and Science of Punishment*, edited by Farah Focquaert et al. Routledge, 2021.
Lee, Youngjae. "Proportionality in Punishment." In *The Palgrave Handbook of Applied Ethics and the Criminal Law*, edited by Larry Alexander and Kimberly Kessler Ferzan. Palgrave Macmillan, 2019.
Leib, Ethan J. "Contract as Vow or Oath." *Legal Theory* 30, no. 1 (2024): 22–44.
Levin, Benjamin. "Guns and Drugs." *Fordham Law Review* 84, no. 5 (2016): 2173–226.
Li, Danny Y. "Antisubordinating the Second Amendment." *Yale Law Journal* 132, no. 6 (2023): 1821–907.
Litman, Harry. "Pretextual Prosecution." *Georgetown Law Journal* 92, no. 6 (2004): 1135–82.
Loader, Ian and Neil Walker. *Civilizing Security*. Cambridge University Press, 2007.
Locke, John. *Second Treatise of Government*, edited by C. B. MacPherson. Hackett Publishing 1980.
Logan, Wayne A. *Knowledge as Power: Criminal Registration and Community Notification Laws in America*. Stanford University Press, 2009.
Logan, Wayne A. "Citizen Searches and the Duty to Report." *Ohio State Law Journal* 83, no. 5 (2022): 939–51.
Lovett, Ian and Adam Nagourney. "Video Rant, Then Deadly Rampage in California Town." *New York Times*, May 24, 2014.
Lynch, Gerard E. "The Lawyer as Informer." *Duke Law Journal* 1986, no. 3 (1986): 491–547.
Lyne, Adrian, dir. *Unfaithful*. 20th Century Fox, 2002.
Lyons, David. "Utility and Rights." In *Theories of Rights*, edited by Jeremy Waldron. Oxford University Press, 1984.
MacCormick, Neil. "Nations and Nationalism." In *Theorizing Nationalism*, edited by Ronald Beiner. State University of New York Press, 1999.
MacIntyre, Alasdair. "Is Patriotism a Virtue?" In *Patriotism*, edited by Igor Primoratz. Humanity Books, 2002.
Mandiberg, Susan F. and Susan L. Smith, *Crimes Against the Environment*. Michie, 1997.
Manning, Chelsea. *README.txt: A Memoir*. Farrar, Straus and Giroux, 2022.
Margalit, Avishai and Joseph Raz. "National Self-Determination." *Journal of Philosophy* 87, no. 9 (1990): 439–61.

Marshall, Sandra and R.A. Duff. "Civic Punishment." In *Democratic Theory and Mass Incarceration*, edited by Albert W. Dzur et al. Oxford University Press, 2016.

McFadden, Robert D. "Daniel Ellsberg, Who Leaked the Pentagon Papers, Is Dead at 92." *New York Times*, June 16, 2023.

McGreal, Chris. "Jared Lee Loughner Note Reveals Aim to Assassinate Gabrielle Giffords." *Guardian*, January 10, 2011.

McMahan, Jeff. "Proportionate Defense." *Journal of Transnational Law & Policy* 23, no. 1 (2014): 1–204.

McMahan, Jeff. "Unjust War in Iraq." *The Pelican Record* 41, no. 5 (2004): 21–33.

Mendlow, Gabriel S. "Why Is It Wrong to Punish Thought?" *Yale Law Journal* 127, no. 8 (2018): 2342–86.

Mendlow, Gabriel S. "The Elusive Object of Punishment." *Legal Theory* 25, no. 2 (2019): 105–31.

Miller, Rudy. "Ex-employee's Deception Led Lehigh Valley Company to Sell $139K in Unapproved Medical Devices, Feds Say." *Lehigh Valley Live*, March 8, 2023. https://www.lehighvalleylive.com/news/2023/03/ex-employees-deception-led-lehigh-valley-company-to-sell-139k-in-unapproved-medical-devices-feds-says.html.

Moore, Mark. "Toward a Balanced Drug Prevention Strategy: A Conceptual Map." In *Drug Addiction and Drug Policy*, edited by Philip B. Heymann and William N. Brownsberger. Harvard University Press, 2001.

Moore, Michael S. *Placing Blame: A Theory of Criminal Law*. Clarendon Press, 1997.

Mosteller, Robert P. "Child Abuse Reporting Laws and Attorney-Client Confidences: The Reality and the Specter of Lawyer as Informant." *Duke Law Journal* 42, no. 2 (1992): 203–78.

Muller, Eric L. *Free to Die for Their Country: The Story of the Japanese American Draft Resisters in World War II*. University of Chicago Press, 2001.

Muller, Eric L. "The Japanese American Cases—A Bigger Disaster than We Realized." *Howard Law Journal* 49, no. 2 (2006): 417–74.

Mumenthaler, Martin S. et al. "Gender Differences in Moderate Drinking Effects." *Alcohol Research & Health* 23, no. 1 (1999): 55–64.

Murphy, Erin. "Manufacturing Crime: Process, Pretext, and Criminal Justice." *Georgetown Law Journal* 97, no. 6 (2009): 1435–507.

Musto, David F. *The American Disease: Origins of Narcotic Control*, 3rd ed. Oxford University Press, 1999.

Natapoff, Alexandra. *Punishment without Crime: How Our Massive Misdemeanor System Traps the Innocent and Makes America More Unequal*. Basic Books, 2018.

Nathan, Daniel O. "Just Looking: Voyeurism and the Grounds of Privacy." *Public Affairs Quarterly* 4, no. 4 (1990): 365–86.

Navarro, Mireya. "Latinos Still Call It Futbol." *New York Times*, July 10, 2002.

Nelson, Valerie J. "Convicted as 'Tokyo Rose,' She Later Received Honors." *Los Angeles Times*, September 28, 2006.

New York Times Editorial Board. "Edward Snowden, Whistle-Blower." *New York Times*, January 1, 2014.

Nielsen, Bjarke and Esben Houborg. "Addiction, Drugs, and Experimentation: Methadone Maintenance Treatment Between 'In Here' and 'Out There.'" *Contemporary Drug Problems* 42, no. 4 (2015): 274–88.

Noah, Lars. "Banning Off-Label Drug Promotion Offends the U.S. Constitution: Making the Strongest Case." *Albany Law Review* 83, no. 1 (2020): 301–12.

Nussbaum, Martha C. "Patriotism and Cosmopolitanism." In *For Love of Country: Debating the Limits of Patriotism*, edited by Joshua Cohen. Beacon Press, 1996.

Nussbaum, Martha C. "Reply." In *For Love of Country: Debating the Limits of Patriotism*, edited by Joshua Cohen. Beacon Press, 1996.

Ohana, Daniel. "Desert and Punishment for Acts Preparatory to the Commission of a Crime." *Canadian Journal of Law and Jurisprudence* 20, no. 1 (2007): 113–42.

Ohana, Daniel. "Administrative Penalties in the *Rechtsstaat*: On the Emergence of the *Ordnungswidrigkeit* sanctioning System in Post-War Germany." *University of Toronto Law Journal* 64, no. 2 (2014): 243–90.

Ohlin, Jens David. *Wharton's Criminal Law*, 16th ed. Thomson Reuters, 2021.

Olsen, Frances. "Statutory Rape: A Feminist Critique of Rights Analysis." *Texas Law Review* 63, no. 3 (1984): 387–432.

Oshima, Shunji. "Individual Differences in Blood Alcohol Concentrations after Moderate Drinking Are Mainly Regulated by Gastric Emptying Rate Together with Ethanol Distribution Volume." *Food and Nutrition Sciences* 3, no. 6 (2012): 732–37.

Ost, Suzanne. *Child Pornography and Sexual Grooming: Legal and Societal Responses.* Cambridge University Press, 2009.

Papandrea, Mary-Rose. "Leaker Traitor Whistleblower Spy: National Security Leaks and the First Amendment." *Boston University Law Review* 94, no. 2 (2014): 449–544.

Paul-Emile, Kimani. "Making Sense of Drug Regulation: A Theory of Law for Drug Control Policy." *Cornell Journal of Law and Public Policy* 19, no. 3 (2010): 691–740.

Pavel, Carmen E. "A Legal Conventionalist Approach to Pollution." *Law and Philosophy* 35, no. 4 (2016): 337–63.

Pembleton, Matthew R. "The Globalization of US Drug Enforcement." In *The Oxford Handbook of Global Drug History*, edited by Paul Gootenberg. Oxford University Press, 2022.

Perlin, Michael L. and Heather Ellis Cucolo. *Shaming the Constitution: The Detrimental Results of Sexual Violent Predator Legislation*. Temple University Press, 2017.

Perry, Stephen R. "Political Authority and Political Obligation." In *Oxford Studies in Philosophy of Law: Volume 2*, edited by Leslie Green and Brian Leiter. Oxford University Press, 2013.

Peter, Fabienne. *The Grounds of Political Legitimacy*. Oxford University Press, 2023.

Pfaff, John. *Locked In: The True Causes of Mass Incarceration and How to Achieve Real Reform.* Basic Books, 2018.

Pincus, Walter. "Catch a Spy—And Look What Happens." *Washington Post*, March 25, 2001.

Pitkin, Hanna. "Obligation and Consent—I." *American Political Science Review* 59, no. 4 (1965): 990–99.

Platt, Elizabeth Reiner. "Gangsters to Greyhounds: The Past, Present, and Future of Offender Registration." *N.Y.U. Review of Law & Social Change* 37, no. 4 (2013): 727–82.

Polson, Michael. "Cultivating Cannabis, Excepting Cannabis." In *The War on Drugs: A History*, edited by David Farber. New York University Press, 2021.

Pozen, David. *The Constitution of the War on Drugs*. Oxford University Press, 2024.

Quong, Jonathan. "The Morality of Defensive Force: Replies to Otsuka, Frowe, Fabre, and Burri." *Criminal Law & Philosophy* 16, no. 3 (2022): 555–74.

Quong, Jonathan. "Proportionality, Liability, and Defensive Harm." *Philosophy & Public Affairs* 43, no. 2 (2015): 144–73.

Radosh, Ronald and Joyce Milton. *The Rosenberg File: A Search for the Truth*, 2nd ed. Yale University Press, 1997.

Ramage, Jane. "Reframing the Punishment Test through Modern Sex Offender Legislation." *Fordham Law Review* 88, no. 3 (2019): 1099–131.

Rawls, John. *A Theory of Justice*, rev. ed. Harvard University Press, 1999.

Raz, Joseph. "The Obligation to Obey the Law." In *The Authority of Law: Essays on Law and Morality*. Oxford University Press, 1979.

Raz, Joseph. "A Right to Dissent? I. Civil Disobedience." In *The Authority of Law: Essays on Law and Morality*. Oxford University Press, 1979.

Raz, Joseph. *The Morality of Freedom*. Claredon Press, 1986.

Raz, Joseph. "Rights and Individual Well-Being." In *Ethics in the Public Domain: Essays in the Morality of Law and Politics*. Oxford University Press, 1994.

Raz, Joseph. "The Obligation to Obey: Revision and Tradition." In *Ethics in the Public Domain: Essays in the Morality of Law and Politics*. Oxford University Press, 1994.

Raz, Joseph. *Practical Reason and Norms*, 2nd ed. Oxford University Press, 1999.

Richman, Daniel C. and William J. Stuntz. "Al Capone's Revenge: An Essay on the Political Economy of Pretextual Prosecution." *Columbia Law Review* 105, no. 2 (2005): 583–640.

Ristroph, Alice. "Respect and Resistance in Punishment Theory." *California Law Review* 97, no. 2 (2009): 1–39.

Ristroph, Alice. "Just Violence." *Arizona Law Review* 56, no. 4 (2014): 1018–63.

Ristroph, Alice. "Regulation or Resistance?: A Counter-Narrative of Constitutional Criminal Procedure." *Boston University Law Review* 95, no. 5 (2015): 1555–1617.

Robbins, Ira P. "Double Inchoate Crimes." *Harvard Journal of Legislation* 26, no. 1 (1989): 1–116.

Roberts, Samuel. "The Impact of the US Drug War on People of Color." In *The Oxford Handbook of Global Drug History*, edited by Paul Gootenberg. Oxford University Press, 2022.

Robinson, Paul H. "Hate Crimes: Crimes of Motive, Character, or Group Terror?" *Annual Survey of American Law* 1992, no. 4 (1992): 605–16.

Rogers, Audrey. "Child Pornography's Forgotten Victims." *Pace Law Review* 28 (2008): 847–63.

Rogers, Audrey. "The Dignitary Harm of Child Pornography—From Producers to Possessors." In *Refining Child Pornography Law: Crime, Language, and Social Consequences*, edited by Carissa Byrne Hessick. University of Michigan Press, 2016.

Rossheim, Matthew E. et al. "Feeling No Buzz or a Slight Buzz Is Common When Legally Drunk." *American Journal of Public Health* 106, no. 10 (2016): 1761–62.

Rossiter, Mike. *The Spy Who Changed the World: Klaus Fuchs, Physicist and Soviet Double Agent*. Skyhorse, 2014.

Sale, Richard. *Traitors: The Worst Acts of Treason in American History from Benedict Arnold to Robert Hanssen*. Berkley Books, 2003.

Samarth, Avinash et al. "Second Class." *Inquest*, November 5, 2021. https://inquest.org/nyc-public-defenders-amicus-second-class/.

Saturday Night Live, "Black Jeopardy with Chadwick Boseman—SNL." Posted April 8, 2018, by Saturday Night Live. YouTube. https://www.youtube.com/watch?v=hzMzFGgmQOc.

Satz, Debra. "Equality of What Among Whom?: Thoughts on Cosmopolitanism, Statism, and Nationalism." In *NOMOS, Vol. 41: Global Justice*, edited by Ian Shapiro and Lea Brilmayer. American Society for Political and Legal Philosophy, 1999.

Savage, Charlie. "Chelsea Manning to Be Released Early as Obama Commutes Sentence." *New York Times*, January 17, 2017.

Scanlon, T. M. *What We Owe to Each Other*. Harvard University Press, 1998.

Schauer, Frederick. *Playing by the Rules: A Philosophical Examination of Rule-Based Decision-Making in Law and in Life*. Clarendon Press, 1991.

Schauer, Frederick. *Profiles, Probabilities, and Stereotypes*. Harvard University Press, 2006.

Scheffler, Samuel. "Conceptions of Cosmopolitanism." In *Boundaries and Allegiances: Problems of Justice and Responsibility in Liberal Thought*. Oxford University Press, 2001.

Scheffler, Samuel. "Liberalism, Nationalism, and Egalitarianism." In *Boundaries and Allegiances: Problems of Justice and Responsibility in Liberal Thought*. Oxford University Press, 2001.

Schwartzberg, Melissa. "Justifying the Jury: Reconciling Justice, Equality and Democracy." *American Political Science Review* 112, no. 3 (2018): 446–58.

Schwarz, Alan. "Expatriate Enthusiasm on Display at Classic." *New York Times*, March 18, 2009.

Scorsese, Martin, dir. *Taxi Driver*. Columbia Pictures, 1976.

Sekar, Satish. *The Cardiff Five: Innocent Beyond Any Doubt*, 2nd ed. Waterside Press, 2017.

Senick, Gerald J. "The Odd and Curious Case of Max Stephan (part one)." *LegalNews.com*, April 17, 2013. https://legalnews.com/Home/Articles?DataId=1375022.

Sese, John with Gerald J. Senick. "Treason in Detroit—The Curious Case of Max Stephan (episode 22, part two)." *LegalNews.com*, March 19, 2021. https://legalnews.com/Home/Articles?DataId=1497500.

Sevel, Michael. "Obeying the Law." *Legal Theory* 24, no. 3 (2018): 191–215.

Shaer, Matthew. "The Long, Lonely Road of Chelsea Manning." *New York Times*, June 12, 2017.

Shelby, Tommie. *Dark Ghettos: Injustice, Dissent, and Reform.* Harvard University Press, 2016.

Shelby, Tommie. *The Idea of Prison Abolition.* Princeton University Press, 2022.

Sherwood, Zach. "Time to Reload: The Harms of the Federal Felon-in-Possession Ban in a Post-*Heller* World." *Duke Law Journal* 70, no. 6 (2021): 1429–72.

Shreefter, Emma Luttrell. "Federal Felon-in-Possession Gun Laws: Criminalizing a Status, Disparately Affecting Black Defendants, and Continuing the Nation's Century-Old Methods to Disarm Black Communities." *City University of New York Law Review* 21, no. 2 (2018): 143–76.

Sidhu, Dave S. "Courts Disagree as to Whether the Federal Felon in Possession Firearm Prohibition Violates the Second Amendment." *Congressional Research Service*, May 28, 2024.

Simester, A. P. *Fundamentals of Criminal Law: Responsibility, Culpability, and Wrongdoing.* Oxford University Press, 2021.

Simester, A. P. and G. R. Sullivan. "On the Nature and Rationale of Property Offences." In *Defining Crimes: Essays on the Special Part of the Criminal Law*, edited by R. A. Duff and Stuart P. Green. Oxford University Press, 2005.

Simester, A. P. and Andreas von Hirsch. *Crimes, Harms and Wrongs: On the Principles of Criminalisation.* Hart Publishing, 2011.

Simmons, A. John. *Moral Principles and Political Obligations.* Princeton University Press, 1979.

Simmons, A. John. "Locke and the Right to Punish." *Philosophy and Public Affairs* 20, no. 4 (1991): 311–49.

Simmons, A. John. *Justification and Legitimacy: Essays on Rights and Obligations.* Cambridge University Press, 2000.

Singer, Peter. *One World: The Ethics of Globalization.* Yale University Press, 2002.

Sklansky, David A. "Cocaine, Race, and Equal Protection." *Stanford Law Review* 47, no. 6 (1995): 1283–322.

Smith, Angela M. "Responsibility for Attitudes: Activity and Passivity in Mental Life." *Ethics* 115, no. 2 (2005): 236–71.

Smolla, Rodeny A. *Smolla and Nimmer on Freedom of Speech*, vol. 1. Clark Boardman Callaghan, 2025.

Snowden, Edward. *Permanent Record.* Metropolitan Books, 2019.

Sood, Avani Mehta. "Attempted Justice: Misunderstanding and Bias in Psychological Constructions of Criminal Attempt." *Stanford Law Review* 71, no. 3 (2019): 593–686.

Spiro, Peter J. *Beyond Citizenship: American Identity after Globalization.* Oxford University Press, 2008.

Spitzer, Robert. *Politics of Gun Control*, 7th ed. Routledge, 2018.

Steiker, Carol S. "Punishing Hateful Movies: Old Wine in a New Bottle Revives Calls for Prohibition." *Michigan Law* Review 97, no. 6 (1999): 1857–73.

Stephen, James Fitzjames. *Liberty, Equality, Fraternity.* Holt & Williams, 1873.

Stevenson, Dru. "In Defense of Felon-in-Possession Laws." *Cardozo Law Review* 43, no. 4 (2022): 1573–1640.

Stilz, Anna. *Liberal Loyalty: Freedom, Obligation, and the State.* Princeton University Press, 2009.

Stone, Geoffrey R. and Lee C. Bollinger, eds. *National Security, Leaks and Freedom of the Press: The Pentagon Papers Fifty Years On.* Oxford University Press, 2021.

Stump, Scott. "Exclusive: Erin Andrews Gets Emotional Remembering When She Called Her Parents About Stalker Recording Her." *Today*, November 22, 2023.

Sullivan, Eileen. "The US Is Easing Marijuana Restrictions. Here's How It Works." *New York Times*, May 16, 2024.
Swan, Sarah. L. "Conjugal Liability." *UCLA Law Review* 64, no. 4 (2017): 968–1037.
Tadros, Victor. *Criminal Responsibility*. Oxford University Press, 2005.
Tadros, Victor. "Crime and Security." *The Modern Law Review* 71, no. 6 (2008): 940–70.
Tadros, Victor. *The Ends of Harm: The Moral Foundations of Criminal Law*. Oxford University Press, 2011.
Tadros, Victor. "Wrongness and Criminalization." In *The Routledge Companion to Philosophy of Law*, edited by Andrei Marmor. Routledge, 2012.
Tadros, Victor. *Wrongs and Crimes*. Oxford University Press, 2016.
Tamir, Yael. *Liberal Nationalism*. Princeton University Press, 1993.
Tan, Kok-Chor. *Justice without Borders: Cosmopolitanism, Nationalism, and Patriotism*. Cambridge University Press, 2004.
Tartt, Donna. *The Secret History*. Alfred A. Knopf, 1992.
Teutsch, Steven M. et al., eds. *Getting to Zero Alcohol-Impaired Driving Fatalities: A Comprehensive Approach to a Persistent Problem*. The National Academies Press, 2018.
Thompson, Sandra Guerra. "The White-Collar Police Force: 'Duty to Report' Statutes in Criminal Law Theory." *William & Mary Bill of Rights Journal* 11, no. 1 (2002): 3–65.
Thorburn, Malcolm. "Criminal Law as Public Law." In *Philosophical Foundations of Criminal Law*, edited by R. A. Duff and Stuart Green. Oxford University Press, 2011.
Thorburn, Malcolm. "Punishment and Public Authority." In *Criminal Law and the Authority of the State*, edited by Antje du Bois-Pedian, Magnus Ulväng, and Petter Asp. Hart Publishing, 2017.
Thorburn, Malcolm. "Criminal Punishment and the Right to Rule." *University of Toronto Law Journal* 70, Supplement 1 (2020): 44–63.
Tsuruoka, Doug. "Did a Forgotten Japanese Journalist Turn the Tide of World War II?" *Asia Times*, August 5, 2015.
Tuori, Kaarlo. "Ultima Ratio as a Constitutional Principle." *Oñati Socio-Legal Series* 3, no. 1 (2013): 6–20.
U.S. Department of Justice, Office of Public Affairs. "Former Employee of Medical Device Manufacturer Pleads Guilty to Forging Two FDA Clearance Letters for Medical Devices." Press Release. July 20, 2023. https://www.justice.gov/opa/pr/former-employee-medical-device-manufacturer-pleads-guilty-forging-two-fda-clearance-letters.
U.S. Department of Justice, Office of Public Affairs. "TD Bank Pleads Guilty to Bank Secrecy Act and Money Laundering Conspiracy Violations in $1.8B Resolution." News Release. October 24, 2021.
U.S. Department of Justice, Office of Public Affairs. "WikiLeaks Founder Pleads Guilty and Is Sentenced for Conspiring to Obtain and Disclose Classified National Defense Information." Press Release. June 25, 2024. https://www.justice.gov/opa/pr/wikileaks-founder-pleads-guilty-and-sentenced-conspiring-obtain-and-disclose-classified.
Valentini, Laura. "The Natural Duty of Justice in Non-Ideal Circumstances: On the Moral Demands of Institution Building and Reform." *European Journal of Political Theory* 20, no. 1 (2017): 45–66.
Valentini, Laura. "The Content-Independence of Political Obligation: What It Is and How to Test It." *Legal Theory* 24, no. 2 (2018): 135–57.
Vitale, Alex S. *The End of Policing*. Verso Books, 2017.
Vizzard, William J. *Shots in the Dark*. Rowan & Littlefield Publishers, 2000.
von Hirsch, Andrew and Andrew Ashworth. *Proportionate Sentencing: Exploring the Principles*. Oxford University Press, 2005.
Waldron, Jeremy. "Rights in Conflict." In *Liberal Rights: Collected Papers 1981–1991*. Cambridge University Press, 1993.
Waldron, Jeremy. "Special Ties and Natural Duties." *Philosophy & Public Affairs* 22, no. 1 (1993): 3–30.

Waldron, Jeremy. *Law and Disagreement*. Clarendon Press, 1999.
Walen, Alec. "Criminalizing Statements of Terrorist Intent: How to Understand the Law Governing Terrorist Threats, and Why It Should Be Used Instead of Long-Term Preventive Detention." *Journal of Criminal Law and Criminology* 101, no. 3 (2011): 803–54.
Walzer, Michael. "Regime Change and Just War." *Dissent* 53, no. 3 (2006): 103–08.
Weiner, Tim et al. *Betrayal: The Story of Aldrich Ames, an American Spy*. Random House, 1995.
Wellman, Christopher Heath. "Political Obligation and the Particularity Requirement." *Legal Theory* 10, no. 2 (2004): 97–115.
Wellman, Christopher Heath. "Rights Forfeiture and *Mala Prohibita*." In *The Constitution of the Criminal Law*, edited by R. A. Duff et al. Oxford University Press, 2013.
Wellman, Christopher Heath. "Toward a Liberal Theory of Political Obligation." *Ethics* 111, no. 4 (2001): 735–59.
Whitman, James Q. *Harsh Justice: Criminal Punishment and the Widening Divide between America and Europe*. Oxford University Press, 2005.
Wigmore, John Henry. *Treatise on the System of Evidence in Trials at Common Law: Including the Statutes and Judicial Decisions of All Jurisdictions of the United States*. Little, Brown, and Company, 1905.
Wilkes, Christopher J. "A Case for Reforming the Anti–Money Laundering Regulatory Regime: How Financial Institutions' Criminal Reporting Duties Have Created an Unfunded Private Police Force." *Indiana Law Journal* 95, no. 2 (2020): 649–82.
Winkler, Adam. "Racist Gun Laws and the Second Amendment." *Harvard Law Review* 135, no. 8 (2022): 537–48.
Wise, David. *Nightmover: How Aldrich Ames Sold the CIA to the KGB for $4.6 Million*. HarperCollins, 1995.
Wise, David. *Spy: The Inside Story of How the FBI's Robert Hanssen Betrayed America*. Random House, 2002.
Wolf, Martin. *Why Globalization Works*. Yale University Press, 2004.
Wolff, Robert Paul. *In Defense of Anarchism*. Harper & Row, 1970.
Yaffe, Gideon. *Attempts: In the Philosophy of Action and the Criminal Law*. Oxford University Press, 2010.
Yaffe, Gideon. "Revisiting the 'But Everyone Does That!' Defense." *Law and Philosophy* 41, no. 2 (2022): 419–40.
Yankah, Ekow N. "Whose Burden to Bear?: Privilege, Lawbreaking and Race." *Criminal Law and Philosophy* 16, no. 1 (2022): 13–28.
Yung, Corey Rayburn. "The Incredible Ordinariness of Federal Penalties for Inactivity." *Wisconsin Law Review* 2012, no. 3 (2012): 841–70.
Zador, Paul L. et al. "Alcohol-Related Relative Risk of Driver Fatalities and Driver Involvement in Fatal Crashes in Relation to Driver Age and Gender: An Update Using 1996 Data." *Journal of Studies on Alcohol* 61, no. 3 (2000): 387–95.
Zielbauer, Paul. "Soccer Upset in Korea, 500 Red Shirts in Flushing." *New York Times*, June 23, 2002.
Zipursky, Benjamin. "Self-defense, Domination, and the Social Contract." *University of Pittsburgh Law Review* 57, no. 3 (1996): 579–614.

Index

For the benefit of digital users, indexed terms that span two pages (e.g., 52–53) may, on occasion, appear on only one of those pages.

Note: Bold page numbers indicate an overarching discussion.